D0215526

MAKING A MATCH

MAKING A MATCH

COURTSHIP IN SHAKESPEARE

AND HIS SOCIETY

Ann Jennalie Cook

PRINCETON UNIVERSITY PRESS

PRINCETON, NEW JERSEY

Copyright © 1991 by Princeton University Press
Published by Princeton University Press, 41 William Street,
Princeton, New Jersey 08540
In the United Kingdom: Princeton University Press, Oxford
All Rights Reserved

Library of Congress Cataloging-in-Publication Data

Cook, Ann Jennalie, 1934-
Making a match : courtship in Shakespeare and his society /
Ann Jennalie Cook.
p. cm.
Includes index.
ISBN 0-691-06842-9 (alk. paper)
1. Shakespeare, William, 1564–1616—Knowledge—
Manners and customs. 2. Shakespeare, William, 1564–1616—
Contemporary England. 3. Courtship—England—History—
16th century. 4. Courtship in literature. I. Title.
PR3069.M3C66 1991
822.3'3—dc20   90–45256 CIP

This book has been composed in Linotron Garamond

Princeton University Press books are
printed on acid-free paper, and meet the guidelines
for permanence and durability of the Committee
on Production Guidelines for Book Longevity
of the Council of Library Resources

Printed in the United States of America by
Princeton University Press, Princeton, New Jersey
10 9 8 7 6 5 4 3 2 1

FOR AMY AND LEE ANN

Contents

Acknowledgments

NO BOOK is an independent creation, but anyone working at the interface of history and literature is especially affected by the revolution of assumptions that has characterized these fields in the past several years. By its very nature a subject like courtship impinges on the controversies challenging both historians and literary critics alike to reassess the theoretical stances that inform all writing. In an effort to reach students and general readers, as well as specialists, I have elected to clarify the premises of the present analysis in a general way rather than move into the more formal discourses of theory. My professional colleagues, however, will readily recognize the origins of my premises and thus the incalculable debt I owe to scholars on both sides of the Atlantic.

My more specific indebtedness in *Making a Match* is also profound. To the staff at the Furness Collection at the University of Pennsylvania I am grateful for access to facsimiles of the entire Short-Title Collection of books printed before 1640 and to everyone at the Folger Shakespeare Library for civilized assistance in using their unique holdings. Several years ago a summer research grant from Vanderbilt University spurred preliminary work that resulted in a residence at the Rockefeller Foundation's Study Center in Bellagio, followed by a Guggenheim Fellowship. An award from Vanderbilt's Research Council provided me with the invaluable editorial skills of Jack and Holly Trotter during the final stages of manuscript preparation, while my departmental secretaries—Carolyn Levinson, Alberta Martin, Florence Muncy, and Virginia Schaefer—labored long and cheerfully on every draft and its revisions. The responses of audiences here and abroad to lectures on courtship have provided an important, broadly based source of encouragement over almost a decade. And the patient, perceptive criticism of my colleagues has forced me to more discriminating judgments. In particular, Nancy Elizabeth Hodge, Marcia MacDonald, Scott Colley, and John Halperin contributed to significant rethinking of my ideas. More personally, I acknowledge the unfailing support of students, friends, daughters, and especially my husband, John D. Whalley.

MAKING A MATCH

Once upon a Time

Wee will say in An English prouerbe, that there belongeth more
to a marriage then two payre of bare legges. [1]
—*Counsel to the Husband*

Your brother and my sister no sooner met but they looked; no
sooner looked but they loved; no sooner loved but they sighed;
no sooner sighed but they asked one another the reason; no
sooner knew the reason but they sought the remedy; and in these
degrees have they made a pair of stairs to marriage, which they
will climb incontinent, or else be incontinent before marriage:
they are in the very wrath of love, and they will together. [2]
—*AYL*, V.ii.31–39

FINDING a mate and then getting married seem to be such universal experiences that audiences suppose they understand exactly what is happening when Shakespeare's characters engage in the rituals of courtship. But was the path couples traveled to the altar much the same then as it is today? In a good part of the world, one now assumes that, in the entirely optional decision to wed, individuals will have had some kind of experience with the opposite sex, perhaps even the intimacy of intercourse. Though conducted to a certain extent in public, the search for an acceptable spouse is largely a private matter. The assistance and approval of friends and family may be highly desirable, but those of age can freely choose whom they like, regardless of external counsel, caution, or cajolery. In this choice, men and women look for shared interests, temperamental compatibility, and physical attraction. Above all else, they look for love, which is regarded as the primary basis for a happy, successful union. Openly to marry for money or status or power seems distasteful, perhaps even a form of prostitution. Indeed, except for the occasional premarital

---

[1] Morris P. Tilley adds, "More belongs to marriage than four bare legs in a bed," *A Dictionary of the Proverbs in England in the Sixteenth and Seventeenth Centuries* (Ann Arbor: University of Michigan Press, 1950), M1146.

[2] All citations are from the *Oxford Shakespeare*, ed. Stanley Wells and Gary Taylor (Oxford: Clarendon Press, 1986). I follow their unconventional spelling of proper names.

agreement, financial arrangements play no formal part in courtship. The only legal document required is an inexpensive license that duly records an exchange of vows made before witnesses. And if the ensuing state of lawful matrimony proves unhappy, then the divorce courts offer a ready means for freeing a husband or wife to begin the process all over again.

However, even a casual look at contemporary customs reveals an immense range of diverse behavior. Some elect not to marry at all, and of those some practice intentional or enforced celibacy while others do not. Homosexual or lesbian unions may share many features of heterosexual marriage. Neither parenthood nor child support nor inheritance nor a division of assets upon parting presupposes a condition of wedlock. Here and there occur such bizarre arrangements as communes with mutually shared partners or guru-decreed mass weddings between virtual strangers. Also, within the more conventional forms of matrimony, such factors as ethnic origin, religion, or wealth may dictate widely divergent rituals. Between a quick ceremony performed by a justice of the peace and a nuptial Eucharist celebrated in a cathedral before hundreds of guests, there is a great difference indeed. The Hasidic wedding of a couple introduced by a professional matchmaker bears scant resemblance to an exchange of individually composed promises in a garden or meadow.

The inevitable alterations wrought by time also demarcate contemporary practices from those of earlier generations. With improved birth control and changing attitudes toward sexual activity, shotgun weddings have become increasingly rare. While the restrictive laws in other states used to make Reno, Nevada, synonymous with divorce, its connotation may eventually require a footnoted explanation, like references to Gretna Green in eighteenth-century literature. Similarly, suits for alienation of affection or breach of promise may one day have meaning only for the antiquarian. And who can say whether a common word like *honeymoon*, much less slang phrases like *popped the question* or *fooled around*, will need definition in some future edition of the *Oxford English Dictionary*? If marital codes change over time and if they vary according to status and belief, then it is naive to suppose that the codes familiar to a Shakespearean audience will be entirely accessible today, regardless of how recognizable their general features may be.

In fact, many of the assumptions that inform Elizabethan and Jacobean wooing seem quite foreign to contemporary society. The situation is further complicated by the fact that different practices characterized different social levels and that each level displayed a spectrum of opinion and be-

havior rather than any absolute uniformity. Yet as spelled out in the ideology of the period, both the state of wedlock and the approved route to
that state were plain enough. Almost without exception, marriage offered
the only venue for morally condoned sexual intercourse or for legitimate
heirs. Although every lawful union was a permanently binding relationship, there were no limits to the number of marriages one could contract,
provided death had ended the previous one. As for the relative importance
of affection and advancement, the factors of wealth, position, and influence could take precedence over liking, love, or lust, especially among the
privileged. In so important an undertaking as matrimony, unstable emotional inclinations often became subservient to the more sober concerns of
kinfolk and allies. Hence the search for a spouse was not necessarily conducted by the future bride or groom, though at some point they had to
assent to the proposed alliance. But the final choice involved far more than
mutual acceptance by the partners and their families, for the stability of
the entire community depended upon financially secure, well-governed
households.

When agreement on such practical terms as monetary support was
reached, with the full concurrence of parents or guardians and the free (or
coerced) consent of the parties to be married, an act of betrothal was performed before witnesses. This espousal signaled that the courtship had
moved into a public arena. Subsequently the banns read from the parish
pulpit, the preparations for the wedding, and the nuptial celebrations
made marriage a communal concern rather than a private one. Among
royalty or nobility, where marital unions carried national or even international implications, court politics came into play. And from the sovereign
on down to the lowliest subject, marriage constituted an irrevocable commitment that only the rare annulment might set aside. Within such a
structure, those who defied the conventions could suffer disgrace, disinheritance, and harsh legal penalties. This ideology of cautious, rational
entry into the estate of matrimony, with all its subsequent responsibilities, was supposed to govern the actions of English subjects in an orderly
commonwealth.

Yet many factors could and did alter the system. Gender certainly
played a role. For most men, marriage was an option they could choose or
refuse, depending on their personal inclinations and income. But for most
women, wedlock was inescapable. Fertility and infant mortality determined which families could provide handsomely for a single child and
which had to apportion resources among several offspring, thereby dimin-

ishing their chances in the marital market. Geography restricted some girls to a handful of possible spouses, in contrast with the oversupply of males ready to snap up wives in London. The accidents of beauty, intelligence, health, riches, birth, or just plain luck all influenced the likelihood of a good match. And religious beliefs affected such matters as premarital chastity, dress, decorum, even whether music accompanied wedding festivities.

However, social status unquestionably exercised the strongest power over the varying practices in English courtship. Among the elite, both women and men, especially heirs, married earlier than those with lesser property attached to their unions. Political considerations dictated which alliances were prudent and which were not. The bride's virginity, too, assumed greater importance where lineage and inheritance of fortune or title were at stake than it did if a husband simply needed a wife to keep his house and share his labors. While unmarried females at the top of society could expect considerable restriction upon their freedom, the masses routinely sent daughters as well as sons into apprenticeship or service. There a master's lax supervision might permit much greater liberties than privileged women enjoyed. In turn, both the separation from family and the interaction with others allowed ordinary folk to choose a spouse instead of taking one chosen by others, as was more often the case with the elite. Concurrence of parents, friends, and masters still counted, but a humble couple's mutual affection could take precedence, provided they had sufficient means to set up a household. Premarital sexual activity resulted in surprisingly little bastardy, although a fair number of village brides went to the altar pregnant.

Though the divergences between the upper levels of society and English subjects of lesser status can be determined with relative success, the practices of those most deviant from the marriage system obstinately resist investigation. A variety of female offenders show up before the church courts as mothers of bastards, but parishes may not have wanted—or been able—to prosecute every illegitimate birth. Moreover, as a result of recurrent economic crises, an unprecedented number of the poor roamed the countryside, coupling and uncoupling with scant regard for moral or legal prescriptions. Even if they wished to assume the responsibilities of conventional wedlock, the dispossessed lacked the means to do so. Poverty could also force women into prostitution as a desperate measure of economic survival. Unlike those who set down written accounts of their lives, these marginal individuals have left behind little or no direct evidence.

However, the subversive threat of their unregulated activity to the insti-
tution of marriage provoked countless diatribes against bawds, harlots,
whoremongers, seducers, rogues, vagrants, and masterless men. Though
the actual extent of such violation of prescribed behavior cannot be determined, its defiance of every convention challenges any easy assumptions
about courtship in Shakespeare or his audiences.

Looking across the whole social spectrum, one can see that every action
relating to courtship was implicitly questioned by alternative possibilities.
The closely chaperoned heiress destined to marry a stranger might envy
her maidservant's freedom to meet and mate with men. Conversely, the
servant, seeing a mistress still in her teens take a husband, could chafe at
her own necessity to delay marriage until she had sufficient savings to set
up housekeeping. If the daring few who eloped cast doubt upon the submission of those who reluctantly accepted a father's spousal candidate, still
the financial security won by such submission stood in marked contrast to
the financial penalties visited upon runaway lovers. The prostitute's easy
availability or even the village girl's dalliance with her betrothed might
have teased at the imagination of the bride who went a virgin to her wedding bed. Yet the respect enjoyed by the chaste wife or maiden deepened
the shame communities accorded loose women. The man marrying for
money without love and the man marrying for love without money mutually judged each other. Even the carnival abandon that marked a wedding feast inherently emphasized the sober restrictions of everyday wedded
life. By their very nature, then, the differences within and between each
social level potentially subverted whatever marital choices people made.

So what does Shakespeare do with courtship as he knew it? Obviously
the subject has considerable importance for him, since every play includes
at least some reference to wooing or wedding, and in most plots it is a
crucial element, frequently dominating the entire action. To say that tales
of love and marriage derive from the sources merely begs the question, for
Shakespeare did not have to employ those particular sources, nor was he
compelled to emphasize the aspects he did. Yet no other segment of human experience commands as much attention as the mating ritual. It
seems fair to suggest, then, that this complex of possibilities exerted a
powerful fascination for the playwright and for theater audiences. Nor is
it difficult to suggest further why the culture focused its gaze there. Not
only did the wedding rites reenact the primal relinquishment of the
daughter by the father to the husband, but all the attendant nuances of
betrothal and matrimony touched on sensitive issues. Sexual maturity and

activity, economic independence, familial and community status, establishment of one's house and line of descent—all found expression in the codes of courtship. Full adulthood for both males and females came only with marriage. Without that, a woman was permanently dependent on her father, her kin, or a master. And if wedlock placed her under a husband's authority, she at least exercised authority over her dwelling, her children, her servants. Similarly, even if a son's financial autonomy was curbed by a still-living father, as a husband he could control some part of his patrimony, govern his household, and command a respectable identity in the commonwealth. By contrast, his unmarried brother had no such scope for wielding patriarchal power, nor could he hope to extend his line into the future. Before wedding, individuals were lesser citizens; afterward, they were incorporated into society at a more responsible level; and in the very act of making a marital choice, they could prove themselves worthy of admiration or contempt.

Even in view of the cultural weight given to the process of taking a spouse, there is reason to think that Shakespeare had special insight into such matters. The circumstances of his personal life reveal how often he stood at the cusp of conflicting codes. Unfettered by the restraints of primogeniture among the elite, Shakespeare's maternal grandfather, Robert Arden, left the bulk of his inheritance to his youngest daughter, Mary. After her marriage to John Shakespeare, that estate enabled him to rise in status, assume public office, and aspire to a coat of arms. Conversely, the forfeiture of a substantial part of Mary's dowry property signaled a decline in family fortunes. As for William Shakespeare, at an age when he should have begun the long process of establishing the financial security marriage required, he found himself hastily wed to a pregnant Anne Hathaway. No evidence for a formal betrothal survives, though the sums required for the special license and sureties are a matter of record, as is the £16 13s. 4d. left the bride for a modest dowry in her father's will. Precociously, William was a husband at eighteen, the father of three before his twenty-first birthday. More typically for her rank, his bride was twenty-six, already with child at the wedding, finished with maternity by thirty. Shakespeare's growing wealth and fame enabled his elder daughter, Susannah, at twenty-four to marry the prosperous, well-educated gentleman John Hall, a respected doctor, though not one of the landed gentry. Poor Judith Shakespeare, a spinster at thirty-one, was at last matched with Thomas Quiney, son of a family friend, in her father's last year of life. Because they failed to get a license for their Lenten marriage, the couple were disciplined by the consistory court. Far worse, the bridegroom had sired an illegitimate child and was still doing penance when Shakespeare died. His will left Judith a marriage portion of £50, which her husband was not allowed to touch, but the chief inheritance passed into the hands of the Halls, while the Quineys had to cope with the shame of yet another of Thomas's bastards.[3]

The cultural variations in sexual stricture and permissiveness, in financial prudence and imprudence, in early or late age at marriage, in the expectations attendant on social rank all swirled about Shakespeare's own life. Although it would be critically naive to suggest that some crude exploration of his unresolved psychological dilemmas is going on in the playwright's creative works, the immediacy with which courtship onstage related to everyone's personal experience, including his own, should not be underestimated. No one walked into a performance ignorant of the ways in which people moved from the unwedded to the wedded state. Even those who could scarcely hope to marry or those who determined never to marry understood the problems and the possibilities of the process. Here is an awareness then shared by everyone but nowadays subtly closed to most people. Simple words like *portion* or *contract* have lost the significance they once held, while terms like *handfasting* or *bride-ale* need a footnote. And who save the scholar really understands the difference between *de praesenti* and *de futuro* spousals?

Hence the first task of *Making a Match* is to reconstruct, insofar as possible, the system of courtship that was familiar to Shakespeare and his audience and thus make a better match between past and present understanding. In this task, the aim is not to flatten out the complexities of experience into a uniform or monolithic construction but to give due acknowledgment of differences, contradictions, subversions. Yet what emerges will still represent only an approximation, a contemporary creation that can never be a faithful re-creation of the past. Even if one could return to the year 1600, the report of such a visit would not render an account of courtship congruent with the Elizabethans' understanding or behavior, for it would be filtered through a twentieth-century sensibility, with its own peculiarities and presuppositions. From the outset, it is best

[3] For a fuller discussion, see S. Schoenbaum, *William Shakespeare: A Documentary Life* (New York: Oxford University Press, 1975); W. Nicholas Knight, "Patrimony and Shakespeare's Daughters," *University of Hartford Studies in Literature* 9 (1977): 175–186; C. L. Barber and Richard P. Wheeler, *The Whole Journey: Shakespeare's Power of Development* (Berkeley: University of California Press, 1986), pp. 43–66.

to admit the impenetrability of history. One can only offer more or less sophisticated hypotheses about the way things were.

Because of the nature of the materials with which the cultural analyst must work, the difficulties intensify. Not only do modern perspectives distort the interpretation of the surviving evidence, but the prejudices and inadequacies of those who produced that evidence affect its reliability. Hence, all the parish records, diaries, poems, manuals, sermons, legal documents, letters, and the like are inherently biased in various ways. Church registers may be incomplete or inaccurate. The writers of diaries and letters invent personas for themselves and others just as the authors of poems and plays invent characters. Sermons and advice books seek to impose limited, codified views upon the rebellious chaos of differing opinions. Laws and legal documents always imply lapses in human behavior, lapses that may or may not be prosecuted with consistency or vigor or effectiveness. Thus, for corroboration, refutation, or qualification, theory and fiction must be juxtaposed against the records of what people actually did. And still there are lacunae. Maddeningly, time seldom preserves adequate answers to the future's questions, for either the answer seemed too obvious to discuss or else the question did not seem significant then. Furthermore, what shards time does preserve are cumulatively subject to the refractions of critical prisms alien to the culture that originally produced those artifacts. Hence, like all history, the description of Elizabethan-Jacobean courtship in this book necessarily makes an imperfect match between what actually prevailed and what now seems to have prevailed.

The second task of *Making a Match*, to analyze the ways in which Shakespeare incorporates the attitudes and experiences of wooing into his plays, also poses a clutch of problems. While all historical evidence and, in fact, all subsequent interpretation of that evidence participate in the creation of fictions, dramatic texts are avowedly fictional, even when they present nonfictional events. Yet, as Sir Philip Sidney recognizes, literature has the imaginative power to reveal a truth superior to any the historian can reveal, so that fictitious situations somehow seem more valid than descriptions in primary documents or scrupulous modern research. Nonetheless, the dramatist is free to depart from what people knew, thought, or did whenever it serves his purposes. What needs to be explored, then, is the extent of Shakespeare's departure, the nature of his treatment, and the aesthetic effect of that treatment, whether it be caricature, criticism, conformity, or sheer fantasy. In other words, what kind of match is being made between social experience and its depiction onstage?

Yet in the interpretive process, one must also be aware that the plays themselves actively participate in creating their culture's understanding of courtship. Although the arrangement of the succeeding chapters, where discussion of the social milieu is followed by discussion of relevant dramatic situations, suggests a privileging of offstage world over onstage world, of a first-order reality over a second-order reality, that is not the underlying premise of this work. The two realms are divided for purposes of clarity only. Indeed, the inclusion of other avowedly fictional materials as part of the historical evidence acknowledges the role literature played (and plays) in shaping cultural assumptions. The worlds are not separate but interpenetrating. Whatever ideas the audiences brought into the theater were to some degree altered by what they viewed there. Possibilities closed to them were enacted, wishes were fulfilled, fears were affirmed, beliefs were attacked, barriers were transcended. Regardless of Shakespeare's motives for depicting the mating game as he did, his dramas entered a vast reservoir of other influences upon all who saw, read, or heard about his works. This playwright did not transform his society; no playwright did—or could. But inevitably his perspectives on courtship, as on other matters, were disseminated through the very acts of performing and eventually of publishing.

However, one must not cast Shakespeare in a godlike role, apart from and above his culture, rendering judgment upon it from some neutral, detached position. Like every playgoer, he too was subject to the restrictions of his own time. As the ensuing chapters will indicate, deeply embedded within his language and action are contemporary codes of speech and conduct. Whether the locale be Elsinore, Venice, or Athens, the signals concerning the status of a marriage suit are invariably English. As was the case with his society, so onstage some marital arrangements never find expression, no matter how fantastic the dramatic circumstances. Polygamy, remarriage after divorce, the duty to father a child for a dead brother's wife—all familiar from situations in the Old Testament—are taboo for both Shakespeare and his countrymen. Other situations, such as incest, he seems disinclined to place at the center of any action, unlike some of his fellow dramatists. Nor does Shakespeare take pains to portray a representative cross section of society. Just as in other literature of the period, royal, noble, or at least gently born lovers dominate the plots, though these ranks constituted no more than 5 to 10 percent of the English population. Only on the fringes do servants, shepherds, country wenches, and whores act out their entanglements. In their emphasis on the upper social levels, the plays recapitulate the imbalance that prevails in the rest of the surviving historical evidence. The further down the social ladder one looks, the harder it becomes to discern the characteristics of human behavior.

Beyond the far-from-simple tasks of explaining what courtship was like in the English Renaissance and what Shakespeare does with courtship in his drama lies the more important issue of the benefit such an analysis can provide. For students, general readers, and playgoers, it offers information that is not widely known but that bears on one's understanding of works throughout the canon. Because Juliet did so, people have long supposed that Elizabethans married at thirteen or fourteen. Many have scorned Petruccio and Bassanio and Claudio as base fortune hunters. And who would suppose, from reading Shakespeare, that love was not then as now the universally accepted basis for marriage? If some scholars, seeing Olivia call Sebastian "husband," think they are married, then others less learned will surely think so too. With more complicated matters, like spousals and elopements and annulments, the subtleties of the problems involved are lost altogether. The evidence made available in the succeeding chapters provides a lens through which one may view the language and action of the plays more nearly as Shakespeare's contemporaries saw them, though an Elizabethan-Jacobean interpretation comprises not *the* meaning but rather *a* meaning of any situation. Even within that meaning lies a complex of possibilities, not unanimous agreement. What happens to a prostitute, a servant, a younger brother, or a prince depends on who is watching, why the events are presented, and how they relate to the rest of the play. As a result, a multidimensional onstage experience interacts with an equally multidimensional offstage consciousness.

For scholars, *Making a Match* will serve other purposes as well. First, it greatly enlarges the scope of historical, demographic, and economic materials generally consulted by literary critics interested in the social context of the plays. All too many begin and end with Lawrence Stone and Peter Laslett, never recognizing the highly controversial status of these historians' theories. The research made available by the Cambridge Group and in many of Stone's publications, not just *The Family, Sex, and Marriage in England, 1500–1800*, can serve a useful function in the assessment of this period, provided one does not accept without question such notions as the lack of affection in the family or the reliability of parish records for a reconstruction of family history.[4] Important, too, is the need to correct mis-

---

[4] For representative criticism of Lawrence Stone's *The Family, Sex and Marriage in En-*

guided ideas about the culture advanced by critics of literature who have not read widely enough to substantiate their hypotheses. For example, the long-standing contention that Puritan thought revolutionized earlier theories about the status of women and freedom of choice in marriage now appears untenable to most social historians.[5] Instead, it would seem that Puritans pursued the same lines of argument as Anglicans and Catholics, both before and after the English Reformation.[6] For that reason, the ensuing study distinguishes among different positions regarding various aspects of courtship, but not between Puritan sources and others on the same subject.

A second area of scholarly significance relates to the extent of the treatment of courtship in Shakespeare. It would be false to claim that no one has pursued this topic before. The fine work of Margaret Ranald and George Hibbard, or even the earlier contributions of Lu Emily Pearson and William Meader, join with the current surge of publications on marriage and the family. But either the focus narrows to a single play, as with

---

gland 1500–1800 (New York: Harper and Row, 1977), see the reviews of Alan Macfarlane in *History and Theory* 18 (1979): 103–126; Keith Thomas, "The Changing Family," *Times Literary Supplement* (21 October 1977): 1226–1227; E. P. Thompson, "Happy Families," *New Society* 41 (8 September 1977): 499–501; Randolph Trumbach, *Journal of Social History* 13 (1979): 136–143; Richard T. Vann, "Review Essay," *Journal of Family History* 4 (1979): 308–315. For sample critiques of both Stone and the Cambridge Group, see Christopher Hill, "Sex, Marriage and Parish Registers" and "Postscript," in *The Collected Essays*, vol. 3 (Amherst: University of Massachusetts Press, 1986), pp. 188–225; Janis Butler Holm, "Toward a History of Women in Early Modern Europe," *Annals of Scholarship* 2 (1981): 110–114; David Levine, *Family Formation in an Age of Nascent Capitalism* (New York: Academic Press, 1977), pp. 153–174.

[5] This view goes at least as far back as William and Malleville Haller's "The Puritan Art of Love," *Huntington Library Quarterly* 5 (1942): 235–272. It has been espoused by Diane Elizabeth Dreher, *Domination and Defiance: Fathers and Daughters in Shakespeare* (Lexington: University of Kentucky Press, 1986), pp. 33–34; Roland M. Frye, "The Teachings of Classical Puritanism on Conjugal Love," *Studies in the Renaissance* 2 (1955): 148–159; Mary Beth Rose, *The Expense of Spirit: Love and Sexuality in English Renaissance Drama* (Ithaca, NY: Cornell University Press, 1988); and most vigorously by Juliet Dusinberre, *Shakespeare and the Nature of Women* (New York: Barnes and Noble, 1975).

[6] See the work of Kathleen M. Davies, "The Sacred Condition of Equality—How Original Were Puritan Doctrines of Marriage?" *Social History* 5 (1977): 563–580; Richard L. Greaves, *Society and Religion in Elizabethan England* (Minneapolis: University of Minnesota Press, 1981); Margo Todd, "Humanists, Puritans, and the Spiritualized Household," *Church History* 49 (1980): 18–34. For analysis of Puritan ideas on emotion, see Edmund Leites, *The Puritan Conscience and Modern Sexuality* (New Haven: Yale University Press, 1986). For a literary critic's attack, see L. T. Fitz, " 'What Says the Married Woman': Marriage Theory and Feminism in the English Renaissance," *Mosaic* 13 (1980): 1–22.

Lynda Boose on *King Lear*, or to a single issue, as with Marilyn Williamson on patriarchy, or else the whole topic is subordinated to some other overriding concern. Thus David Bevington looks at betrothal and marriage under the rubric of stage gesture, and Carol Neely sees them in the light of feminist strategies. For Marjorie Garber, they are rites of passage; for Jonathan Goldberg, political actions. No one looks at the intricacies of the entire process, from the point of eligibility to the consummated union, and no one looks at Shakespeare's entire canon. Indeed, some critics ignore the historical context altogether, as if the world of the plays were separable from its own time and communicated only with present time. An awareness of culture-bound codes would prevent otherwise astute interpreters from claiming that Baptista is trying to avoid support of his shrewish daughter Kate should she be widowed, or that in *1 Henry VI* "Margaret appears as a . . . modest and proper young woman," or that Paris "wants to become a Capulet by marrying Juliet."[7] As the notes will indicate, scholars not only disagree about the meaning of particular situations, but in hundreds of instances they are simply wrong because of their ignorance regarding courtship.

None of the subsequent discussion is intended to deny the value and validity of other theoretical approaches. Nor is the primacy of history being asserted here. In one sense, Richard Levin speaks the blunt truth when he says that historical research is "preinterpretative."[8] For scholars, part of the usefulness of *Making a Match* comes under the heading of homework, the essential if time-consuming task of finding out what certain kinds of behavior once signified. In a way, it is the relearning of a partly intelligible language. But with mastery of that language can come a fuller critical power. Feminists will find here a much richer body of evidence to support their views. Psychological critics can discuss emotional discordances with a better understanding of the cultural roots for such conflicts. Those who explain by extended application of a single historical vignette can select incidents with greater sensitivity to their appropriateness. Political think-

---

[7] Coppélia Kahn, "*The Taming of the Shrew*: Shakespeare's Mirror of Marriage," *Modern Language Studies* 5 (1975): 91; Marilyn French, *Shakespeare's Division of Experience* (New York: Summit Books, 1981), p. 48; Northrop Frye, *Northrop Frye on Shakespeare* (New Haven: Yale University Press, 1986), p. 16.

[8] Richard Levin, *New Readings vs. Old Plays: Recent Trends in the Reinterpretation of English Renaissance Drama* (Chicago: University of Chicago Press, 1979), p. 146. Among those who have shown the crucial importance of such "pre-interpretive" work is J. Leeds Barroll, in "A New History for Shakespeare and His Time," *Shakespeare Quarterly* 39 (1988): 441–464.

ers will see with subtler refinement how power operated in marital matters. Proponents of carnival will discover additional ways in which rules were flouted and propriety challenged. Theorists of discourse will have a more sophisticated lexicon to work with. And those who wish to deconstruct the entire critical enterprise can dismantle yet another set of possibilities. The present study of courtship in Shakespeare and his society, then, seeks neither to quarrel with nor to supersede other perspectives. Its goal is to provide a source of information about the culture that will in turn make more intelligible the scenes of wooing and wedding in the plays. For those with particular ideological or theoretical approaches, the task remains to translate the materials made available here into their own interpretations of its significance.

For purposes of clarity, the ensuing chapters will move topically through the various aspects of courtship rather than subordinating the social system to such literary arrangements as Shakespearean chronology or genre. Hence each play will be considered whenever it relates to a given aspect of the system. Emerging from that complicated matrix are the general issues of the age and status of prospective spouses, the roles played by personal affection and parental authority, the intervention of friends and other outsiders in making the match, the financial arrangements for marriage, the publicly approved route to the altar, the alternative shortcuts and short circuits, and finally the political functions served by matrimony. Each topic will be analyzed in turn. Though both the social history and the plays carry an intrinsic interest, that interest intensifies when they illuminate each other.

However, such illumination occurs only when due weight is given to the cultural context as well as to the plays. The subtitle of this book—*Courtship in Shakespeare and His Society*—is intended to signal a relatively equal treatment of social history and Shakespearean drama, rather than a brief summary of matrimonial practices or reference to them merely as required by a specific situation. Not only would such a procedure distort the complexity of the issues involved, but it would make the research presented here less useful to those whose primary interests may not lie with Shakespeare. As they stand, the first half of chapters 2 through 9 presents a detailed explanation of the Elizabethan-Jacobean courtship system not readily available anywhere else. Using wherever possible the language of the primary documents, the analysis moves from contemporary opinions to legalities to fictional treatments to records of individual or group behavior. Not only will this material assist literary critics working on other writers, genres, and problems of the period, but it should also interest students of history, anthropology, demography, art, and other Renaissance subjects. The extensive notes make accessible the enormous range of sources from which the evidence was drawn. Shakespeareans should bear in mind, while they work through the historical evidence, that the analysis of the plays will be clearer for them if it follows a full examination of the cultural milieu. And those readers from other disciplines, who might prefer to skip the dramatic criticism, will discover that it provides cautionary examples regarding the appropriate use of literary evidence in interpreting history. The historical texts and the theatrical texts must be treated with equal integrity if their complicated match is to be presented with integrity.

The Age of Marriageability

For an vnnatural & vnhonest thing is it, to mary yong folkes,
which yet haue not attained to their lawful & iust yeres.
—Heinrich Bullinger, *The Christian State of Matrimony*

My child is yet a stranger in the world;
She hath not seen the change of fourteen years.
Let two more summers wither in their pride
Ere we may think her ripe to be a bride.
—*Rom.*, I.ii.8–11

BECAUSE Juliet marries just before her fourteenth birthday, many have assumed that such early alliances were quite common in Shakespeare's England.[1] As a result, only with the patient work of demographers in recent years have the period's normative practices been established with any reliability. And those practices differ markedly from the situation presented in *Romeo and Juliet*. From the top to the bottom of the social scale, the vast majority of English couples conformed to the northwest European pattern, in which marriage was deferred, sometimes for ten years or more beyond puberty.[2] Specific studies show that, except among the gentility, the average age when women first married was the mid-twenties, while

---

[1] Such assumptions began with the findings of F. J. Furnivall, ed., *Child-Marriages, Divorces, and Ratification 1561–6*, Early English Text Society, vol. 108 (London: Kegan Paul, Trench, Trübner, 1897). See also Carroll Camden, *The Elizabethan Woman* (Houston: Elsevier Press, 1952), p. 91; Christina Hole, *The English Home-Life, 1500 to 1800* (London: B. T. Batsford, 1947), p. 56; G. E. Howard, *A History of Matrimonial Institutions* (Chicago: University of Chicago Press, 1904), 1:399–403; William G. Meader, *Courtship in Shakespeare: Its Relation to the Tradition of Courtly Love* (New York: Columbia University, King's Crown Press, 1954), pp. 53–57; Chilton Latham Powell, *English Domestic Relations, 1487–1653* (New York: Columbia University Press, 1917), e.g., pp. 14ff., 124.

[2] See, e.g., John Hajnal, "European Marriage Patterns in Perspective," in *Population in History: Essays in Historical Demography*, ed. D. V. Glass and D.E.C. Eversley (Chicago: Aldine Publishing Company, 1965), p. 101; idem, "Two Kinds of Pre-Industrial Household Formation System," in *Family Forms in Historic Europe*, ed. Richard Wall, Jean Robin, and Peter Laslett (Cambridge: Cambridge University Press, 1983), p. 65.

men married a few years later (see Appendix).[3] Even the privileged did not rush to the altar as adolescents. The gentry married off their daughters at about twenty, sons at twenty-five or so. While only 5 to 6 percent of peers wed at fifteen or younger, during the period the age at marriage among this group showed a notable shift toward the early twenties.[4] More surprisingly, perhaps, of children with ducal and royal parents, 45 percent of the females and 79 percent of the males remained single until twenty or later.[5]

A wide range of legal structures and social practices combined to support the pattern of late marriage. Before their majority, children were lawfully under the control of parents, guardians, or masters and hence not free to bestow themselves in marriage. By 1604, canon law forbade a priest to marry anyone under the age of twenty-one without the assurance of parental consent, upon pain of suspension from his office.[6] Moreover, debates raged as to whether one attained adulthood at the beginning or the end of the twenty-first year, and there were attempts to raise the threshold of

[3] This research confirms the earlier report by Peter Laslett in his 1965 ed. of *The World We Have Lost* and reasserted in *The World We Have Lost, Further Explored* (London: Methuen, 1983), p. 83, setting ages 23–24 for women and 27–28 for men at first marriage. D'Orsay Pearson, "Renaissance Adolescent Marriage: Another Look at Hymen," *Cithara* 23 (1983): 17, takes issue with these studies because a mean age does not take into account the youngest age. However, much of the research does provide age cohorts.

[4] Lawrence Stone, "Marriage among the English Nobility in the 16th and 17th Century," *Comparative Studies in Society and History* 3 (1960–1961): 198; idem, *The Crisis of the Aristocracy, 1558–1641* (Oxford: Clarendon Press, 1965), p. 653; idem, *The Family, Sex and Marriage in England 1500–1800* (New York: Harper and Row, 1977), p. 46. In "Social Mobility in England, 1500–1700," in *Seventeenth-Century England: Society in an Age of Revolution*, ed. Paul Seaver (New York: New Viewpoints, 1976), p. 49, Stone says that during the late sixteenth century, peers' eldest sons married at about 21, but the average age for all children and grandchildren of the peerage was 25 or 26. T. H. Hollingsworth, "The Demography of the British Peerage," Supplement to *Population Studies* 18, no. 2 (1964): 11, further refines that figure for the years 1575–1624 to show sons of peers wedding at a mean age of 29, daughters at a mean age of 22 or 23. Laslett, *World*, p. 82, sets 20 and 25 as the norms for women and men in the elite. Ralph A. Houlbrooke, *The English Family, 1450–1700* (London: Longman, 1984), p. 66, says that 21 percent of peers and heiresses were married by 17 during the period 1540–1599, but only 12 percent during the years 1600–1659.

[5] Hajnal, "European Marriage," p. 113.

[6] Edmund Gibson, *Codex Juris Ecclesiastici Anglicani* (Oxford: Clarendon Press, 1761), 1:421; *Constitutions and Canons Ecclesiastical 1604* (Oxford: Clarendon Press, 1923), L3ᵛ–L4, 3ᵛ.

majority even higher.[7] Parents frequently specified an age of inheritance later than twenty-one, so that the financial support for a marriage did not pass into an heir's own hands until he was deemed fully mature.[8] And of course the Statute of Artificers governing apprenticeship had the same effect, since the training period lasted until young men reached twenty-four.[9] After 1556, freedom of the City of London, which marked the entry into one's trade and the end of apprenticehood, was delayed to this age specifically to curb "over-hasty marriages and soon setting up of households by the youth."[10] Other restrictions often kept craftsmen from independent practice until they were thirty.[11] In a less formally regulated way, village marriages often had to wait until a living, or a cottage and plot of land became available.[12]

However, certain peculiarities of civil and canon law, inherited from the medieval period and before that from the Romans, have tended to shift attention away from actual practice toward theoretical possibilities.[13] Technically, parents could promise future marriage for children as young as seven, but such early vows had to be confirmed by the prospective bride and groom after they reached the ages of twelve and fourteen, respectively.[14] Yet so qualified are these laws that they clearly refer to unusual

---

[7] Keith Thomas, "Age and Authority in Early Modern England," *Proceedings of the British Academy* 62 (1976): 206, 226–227.

[8] Ibid., p. 228.

[9] 5 Eliz. c. 4.

[10] Lawrence Manley, ed., *London in the Age of Shakespeare* (University Park: Pennsylvania State University Press, 1986), p. 273.

[11] Thomas, "Age and Authority," pp. 216–217; Margaret Gay Davies, *The Enforcement of English Apprenticeship* (Cambridge: Harvard University Press, 1956), pp. 19n.4, 193–194; William Sheppard, *Englands Balme* (London, 1657), p. 203; *Tudor Economic Documents*, ed. R. H. Tawney and Eileen Power (London: Longmans, Green, 1924), 1:354, 356, 358.

[12] For a look at the effects of economic conditions on rural marriages, see Peter Clark, *English Provincial Society from the Reformation to the Revolution: Religion, Politics and Society in Kent 1500–1640* (Hassocks, Sussex: Harvester Press, 1977), p. 244; W. C. Howson, "Plague, Poverty and Population in Parts of North-west England, 1580–1720," *Transactions of the Historic Society of Lancashire and Cheshire* 112 (1960): 29–55.

[13] Steven Ozment, *When Fathers Ruled: Family Life in Reformation Europe* (Cambridge: Harvard University Press, 1983), p. 25; Furnivall, *Child-Marriages*, p. xxxix; J.-L. Flandrin, "Repression and Change in the Sexual Life of Young People in Medieval and Early Modern Times," *Journal of Family History* 2 (1977): 197.

[14] *The Lawes Resolutions of Womens Rights* (London, 1632), p. 7; Henry Swinburne, *A Treatise of Spousals, or Matrimonial Contracts* (London, 1686), pp. 19–20 (this work, pub-

circumstances and, even more clearly, are tied to the age of puberty. Thus, twelve and fourteen are called "Ripe Age," a contemporary term denoting physical maturity, which brings the "abilitie and fitnesse for procreation."[15] If quite youthful affianced partners had sexual intercourse (prima facie evidence of maturation), that act carried with it the presumption of consent to their union, and there was even a proviso that lawful marriages could occur at ages younger than twelve if puberty had been attained. Elizabethans and Jacobeans thereby recognized that adulthood could not be defined by a set number of years, as could wardship or legal minority.[16]

When one seeks evidence for the true age of sexual maturity, it becomes increasingly obvious that twelve and fourteen probably represented the very earliest points at which feminine and masculine puberty arrived. Thanks to improved nutrition and medical care, the onset of adolescence has dropped markedly in the twentieth century, so that now female menses begin on average at twelve but may start as early as eight or nine.[17] By contrast, in Shakespeare's day maturation came much later. Medical handbooks specify the span of menstruation as extending from fourteen or fifteen to forty-six or fifty,[18] and other works routinely refer to the years from fourteen or fifteen to twenty-five as "youth,"[19] or adolescence. It was acknowledged, however, that male sexuality might develop as late as eigh-

---

lished long after Swinburne's death in 1624, details the practices of his own time); William Harrington, *The Comendacions of Matrymony* (London, 1528), C3ᵛ–C4. Then, as now, girls reached puberty earlier than boys; see Ozment, *When Fathers Ruled*, p. 11; Ian Maclean, *The Renaissance Notion of Woman* (Cambridge: Cambridge University Press, 1980), pp. 32, 35. Powell, *English Domestic Relations*, p. 5n, presumes that twelve and fourteen were the customary ages of puberty.

[15] Swinburne, *Treatise*, p. 24; William Perkins, *Christian Oeconomie*, trans. Thomas Pickering (London, 1609), p. 54.

[16] *Lawes*, p. 57; Swinburne, *Treatise*, p. 51.

[17] E. Pearlman, "Historical Demography for Shakespeareans," *Shakespearean Research Opportunities* 7–8 (1972–1974): 70, points out that the menarche has been dropping four months per decade since 1830; seventeen was not an uncommon age for the onset of menstruation in the nineteenth century. See also R. E. Behrman, V. C. Vaughn, and W. E. Nelson, eds., *Nelson Textbook of Pediatrics*, 17th ed. (Philadelphia: W. B. Saunders, 1987), p. 1231.

[18] Thomas Cogan, *The Haven of Health* (London, 1584), p. 255. Nicholas Culpeper, *A Directory for Midwives* (London, 1671), says "never before the twelfth" year, p. 71, and "none till after twelve," p. 75. See also John Sadler, *The Sick Womans Private Looking-Glasse* (London, 1636), p. 13.

[19] Susan Brigden, "Youth and the English Reformation," *Past and Present* 95 (1982): 37;

teen, after which time a woman could legally ask for a dissolution of marriage on the grounds of impotence.[20] The attempt in 1571 to raise the minimum ages of consent to marriage from twelve and fourteen to either fourteen and sixteen or fifteen and seventeen may well reflect a move to bring this regulation in line with the average onset of puberty rather than the earliest.[21] And the change in church canons deferring the deadline for compulsory communion to sixteen may also represent an adjustment to a more realistic assessment of maturity.[22]

When one looks to specific cases, Dr. Simon Forman affirms that in October after her marriage "my wife's course came down and it was the first time that ever she had them."[23] Mistress Forman's age is a matter of dispute; she may have been as young as fifteen or as old as nineteen.[24] Sir Simonds D'Ewes more indirectly hints at the belated maturation of both his mother and his wife. The elder woman "remained barren about six years after her marriage (which partly was occasioned by reason she married very early, being scarce fourteen years old. . . .)," and her future daughter-in-law followed much the same pattern. Not quite fourteen when she wed Sir Simonds, the girl "was, since my marriage, within the space of some nine months, much grown in stature, and improved in handsomeness." Nonetheless, the couple had "been partakers of the nuptial rites about two years, and yet had as little expectation of issue as in the first

---

Cogan, *Haven*, p. 193; William Gouge, *Of Domesticall Duties* (London, 1622), p. 526; James Osborn, ed., *The Autobiography of Thomas Whythorne* (Oxford: Clarendon Press, 1961), p. 80; Thomas Pritchard, *The Schoole of Honest and Vertuous Lyfe* (London, ca. 1579), p. 23.

[20] Swinburne, *Treatise*, p. 49. Precisely this charge was brought against the Earl of Essex in Francis Howard's notorious suit for annulment in 1613.

[21] Thomas, "Age and Authority," p. 226. The effort was temporarily approved in 1653.

[22] *Constitutions*, R4, S1; Thomas, "Age and Authority," p. 224.

[23] A. L. Rowse, *Sex and Society in Shakespeare's Age: Simon Forman the Astrologer* (New York: Charles Scribner's Sons, 1974), p. 95. Forman was frequently asked to examine girls, some as old as eighteen, because they had not begun menstruation. See, e.g., Ashmolean MSS 195.45ᵛ, 195.214, 206.433; citations generously supplied by Barbara Traister in private correspondence.

[24] Traister says 15; Richard Greaves says 16, in *Society and Religion in Elizabethan England* (Minneapolis: University of Minnesota Press, 1981), p. 145; Kathy Lynn Emerson says 18, in *Wives and Daughters: The Women of Sixteenth-Century England* (Troy, NY: Whitston Publishing Company, 1984), p. 7; Rowse, *Sex*, says 19, p. 78, then later says 17 or 18, p. 92.

eight months of our continence next after marriage." A daughter finally arrived three and a half years after their wedding.[25]

Quite aside from the physical, financial, or legal ability to marry is the rhetoric attending the question of when individuals were old enough for matrimony. Here one finds a torrent of opposition to Romeo-and-Juliet marriages. The objections, whether private or public, center on issues of health, money, and discretion. Parents are repeatedly urged not to "marre their children by marying them, during their minorities" or, worse yet, "in their child hood, before either bloud or affection ripen them."[26] Indeed, "infancie," along with disease and other impediments, could be advanced as a ground for breaking betrothal contracts.[27] The Elizabethans further object to early consummation because it presumably causes sterility, difficult childbirth, and defective children. Citing reasons for long, difficult deliveries, Eucharius Roeslin begins, "Fyrst when the Woman that laboreth is conceyued ouer yonge/as before .xii yee[r] or xv. yere of aege/which chãceth somtyme/though not verye often."[28] The law's laxity in allowing those as young as twelve or fourteen to marry "is the cause that men and women in these days are both weake of body, and small of stature," according to Thomas Cogan, another medical authority.[29]

Critics also denounce early marriages contracted for financial advantage. Thus they object to noblemen who "for the moste parte marrye theyr chyldren at theyr pleasure whan they are verye yonge, euen to suche as

[25] Sir Simonds D'Ewes, *The Autobiography and Correspondence*, ed. James Orchard Halliwell (London: Richard Bentley, 1845), 1:2, 358, 417.

[26] William Vaughan, *The Golden-grove* (London, 1600), N8 (note the echo of *Rom.*'s "and too soon marred," I.ii.13); Alexander Niccholes, *A Discourse of Marriage and Wiving* (London, 1620), p. 11. See also Thomas Becon, *The Golden Boke of Christen Matrimonye* (London, 1543), C5.

[27] Robert Cleaver, *A Godly Form of Householde Government* (London, 1598), p. 127.

[28] Eucharius Roeslin, *The Byrth of Man-Kynde* (London, 1540), p. xiiii. The youngest recorded aristocratic mother was the Countess of Exeter, who delivered a child in 1589 when she was fourteen and a half; E. W. Ives, "Shakespeare and History: Divergencies and Agreements," *Shakespeare Survey* 38 (1985): 28.

[29] Cogan, *Haven*, p. 255. See also Heinrich Bullinger, *The Christian State of Matrimony*, trans. Miles Coverdale (London, 1575), p. 16ᵛ; D'Ewes, *Autobiography*, 1:319; Gouge, *Domesticall Duties*, p. 180; Niccholes, *Discourse*, p. 11; Juan Luis Vives, *The Office and Duetie of an Husband*, trans. Thomas Paynell (London, 1553), I3–I3ᵛ; Greaves, *Society*, p. 239; Ozment, *When Fathers Ruled*, p. 103; Stone, "Marriage," p. 199. However, it was also thought that intercourse helped cure menstrual difficulties, according to Hilda Smith, "Gynecology and Ideology in Seventeenth-Century England," in *Liberating Women's History*, ed. Berenice A. Carroll (Urbana: University of Illinois Press, 1976), p. 101.

wyll geue them most mony for them."[30] However, moralists find equally offensive the youths who wed with no thought of financial support for their union: "And besides this, you shal haue euery saucy boy, of ten, fourteene, sixteen, or twenty yeares of age, catch vp a woman & mary her . . . without any respect how they may liue together, with sufficient maintenance for their callings and estate."[31] Ideally, tender years should neither excuse monetary irresponsibility nor promote monetary gain at the expense of all other considerations.

Above everything else, the theorists insist that partners attain both "rype yeeres and good discretion"[32] before entering a marriage. For women, the recommended age varies from seventeen to twenty-two, and for men from twenty to thirty-five or so.[33] Interestingly, Lord Burghley planned for his son Thomas Cecil to marry at twenty, perhaps to exert control over a match just before Thomas reached his majority, but Sir Walter Raleigh thought thirty a better age.[34] "When you haue past your minority, or serued your Apprentisships vnder the gouernment of others, when you begin the world for your selues"[35] seems to another authority the appropriate time for a man to take a wife. From a practical standpoint, spouses still in their teens are deemed incompetent to manage a household. A letter of the period written to a newly married man counsels thus: "I understand you conceived unkindly of your father, that he would not suffer you to marry sooner. If you knew what it were for a wife of fifteen years, and a husband of seventeen to entertain the charge and government of a family, you would say your father were cruel in marrying you so soon, and

---

[30] Thomas Becon, *Worckes* (London, 1564), 1:cccclxiiii. See also Gouge, *Domesticall Duties*, p. 565.

[31] Phillip Stubbes, *The Anatomie of Abuses* (London, 1595), p. 65.

[32] Bartholomaeus Batty, *The Christian Man's Closet*, trans. William Lowth (London, 1581), p. 95ᵛ. See also Dudley Fenner, *The Artes of Logike and Rethorike* (London, 1584), Cᵛ; John Stockwood, *A Bartholomew Fairing for Parentes* (London, 1589), p. 50.

[33] The preferred ages correspond closely with those presumed ideal for conception—twenty for females, thirty for males; see Greaves, *Society*, p. 239. See also Batty, *Christian Man's Closet*, p. 97ᵛ; Cogan, *Haven*, p. 248; Robert Crofts, *The Lover, or Nuptiall Love* (London, 1638), B2ᵛ; Elizabeth Grymeston, *Miscelanea, Meditations, Memoratives* (London, 1604), A4; Richard Jones, *The Passionate Morrice*, ed. F. J. Furnivall, New Shakspere Society, ser. 6, no. 2 (London: M. Trübner, 1876): 51; Pierre de la Primaudaye, *The French Academie* (London, 1586), p. 496; Joseph Swetnam, *The Araignment of Lewde, Idle, Froward, and Unconstant Women* (London, 1615), p. 46.

[34] *Advice to a Son: Precepts of Lord Burghley, Sir Walter Raleigh, and Francis Osborne*, ed. Louis B. Wright (Ithaca, NY: Cornell University Press, 1962), pp. xiv, 22.

[35] Ester Sowernam, *Ester Hath Hangd Haman* (London, 1617), A3ᵛ–A4.

yourself unadvised in entering so hastily into so weighty a charge."[36] Satirically, writers claim, "The forward Virgins of our age are of opinion, that this commodity [marriage] can neuer be taken vp too soone, and . . . they will resolue you foureteene is the best time of their age, if thirteene bee not better."[37] The commentators' caustic tone implicitly condemns these adolescents so eager to be wives.

While no one seems to favor a child bride, a woman somewhat younger than her husband does merit acceptance, primarily because she will be more malleable to his wishes.[38] At the other extreme, those delaying marriage overlong come in for censure too: "he that marrieth late marrieth euill, infinuate vnto us."[39] Especially foolish were women "who many times deferre making their choyce, till age bring them to contempt, and excludes them from all choyce."[40] Some aver that children not wedded by the age of twenty-five can independently seek their own partners,[41] although such action brings "for the most part disaster and penurie."[42] For women, the fact that a younger married sister would take social precedence over a yet-unmarried elder sister emphasizes the desirability of finding a

---

[36] Sir Harris Nicolas, *Memoirs of the Life and Times of Sir Christopher Hatton* (London: Richard Bentley, 1847), p. xliv. See also Giovanni M. Bruto, *The Necessarie, Fit, and Convenient Education of a Yong Gentlewoman*, trans. W. P. (London, 1598), G2ᵛ; Thomas Carter, *Carters Christian Commonwealth: Domesticall Dutyes Deciphered* (London, 1627), p. 205; *The Court of Good Counsell* (London, 1607), B3ᵛ; Thomas Gataker, *Marriage Duties Briefely Couched Together* (London, 1620), p. 21; Primaudaye, *French Academie*, p. 496; Robert Snawsel, *A Looking Glasse for Maried Folkes* (London, 1610), D5ᵛ–D7ᵛ; Hercules and Torquato Tasso, *Of Mariage and Wiving*, trans. R. T. (London, 1599), F1; John Wing, *The Crowne Conjugall or, The Spouse Royall* (Middleburgh, 1620), pp. 128–129.

[37] Niccholes, *Discourse*, p. 11. See also Henry Parrott, "A young Nouices new yonger wife," in *Cures for the Itch. Characters, Epigrams, Epitaphs* (London, 1626); John Marston, *The Scourge of Villanie* (London, 1598), D5; Samuel Rowlands, *Tis Merrie When Gossips Meete* (London, 1602), C2ᵛ, D3; Wye Saltonstall, *Picturae Loquentes* (London, 1631), no. 4.

[38] Leone B. Alberti, *Hecatonphila, The Arte of Love* (London, 1598), pp. 7, 18; *Court*, B3ᵛ; Gouge, *Domesticall Duties*, p. 188; Stefano Guazzo, *The Civile Conversation*, trans. George Pettie (London: Constable, 1925), 2:18; Tasso, *Mariage*, p. 10. Hollingsworth, "Demography," p. 13, says that this kind of age discrepancy was the norm, as does Ruth Kelso, *Doctrine for the Lady of the Renaissance* (Urbana: University of Illinois Press, 1956), p. 81.

[39] Thomas Nashe, *The Anatomie of Absurditie* (London, 1589), A3. See also Morris P. Tilley, *A Dictionary of the Proverbs in England in the Sixteenth and Seventeenth Centuries* (Ann Arbor: University of Michigan Press, 1950), M699 and L74.

[40] Richard Brathwait, *The English Gentlewoman* (London, 1631), p. 146. See also Niccholes, *Discourse*, p. 11.

[41] Batty, *Christian Man's Closet*, p. 27ᵛ; Gouge, *Domesticall Duties*, pp. 564–565.

[42] Thomas Heywood, *A Curtaine Lecture* (London, 1637), p. 99.

husband sooner rather than later.[43] Regardless of which partner is older, the May-December relationship draws virtually unanimous criticism. "Touching the difference in yeeres, me thinks it is an unseemely thing, to see a yong woman matched with a man that carryeth a countenaunce rather to be her father than her husband, and I am perswaded, that yong dainty damsels go as willinglye to such husbandes, as they woulde doe to their graves."[44] One reason for objection to this kind of union is that "Virilitie" and fertility end at "Olde Age."[45]

Yet human rhetoric and human behavior do not necessarily coincide. What parents, preachers, satirists, and social critics prescribe or describe can differ markedly from what people actually do. Thus it is useful to consider at least some specific individuals to see in what respects their marital practices reflect the ideals set forward in contemporary writings. And if one looks for examples of extremely youthful marriages, they are easy enough to find. Sir Ralph Verney and Mary Bucknell were wed at the respective ages of sixteen and thirteen, while Katherine Grey was thirteen and Lord Henry Herbert sixteen, and at fourteen or fifteen Grace Sherrington married Anthony Mildmay.[46] At the social apex, the much-sought-after Princess Elizabeth took the Elector of the Palatinate as her husband when she was sixteen. There are also plenty of instances of marriage deferred to a very late age, such as that of Michael Hickes, who found a

---

[43] Gouge, *Domesticall Duties*, p. 211; William Whately, *A Care-Cloth, or a Treatise of the Cumbers and Troubles of Marriage* (London, 1624), p. 61.

[44] Guazzo, *Civile Conversation*, 2:4; *Court* quotes this passage almost verbatim. See also Angel Day, *The English Secretary* (London, 1607), pp. 138–140; D'Ewes, *Autobiography*, 1:229; Lord Dudley North, *Observations and Advices Oeconomical* (London, 1669), p. 6; Perkins, *Christian Oeconomie*, p. 63; Henry Smith, *A Preparative to Mariage* (London, 1591), p. 15; Torquato Tasso, *The Housholders Philosophie*, trans. T. K. (London, 1588), pp. 10–10ᵛ; Tilley, *Dictionary*, P421; Edmund Tilney, *A Brief and Pleasant Discourse of Duties in Mariage, Called the Flower of Friendshippe* (London, 1568), B4; Geffrey Whitney, *A Choice of Emblemes, and Other Devises* (Leyden, 1586), p. 99; L. Wright, *Display of Dutie* (London, 1621), D3ᵛ; Janet C. Stavropoulos, "Love and Age in *Othello*," *Shakespeare Studies* 19 (1987): 125–128.

[45] Pritchard, *Schoole*, pp. 26, 27. See also Perkins, *Christian Oeconomie*, p. 63.

[46] Miriam Slater, *Family Life in the Seventeenth Century: The Verneys of Claydon House* (London: Routledge and Kegan Paul, 1984), p. 13; Pearson, "Renaissance Adolescent Marriage," p. 19; Retha M. Warnicke, *Women of the English Renaissance and Reformation* (Westport, CT: Greenwood Press, 1983), p. 149; Rachel Weigall, ed., "The Journal of Lady Mildmay, circa 1570–1617," *The Quarterly Review* 215 (1911): 122. See also Sara Heller Mendelson, *The Mental World of Stuart Women: Three Studies* (Amherst: University of Massachusetts Press, 1987), p. 67, for the Earl of Cork's handling of his daughters' early marriages.

spouse at fifty-one, and of May-December unions like Sir Francis Bacon's alliance with Alice Barham when she was fourteen and he forty-five.[47] However, virtually all the cases of marriage at an early age involved questions of property, with the alliance arranged to secure a dowry or inheritance or income before one's child or ward could reach legal majority.[48] Moreover, it was not uncommon to put such children through a wedding ceremony and then separate them for a period of years—the groom was often sent abroad—before they actually began cohabiting. This practice was followed not only with the Earl of Essex but with such lesser-known individuals as Sir Thomas Berkeley (married at thirteen) and Francis, son of the Earl of Cork (married at sixteen), together with a good many others.[49]

Overwhelmingly more numerous than the unusual circumstances just rehearsed were the situations in which individuals did not marry until they had reached physical and emotional maturity. Had he "bene caught by the combination of frēds and followers" in his youth, the Earl of Northumberland would "have bene married to a long sorrow." Instead, "In my choise of a wyfe, it was long or I made it; I had told 31 years or I tooke one."[50]

---

[47] Alan G. R. Smith, *Servant of the Cecils: The Life of Sir Michael Hickes, 1543–1612* (Totowa, NJ: Rowman and Littlefield, 1977), p. 100; George R. Hibbard, "Love, Marriage and Money in Shakespeare's Theatre and Shakespeare's England," in *Elizabethan Theatre VI*, ed. Hibbard (Toronto: Macmillan of Canada, 1975), p. 137. See also Rowse, *Sex*, p. 78, with reference to n.24 above for the disagreement about Mrs. Forman's exact age. Martin Ingram, *Church Courts, Sex, and Marriage in England, 1570–1640* (Cambridge: Cambridge University Press, 1987), p. 140, discusses the factors that could make May-December marriages acceptable.

[48] Even Furnivall recognizes this factor, *Child-Marriages*, pp. xv–xxii, as does Powell, *English Domestic Relations*, p. 15. See also J. P. Cooper, "Patterns of Inheritance and Settlement by Great Landowners from the Fifteenth to the Eighteenth Centuries," in *Family and Inheritance: Rural Society in Western Europe, 1200–1800*, ed. Jack Goody, Joan Thirsk, E. P. Thompson (Cambridge: Cambridge University Press, 1976), p. 211. The authority on wardship is Joel Hurstfield, *The Queen's Wards: Wardship and Marriage under Elizabeth I*, 2d ed. (London: Frank Cass, 1973). See as well H. E. Bell, *An Introduction to the History and Records of the Court of Wards and Liveries* (Cambridge: Cambridge University Press, 1953), esp. pp. 114–115, to see how trafficking in wards increased during the period.

[49] Gouge, *Domesticall Duties*, decries this practice, p. 203. So do Gataker, *Marriage Duties*, pp. 38–39; Daniel Rogers, *Matrimoniall Honour* (London, 1642), p. 94; and Wing, *Crowne Conjugall*, p. 129. Stone gives many specific examples in "Marriage," pp. 198–200, and *Crisis*, pp. 657–659. See also D'Ewes, *Autobiography*, 1:320; Gervase Holles, *Memorials of the Holles Family, 1493–1656*, ed. A. C. Wood, Camden Society Publications, 3d ser., 55 (1937): 229.

[50] Henry Percy, ninth Earl of Northumberland, "Instructions . . . to his Son," *Archaeologia* 27 (1838): 345, 333.

Sir William Wentworth describes his father's death with a casual reference to his own marital status: "My father liued till I was aboutt 27 years old, I being then unmaryed."[51] Katherine Knyvett did not wed Edmund Paston until she was twenty-five, while Sir Anthony Coke's daughters all married rather late (Anne was nearly thirty at her wedding).[52] And time after time one finds wards or heirs and heiresses united not as mere children but shortly before reaching their majority—Lady Anne Clifford to Richard Sackville when she was nineteen and he twenty, Sir Robert Drury to the daughter of Sir Nicholas Bacon when he was seventeen and Anne nineteen.[53] The list could go on indefinitely, but so could the list of those for whom marriage was postponed until they were even older.

What can distract the Shakespeare critic is the example of Shakespeare himself. At twenty-six, Anne Hathaway married at an age typical for her social station, but at eighteen her husband departed radically from the standard pattern. His early commitment might seem less anomalous had he possessed notable fame, fortune, or family in 1581, but he did not. Nevertheless, it skews a modern assessment of Elizabethan custom to regard either William Shakespeare or a handful of his contemporaries as normative when in fact they represent an extreme on the spectrum of age at first marriage. Against any analysis of fictional courtships onstage should be set the expectations of what was considered usual or unusual offstage. And while demographic evidence shows that privileged Englishmen married somewhat younger than ordinary folk, public opinion opposed the union of virtual children with considerable unanimity. It seems clear that extraordinary measures were often taken to protect the occasional juvenile spouse from premature sexual intercourse and that the onset of puberty occurred three or four years later than it does now. Legal statutes too put marriage for minors under the control of parents or guardians. Hence, with few exceptions, law, biology, and custom combined to make the average age when men and women first wed much later than one would suppose by looking at Shakespeare himself or at his Juliet.

[51] *Wentworth Papers, 1597–1628*, ed. J. P. Cooper, Camden Society Publications, 4th ser., 12 (1973): 29.

[52] Ruth Hughey, ed., *The Correspondence of Lady Katherine Paston, 1603–1627*, Norfolk Record Society 14 (1941): 15–16; Minna F. Weinstein, "Reconstructing Our Past, Reflections on Tudor Women," *International Journal of Women's Studies* 1 (1978): 135.

[53] Emerson, *Wives*, pp. 149, 203, 220, 223, 233, 234, 235, 237. For more comprehensive accounts of who married whom and at what age, see Ann Hoffmann, *Lives of the Tudor Age, 1485–1603* (New York: Barnes and Noble, 1977); Edwin Riddell, ed., *Lives of the Stuart Age, 1603–1714* (New York: Barnes and Noble, 1976); Alan and Veronica Palmer, *Who's Who in Shakespeare's England* (New York: St. Martin's Press, 1981).

When introducing a very young heroine, Shakespeare takes particular care to specify how old she is, perhaps as a signal to his audience that they should regard her in a special way. For example, in *Richard II* and *Romeo and Juliet*, both written about 1595, Shakespeare alters the ages of important female characters. Historically, Isabella was only eight at her marriage to Richard some two years after his first wife, Anne of Bohemia, had died. For the purposes of the play, however, the queen (whose name is never specified) cannot be a mere child. The charges that Bushy and Green "Made a divorce betwixt his queen" and Richard and "Broke the possession of a royal bed" (*R2*, III.i.12–13) sound absurd if Bolingbroke refers to a little girl. Moreover, the pathetic effects of the garden scene and the wrenching farewell scene cannot be obtained with a child wife, no matter how precocious. Thus Shakespeare remains silent about this character's age, identifies her neither as Anne nor as Isabella, and endows her with the qualities of a grown woman. Here, where history itself provides the authority for an astonishingly young wife, the playwright instead creates an adult. Certainly, as I have suggested, the alteration fits in with the aesthetic demands of *Richard II*, but Shakespeare may also have felt that his spectators would be offended by blunt reminders that an English sovereign would have married a mere child, when such a practice was frowned upon in Elizabethan society. Thus Richard's queen is silently transformed from child to woman.

Not so with Juliet. In Arthur Brooke's poem, the play's immediate source, the heroine is sixteen, and in William Painter's earlier prose translation of Bandello, she is eighteen.[54] Yet in the first act Shakespeare's text specifies an even younger age. As Lady Capulet says, "She's not fourteen," with the Nurse echoing, "she's not fourteen." "Come Lammas Eve at night shall she be fourteen," she repeats, and again, "On Lammas Eve at night shall she be fourteen" (I.iii.13, 15, 19, 23). Moreover, Lady Capulet confirms such an age as common for marrying.

> Well, think of marriage now. Younger than you
> Here in Verona, ladies of esteem,

---

[54] In Brooke's *The Tragicall Historye of Romeus and Juliet*, even at sixteen, Juliet is "too yong to be a bryde" (line 1860), while Romeo is older and more experienced: "I, as a ravisher, thou, as a careless child" (line 1651); Geoffrey Bullough, *The Narrative and Dramatic Sources of Shakespeare* (London: Routledge and Kegan Paul, 1957), 1:334, 328. Jill Levenson's otherwise full explication of the earlier versions of the story does not note the significance of the protagonists' ages; "Romeo and Juliet before Shakespeare," *Studies in Philology* 81 (1984): 325–347.

Are made already mothers. By my count,
I was your mother much upon these years
That you are now a maid.

(71–75)

Paris also affirms that the custom exists: "Younger than she are happy mothers made" (I.ii.12). However, her father initially refuses to consider a union for Juliet until she is two years older. The information in the opening scenes is straightforward, repeated several times lest the facts be overlooked. Yet these "facts" directly contradict the usual English marriage practices. What does Shakespeare achieve by deliberate alteration of both his sources and social custom?

One obvious effect is to lessen the responsibility of Romeo and Juliet for the disastrous consequences of their actions. In the play's sources the lovers incur harsh censure for rash, disobedient behavior. Brooke's poem, in fact, ends with a moral diatribe against defying one's elders. However, Shakespeare's tragedy evokes sympathy for the protagonists, even though between them they violate their parents' trust, contract a hasty secret marriage, kill two noblemen, break several laws, and commit the mortal sin of suicide. Yet because of their extreme youth, the blame for such behavior is largely displaced upon others—the kinsmen who perpetuate the feud, the Nurse who lacks discretion, Friar Laurence who connives at a clandestine wedding and its cover-up. Juliet, after all, is scarcely more than a child, her weaning and infancy still vivid memories. Instead of being attended by companions her own age, as are Portia or Hero, she remains entrusted to a nurse. And Romeo is a mere youth, initially indulging in the pleasurable pains of unrequited adolescent love. His friends Benvolio and Mercutio jeer at romance and give no thought to marriage, nor does Tybalt: they are too young, too busy crashing parties and playing jokes and provoking quarrels. As is consistent with the other tragic motifs, the protagonists' rash, premature assumption of maturity plunges them into the bitterly complicated consequences that always attend adult behavior. Ready or not, they must deal with the results of what they have done, and they must do so virtually alone. The star-crossed lovers cannot escape the aftermath of their impulsive actions, but their tender ages do mitigate the blame that would fall on adults acting in the same way.[55]

The extreme youth of Romeo and Juliet also underscores the aestheti-

[55] Marianne Novy, *Love's Argument: Gender Relations in Shakespeare* (Chapel Hill: University of North Carolina Press, 1984), among others, sees that "the extreme youth of the lovers emphasizes their innocence and inexperience," p. 109.

cally lush, hot, sensuous atmosphere of Verona. In a place where all passion is at the boil—choler, grief, hatred—sexual passion is unbridled too. The urge to couple is as furious as the urge to quarrel. Emotional intensity so pervades the society that it constantly erupts into public broils, private highjinks, secret sorrows, magical fantasies, dark premonitions. For the youngest and most innocent, of course, the sensations seem most intense. Moreover, in this tragedy where family (or house) determines destiny, Juliet in particular recapitulates her parents' patterns. Like her father, she bursts into fits of anger and grief, rushes into premature commitments; like her mother, she is wed before she reaches fourteen.[56] And how emotionally seductive for an Elizabethan audience to enter into a world where beautiful women, already blooming at thirteen or fourteen, might be impetuous enough to marry a young blood not yet twenty. Comprising titillating yet condemned practices, the exotic-erotic milieu of Verona could elicit a complex response in an English society where most marriages were delayed until adulthood.[57]

Yet the precocious satisfaction of sexual desire, regardless of its power over the imagination, carries certain dangers in real life. Elizabethans objected to matrimony for extremely young girls partly on the grounds that it added to the dangers of childbearing. *Romeo and Juliet* suggests that Lady Capulet's early union and the subsequent birth of Juliet may have had damaging consequences, for she has produced no other living children. As her spouse observes, "And too soon marred are those so early made" mothers (I.ii.13).[58] It is not necessary to invent an earlier marriage for Old Capulet, as some critics have done, to explain why the grave "hath swallowèd all my hopes but she," why all his offspring "but this only child" are dead (III.v.165).[59] Rather, his own marriage resembles the one he fi-

[56] Irene G. Dash, *Wooing, Wedding, and Power: Women in Shakespeare's Plays* (New York: Columbia University Press, 1981), sees the situation as more intentional on the parents' part, Lady Capulet "saddling the child with her own destiny," pp. 70–71.

[57] E. Pearlman, "Historical Demography," pp. 70–71, says Juliet's "physical precocity" is typical of Shakespeare's "Italianate atmosphere" and allows her to be "both passionate and silly." Pearson, "Renaissance Adolescent Marriage," p. 24, discusses the decadently erotic nature of Italy in Elizabethan eyes, as does John L. Lievsay, *The Elizabethan Image of Italy* (Ithaca, NY: Cornell University Press, 1964), p. 5.

[58] Almost alone, Coppélia Kahn, *Man's Estate: Masculine Identity in Shakespeare* (Berkeley: University of California Press, 1981), p. 94, feels Capulet may mean "that pregnancies are more likely to be difficult for women in early adolescence."

[59] See, e.g., John Hankins's introduction in *The Pelican Shakespeare*, ed. Alfred Harbage (Baltimore: Penguin Books, 1969), p. 856. Harbage, like most editors, includes the line

nally approves for his adolescent daughter and her more mature suitor, the County Paris. Though Lady Capulet, having borne Juliet at fourteen or fifteen, would be approaching thirty, her husband last danced in a youthful bachelor's mask some thirty years ago (I.v.33). With such a discrepancy in age between himself and his wife, he can easily advise Paris to wait before wedding Juliet. Yet in a subtle subtext Shakespeare may also be confirming his compatriots' belief that old age, like immaturity, mars the reproductive function. Perhaps it is Capulet's depleted vigor that has produced but one surviving child in a May-December union. Perhaps, too, the play may thereby suggest that adulthood does not necessarily arrive in a stated number of years. Age offers no guarantee against childishness, and by the time Romeo confronts Paris at the tomb, calling him "youth" and "boy" (V.iii.59, 61, 70), Juliet's young husband is surely far more experienced than his older rival.

Romeo's youth, though unstated, is not difficult to infer, but Count Bertram's wardship to the King of France unmistakably marks him as less than twenty-one, as does Helen's similar wardship to the Countess of Roussillon. The immaturity of the two leading characters in *All's Well* may have much to do with their headstrong behavior, which some have found so repellent.[60] As for the ages of other characters, Troilus "ne'er saw three-and-twenty" and "has not past three or four hairs on his chin" (I.ii.232, 108). Though old enough to be legally responsible for his actions, he is young enough to lust after Cressida in much the same way Bertram lusts after Diana. At twenty-five (I.i.125, V.i.311, 322–323), one Antipholus conducts an aggressive courtship in *The Comedy of Errors*, while his twin copes with a demanding new wife.[61] Similarly, their twin servants, virtually the same age, remain bachelors, though one has espoused himself to the great greasy Luce. Having eschewed marriage for many years before wedding Desdemona, Othello disclaims the youthful

---

"Earth hath swallowèd all my hopes but she" (I.ii.14), which appears in Q2–Q5 and in the Folio but is omitted from the Oxford edition.

[60] Among the critics with negative views on Bertram's youth are Robert G. Hunter, *Shakespeare and the Comedy of Forgiveness* (New York: Columbia University Press, 1965), p. 118; Arthur Kirsch, *Shakespeare and the Experience of Love* (Cambridge: Cambridge University Press, 1981), p. 117; Hugh Richmond, *Shakespeare's Sexual Comedy: A Mirror for Lovers* (New York: Bobbs-Merrill, 1971), p. 81; Peggy Muñoz Simonds, "Sacred and Sexual Motifs in *All's Well That Ends Well*," *Renaissance Quarterly* 42 (1989): 38.

[61] Ernest Pettet, *Shakespeare and the Romance Tradition* (New York: Staples Press, 1949), p. 70, deems each twin "somewhat old for the typical Shakespearean lover," but he thinks they are thirty-three.

"heat" of "appetite"—"the young affects / In me defunct" (I.iii.262–264).[62] Their May-December union brings disaster as surely as the one between Saturninus and Tamora, who promises to be "A loving nurse, a mother to his youth" (I.i.329). After bearing children to Antigonus and keeping a sixteen-year vigil, Paulina can term herself an "old turtle" (V.iii.133) just before she unexpectedly espouses Camillo at the end of *The Winter's Tale*. But aside from scattered clues of this kind, Shakespeare provides information as to specific ages in wooing only under special circumstances.

In situations where characters' maturity might be in doubt, indirect evidence tells spectators that they are not watching the actions of adolescents. In *The Taming of the Shrew*, Bianca has long been pursued by suitors, and Kate is her elder sister. At Belmont, from all over the world, "many Jasons come in quest" (I.i.172) of Portia, who capably manages her estate as an adult without benefit of the guardian required by minors. In *Much Ado about Nothing*, the wittily controlled dialogue between Hero's set of young women and the various men in the comedy indicates considerable experience with such repartee, an experience further confirmed by Margaret's involvement with Borachio and Beatrice's former attachment to Benedick. Cordelia and Desdemona are old enough to be formally wooed, the one by the rulers of France and Burgundy, the other by the "wealthy curlèd darlings" of Venice (I.ii.69).[63] In a borderline case like Viola's, the Elizabethan audience would know at once that the voyage which shipwrecks her in Illyria could not have been made under her brother's sole protection, nor could Sebastian independently accept a proposal from Olivia, unless the twins were at least twenty-one.[64] The same holds true for Olivia, who heads her own household after her brother's death and contracts a marriage for herself. Here in *Twelfth Night* the spectacle of four young adults, unfettered by parents or guardians, adds to the fun. However, all these signals—so clear to Renaissance spectators, regardless of whether they ignored them in a theatrical suspension of expectation—have

---

[62] For other references to Othello's age, see I.i.88, I.iii.349, and II.i.230.

[63] Marvin Rosenberg, *The Masks of King Lear* (Berkeley: University of California Press, 1972), p. 47, speculates that Goneril and Regan may not be much older than Cordelia, perhaps too young to bear the children they manifestly do not have.

[64] Meader, *Courtship*, supposes that Viola is about fifteen and that she and her brother might have gone to sea because of their father's death, p. 55. Derek Brewer, *Symbolic Stories: Traditional Narratives of the Family Drama in English Literature* (Totowa, NJ: Rowman and Littlefield, 1980), p. 117, thinks the twins and Olivia are probably seventeen, Orsino eighteen.

become blurred to modern audiences with quite different assumptions about the age when courtship takes place.

Shakespeare presents adult lovers in all his dramas except *All's Well*, *Romeo and Juliet*, the late romances, and possibly *The Merry Wives of Windsor*. In this last play, the opening scene, characteristically conveying important information, provides the following report of Anne Page: "And seven hundred pounds of moneys, and gold and silver, is her grandsire upon his death's-bed—Got deliver to a joyful resurrections—give, when she is able to overtake seventeen years old" (I.i.46–49). Evans's wretched grammar makes it difficult to tell whether Anne has yet overtaken seventeen.[65] However, the swarm of suitors anxious for her hand—Abraham Slender, Dr. Caius, and Master Fenton—suggests that the girl is at least old enough to have her legacy in hand. Moreover, in her conversations she seems remarkably self-assured for a girl in her teens. Even if she has reached her majority, the fact that both parents are living (a circumstance unusual in Shakespeare)[66] would account for her reluctance to choose Fenton over their objections. Her secret nuptials at the comedy's conclusion may indicate that, as an adult, she can legally bind herself to Fenton. Equally likely, the wedding may simply imply that Windsor's vicars, like its schoolmasters and doctors, are less than scrupulous. Perhaps here too is a purely English possibility that would have appealed to its audience's longings, however unrealistic, for a youthful marriage, with none of the fatal consequences attending the adolescent union of Romeo and Juliet. Amid the frolics of dumping, thumping, and pinching Falstaff, the irregular matrimony of a pretty heiress, even at seventeen or so, cannot seem like a serious transgression.

Shakespeare's late romances repeatedly employ the figure of the child bride. Marina is fourteen, Perdita sixteen, and Miranda almost fifteen. As with Juliet, their ages are all clearly specified. The reasons for the reappearance of the very young heroine lie partly in the sources and partly in the peculiar nature of this kind of drama. For one thing, the cyclical, familial context of the plays is more manageable with immature offspring than with a second generation of fully grown adults. Then, too, the fairytale quality of unreality that pervades the tragicomedies is enhanced by a heroine far too young and unworldly to face matrimony in everyday

---

[65] Meader, *Courtship*, p. 55, thinks she is not yet seventeen.

[66] On this point, see Maynard Mack's seminal "Rescuing Shakespeare," International Shakespeare Association Occasional Paper no. 1 (1979), p. 7.

terms.[67] By comparison, Juliet's passionate haste to consummate her wedding vows and Anne Page's deft handling of her multiple wooers seem warmly human. But Marina, Perdita, and Miranda emerge as figures from remote realms, innately pure and strangely wise though scarcely past childhood. Part of the appeal to audiences may well derive from the distance between such a heroine and an eligible, flesh-and-blood English female. Young men might dream of these maidens, but they generally married women of twenty or more, not girls of fourteen or sixteen. They might spin fantasies of loving a shepherdess or a virgin in a brothel or a damsel on an enchanted island, each a princess, of course. Yet the majority actually married wives of suitable age and suitable background from suitable families. The extreme youth of Marina, Perdita, and Miranda, then, makes an essential contribution to the atmosphere of fantasy engendered by the romances.

The heroines' youth also reinforces other aspects of these plays. In all the tragicomedies Shakespeare deals with the motif of endangered chastity. The younger the girl, the stronger the sense of both innocence and peril. Worst of all looms the ominous specter of incest.[68] With *The Winter's Tale*, Shakespeare retreats from an explicit opportunity for a father-

[67] Among those noting the otherworldly quality of the romances are Joan Hartwig, *Shakespeare's Tragicomic Vision* (Baton Rouge: Louisiana State University Press, 1972), pp. 5–6, 15, and passim; Barbara A. Mowat, *The Dramaturgy of Shakespeare's Romances* (Athens: University of Georgia Press, 1976), p. 1; Pettet, *Shakespeare and the Romance*, p. 188; Leah Scragg, *Discovering Shakespeare's Meaning* (Totowa, NJ: Barnes and Noble, 1988), pp. 76–80; Paul N. Siegel, *Shakespeare in His Time and Ours* (Notre Dame, IN: University of Notre Dame Press, 1968), p. 206.

[68] Critics discussing the incestuous possibilities in these plays include Linda Bamber, *Comic Women, Tragic Men: A Study of Gender and Genre in Shakespeare* (Stanford, CA: Stanford University Press, 1982), p. 175; C. L. Barber and Richard P. Wheeler, *The Whole Journey: Shakespeare's Power of Development* (Berkeley: University of California Press, 1986), p. 301; Lynda E. Boose, "The Father's House and the Daughter in It," in *Daughters and Fathers*, ed. Boose and Betty S. Flowers (Baltimore: Johns Hopkins University Press, 1989), pp. 30–31, 69; Stanley Cavell, *Disowning Knowledge: In Six Plays of Shakespeare* (New York: Cambridge University Press, 1987), pp. 216–217; Barbara Melchiori, " 'Still harping on my daughter,' " *English Miscellany* 11 (1960): 67–68; Carol Thomas Neely, *Broken Nuptials in Shakespeare's Plays* (New Haven: Yale University Press, 1985), pp. 167–170; Ruth Nevo, *Shakespeare's Other Language* (London: Methuen, 1987), p. 37ff; Kay Stockholder, *Dream Works: Lovers and Families in Shakespeare's Plays* (Toronto: University of Toronto Press, 1987), p. 174; Mark Taylor, *Shakespeare's Darker Purpose: A Question of Incest* (New York: AMS Press, 1982), passim; Leonard Tennenhouse, *Power on Display: The Politics of Shakespeare's Genres* (London: Methuen, 1986), p. 176. See also Marc Shell, *The End of Kinship: "Measure for Measure," Incest, and the Ideal of Universal Siblinghood* (Stanford, CA: Stanford University Press, 1988); Margaret Loftus Ranald, *Shakespeare and His Social Context* (New York: AMS Press, 1987), pp. 41, 95.

daughter liaison set up by the source, where the king actually woos his long-lost child until her identity is revealed.[69] The only vestige remaining is a passage during the first encounter of Leontes and the runaway lovers, when he vows he would "beg your precious mistress" (V.i.222) of Florizel until Paulina rebukes him for such a betrayal of Hermione. "I thought of her / Even in these looks I made" (227–228) is the father's oblique response. By comparison with this near-suppression of incest, *Cymbeline* edges closer to the possibility of a sexual relationship between siblings. In a sense, Posthumus is a foster-brother to Innogen because they have been reared in the same household, though no blood kinship unites them. To Cloten, however, Innogen is related by marriage if not by birth, since he is her stepbrother, living at court as she does. More disturbing still are the undertones to her arrival in male disguise at the forest home of her missing brothers:

> GUIDERIUS.   Were you a woman, youth,
> I should woo hard but be your groom in honesty,
> Ay, bid for you as I'd buy.
> ARVIRAGUS.   I'll make't my comfort
> He is a man, I'll love him as my brother.
>
> (III.vi.66–69)

Such hints never move beyond hinting, but in the context of the other romances, they do suggest a subtext of incest as the most dangerous sexual menace to the very young female.

Ominously, the Prologue of *Pericles* describes such a relationship between Antiochus and his daughter: "Bad child, worse father, to entice his own. . . . / By custom what they did begin / Was with long use account' no sin" (sc. 1, 27, 29–30). While this unnatural union constitutes the most overt attack of an incestuous nature, no child can be safe from other kinds of attack in the play's world. Upon the death of Lychorida, her nurse-protectress, Marina escapes a murder ordered by her envious foster-mother, Dioniza, only when the girl is kidnapped by pirates. At the brothel to which she is sold, other children too are coarsely violated:

> BAWD. . . . 'Tis not our bringing up of poor bastards—as I think I have
>   brought up some eleven—
> BOULT. Ay, to eleven, and brought them down again.
>
> (sc. 16, 13–15)

---

[69] Bullough, *Narrative and Dramatic Sources*, vol. 8 (1975), 193–196.

When the fourteen-year-old Marina's virtue repeatedly quenches the lust of customers, the Pander commands, "Boult, take her away. Use her at thy pleasure. Crack the ice of her virginity, and make the rest malleable" (sc. 19, 166–168). The effect of such brutal, violent danger is heightened when directed at a mere girl, bereft of nurse or parents or guardians, though the peril can be just as menacing at a royal court, where kings seduce their daughters, and queens order foster-daughters murdered.

Similarly, though more subtly, in *The Tempest* Shakespeare also emphasizes the vulnerability of the naive, unprotected virgin. In the past Miranda, now scarcely fifteen, has been attacked by Caliban, again a kind of proto-brother.[70] Propero rages, "Filth as thou art, . . . thou didst seek to violate / The honor of my child." Unrepentant, Caliban boasts, "O ho, O ho! Would't had been done! / Thou didst prevent me; I had peopled else / This isle with Calibans" (I.ii.349–353). And the man-beast would just as willingly hand over Miranda to the drunken Stephano: "She will become thy bed, I warrant, / And bring thee forth brave brood" (III.ii.105–106). The image of a Caliban or a Stephano coupling with Miranda to produce more monsters or fools powerfully represents the loathsome kind of sexual menace to maidenhood conjured up in the romances. It also helps to account for Prospero's repeated insistence on Ferdinand's restraint, an insistence that may or may not imply a covert incestuous attraction to his daughter.[71]

> PROSPERO. Look thou be true. Do not give dalliance
> Too much the rein. The strongest oaths are straw
> To th' fire i'th' blood. Be more abstemious,
> Or else good night your vow.

[70] Paul Brown, " 'This thing of darkness I acknowledge mine': *The Tempest* and the Discourse of Colonialization," in *Political Shakespeare: New Essays in Cultural Materialism*, ed. Jonathan Dollimore and Alan Sinfield (Ithaca, NY: Cornell University Press, 1985), p. 62, feels that Prospero is trying to "circumvent Caliban's version of events by reencoding his [Caliban's] boundlessness as rapacity . . . as a desire to violate the chaste virgin, who epitomizes courtly property."

[71] For negative views of Prospero's injunctions, see Bamber, *Comic Women*, pp. 175, 182; Paula S. Berggren, "The Woman's Part: Female Sexuality as Power in Shakespeare's Plays," in *The Woman's Part: Feminist Criticism of Shakespeare*, ed. Carolyn Lenz, Gayle Greene, Carol Thomas Neely (Urbana: University of Illinois Press, 1980), p. 30; David Shelley Berkeley, *Blood Will Tell in Shakespeare's Plays* (Lubbock: Texas Tech University Press, 1984), p. 13; Stockholder, *Dream Works*, p. 208. Marjorie Garber, *Coming of Age in Shakespeare* (New York: Methuen, 1981), pp. 139–140, finds Prospero's injunctions "natural and appropriate."

FERDINAND.   I warrant you, sir,
   The white cold virgin snow upon my heart
   Abates the ardor of my liver.[72]

(IV.i.51–56)

Though not a brothel, Prospero's desert island affords no protection for Miranda's virginity save Ferdinand's honor and her father's watchfulness. Since the age of three, this lone girl has had no nurse, no woman companion, no experience with young men, not even the shelter of a house, much less the safeguards due a princess.[73] Her utter innocence—intensified far beyond Perdita's or Marina's—combines with the force of first love to render Miranda unusually vulnerable to Ferdinand. Artlessly she offers, "I am your wife, if you will marry me," and adds, "To be your fellow / You may deny me, but I'll be your servant / Whether you will or no." As she confesses, "I prattle / Something too wildly, and my father's precepts / I therein do forget" (III.i.83–86, 57–59). By his own admission, the Neapolitan prince is experienced with women:

> Full many a lady
> I have eyed with best regard, and many a time
> Th'harmony of their tongues hath into bondage
> Brought my too diligent ear. For several virtues
> Have I liked several women. . . .

(39–43)

Were he a Caliban or even a Bertram, Ferdinand could easily take advantage of Miranda's trusting love. Heedless of Prospero's commands and ignorant of accepted behavior, the girl is virtually defenseless unless her wooer exercises more discipline than she seems capable of.

To assume that the vulnerable young heroines of Shakespeare's late plays are entering upon courtship, marriage, or sexual activity at the usual age inevitably lessens the sense of wonder and distance the romances should evoke. But even modern audiences need only consider the effect of a twenty-five-year-old Marina or Perdita or Miranda to see the shattering difference that would result. Could a grown woman convincingly preside, like Perdita, as an innocent virginal queen over sheepshearing rites where

---

[72] Note Prospero's earlier, longer injunction, IV.i.15–23.

[73] Melchiori, " 'Still harping,' " p. 66, is one of the few who note that Miranda has no watchful companions. Peter Erickson, *Patriarchal Structures in Shakespeare's Drama* (Berkeley: University of California Press, 1985), pp. 8–9, merely feels that her "isolation as a woman" deprives her of a role model.

earthy hanky-panky provides half the fun? Or could an adult convert brothel customers to penitents at first encounter as does the saintly little Marina? Could a mature female possibly exclaim, with Miranda, "O brave new world / That has such people in't" (V.i. 186–187)? Surely not. In all these works the dramatic requirement for an unusually young heroine leads Shakespeare to specify her age, ensuring that his audience sees a girl scarcely beyond childhood rather than one of years suitable for conventional courtship.

In plays with other aesthetic demands, lovers may be either mature or immature in order to meet the needs of the action appropriately. Their adolescence must figure into the critical assessment of Romeo and Juliet, Bertram and Helen, while their more advanced years must figure into an assessment of Othello or Duke Vincentio. Whether the comic venue is Illyria or Windsor or Syracuse, Shakespeare always provides clues to let spectators know when wooers are old enough to play matrimonial games. At the highest social levels, where kingdoms go with marriage, a prospective bride like Cordelia or Ophelia may be relatively young, but she is never a child and her royal suitor is always an adult. Even in an instance where history gives authority for a child queen, Shakespeare substitutes a grown woman for Richard II's wife. With a subtlety now obscure to audiences, he threads his way through the elaborate web of expectations governing the age when individuals become eligible for wedlock, both in his fictional sources and in his own social milieu. A recovered awareness of that subtlety can add significant nuances to interpretation of the plays. At the very least, it can caution critics against casually generalizing, "Shakespearean heroines marry very young, in their teens."[74]

[74] Stephen Orgel, "Prospero's Wife," in *Rewriting the Renaissance*, ed. Margaret W. Ferguson, Maureen Quilligan, Nancy J. Vickers (Chicago: University of Chicago Press, 1986), p. 57. He also says Anne Hathaway was twenty-four when she married; she was twenty-six.

The Social Status of Prospective Partners

He that a fit wife to himselfe doth wed,
· In minde, birth, age, keepes long a quiet bed.
—Alexander Niccholes, *A Discourse of Marriage and Wiving*

Equals to equals, good to good is joined.
—*Per.*, sc. 9, 88

BESIDES expecting sufficient maturity in brides and grooms, the Elizabethans also shrewdly calculated other desirable qualities. Such factors as rank, lineage, family, power, wealth, education, appearance, health, upbringing, virtue, intelligence, and religious persuasion all entered into the process of choosing a mate. Echoing the generally accepted wisdom of his subjects, in 1599 King James formally advises his son thus:

> The three accessories, whiche as I haue saide, ought also to be respected . . . are beautie, riches, and friendship by alliance, whiche are al blessings of God. For beautie increaseth your loue to your Wife, contenting you the better with her, without caring for others: and riches & great alliance, doe both make her the abler to be a helper vnto you. But. . . . beautie without bountie, wealth without wisdome, and great friendship without grace and honestie; are but faire shewes, and the deceatfull masques of infinite miseries.[1]

Further, James insists on a bride of the same faith who comes from a healthy stock with no "hereditary sicknesses." However, a prince cannot choose his wife from just any family, for "if he Marie firste basely beneath his rank, he will euer be the lesse accounted of there-after."[2] To a striking degree, other writers of the period reiterate the same ideals and reservations regarding a suitable spouse.[3]

[1] James I, *Basilicon Doron*, ed. James Cragie (Edinburgh: William Blackwood and Sons, 1944), 1:127–129.

[2] Ibid., p. 131. For Elizabeth's similar views regarding equality of rank, see Julia Briggs, *This Stage-Play World: English Literature and Its Backgrounds 1580–1625* (New York: Oxford University Press, 1983), p. 49.

[3] Besides the works subsequently cited, see Jean Bodin, *The Six Bookes of a Commonweale*,

In particular, Englishmen preach the advisability of equal social status between husbands and wives. As experts recommend, "But rather followe that olde and wise Prouerbe: *Equalem tibi muherem inquire*. Search out a woman that is thine equall. And as the Poet saith: *Si vos nubere, nube pari*. If thou wilt needes marry, then marry thy matche."[4] Another says to "choose such as are of equall yeeres, birth, fortunes, and degree, of good parentage, and kindred, of such a countenance, complexion and constitution, as best agrees to our love and disposition."[5] Accompanying these exhortations are dire warnings of the evils that ensue from pairing like with unlike. A mild remonstrance claims, "When a poore party meets with a rich, a well-bred one with a rude and illiberal, a curteous with a froward, a bountiful with a miserly, a noble with a base; one from the Court with another from the cart or the shop; a proper and personable, with a deformed, crooked or dwarfe, what a disproportion doth it cause, and a kind of loathsomnesse?"[6] A translation from Torquato Tasso insists

---

trans. Richard Knolles (London, 1606), p. 20; Patrick Hannay, *A Happy Husband, To Which Is Adjoyned the Good Wife* (London, 1619), A4, B^v–B2; Dorothy Leigh, *The Mother's Blessing* (London, 1616), p. 52; Alexander Niccholes, *A Discourse of Marriage and Wiving* (London, 1620), B^v; John Norden, *The Fathers Legacie* (London, 1625), A5^v; William Perkins, *Christian Oeconomie*, trans. Thomas Pickering (London, 1609), pp. 62–64; Thomas Wilson, *The Arte of Rhetorique* (London, 1553), pp. 22, 34. For literary presentations of these ideas, see Nicholas Breton, *The Mother's Blessing* (London, 1621), D^v, D4–D4^v; Sir Geoffrey Fenton, *Monophylo . . . A Philosophicall Discourse and Division of Love* (London, 1572), pp. 17, 20; Charles Gibbon, *A Work Worth the Reading* (London, 1591), pp. 1–12; Sir Thomas Overbury, "Of the choyce of a Wife," in *His Wife* (London, 1616). Shakespeareans may also wish to consult Ralph Berry, *Shakespeare and Social Class* (Atlantic Highlands, NJ: Humanities Press International, 1988); Frank Whigham, *Ambition and Privilege: The Social Tropes of Elizabethan Courtesy Theory* (Berkeley: University of California Press, 1984).

[4] Bartholomaeus Batty, *The Christian Man's Closet*, trans. William Lowth (London, 1581), p. 97^v; see also p. 99^v.

[5] Robert Crofts, *The Lover, or Nuptiall Love* (London, 1638), B2, E3^v. See also, e.g., *A Discourse of the Married and Single Life* (London, 1621), pp. 21, 29; Desiderius Erasmus, *A Modest Meane to Mariage* (London, 1568), B6; Dudley Fenner, *A Short and Profitable Treatise of Lawfull and Unlawfull Recreations* (Middleburgh, 1590), A4–A4^v; Matthew Griffith, *Bethel, or A Forme for Families* (London, 1633), pp. 253–254; Elizabeth Grymeston, *Miscelanea, Meditations, Memoratives* (London, 1604), A3^v; Stefano Guazzo, *The Civile Conversation*, trans. George Pettie (London: Constable, 1925), 2:18; *The Court of Good Counsell* (London, 1607), C^v (repeats Guazzo almost verbatim); Thomas Pritchard, *The Schoole of Honest and Vertuous Lyfe* (London, ca. 1579), pp. 56–57; Torquato Tasso, *The Housholders Philosophie*, trans. T. K. (London, 1588), p. 11^v; Hercules and Torquato Tasso, *Of Mariage and Wiving*, trans. R. T. (London, 1599), B2–B2^v, L; William Whately, *A Care-Cloth, or a Treatise of the Cumbers and Troubles of Marriage* (London, 1624), p. 73; L. Wright, *Display of Dutie* (London, 1621), D3^v.

[6] Daniel Rogers, *Matrimoniall Honour* (London, 1642), p. 61; also p. 69. See as well

that "two Palfreys or two Oxen of vnequall stature cannot be coupled vnder one selfe yoake" but then contradictorily requires that when such disparate unions do occur, the partner of higher status should "more honor and esteeme" the spouse because "Matrimonie maketh equall many differences."[7] Aside from this rare exception, however, most writers are not so charitable. The general antipathy toward disparity in age, discussed in the previous chapter, extends to disparity in all other matters.

To read the advice literature, one would suppose that virtue counted more than anything else, for theorists repeatedly insist upon the superiority of intrinsic nobility over worldly assets. As the conventional counsel puts it, "Let hir person be sought, not hir substance, craue hir vertues, not hir riches."[8] Among those virtues, writers especially commend piety, chastity, humility, and industry. Hence a man is advised to "choose such an one as may be more commended for humility than beauty. A good housewife is a great patrimony; and she is most honourable that is most honest."[9] What this particular strain of didacticism claims is that the criterion of moral worth should outweigh such advantages as birth, wealth, appearance, and the like. Yet a good deal of the exhortation is moral window dressing. Again and again comes the cynical echo, "Few take wives for God's sake."[10] While no one advocates marriage to a wicked partner, most of the prevailing advice seriously undercuts the notion that ethical

---

Advice to a Son: Precepts of Lord Burghley, Sir Walter Raleigh, and Francis Osborne, ed. Louis B. Wright (Ithaca, NY: Cornell University Press, 1962), p. 69; Thomas Dekker, "The Batchelors Banquet," in *The Non-Dramatic Works*, ed. Alexander B. Grosart (1884; reprint, New York: Russell and Russell, 1963), 1:197–209; John Ferne, *The Blazon of Gentrie* (London, 1586), pp. 9–10; Richard Mulcaster, *Positions* (London, 1581), p. 180; and Whately, *Care-Cloth*, p. 74.

[7] Tasso, *Housholders Philosophie*, pp. 9ᵛ–10. Robert Cleaver, *A Godly Form of Householde Government* (London, 1598), pp. 145–146, follows Tasso.

[8] Edmund Tilney, *A Brief and Pleasant Discourse of Duties in Mariage, Called the Flower of Friendshippe* (London, 1568), B5. See also Richard Brathwait, *The English Gentlewoman* (London, 1631), p. 148; Heinrich Bullinger, *The Christian State of Matrimony*, trans. Miles Coverdale (London, 1575), pp. 50ᵛ–51; Thomas Carter, *Carters Christian Commonwealth: Domesticall Dutyes Deciphered* (London, 1627), pp. 8–9; Guazzo, *Civile Conversation*, 2:7; Edward Hake, *A Touchestone for This Time Present* (London, 1574), E2; *The Mothers Counsell* (London, 1631), p. 3; Joseph Swetnam, *The Araignment of Lewde, Idle, Froward, and Unconstant Women* (London, 1615), p. 43; Tasso, *Of Mariage*, Lᵛ.

[9] John Lyly, *Euphues: The Anatomy of Wit; Euphues and His England*, ed. Morris William Croll and Harry Clemons (1916; reprint, New York: Russell and Russell, 1964), p. 209. See also Richard Greenham, *Works* (London, 1599), p. 35; Thomas Taylor, *A Good Husband and a Good Wife* (London, 1625), p. 9.

[10] Morris P. Tilley, *A Dictionary of the Proverbs in England in the Sixteenth and Seventeenth Centuries* (Ann Arbor: University of Michigan Press, 1950), F199.

rectitude alone compensates for disparity in other attributes. Overwhelmingly, authorities recommend a union of equals and frown upon unions
perceived as unequal.

Concern especially attached to marrying outside one's degree of birth or
riches if the primary motive behind such matrimony seemed to be ambition or avarice. Critics chastise unscrupulous fathers who debase their
status: "For men will sooner match their daughters with my yong maister,
a rich Coblers Sonne, though they be their heires, then with a Gentleman
of a good house, being a younger Brother. Heerby comes the decay of
ancient gentilitie, and this *the* making of vpstart houses."[11] They warn that
those who are "too greedie of honour, worship, or wealth, intending to
haue the gold, and catching the hotte coales doo burne themselues without
recouerie."[12] Yet despite objections from many quarters, countless brides
and grooms were chosen primarily for their wealth rather than their birth
or education or even virtue. In short, "the greedines of the world is so
great at this day, that a man . . . careth not though his wife be ill brought
vp and worse borne, so that she be rich enough."[13] Much specific advice
bluntly asserts the primacy of riches, most notably these thoughts of the
Earl of Northumberland, who declares that a wife "should bringe with her
meate in her mouthe to mayntaine her expence" and "that her frends
should be of that eminency that they might probably appere to be stepps
for yow to better yowr fortun."[14] Like advice advocating the virtuous
spouse, these recommendations for a rich spouse may reflect a desired

[11] Richard Jones, *The Passionate Morrice*, ed. F. J. Furnivall, New Shakspere Society, ser.
6, no. 2 (London: N. Trübner, 1876): 98–99.

[12] Cleaver, *Godly Form*, p. 143, echoing Bullinger, *Christian State*, p. 51. See also Hen-
ricus Cornelius Agrippa, *The Commendation of Matrimony* (London, 1540), C6ᵛ; Bullinger,
Christian State, pp. 51–52; Angel Day, *The English Secretary* (London, 1607), p. 138; *Dis-
course*, pp. 20–21; Desiderius Erasmus, "The Unequal Marriage," in *Colloquies*, trans.
N. Bailey and ed. E. Johnson (London: Gibbings and Company, 1900), 3:61; Thomas
Gataker, *A Good Wife Gods Gift: and, A Wife Indeed* (London, 1623), pp. 16, 24; William
Gouge, *Of Domesticall Duties* (London, 1622), p. 190; Griffith, *Bethel*, pp. 255–256;
Thomas Heywood, *A Curtaine Lecture* (London, 1637), p. 100; Pierre de la Primaudaye,
The French Academie (London, 1586), p. 482; Pritchard, *Schoole*, p. 55; Rogers, *Matrimo-
niall Honour*, p. 45; Tilney, *Duties*, B2ᵛ; Juan Luis Vives, *The Office and Duetie of an Hus-
band*, trans. Thomas Paynell (London, 1553), D6; John Wing, *The Crowne Conjugall or,
The Spouse Royall* (Middleburgh, 1620), p. 105.

[13] *Court*, B2. See also Gataker, *Good Wife*, p. 18.

[14] Henry Percy, ninth Earl of Northumberland, "Instructions . . . to his Son," *Archaeo-
logia* 27 (1838): 333. See also *Advice*, pp. 10, 68, 69; William Cecil, Lord Burleigh,
Precepts (London, 1636), p. 2; Antonia Fraser, *The Weaker Vessel* (New York: Alfred A.
Knopf, 1984), p. 11; Swetnam, *Araignment*, p. 46.

rather than an actual form of behavior, but both notions feed into the culture's general conceptions about courtship.

One should of course discriminate between blatant fortune hunting or status seeking and a prudent awareness of the economic resources required to maintain one's rank. At the same time, it is important to recognize that, for many, a trade-off between birth and riches offered the only way to rise or to survive in the society.[15] These aspects of the marital market provided a ready target for literary satire. Thus, Francis Lenton twits the young schoolmaster, the gallant courtier, the fledgling barrister, and the country widow alike for seeking to ally wealth with position, while Wye Saltonstall presents a vulnerable heir, whose "knowne estate in the countrey proposes him varieties of matches, and his wealth, not his witt win's him affection."[16] Advice from fictional fathers parallels that of historical fathers, declaring, "Let a wench be wealthy, and set out in her brauerie, though she bee painted for her beautie, and scarce gentill for her parentage, yet, if she catch the name of a Lady, she must bee honoured like Queene *Guineuer*," because "Gold is halfe a God on the earth."[17] And no moralist could put the case more succinctly than the poet who observes,

> Yet manie are, who not the cause regarde,
> The birthe, the yeares, nor vertues of the minde:
> For goulde is first, with greedie men prefer'de,
> And loue is laste, and likinge set behinde.[18]

Besides wealth, beauty also attracts a good deal of contemporary attention, most of it negative. Underlying the suspicion of beauty is an awareness of its power to sway the judgment of a partner's fitness, as well as the long cultural history of ambivalence toward women. Hence, the proverbial advice counsels a suitor to "use as well his Ear as his Eye, that is, let him rather trust to his discretion according to what he hears than to his affection kindled by sight, that she may be no lesse useful in the day than agreeable at night."[19] A sermon warns, "Beautie is but painting, age and

---

[15] See, e.g., Rogers, *Matrimoniall Honour*, pp. 62–63.

[16] Francis Lenton, *Characterismi: or, Lentons Leasures* (London, 1631), nos. 2, 3, 7, 16; Wye Saltonstall, *Picturae Loquentes* (London, 1631), no. 9. See also Edward Blount, *Micro-Cosmographie, or, a Peece of the World Discovered* (London, 1628), nos. 9, 19.

[17] Nicholas Breton, *An Olde Mans Lesson and a Young Mans Love* (London, 1605), B4.

[18] Geffrey Whitney, *A Choice of Emblemes, and Other Devises* (Leyden, 1586), p. 99. See also Henry Willoby, *Willobie his Avisa, or the True Picture of a Modest Maid, and of a Chast and Constant Wife* (London, 1594), pp. 2ᵛ, 4.

[19] Lord Dudley North, *Observations and Advices Oeconomical* (London, 1669), p. 4. The advice regarding ears rather than eyes was ubiquitous; see, e.g., Tilney, *Duties*, B4ᵛ.

sicknesse will weare it away, why should any man make that his guide in chusing a wife?"[20] But more worldly figures see a worse danger in fair wives, for "their nature is so fraile and variable and temptations so ryfe as nether for anie worde nor othes will a wise man trust them for constancy."[21] Only in fiction are women lauded "for bewty and shape of body . . . well worthy to haue lien by a Prince."[22] For several observers, the most desirable form of comeliness consists of health in mind and body because these qualities can be passed on to one's children. Lord Burghley's dictum, "Make not choise of a Dwarfe or a Foole, for from the one you may beget a race of *Pigmeyes*, as the other will be your daily griefe and vexation," is repeated by several other fathers.[23]

Since, theologically, marriage is ordained of God to ensure "the procreation of children. . . . and to avoid fornication,"[24] external conditions like appearance or wealth or rank hold no necessary primacy in the selection of a spouse. However, a discrepancy prevails between high-minded theory and hardheaded practicality. Even a staid legal explication reveals the inherent contradictions of the social system, averring that "whosoeuer marryeth for beautie, age, order, splendour of birth, or for riches . . . doth very peruersely, though it be not expressly disallowed, but Marriage may be for the[se] other things also, and the Consent may be giuen for them."[25] Certainly when one turns from fictional or didactic literature to records of actual human behavior, the evidence shows overwhelmingly that, for those in the more privileged levels of society, rank and riches did outweigh other considerations. Above all else, Sir Simonds D'Ewes insisted on an ancient, honorable lineage in addition to an inheritance, while Sir Francis Bacon primarily required money to pay his debts and maintain his position ade-

[20] Whately, *Care-Cloth*, p. 22. See also Batty, *Christian Man's Closet*, p. 98ᵛ; Bullinger, *Christian State*, p. 50; Cleaver, *Godly Form*, pp. 141–143; *Court*, H3ᵛ; Thomas Gataker, "A Good Wife," in *Two Mariage Sermons* (London, 1620), p. 17; Grymeston, *Miscelanea*, A3ᵛ; Michel Eyquem de Montaigne, "On Some Verses of Virgil," in *The Complete Works*, trans. Donald M. Frame (Stanford, CA: Stanford University Press, 1948), p. 646; North, *Observations*, p. 6; Swetnam, *Araignment*, p. 52; Wright, *Display*, D2.

[21] *Wentworth Papers 1597–1628*, ed. J. P. Cooper, Camden Society Publications, 4th ser., 12 (1973): 22. See also Percy, "Instructions," p. 346; *Advice*, pp. 20–21.

[22] Erasmus, *Modest Meane*, B4.

[23] Cecil, *Precepts*, p. 4. See also *Advice*, p. 21; Percy, "Instructions," pp. 333, 346; and, more theoretically, Pritchard, *Schoole*, p. 70.

[24] *The Book of Common Prayer, 1559*, ed. John Booty (Charlottesville: University Press of Virginia, 1976), p. 290.

[25] *The Lawes Resolutions of Womens Rights* (London, 1632), p. 63. See also William Harrington, *The Comendacions of Matrymony* (London, 1528), A4.

quately.[26] Now and again a Sir Walter Raleigh or a John Donne would elope with little thought of the social consequences, but such individuals represented the exception and not the norm. Often they paid dearly for their imprudence.

Far more typical were marriages like that described by Philip Gawdy: "I writt to yow that my Lo: of Pembroke had marryed my Lady Mary and now my Lo. Dauers [Danvers] shall marry her sister my lady Alathia. . . . It is thought very fytt and conuenyent that euery man now sholde marry within his owne element."[27] In their extensive correspondence the Barrington family weighed prospective matches with a careful eye toward wealth, religion, birth, and connections. Praise went to the cousin who chose "a gentlewoman of portion, education and proportion paralel to his estate," and contempt to the man's sister, who wed "an apothecarye's sonn who hath but 700^{ls} [pounds] per annum assured him."[28] The objection advanced to Catherine Nicholls's match with John Wilde acknowledged him "of honest parentage . . . life and conversation" but decried the "great disparity betwixt the said parties . . . as well in respect of birth and descent as of estate and livelihood."[29] Carrying out the injunctions of their age and of their own writings, the clergy tended to marry daughters of other clergymen, and not even bishops married into the nobility.[30]

---

[26] Sir Simonds D'Ewes, *The Autobiography and Correspondence*, ed. James Orchard Halliwell (London: Richard Bentley, 1845), 1:308–309, 311, 325, 420; he discusses his wife's derivation at considerable length, pp. 326–346. For Bacon, see George R. Hibbard, "Love, Marriage and Money in Shakespeare's Theatre and Shakespeare's England," in *Elizabethan Theatre VI*, ed. Hibbard (Toronto: Macmillan of Canada, 1975), pp. 134, 136–138.

[27] Philip Gawdy, *Letters of Philip Gawdy*, ed. Isaac Herbert Jeayes (London: J. B. Nichols and Sons, 1906), pp. 147–148. In fact, Lord Danvers died unmarried. For similar contemporary reports, see Arthur Searle, ed., *Barrington Family Letters, 1628–1632*, Camden Society Publications, 4th ser., 28 (1983): 235; Norman Egbert McClure, ed., *The Letters of John Chamberlain* (Philadelphia: American Philosophical Society, 1939), 1:512.

[28] Searle, *Barrington*, pp. 124, 247; see also pp. 116, 119. For comparable appraisals, consult D'Ewes, *Autobiography*, 1:228; James Osborn, ed., *The Autobiography of Thomas Whythorne* (Oxford: Clarendon Press, 1961), p. 185; Sir Harris Nicolas, *Memoirs of the Life and Times of Sir Christopher Hatton* (London: Richard Bentley, 1847), p. xlv.

[29] Cited in Martin Ingram, *Church Courts, Sex, and Marriage in England, 1570–1640* (Cambridge: Cambridge University Press, 1987), pp. 203–204.

[30] M. K. Ashby, *The Changing English Village: A History of Bledington, Gloucestershire in Its Setting 1066–1914* (Kineton: Roundwood Press, 1974), p. 97; Joel Berlatsky, "Marriage and Family in a Tudor Elite: Familial Patterns of Elizabethan Bishops," *Journal of Family History* 3 (1978): 12, 7; B. C. Blackwood, "Marriages of Lancashire Gentry," *Genealogists' Magazine* 16 (1970): 324.

While modern scholars have recognized the particular attractions that counted most strongly, they also recognize the Elizabethans' increasing difficulty in adhering to either the ideal of intrinsic worth or the ideal of absolute equality in the choice of a mate.[31] Englishmen faced some uncomfortable truths. After all, a younger son frequently had to marry money to maintain the dignity of his birth.[32] And since daughters, unlike their brothers, had almost no option save marriage, their disproportionate numbers on the matrimonial market often necessitated compromises in a husband's qualifications.[33] Similarly, the increasing costs of their rank led peers to seek heirs or heiresses as spouses. As for the ambitious, wedding the right mate offered a ready shortcut to status and power. Lawrence Stone's research shows the growing supremacy of wealth in aristocratic marriages, though it reveals decided limits on how far down the social scale a noble family would go, regardless of the lure of riches.[34] T. H. Hollingsworth has also found that the proportion of nobly born spouses for peers' children reached an apex during this period, indicating that high expectations as to rank accompanied the need for wealth.[35] Below the level

---

[31] Michael D. Bristol, *Carnival and Theatre: Plebeian Culture and the Structure of Authority in Renaissance England* (New York: Methuen, 1985), p. 163; Richard L. Greaves, *Society and Religion in Elizabethan England* (Minneapolis: University of Minnesota Press, 1981), pp. 130–143; Lu Emily Pearson, *Elizabethans at Home* (Stanford, CA: Stanford University Press, 1957), pp. 311–312.

[32] For the status of younger brothers, see Sir Thomas Wilson, "The State of England (1600)," ed. F. J. Fisher, *Camden Miscellany*, 3d ser., 52 (1936): 24; Miriam Slater, "The Weightiest Business: Marriage in an Upper-Gentry Family in Seventeenth-Century England," *Past and Present* 72 (1976): 40–43; Lawrence Stone, *The Crisis of the Aristocracy, 1558–1641* (Oxford: Clarendon Press, 1965), pp. 599–600; Joan Thirsk, "Younger Sons in the Seventeenth Century," *History* 54 (1969): 358–377.

[33] T. H. Hollingsworth, "The Demography of the British Peerage," Supplement to *Population Studies* 18, no. 2 (1964): 9, shows that in the peerage fewer men than women compromised on rank.

[34] Lawrence Stone, "Marriage among the English Nobility in the 16th and 17th Centuries," *Comparative Studies in Society and History* 3 (1960–1961): 194–197; idem, *Crisis*, pp. 632–649; idem, *The Family, Sex and Marriage in England 1500–1800* (New York: Harper and Row, 1977), pp. 60–61, 86–87; idem, "Social Mobility in England, 1500–1700," in *Seventeenth-Century England: Society in an Age of Revolution*, ed. Paul Seaver (New York: New Viewpoints, 1976), p. 43.

[35] Hollingsworth, "Demography," p. 9, says that nobly born wives represented 25 percent (1550–1574), 37.6 percent (1575–1599), 41.3 percent (1600–1624), 38 percent (1625–1649) of the total. Nobly born husbands constituted 34.5 percent (1550–1574), 29.5 percent (1575–1599), 31.2 percent (1600–1624), 33 percent (1625–1649) of the total.

of the nobility, some Londoners moved out into country areas and established themselves—often to advantage—by marrying into local families with ancient roots.[36] Still further down the social ranks certain other Londoners had disproportionate opportunities to move upward. Because men greatly outnumbered women there, both native daughters and yeomen's daughters up from the countryside tended to make more advantageous marriages than would ordinarily have been the case,[37] including instances when a servant wed her master, especially just after his wife had died.[38] In this regard, some 40 percent of those born outside London who became wives of City widowers had been servants, sometimes in the same household, while apprentices had similar fortune with their masters' widows.[39]

On balance, then, both historical research and contemporary records do confirm the existence of alliances between those of unequal rank, wealth, or personal gifts. Yet neither the number nor the range must be exaggerated, for both were rather limited. Between the zenith of choice based on virtue alone and the nadir of choice based on venality alone lay the great majority of marital partnerships. Rhetorically and practically, the normative pattern was an essential parity between husband and wife, with some allowance for balancing an advantage in one spouse against a differing advantage in the other spouse. The scales rarely tipped far in either direction, regardless of whether the match joined nobility or commoners.

Shakespeare's pairing of marriage partners runs the full social gamut, from the occasional union of servants, like Dromio of Ephesus and the fat kitchen wench Nell, to the wedding of royalty, like Pericles and Thaisa. The couples also span the spectrum from absolute social equality to pronounced disparity in rank. Apparently the playwright again seems content to work out the consequences of any particular situation according to the

[36] Peter Clark, *English Provincial Society from the Reformation to the Revolution: Religion, Politics and Society in Kent 1500–1640* (Hassocks, Sussex: Harvester Press, 1977), p. 127; Lawrence and Jeanne C. Fawtier Stone, *An Open Elite? England 1540–1880* (Oxford: Clarendon Press, 1984), pp. 247–251.

[37] Vivien Brodsky Elliott, "Single Women in the London Marriage Market: Age, Status and Mobility, 1598–1619," in *Marriage and Society: Studies in the Social History of Marriage*, ed. R. B. Outhwaite (New York: St. Martin's Press, 1981), p. 99. Oddly, the migrant daughters of gentlemen, tradesmen, and craftsmen do not seem to have enjoyed a similar advantage.

[38] Marjorie K. McIntosh, "Servants and the Household Unit in an Elizabethan English Community," *Journal of Family History* 9 (1984): 21.

[39] Elliott, "Single Women," p. 88; Lawrence Manley, ed., *London in the Age of Shakespeare* (University Park: Pennsylvania State University Press, 1986), p. 272.

requirements of its dramatic context, just as he does with the ages of wooers.

In certain plays social parity is clearly demanded. The indistinguishability of the twin Antipholi in *A Comedy of Errors*, for example, is enhanced by their eventual union to sisters, Adriana and Luciana. The very language of the wooing scene reinforces the doubleness, the merging of sexual and kinship identity, that forms the comedy's aesthetic core:

> LUCIANA. Why call you me "love"? Call my sister so.
> ANTIPHOLUS S. Thy sister's sister.
> LUCIANA.   That's my sister.
> ANTIPHOLUS S.   No,
> It is thyself, mine own self's better part,
> Mine eye's clear eye, my dear heart's dearer heart,
> My food, my fortune, and my sweet hope's aim,
> My sole earth's heaven, and my heaven's claim.
> LUCIANA. All this my sister is, or else should be.
> ANTIPHOLUS S. Call thyself, sister, sweet, for I am thee.
> Thee will I love, and with thee lead my life.
>
> (III.ii.59–67)

Repeatedly, the play voices the indivisibility of husband and wife, of twin and twin, and here of sister and sister, wooer and beloved. Such pronounced symmetry requires a wife for the unmarried Antipholus as like as possible to the wife of the married Antipholus. Even the twins' slight differences of temperament dictate that the fiery Ephesian is matched to the hot-tempered Adriana, while the calmer Luciana will wed the more cautious Syracusan.

In other plays, too, the dramatic balance would be radically upset by pairing any but equal partners. Falstaff may outrageously suggest that Poins plans to marry Hal to his sister Nell, but for Henry V, epitome of English sovereignty, only his foreign rival's heiress, Catherine of France, can properly become queen. A king and three noble courtiers symmetrically pursue a royal princess and her three noble attendants across the chessboard of *Love's Labour's Lost*. And the pathos of *Romeo and Juliet* is intensified by the fact that, were it not for the feud, these two lovers would be perfectly, if prematurely, matched. Sole heirs, male and female, of "Two households, both alike in dignity," "Of honorable reckoning are you both" (Pro., 1; I.ii.4). Throughout the tragedy the lovers mirror each other in youth, beauty, rashness, death, love, grief: "O, he is even in my mistress' case / Just in her case! . . . Even so lies she, / Blubb'ring and weeping, weeping and blubb'ring" (III.iii.84–87). Here no difference in age or wealth or social standing or temperament or affection mars the fitness of this precocious union—only the fatal difference between their names and houses.

In more comic terms, a similar parallelism attends the merits of the suitors in *A Midsummer Night's Dream*.

> THESEUS. Demetrius is a worthy gentleman.
> HERMIA. So is Lysander.
>
> . . . .
>
> LYSANDER. I am, my lord, as well derived as he,
> As well possessed. My love is more than his,
> My fortunes every way as fairly ranked,
> If not with vantage, as Demetrius.
>
> (I.i.52–53, 99–102)

Helena, too, stands equal in worth and beauty to Hermia: "Through Athens I am thought as fair as she" (227). Despite a disparity in height, their sameness echoes that of the males:

> We, Hermia, like two artificial gods
> Have with our needles created both one flower,
> Both on one sampler, sitting on one cushion,
> Both warbling of one song, both in one key,
> As if our hands, our sides, voices, and minds,
> Had been incorporate. So we grew together,
> Like to a double cherry: seeming parted,
> But yet an union in partition,
> Two lovely berries moulded on one stem.
>
> (III.ii.204–212)

Were it not for the caprice of the eye, which operates quite as arbitrarily as the Capulet-Montague feud, the lovers could be paired in any pattern, as the night's events demonstrate and as every critic has noted. To work effectively, however, this comic fugue requires sets of precisely matched partners.

Even in a modern social milieu that does not emphasize rank or the desirability of marrying within one's rank, audiences see the extraordinary equality of some partners in Shakespeare. However, when his plays move into situations of apparent or actual disparity, twentieth-century spectators may miss subtle points of conventionality, as well as more radical breaches of convention. In some cases the misyoking is merely apparent. The romances, for example, make it clear that, despite their surroundings, Marina, Perdita, and Miranda spring from royal blood and therefore are equally mated with Lysimachus, Florizel, and Ferdinand. However, in works where some genuine difference in birth appears, the romantic involvement receives careful handling. Thus, when Beatrice goes too far in bantering with Don Pedro, the Prince of Aragon, she must extricate herself:

> BEATRICE. I may sit in a corner and cry "Heigh-ho for a husband."
>
> DON PEDRO. Lady Beatrice, I will get you one.
>
> BEATRICE. I would rather have one of your father's getting. Hath your grace ne'er a brother like you? Your father got excellent husbands if a maid could come by them.
>
> DON PEDRO. Will you have me, lady?
>
> BEATRICE. No, my lord, unless I might have another for working days. Your grace is too costly to wear every day. But I beseech your grace, pardon me.
>
> (*Ado*, II.i.299–308)

Any mere gentlewoman who aspires to the hand of a prince "is no equal for his birth," "A very forward March chick" (155, I.iii.51), as Don John mistakenly observes of Hero.[40] In actuality, Beatrice and Hero more appropriately marry courtiers, not sovereigns—their equals, not their betters.

The lessons of history itself, at least as presented by Shakespeare, testify to the dangers of rulers' wedding beneath them, especially Henry VI's choice of Queen Margaret and Edward IV's of Lady Gray. What a delicate problem, then, presents itself in *Henry VIII*, where Shakespeare tells of the English king who set aside Queen Katherine, Princess of Spain, to marry Anne Boleyn, an untitled subject. The problem is made even more difficult in that the events portrayed had occurred less than a century earlier,

---

[40] Harry Berger, Jr., "Against the Sink-a-Pace: Sexual and Family Politics in *Much Ado About Nothing*," *Shakespeare Quarterly* 33 (1982): 304, says of Hero, "I think we are allowed at least a momentary doubt as to whether she and Leonato would not have preferred the Prince to Claudio, especially when she hears the Prince casually offer himself to Beatrice." I suspect Berger mistakes banter here for a serious proposal, as Beatrice does not. In totally different terms, Linda Bamber, *Comic Women, Tragic Men: A Study of Gender and Genre in Shakespeare* (Stanford, CA: Stanford University Press, 1982), says of Beatrice's refusal, p. 40, "The feminine Other, lacking the ambition to be more than she is to begin with, is naturally free from the comic disgrace of status-seeking."

and Anne's child, Elizabeth, had been dead but ten years, the memory of her presence still powerful to a London audience. Miraculously, the play manages to avoid disparagement of Katherine, Anne, or Henry. Only Wolsey objects to the new queen's lowly rank—and his self-serving plans for the king's second marriage are clear enough:

> It shall be to the Duchess of Alençon,
> The French King's sister—he shall marry her.
> Anne Boleyn? no! I'll no Anne Boleyns for him.
> There's more in't than fair visage. Boleyn?
> No, we'll no Boleyns!
>
> . . . .
>
> The late Queen's gentlewoman? a knight's daughter
> To be her mistress' mistress? the Queen's queen?
>
> (III.ii.86–90, 95–96)

Yet Wolsey admits, "I know her virtuous / And well-deserving" (98–99), while others repeatedly stress Anne's beauty and her virtues, with no mention of her birth. "The fairest hand I ever touched. O beauty, / Till now I never knew thee" (I.iv.76–77), they say, and "Beauty and honour in her are so mingled / That they have caught the King" (II.iii.76–77). Finally, this lushly sensuous passage expresses Anne's superhuman perfection in terms of the period's most valuable coin, the angel,[41] and its most fabled wealth, the Indies: "Sir, as I have a soul, she is an angel. / Our King has all the Indies in his arms, / And more, and richer, when he strains that lady" (IV.i.44–46).

The praiseworthy image of Anne is enhanced by the only private scene allowed her in the play, a scene not in Shakespeare's sources. Here, her aversion to ambition itself—she has clearly never coveted a share of the throne—contrasts with the coarse greed of her attendant.

> ANNE.   By my troth and maidenhead,
>   I would not be a queen.
> OLD LADY.   Beshrew me, I would—
>   And venture maidenhead for't; and so would you,
>   For all this spice of your hypocrisy.
>
>   . . . .
>
>   Yes, troth and troth. You would not be a queen?

---

[41] An angel was a gold coin worth 11*s.* by 1610; see Sandra K. Fischer, *Econolingua: A Glossary of Coins and Economic Language in Renaissance Drama* (Newark: University of Delaware Press, 1985), p. 41.

ANNE. No, not for all the riches under heaven.

OLD LADY. 'Tis strange; a threepence bowed would hire me,
  Old as I am, to queen it.

  . . . .

ANNE. I swear again, I would not be a queen
  For all the world.

OLD LADY.   In faith, for little England
  You'd venture an emballing; I myself
  Would for Caernarfonshire, although there 'longed
  No more to th' crown but that.

(II.iii.23–26, 34–37, 45–49)

When word comes at just this point that the king has made Anne Marchioness of Pembroke with an annual income of a thousand pounds, she responds with confusion, still displaying no trace of ambition: "Would I had no being, / If this salute my blood a jot. It faints me / To think what follows" (103–105). By carefully editing what Anne says and what others say of her, by keeping her silent during the splendor of her own coronation and thereafter barring her from the stage altogether, Shakespeare seems to be minimizing doubts regarding her fitness to be a queen—especially by comparison with Katherine. Even more important, the final baptismal scene emphasizes the greatness of Anne's offspring and of Elizabeth's successor, James. Though hyperbolic flattery, Cranmer's language here does help to obscure the awkward fact that the legendary Virgin Queen springs from the union of Henry VIII with a mere knight's daughter, who would subsequently be executed for treasonous infidelity.

Only indirectly does Shakespeare hint at the disastrous conclusion of Henry's alliance to Anne Boleyn. At least some in the audience, however, would hear echoes of *Othello*, with the Old Lady and Anne's closet scene evoking that of Emilia and Desdemona, both centering on the relative rewards of sexual virtue and sexual surrender. Also, Wolsey's line, "This candle burns not clear; 'tis I must snuff it, / Then out it goes" (III.ii.97–98), conjures up Othello's "Put out the light" speech (V.ii.7ff.). These passages perhaps subtly remind spectators that both Desdemona and Anne will die for presumed adultery at the hands of a once-adoring husband— the one strangled, the other under a headsman's ax. It may be relevant in this connection that the fatal marriage in *Othello* is also an unequal union. If, as the Moor claims, "I fetch my life and being / From men of royal siege" (I.ii.21–22), then he has wed beneath his rank.[42] As for Desde-

---

[42] Mark Taylor, *Shakespeare's Darker Purpose: A Question of Incest* (New York: AMS Press,

mona, Brabanzio finds it inconceivable "For nature so preposterously to err" (I.iii.62) that a Venetian senator's daughter could choose Othello "in spite of nature, / Of years, of country, credit, everything" (96–97). Confirming this view of the marriage, Iago also emphasizes the lack of "sympathy in years, manners, and beauties, all which the Moor is defective in" (II.i.230–231). The tragedy of course does not make the perspectives of Brabanzio or Iago normative, but their feeling that the match flies in the face of conventional parity between spouses would find confirmation in most English opinion. Not only do years and race divide Othello and Desdemona, but so do temperament, upbringing, occupation, family, nationality, and custom. Such profound differences finally help to ensure that the Moor cannot know his wife well enough to determine whether she is honest—that highest form of virtue which is the asset she brings to the marriage greater than her social status or her forfeited inheritance.

In dramatizing fictional marriages between men and women of unequal rank, Shakespeare hews to no single pattern. Occasionally, the difference simply seems to touch on the realities of ordinary life. In *The Merry Wives of Windsor*, for instance, a gentlewoman with rich parents and money in her own right represents a desirable prospect, as she would in any English town. Her father's choice for Anne Page is the simpleton Slender, an alliance that strengthens long-standing friendships with his neighbors, keeps his daughter close at hand, and provides her a secure living. "O, what a world of vile ill-favoured faults," laments poor Anne, "Looks handsome in three hundred pounds a year" (III.iv.31–32). Nor is Master Page less calculating than his wife; she favors Doctor Caius, who "is well moneyed, and his friends / Potent at court. He, none but he, shall have her / Though twenty thousand worthier come to crave her" (IV.iv.86–88). Despite its salty burlesque qualities, this comedy reflects the comparative considerations of status and fortune that actually entered into Elizabethan marriage negotiations. Part of the humor in *Merry Wives* lies in Page's rejection of the very qualities in Fenton, his daughter's choice, that might have recommended the young man. With little or no money, this suitor boasts high birth and breeding, he is well educated, and he has far more important connections than Caius through his past friendship with Prince Hal. "He capers, he dances, he has eyes of youth; he writes verses, he speaks holiday, he smells April and May" (III.ii.61–62). In short, Fenton em-

---

1982), p. 111, takes the position that, as a senator's daughter, Desdemona marries below her rank. However, rank is the one ground of inequality not charged against her for this marriage.

bodies everything a father of indifferent birth might wish for his heiress daughter.

Yet Page, like many Elizabethans, distrusts the wooer's superior rank and intelligence—"He is of too high a region; he knows too much" (67–68). In particular, he suspects Fenton's motives, declaring, "No, he shall not knit a knot in his fortunes with the finger of my substance" (68–69). The young man entertains no illusions concerning Page's objections, nor indeed about the exigencies of his situation.

> FENTON. He doth object I am too great of birth,
>   And that, my state being galled with my expense,
>   I seek to heal it only by his wealth.
>   Besides these, other bars he lays before me—
>   My riots past, my wild societies;
>   And tells me 'tis a thing impossible
>   I should love thee but as a property.
> ANNE. May be he tells you true.
> FENTON. No, heaven so speed me in my time to come!
>   Albeit I will confess my father's wealth
>   Was the first motive that I wooed thee, Anne,
>   Yet, wooing thee, I found thee of more value
>   Than stamps in gold or sums in sealèd bags.
>
> (III.iv.4–16)

As with Claudio or Bassanio, Fenton here expresses genuine affection for his beloved, although he would not be wooing her were she poor, nor would Caius or Slender. The pragmatic tone of *Merry Wives*, the manifest inferiority of Anne's other suitors, not to mention the play's final outcome, emphasize the fitness of this match, with the bride's good estate balanced by her husband's good blood.[43]

---

[43] Marilyn French, *Shakespeare's Division of Experience* (New York: Summit Books, 1981), p. 107, denigrates the play because "property is *all* it is about," terming Fenton as well as Falstaff "a down-at-heels aristocrat (foreigner) who is attempting to 'steal' from the propertied men of Windsor." She even claims that Slender "agrees to marry Anne Page for her money," p. 106. However, it is not Slender but his backers, Shallow and Evans, who are attracted by her inheritance, and it is Page who promotes the match to secure Slender's income for his daughter. J. A. Bryant, Jr., "Falstaff and the Renewal of Windsor," *PMLA* 89 (1974): 300, says, "Monetary concerns are defeated, biology wins out," neatly ignoring Fenton's financial success. Similarly, Larry S. Champion, *The Evolution of Shakepeare's Comedy: A Study in Dramatic Perspective* (Cambridge: Harvard University Press, 1970), sees Fenton as "the aristocrat who woos for love rather than material gain," p. 61. Peter Erickson,

Yet in many of Shakespeare's plays no such prosaic trade-off character-izes the discrepancies between marriage partners. In the early comedy *Two Gentlemen of Verona*, Sylvia, daughter to the Duke of Milan, outranks her three suitors to a much greater extent than Fenton outranks Anne. Though titled equally with Sir Proteus and Sir Valentine, Sir Thurio has the ad-vantages of wealth and parental favor. He is the "foolish rival, that her father likes / Only for his possessions are so huge" (II.iv. 172–173). But he abandons his courtship rather than risk his life: "I hold him but a fool that will endanger / His body for a girl that loves him not" (V.iv.131–132). Similarly, Valentine violates his lord's trust by wooing Sylvia secretly and later offers to hand her over to Proteus—who betrays his closest friend, deceives both the Duke and Thurio, breaks his vows to Julia, forces his suit on Sylvia, and finally attempts to rape her in the forest. The play's farcically improbable events, during which the same girl is casually passed back and forth among all three unworthy suitors, make it comically ap-propriate to bestow her upon Valentine, reduced to a penniless outlaw chief. In this mad world, rank scarcely matters, although the Duke takes great care at the end to degrade Thurio, to elevate Valentine, and to reca-pitulate his own and Sylvia's status.

> The more degenerate and base art thou [Thurio]
> To make such means for her as thou hast done,
> And leave her on such slight conditions.
> Now by the honor of my ancestry
> I do applaud thy spirit, Valentine,
> And think thee worthy of an empress' love.
>
> .   .   .   .
>
> Thou art a gentleman, and well derived.
> Take thou thy Sylvia, for thou hast deserved her.
>
> (134–139, 144–145)

Like his rivals, Valentine no more deserves this—or any—lady than he deserves to be called a gentleman. In such a context, the grotesque social mismatch emphasizes the obvious discrepancies upon which the play's per-verse humor depends.

In comedies less farcical, Shakespeare uses other techniques to account

---

"The Order of the Garter, the Cult of Elizabeth, and Class-Gender Tension in *The Merry Wives of Windsor*," in *Shakespeare Reproduced: The Text in History and Ideology*, ed. Jean How-ard and Marion O'Connor (New York: Methuen, 1987), more sophisticatedly identifies class and gender as the chief ideological centers of *Wiv.*, p. 118.

for socially unequal marriages. With its insistent financial emphasis, *The Merchant of Venice* pairs a debt-ridden aristocrat and a fabulously wealthy heiress.[44] Bassanio is the very embodiment of a reckless gallant who has outspent his small inheritance—no uncommon phenomenon in London or in Venice.

> 'Tis not unknown to you, Antonio,
> How much I have disabled mine estate
> By something showing a more swelling port[45]
> Than my faint means would grant continuance,
> Nor do I now make moan to be abridged
> From such a noble rate; but my chief care
> Is to come fairly off from the great debts
> Wherein my time, something too prodigal,
> Hath left me gaged. To you, Antonio,
> I owe the most in money and in love,
> And from your love I have a warranty
> To unburden all my plots and purposes
> How to get clear of all the debts I owe.
>
> (I.i.122–134)

Critical disparagement of Bassanio either overlooks or misunderstands his desire to repay rather than ignore his indebtedness and to do so "fairly" and "within the eye of honor," as Antonio puts it (128, 137).[46] For a

---

[44] Frank Whigham, "Ideology and Class Conduct in *The Merchant of Venice*," *Renaissance Drama*, n.s., 10 (1979), asserts, "The marriage plot chronicles Bassanio's courtship of and assimilation into the elite," claiming that he "compels desert by the manipulation of the systems of courtesy," pp. 94, 107. However, Bassanio is called "lord" (I.i.69) by his friends long before he wins Portia. Moreover, he has been a soldier-scholar-courtier (I.ii.110–111) like Claudio in *Ado*, following a career familiar among the elite. Portia supplies land and wealth to a husband already an aristocrat. Robert Ornstein, *Shakespeare's Comedies: From Roman Farce to Romantic Mystery* (Newark: University of Delaware Press, 1986), p. 162, notes that both Bassanio and Portia are aristocrats, as does Richard A. Levin, *Love and Society in Shakespearean Comedy* (Newark: University of Delaware Press, 1985), p. 38.

[45] Besides relating to the play's mercantile imagery, Bassanio's use of the word "port" echoes Sir Thomas Smith's classic, if circular, definition of a gentleman as one who can "beare the Port, charge and countenance of a Gentleman," *The Common-wealth* (London, 1640), p. 55.

[46] Critics are split pretty evenly over Bassanio. Among his defenders, Ornstein, *Shakespeare's Comedies*, p. 92, notes that Gianetto in *Il Pecorone*, the play's source, is much more venal than Bassanio, while Stone, *Crisis*, pp. 582–583, tells us that the character's prodi-

gentleman with no profession, no connections at court, no mercantile investments, and no further inheritance, matrimony represents the only ethical hope for restoration to solvency. Moreover, Bassanio pursues a virtuous heiress who has already evinced a possible attraction to him: "Sometimes from her eyes / I did receive fair speechless messages" (163–164). In his situation Bassanio would be foolish not to seek "a lady richly left" (161). Nor does he stand alone in his desire: "For the four winds blow in from every coast / Renownèd suitors" (168–169). The idea of competing on the same terms with princes for such a treasure and, amazingly, at the express orders of the lady's father would seem to exercise a particularly powerful appeal at a time when heiresses almost never married poor gentlemen, and parents never bestowed their rich daughters so capriciously.

Moreover, Shakespeare does not portray this alluring courtship as a purely mercenary arrangement. Portia cannot choose or refuse as she likes,[47] yet her conversation with Nerissa clearly reveals a long-standing interest in Bassanio.

> NERISSA. Do you not remember, lady, in your father's time, a Venetian, a scholar and a solder, that came hither in company of the Marquis of Montferrat?
>
> PORTIA. Yes, yes, it was Bassanio—as I think, so was he called.
>
> NERISSA. True, madam. He, of all the men that ever my foolish eyes looked upon, was the best deserving a fair lady.
>
> PORTIA. I remember him well, and I remember him worthy of thy praise.
>
> (I.ii.109–118)

In the subsequent dialogue with Bassanio, one sees that Portia's favorable recollections have deepened into love. To his credit, her suitor admits his impoverished condition: "I freely told you all the wealth I had / Ran in my veins: I was a gentleman" (III.ii.252–253). And the extent of his own commitment and courage are tested by the caskets far more severely than those of any other rival for Portia's hand. Under the terms of her father's will, a man who makes the wrong choice is enjoined "never in my life / To woo a maid in way of marriage" (II.ix.12–13), a detail Shakespeare adds to his source. For the other wooers, Morocco and Aragon, permanent

---

gality is petty compared to the excesses of Rutland, Southampton, Oxford, Essex, and Northumberland.

[47] In this regard, it is hard to see why French, *Shakespeare's Division*, p. 102, sees Portia as a purchaser of love. With all her money, she cannot buy or even choose the man she loves because of her father's restrictions.

bachelorhood still leaves intact their titles, social position, and fortunes. But for Bassanio, renunciation of marriage means sacrificing everything, including the last hope for maintaining his honor and status. He alone, of all the suitors, "must give and hazard all he hath" (20).[48] And, as with the caskets, Bassanio's unpromising, leaden exterior—his poverty, his debts, his risks—mysteriously encloses those qualities Portia's father requires in her husband.[49]

Shakespeare combines realistic and unrealistic elements quite differently in *As You Like It* in order to pair off a duke's daughter, rightful heiress to the entire realm, with the younger son of a mere knight.[50] The comedy opens with a starkly recognizable situation that emphasizes the hero's lowly status. By the terms of his will, Sir Rowland de Bois has bequeathed Orlando a modest thousand crowns and "charged my brother on his blessing to breed me well—and there begins my sadness. My brother Jaques he keeps at school, and report speaks goldenly of his profit. For my part, he keeps me rustically at home. . . . He lets me feed with his hinds, bars me the place of a brother, and as much as in him lies, mines my gentility with my education" (I.i.3–9, 17–19). Denied his inheritance and the upbringing appropriate to his rank, Orlando seeks relief by trying for preferment at court. He hopes that a successful show at wrestling, one of the few sports practiced by wellborn and lowborn alike,[51]

---

[48] Sylvan Barnet, "Prodigality and Time in *The Merchant of Venice*," *PMLA* 87 (1972): 28–29, here distinguishes between virtue, which entails risk, and usury, which carries no risk. Levin, *Love and Society*, p. 59, thinks Bassanio "has nothing to lose, since Portia has apparently not repeated the key stipulation that a losing suitor must vow never to marry." However, since the audience has already heard the conditions, there is no reason to assume that she has suddenly altered her father's rules. Elliot Krieger, *A Marxist Study of Shakespeare's Comedies* (New York: Barnes and Noble, 1979), pp. 26–27, presumes Bassanio risks nothing since, if he loses, he is still a gentleman. But not even his status can be maintained with poverty and debts.

[49] Carol Thomas Neely, *Broken Nuptials in Shakespeare's Plays* (New Haven: Yale University Press, 1985), p. 11, regards the father's will as less restrictive and more imaginative than those of a good many Elizabethan fathers.

[50] For a longer and richly rewarding analysis of this play in the Elizabethan context of the younger brother, see Louis Adrian Montrose, " 'The Place of a Brother' in *As You Like It*: Social Process and Comic Form," *Shakespeare Quarterly* 32 (1981): 28–54.

[51] See Lilly C. Stone, *English Sports and Recreations* (Charlottesville: University Press of Virginia, 1960), pp. 10–12, 14–17; she notes that Castiglione advises courtiers not to compete with an inferior unless they are "sure to get the victory." According to Edward Hall, Henry VIII included wrestling among his many exercises, and Robert Burton includes wrestling in his list of sports for country folk and artisans. See also Ruth Kelso, *The Doctrine of the English Gentleman in the Sixteenth Century*, University of Illinois Studies in

will attract Duke Frederick's attention and gain him some suitable post of service.[52] His hopes, of course, are dashed when the usurper-duke learns of Orlando's parentage and peremptorily exiles him, even as Oliver plots his murder. Initially, then, the play is rooted in the realpolitik of Elizabethan England, where younger sons of gentle birth had a difficult struggle even for recognition, let alone for a spouse.

But Shakespeare deliberately intensifies Orlando's situation. In Thomas Lodge's *Rosalynde*, the father has bequeathed more land to the younger brother than to the older, thus partly justifying the firstborn's enmity. By altering his source, the playwright creates an even more improbable courtship between a duke's daughter and a knight's banished younger son, who is penniless and ill-educated—as his complaints and his verses prove. Certain parallels foster the illusion of a union of equals: both Orlando and Rosalind depend upon the goodwill of a hostile guardian, both are barred from lawful inheritance, and both receive support from a loyal companion. Furthermore, the pastoralism, the artificiality, the obvious removal of the Arden world from anything remotely resembling reality facilitate the audience's pleasurable acceptance of a patently impossible match. Though the never-never-land qualities of *As You Like It* are much noted,[53] only a

Language and Literature 14 (1929): 149. William G. Meader, *Courtship in Shakespeare: Its Relation to the Tradition of Courtly Love* (New York: Columbia University, King's Crown Press, 1954), p. 65, says that the play stresses Orlando's poetry writing rather than his wrestling as a way of elevating his status, missing the point that the hero is far better at the latter than the former. Margaret Loftus Ranald, *Shakespeare and His Social Context* (New York: AMS Press, 1987), wrongly asserts that "wrestling was not considered fit employment for the nobly born," p. 77.

[52] Thomas Kelly, "Shakespeare's Romantic Heroes: Orlando Reconsidered," *Shakespeare Quarterly* 24 (1973): 17, thinks the chain she gives him bestows upon "Orlando a place equal in every respect to Rosalind's." However, not only is her gift far less than what the duke should have awarded Orlando for this victory, even if he withheld a position at court, but it is a present from a superior to an inferior, a mark of their social inequality.

[53] See, e.g., Richard Knowles, ed., *The New Variorum Edition of "As You Like It"* (New York: Modern Language Association of America, 1977), pp. 539–545; Kenneth Muir, *Shakespeare's Comic Sequence* (New York: Barnes and Noble, 1979), p. 89; Phyllis Rackin, "Androgyny, Mimesis, and the Marriage of the Boy Heroine on the Renaissance Stage," *PMLA* 102 (1987): 34; Kent Talbot van den Berg, "Theatrical Fiction and the Reality of Love in *As You Like It*," *PMLA* 90 (1975): 885–893. Judy Z. Kronenfeld, "Social Rank and the Pastoral Ideals of *As You Like It*," *Shakespeare Quarterly* 29 (1978): 343, cautions that the pastoral here is still rooted in social reality, with the restoration of a patron-servant relationship involved in the purchase of a living and the employment of Corin by Rosalind and Celia. She might also have added that the cousins take along jewels, Adam and Orlando the former's life savings to support themselves in Arden. Ranald, *Shakespeare and His*

few scholars observe that the pairing of Rosalind and Orlando—with their great disparity in rank, their unrestricted courtship, her father's consent so lightly granted—marks perhaps the high point of fanciful invention in the comedy.[54] Indeed, the movement toward this form of wish fulfillment gives the comedy its primary direction.

Only slightly less improbable than the Rosalind-Orlando match is the union of the aristocratic Celia with Oliver, who does not have even a minor title, as did his father. That subtle point is comically underlined by the fact that the ignorant country curate is "Sir" Oliver, while Celia's beloved is not. In this context, the misyoking of Touchstone and Audrey appears no more disparate than the marriages of the social sophisticates; the former is merely more obvious nowadays. Ironically, the only equals who do marry are Silvius and Phoebe, despite their decidedly unequal affection for each other. To ensure that no one accepts these preposterous pairings as anything but romantic fiction, Shakespeare employs Hymen to solemnize the nuptials. Not present in the source, that curious figure, variously attacked and defended, is aesthetically appropriate for a fantasy wedding between those who would never have joined in real life.[55] Merely to imagine the jarring effect of bringing onstage a clergyman, like the priest in *Much Ado*, is to understand Hymen's fitness. Yet in a modern society that insists upon everyone's fundamental equality, playgoers do not fully savor the comic delights of a stage world where one can marry without regard for barriers of rank.

Social Context, p. 75, points out that references to threatened evictions and to harsh seasons are means by which "Shakespeare avoids cloying sentimentality."

[54] Among those who at least note the unrealistic difference in rank are Edward I. Berry, *Shakespeare's Comic Rites* (Cambridge: Cambridge University Press, 1984), p. 45; Hibbard, "Love," p. 135; Leo Salingar, *Shakespeare and the Traditions of Comedy* (Cambridge: Cambridge University Press, 1974), p. 298; David Lloyd Stevenson, *The Love-Game Comedy* (New York: Columbia University Press, 1946), pp. 199–200.

[55] References to Hymen's mysterious nature include William C. Carroll, *The Metamorphoses of Shakespearean Comedy* (Princeton: Princeton University Press, 1985), p. 134; Krieger, *Marxist Study*, p. 84; Agnes Latham, ed., *As You Like It*, Arden Shakespeare (London: Methuen, 1975), pp. xxi–xxiiii; Alexander Leggatt, *Shakespeare's Comedy of Love* (London: Methuen, 1974), pp. 190–191, 213; Marianne L. Novy, " 'And You Smile Not, He's Gagged': Mutuality in Shakespearean Comedy," *Philological Quarterly* 55 (1976): 184; Joseph Westlund, *Shakespeare's Reparative Comedies: A Psychoanalytic View of the Middle Plays* (Chicago: University of Chicago Press, 1984), p. 78. Marvin Felheim and Philip Traci, *Realism in Shakespeare's Romantic Comedies: "O Heavenly Mingle"* (Washington, DC: University Press of America, 1980), almost alone, call the wedding "realistic (neither cynical nor romantical)," p. 7.

Besides the magical realms of Belmont and the imaginary Forest of Arden, Shakespeare also uses occasions of holiday escape for matrimony between the aristocracy and those of lesser birth. In *Twelfth Night*, Viola and Sebastian come of a "Right noble" (V.i.262) Messaline family, well known to the Illyrian ruler: "Orsino. I have heard my father name him" (I.ii.24). Yet the twins do not have even lesser titles, like Olivia's kinsman Sir Toby Belch and her hapless wooer Sir Andrew Aguecheek. On the face of things, Orsino, "A noble duke, in nature / As in name" (22–23), should rightly marry Olivia, "A virtuous maid, the daughter of a count" (32). Male and female, of almost equal rank, each the head of a great household, the two aristocrats are already engaged in a fruitless courtship when the comedy begins.[56] However, they marry not each other but Viola and Sebastian, the sister a servant to the duke, the brother also seeking service in the same court. The twins' elevation in status is formally delineated by Orsino and ratified by Olivia:

> ORSINO.   You shall from this time be
>   Your master's mistress.
> OLIVIA.   A sister, you are she.
>
> (V.i.322–323)

Of course companionate service in a noble or royal household never represented a disparagement to one's birth. Shakespearean plays from *Two Gentlemen* onward offer many examples, as do countless other works and historical practices of the period. Nonetheless, in this particular comedy, the lines between masters and servants are repeatedly blurred. Olivia's steward aspires "To be Count Malvolio," reveling in his imagined advancement: "There is example for't: the Lady of the Strachey married the yeo-

---

[56] French, *Shakespeare's Division*, p. 116, wrongly considers Viola to be Olivia's "social equal," Orsino their "social superior." Ornstein, *Shakespeare's Comedies*, p. 174, thinks Viola, like Helen, must "adore a great nobleman who is far above their station in life." Levin, *Love and Society*, p. 25, says that Orsino and Olivia "can afford to be self-indulgent" in their choice because they stand at the top of the social ladder. Leonard Tennenhouse, *Power on Display: The Politics of Shakespeare's Genres* (London: Methuen, 1986), p. 66, who credits Olivia's recognition of the preeminent "iconic value of blood," does not deal with the significance of title in designating rank. Stephen Greenblatt, *Shakespearean Negotiations: The Circulation of Social Energy in Renaissance England* (Oxford: Clarendon Press, 1988), p. 66, refers to "the scandal of a marriage contracted so far beneath a countess's station," which is rendered "illusory," p. 72, by Orsino's assurance of the twins' noble blood in act V. Since Viola says at her first appearance that Orsino is well known to her father and promises bounteous payment to the captain, it is established from the outset that her brother's alliance with Olivia would not threaten a "scandal," as does Malvolio's scheme.

man of the wardrobe. . . . Having been three months married to her, sitting in my state—. . . . Calling my officers about me, in my branched velvet gown. . . . telling them I know my place, as I would they should do theirs" (II.v.33, 37–38, 42–43, 45–46, 51–52). The irony of Malvolio's soliloquy, of course, is that while he assumes *his* servants would know their place, he does not know his own, and neither does any other character. Orsino neglects his duties as a ruler to pine over an unrequited love, Olivia first vows seven years of mourning and then goes chasing after a handsome young courtier, Sir Andrew is gulled into wooing a countess, and Viola forsakes her identity as a woman to become Cesario. In the topsy-turvy holiday world of *Twelfth Night*, not only do servants marry masters—Maria's and Sir Toby's nuptials the comic counterpart of the other two matches—but, paradoxically, order is thereby restored. They may not have titles, but Maria is assuredly a good-natured curb on Sir Toby's riotous indulgences, Viola the very pattern of restraint for a self-indulgent Orsino, and Sebastian the forceful male needed to manage Olivia's chaotic household. Moreover, while some of lesser status do wed their social betters, not one of them actively pursues such advancement.[57] Inferior birth here brilliantly balances superior personal qualities. The lack of these qualities, together with their own absurdly ambitious hopes, dooms the aspirations of Malvolio and Sir Andrew.

While it is easy to applaud the good fortune of Viola and Orsino, Sebastian and Olivia, many might have sympathized with Bertram's reluctance to accept Helen in *All's Well That Ends Well*. Here, in Shakespeare's longest, most direct exploration of inequality in birth and rank, the heroine herself acknowledges the lowliness of her status as compared with her beloved's.[58]

---

[57] Levin, *Love and Society*, p. 25, claims that Maria, like Malvolio, hopes to rise by marrying a titled spouse, destroying Sir Toby's rival, Malvolio, as part of her campaign. But only Sir Toby, not Maria, mentions marriage—and then out of her presence. Levin saves his harshest criticism for Viola, "an *arriviste*," corrupt, ambitious, and calculating, like Helen in *All's Well*, pp. 121–122, 128–129. He traces this judgment to her inquiry about Orsino's marital status in I.ii, but he misses the point here. Shipwrecked, her brother presumed dead, Viola first wishes to enter the household of the similarly bereaved Countess Olivia. With that possibility foreclosed, Orsino's bachelor status determines that her service to him (her only option at this point) must be in male disguise, as it need not have been had he possessed a wife. Precisely this kind of point can be clarified by the historical research Levin dismisses.

[58] For a summary of critical responses to Helen and her social inferiority, see Neely, *Broken Nuptials*, p. 227n.14; Michael Taylor, "Persecuting Time with Hope: The Cynicism of Romance in *All's Well That Ends Well*," *English Studies in Canada* 11 (1985): 293n.7.

'Twere all one
That I should love a bright particular star
And think to wed it, he is so above me.
In his bright radiance and collateral light
Must I be comforted, not in his sphere.
Th'ambition in my love thus plagues itself.

(I.i.84–89)

Repeatedly, she dwells on the "difference betwixt their two estates" (I.iii.109). Hence, it should come as no surprise that, confronted with her election of him as husband, Bertram responds, "A poor physician's daughter, my wife? Disdain / Rather corrupt me ever" (II.iii.116–117). Were the issue so narrowly defined, most Elizabethans would probably have sided with the count's son. However, Shakespeare places even more weight upon the other side of the question. Unlike the tale in Boccaccio, where Giletta is an heiress but not noble, the king reluctant to bestow her, and Beltramo affronted by a bride lacking "a stock convenable to his nobility,"[59] the play's heroine is presented much more sympathetically. To do her justice, the father of "this gentlewoman" was the famed Gerard de Narbon, "whose skill was almost as great as his honesty" (I.i.34–35, 17–18) and whose death is noted even by the king (I.ii.69–71). Like Bertram, Helen has been properly reared in the household of his mother, the Countess of Roussillon, who says of her charge, "She derives her honesty and achieves her goodness" (I.i.42–43). Though reserving explicit, formal approval for a marriage,[60] her guardian does approve Helen's mission to the French court, where Bertram serves: "What I can help thee to, thou shalt not miss" (I.iii.255). The countess's tacit goodwill thus reinforces a sense of Helen's inherent worth, as does the advance report of her to the ailing king: "I have spoke / With one that in her sex, her years, profession, / Wisdom and constancy, hath amazed me . . ." (II.i.81–83).

Among subsequent critics, see C. L. Barber and Richard P. Wheeler, *The Whole Journey: Shakespeare's Power of Development* (Berkeley: University of California Press, 1986), p. 15; Lisa Jardine, "Cultural Confusion and Shakespeare's Learned Heroines: 'These are old paradoxes,' " *Shakespeare Quarterly* 38 (1987): 9–11; Ranald, *Shakespeare and His Social Context*, p. 34; Peggy Muñoz Simonds, "Sacred and Sexual Motifs in *All's Well That Ends Well,*" *Renaissance Quarterly* 42 (1989): 38.

[59] Geoffrey Bullough, *The Narrative and Dramatic Sources of Shakespeare* (London: Routledge and Kegan Paul, 1958), 2:391.

[60] Indeed, she has no authority to give such approval because, as a royal ward, Bertram can be bestowed in marriage only by the king. See chap. 4.

Yet even in a problematic comedy dealing overtly with the issue of rank, Shakespeare sets some limits. Helen specifically rules out a royal husband:

> Exempted be from me the arrogance
> To choose from forth the royal blood of France,
> My low and humble name to propagate
> With any branch or image of thy state.
>
> (195–198)

Without doubt, however, the grateful sovereign, miraculously cured of his fistula, thinks her fit for any among his nobly born wards—"Who shuns thy love shuns all his love in me" (II.iii.74). His view is echoed by the more dispassionate courtier Lafeu: "I had rather be in this choice than throw ambs-ace for my life" (79–80).[61] Her selection made, the king further promises to elevate Helen's worldly standing in order to satisfy Bertram's objection, after which point she never again protests any inferiority in status. Her benefactor proclaims, " 'Tis only title thou disdain'st in her, the which / I can build up" (118–119). Then follows a lengthy speech on virtue, which might have been lifted directly from the countless manuals on nobility and which ends with another pledge to enlarge Helen's rank and fortune.

> If she be
> All that is virtuous, save what thou dislik'st—
> "A poor physician's daughter"—thou dislik'st
> Of virtue for the name. But do not so.
> From lowest place when virtuous things proceed,
> The place is dignified by th' doer's deed.
>
> . . . .
>
> I can create the rest. Virtue and she
> Is her own dower; honor and wealth from me.
>
> (122–127, 144–145)

As the subsequent action reveals, the hero has neither the inherent nobility of Helen nor the inherited nobility of his parents. He deserts his wife, disobeys the king, follows the corrupt Paroles, attempts to seduce

---

[61] Ornstein, *Shakespeare's Comedies*, p. 178, points to Lafeu's attitude when he claims that Helen's "difference of rank matters only to Bertram." Joseph G. Price, *The Unfortunate Comedy: A Study of "All's Well That Ends Well" and Its Critics* (Liverpool: Liverpool University Press, 1968), p. 155, on the other hand, thinks Lafeu's remarks, which seem to show a rejection of Helen by all the king's wards, indicate a tone of voice or stage action that belies their polite words to her.

Diana, and then slanders the girl. All interpreters of this play have trouble with Bertram's behavior. What they fail to see, perhaps, is the difficulty of dealing effectively or persuasively with a union that would, in fact, have represented a disparagement of birth. In *All's Well* there is no comfortable excuse of holiday frivolity as in *Twelfth Night*, or of village highjinks as in *Merry Wives*. Forsaking the distance of romance or legend or fantasy, this work must find other ways to deal with the mismatch around which the plot revolves. Endowing Helen with virtue, resourcefulness, and aristocratic approval while emphasizing Bertram's immaturity and immorality has seldom pleased modern audiences. But Shakespeare's own spectators may have required clear proof of a nobleman's ignobility in order to accept his marriage to a heroine of common birth when the union is presented in a sober courtly context.

Rank continues to be a significant issue, even in the faraway realm of the romances. While some matches, proposed or consummated, follow the pattern of equality in birth, some may appear to violate that pattern. Thus, Leontes, King of Sicilia, is married to Hermione, daughter of the King of Russia, and presumably Polixenes has an equally appropriate wife. By the time Paulina weds Camillo, who initially has been raised from humbler status to steward, he enjoys a royal confidence that equals both her stature and that of her first husband, Antigonus. However, other courtships in the late plays seem more problematic. Without knowing Miranda's lineage, Ferdinand unhesitatingly promises to make her Queen of Naples and thus unwittingly allies himself to the heiress of Milan's realm in *The Tempest*. In wooing Antiochus's daughter, Pericles discovers a sexual sin that cancels even the highest rank, but in choosing an unknown knight, Thaisa wins a kingly mate. By contrast, *Pericles* presents Lysimachus as considerably less than perfect. Though governor of Mitylene, he first appears as a customer in a brothel. Despite rewarding Marina's virtue with gold, he does not rescue her, and he seems unconcerned that the profits of the girl's honest labors go to fatten the bawd's purse. Hardly a saint himself, he still will not marry an unknown maiden he has met in the stews, though "She's such a one that were I well assured / Came of a gentle kind and noble stock, / I'd wish me no better choice, and think me rarely wed" (sc. 21, 57–59). Goodness alone will not suffice for Lysimachus.[62]

---

[62] Muir, *Shakespeare's Comic Sequence*, p. 153, acknowledges that Lysimachus "has to be something of a rake" because of the brothel visit but still "fundamentally decent . . . to marry Marina." By contrast, Neely, *Broken Nuptials*, p. 185, thinks Lysimachus "a deco-

Nor, in King Cymbeline's opinion, will it suffice for his daughter, Innogen, who has married the "poor but worthy" (I.i.7) Posthumus rather than Prince Cloten, "the sole son of my queen" (139). Her father rages, "Thou took'st a beggar, wouldst have made my throne / A seat for baseness" (142–143).[63] As all the courtiers know,

> He that hath missed the Princess is a thing
> Too bad for bad report, and he that hath her—
> I mean that married her—alack, good man,
> And therefore banished!—is a creature such
> As, to seek through the regions of the earth
> For one his like, there would be something failing
> In him that should compare.
>
> (16–22)

While Cloten fully confirms his base reputation, Posthumus, like Bertram, reveals a flawed character, not entirely commensurate with this initial report of him.[64] Although her husband eventually redeems himself by sincere repentance as well as by notable bravery in battle, his actions still do not necessarily qualify him to rule Britain at Innogen's side. Significantly, at least for Shakespeare's audience, the king never acknowledges Posthumus as "son-in-law" (V.vi.423) until after the lost princes are discovered. As Cymbeline tells his daughter, "O Innogen, / Thou hast lost by this a kingdom" (374–375). With two brothers ahead of her in the

---

rous governor who observes proprieties by asking for Marina's hand only when he has learned her origins." While this kind of propriety generally marks the earlier comedies, I do not think it is consistent with the blinder commitment to inherent worth characteristic of the romances.

[63] Kay Stockholder, *Dream Works: Lovers and Families in Shakespeare's Plays* (Toronto: University of Toronto Press, 1987), p. 177, claims Posthumus "is, in short, a social climber." Yet David Bergeron, *Shakespeare's Romances and the Royal Family* (Lawrence: University Press of Kansas, 1985), p. 143, wonders "how Cymbeline can regard Posthumus as 'base,' having himself nurtured Posthumus at court." However, not every royal ward, particularly one poor and untitled, would have been considered a fit match for the heiress to the throne. Dynastic considerations clearly figure into the promotion of Cloten's suit, as Bergeron recognizes, pp. 142–145. David Shelley Berkeley, *Blood Will Tell in Shakespeare's Plays* (Lubbock: Texas Tech University Press, 1984), pp. 71–80, suggests that Cloten, whose status derives solely from the marriage of his unnamed mother, the Queen, may have no valid claim to noble or even gentle birth.

[64] Ornstein, *Shakespeare's Comedies*, p. 198, traces Posthumus's faults to his feelings of social inferiority. Tennenhouse, *Power*, pp. 176, 180, disagrees, viewing Jupiter's show as confirmation of the young man's worthiness.

succession, the princess's marriage becomes "more equal ballasting" (III.vi.75) and no longer threatens to enthrone a commoner, however worthy. In romance, too, the higher the social level, the more serious any disparity in birth.

Thus, in *The Winter's Tale*, when Polixenes rages, "Thou art too base / To be acknowledged. Thou, a sceptre's heir, / That thus affects a sheephook" (IV.iv.417–420), his anger is at least understandable.[65] Neither the king nor Camillo expresses any disapproval so long as the prince merely loves the pretty country lass, but marriage to one "Worthy enough a herdsman" (435) is another matter entirely. Florizel flouts every rule by contracting himself to a shepherdess, while Perdita's presumed father is an "old traitor" (420) deserving of the gallows for promoting such a match. Knowing the heroine's true identity, spectators understand the appropriateness of the betrothal. What they may miss, however, is the reckless courage Florizel displays by remaining faithful to his love without knowing her rank:

> Not for Bohemia, nor the pomp that may
> Be thereat gleaned; for all the sun sees, or
> The close earth wombs, or the profound seas hides
> In unknown fathoms, will I break my oath
> To this my fair beloved.

(488–492)

A spouse's inherent value is not sufficient for Bertram or Lysimachus or Cymbeline, but it is for Florizel. And such absolute faith is required to redeem the tragic losses born of unfaith. Nonetheless, Perdita's royal birth finally allies *The Winter's Tale* with those plays in which like mates with like, as was usually the case in Renaissance England. Only in carefully qualified circumstances or in patently unrealistic situations do characters marry without regard for rank or riches.

For Shakespeare, then, the question of relative status between marriage partners roots itself in complicated cultural demands. Where absolute equality prevails, it can enhance a sense of interchangeability, as in *The*

---

[65] For very different interpretations of the king's tirade, see Barber and Wheeler, *Whole Journey*, p. 300; Howard Felperin, *Shakespearean Romance* (Princeton: Princeton University Press, 1972), p. 238; Neely, *Broken Nuptials*, pp. 195–196; Irving Singer, *The Nature of Love: Courtly and Romantic* (Chicago: University of Chicago Press, 1984), 2:236; Stockholder, *Dream Works*, p. 192; Joseph H. Summers, *Dreams of Love and Power: On Shakespeare's Plays* (Oxford: Clarendon Press, 1984), p. 36; Taylor, *Shakespeare's Darker Purpose*, pp. 78–80.

Comedy of Errors, or redouble a sense of loss, as in *Romeo and Juliet*. Where an apparent disparity exists, it can test faith, as in *The Winter's Tale* or *Pericles* or *The Tempest*. In cases of discrepancy between birth and wealth, it seems difficult for contemporary audiences to approve the rich matches won by a Fenton or a Bassanio, though the Elizabethans knew well enough the pressures upon impoverished noblemen. By contrast, when an extreme difference of status separates Orlando and Rosalind, Bertram and Helen, modern spectators seem blind to the former situation and sharply critical of the latter. They miss the lengths to which Shakespeare goes in emphasizing the fantasy of the *As You Like It* union and in questioning the nature of nobility in *All's Well*. But whatever the techniques employed in comedy to deal with disparate pairings, certain limits still prevail. Fictional counts or dukes may marry beneath their rank, but when heirs to thrones seem to, their consorts turn out to be of equal birth. For historical sovereigns, the plays can spell out the folly of Henry VI and Edward IV in taking queens of lesser status or affirm the choice of Henry V or minimize the inferior birth of Anne Boleyn. Viewed through the lenses of tragedy, the marriage of a man and woman differing in age, birth, upbringing, temperament, nationality, and race can wreak disaster in *Othello*. Even when Shakespeare does not deal specifically with the issue of status between marital partners, casual references reflect his society's views. A rich merchant wants "an heir more raised / Than one which holds a trencher" (*Tim.*, I.i.121–122) and so objects to the courtship of his only daughter by a mere servant. Lovers wail, "The course of true love never did run smooth" because "it was different in blood— / O cross!—too high to be enthralled to low" (*MND*, I.i.134–135). And the worst insult Shylock can fling at his Christian tormenters advises that they free slaves and "marry them to your heirs" (*MV*, IV.i.93). Onstage as offstage, crossing barriers of rank in courtship incurred difficulties most couples never faced because they did not cross those barriers.

Parental Authority and Personal Affection

> But howsoeuer the case be, I suppose our marriage shall bee the
> more luckie, if it be made by the authoritie of our parents.
>
> —Erasmus, *A Modest Meane to Mariage*

> This youthful parcel
> Of noble bachelors stand at my bestowing,
> O'er whom both sovereign power and father's voice
> I have to use.
>
> —*AWW*, II.iii.53–56

CIRCUMSCRIBING the range of possible marital partners was a theoretical system of checks and balances designed to protect the interests of both the bridal couple and their respective families. On the one hand, those in authority—parents or guardians of minor children and masters of servants—had to give formal consent to the marriage of their charges. On the other hand, those charges had to agree to any proposed match and could dissent if it displeased them.[1] The absolute right of a free choice belonged only to single adults without masters or living parents, to widowers, and to most widows. However, because many among the English populace with little or no property spent several years of comparative independence before marrying, they effectively chose for themselves too. By law and custom, everyone was supposed to consider the wishes of others with vested concerns in a union. But since marriages, then as now, consist of more than legal niceties or social conventions, autonomy in making a match varied considerably.

Of all ideological mandates, none enjoyed wider acceptance than the

---

[1] Three books deal extensively with these and related issues in Shakespeare: Diane Elizabeth Dreher, *Domination and Defiance: Fathers and Daughters in Shakespeare* (Lexington: University Press of Kentucky, 1986); Peter Erickson, *Patriarchal Structures in Shakespeare's Drama* (Berkeley: University of California Press, 1985); Marilyn L. Williamson, *The Patriarchy of Shakespeare's Comedies* (Detroit: Wayne State University Press, 1986). All rely heavily upon the work of Lawrence Stone, and while each critic has looked at a limited range of primary and secondary sources, none has examined anything like the full spectrum of evidence, and none sets the issues into the wider matrix of courtship.

obligation of father or guardian to provide a proper mate for child or ward. As the two previous chapters indicate, there was abundant advice on the appropriate time to seek a spouse and the qualities to look for. But implicit in the injunctions against wedding children too young or wedding them to unworthy partners lies the presupposition of the parental right to arrange matches, even for the wrong reasons. The ubiquity of phrases like "If the Father meane to marry his Daughter to a Courtier" or "fathers to marry a son"[2] shows a powerful assumption that the older generation should determine marital choices for the younger generation. Thus fathers are urged to "runne and ride to seeke out good matches for their children."[3] And who better to make this decision? After all,

> parents by the instinct of nature louing their children as well as children loue themselues, and hauing by much experience better vnderstanding of a meete helpe, and better able to vse their discerning gift in this case, because it is not their owne case, and yet the case of one whom they loue as themselues, and to whom they wish as much good as to themselues; is it not meete euen for the childs good, that in a matter of such moment as mariage, the parent should haue a stroake?[4]

Yet in addition to the claims of experience and affection, patriarchal power in this decision also derived from the hierarchical conception of society, with its insistence on the subjection of all individuals to those set in command above them.[5] As many now recognize, the stridency of the

[2] *The Court of Good Counsell* (London, 1607), H3v; Thomas Heywood, *A Curtaine Lecture* (London, 1637), p. 97. See also Bartholomaeus Batty, *The Christian Man's Closet*, trans. William Lowth (London, 1581), p. 95v; *A Discourse of the Married and Single Life* (London, 1621), pp. 29–30; Desiderius Erasmus, "The Unequal Marriage," in *Colloquies*, trans. N. Bailey and ed. E. Johnson (London: Gibbings and Company, 1900), 3:65; Lord Dudley North, *Observations and Advices Oeconomical* (London, 1669), p. 18; Henry Percy, ninth Earl of Northumberland, "Instructions . . . to his Son," *Archaeologia* 27 (1838): 331; Philip Stubbes, *The Anatomie of Abuses* (London, 1595), p. 65.

[3] Daniel Rogers, *Matrimoniall Honour* (London, 1642), p. 80. See also *Court*, Cv, H3–H3v; Joseph Swetnam, *The Araignment of Lewde, Idle, Froward, and Unconstant Women* (London, 1615), p. 53 (repeats *Court*, Cv); William Perkins, *Christian Oeconomie*, trans. Thomas Pickering (London, 1609), p. 143.

[4] William Gouge, *Of Domesticall Duties* (London, 1622), p. 449. See also Robert Cleaver, *A Godly Form of Householde Government* (London, 1598), p. 149; Dudley Fenner, *The Artes of Logike and Rethorike* (London, 1584), Cv; Juan Luis Vives, *A Verie Fruitfull and Pleasant Booke Called the Instruction of a Christian Woman*, trans. Richard Hyrde (London, 1540), R4.

[5] See, e.g., Keith Thomas, "Age and Authority in Early Modern England," *Proceedings of the British Academy* 62 (1976): 205–248.

argument betrays both the fear of and the presence of resistance to such a view. But the force of so many voices dictating conformity to the system should not be minimized. Hence the authorities say that servants ought not to marry "vnlesse their master giue consent thereto," and that guardians must see their wards "well maried."[6] Not only in their minority, but even "when they are once grown vp [children] are bound, but with a much more straiter bond, to loue, reuerence, serue, and nourish their Father, and in all things to shew themselues dutifull and obedient."[7] Furthermore, "This obedience must shew it selfe especially in being gouerned by them in the matter of calling, and mariage."[8] Under such an ideology, the lines blurred between careful provision for future well-being and a tyrannical exertion of paternal will—as did the lines between respectful deference and slavish subjugation.

At the far end of the spectrum lay compelled marriage, "the extreamest bondage that is," when "those that hate, inforced are to ioyne."[9] A sufficient number of complaints survives to suggest that some fathers did arrange unions with scant regard for their children's wishes. "Yet now consider," says one observer, that "when matches are made by the Parentes . . . before the young couple haue any knowledge of it, & so many times are forced against their mindes, fearing the rygor and displeasure of their parents, they often promise with their mouthes that which they refuse with their hearts."[10] Among the unfortunate consequences of these love-

[6] William Whately, *A Care-Cloth, or a Treatise of the Cumbers and Troubles of Marriage* (London, 1624), A4; Gouge, *Domesticall Duties*, p. 605. See also Cleaver, *Godly Form*, p. 130; Gouge, *Domesticall Duties*, pp. 451, 605, 662–664; Perkins, *Christian Oeconomie*, p. 85.

[7] Jean Bodin, *The Six Bookes of a Commonweale*, trans. Richard Knolles (London, 1606), pp. 20–21; see also p. 14. Further authorities include Thomas Carter, *Carters Christian Commonwealth: Domesticall Dutyes Deciphered* (London, 1627), pp. 129–132; Rogers, *Matrimoniall Honour*, p. 73; William Vaughan, *The Golden-grove* (London, 1600), N8ᵛ.

[8] Fenner, *Artes*, F8ᵛ. See also Heinrich Bullinger, *The Christian State of Matrimony*, trans. Miles Coverdale (London, 1575), pp. 12–12ᵛ; John Stockwood, *A Bartholomew Fairing for Parentes* (London, 1589), pp. 18, 34, 35. William Perkins, *Workes* (Cambridge, 1618), 3:696, even called for parental approval of remarriage by widows.

[9] George Whetstone, *An Heptameron of Civill Discourses* (London, 1582), F1; Geffrey Whitney, *A Choice of Emblemes, and Other Devises* (Leyden, 1586), p. 99. See also Henricus Cornelius Agrippa, *The Commendation of Matrimony* (London, 1540), C4ᵛ; Erasmus, "Unequal Marriage," p. 61.

[10] Swetnam, *Araignment*, pp. 51–52, following Stefano Guazzo, *The Civile Conversation*, trans. George Pettie (London: Constable, 1925), 2:5; Swetnam alters his source only slightly. See also Gouge, *Domesticall Duties*, p. 585; Rogers, *Matrimoniall Honour*, pp. 93–94.

less, autocratically arranged weddings, contemporaries predict "discontent and misery," "wretchednes," "barrenness [due] to compeld copulation," the transformation of men into "monsters," women into "devills," and "that abhominable act of adultery."[11] Nonetheless, the insistence upon parental primacy in contracting matrimony often implies that children should have little or no say in the selection of a mate. Juan Luis Vives declares "that it becometh nat a mayde to talke / where her father and mother be in coṁunication / about her mariage: but to leaue all that care and charge holly vnto them."[12] In some cases, offspring actually become equated with property, to be disposed of at the owner's pleasure: "For the childe (in respect of the body) is part of the parents goods."[13] Acting on the basis of these views, parents could feel justified in making whatever matches seemed best and in expecting docile compliance from their sons or daughters.

Theoretically, at least, the exercise of authority in matrimony was limited to the issue of consent, required of both parents and children, which formed the basis for all valid marriages (*consensus nuptialis*). It did not matter who made the initial choice, so long as the arrangement met with agreement from everyone involved. As one writer describes the situation,

> The first liking is sometimes on the parents or other friends part, and then by them made knowne to the partie to be maried. . . . Sometimes againe the first liking is on the parties part that is to be maried: and then if that partie be vnder the gouernment of parents, the matter must be moued to them, before there be any further proceeding therein.[14]

Under ideal circumstances, the final commitment was *"a voluntarie promise of marriage, mutually made betweene one man and one woman, both beeing meete and free to marry one another, and therefore allowed so to do by their Parents."*[15]

---

[11] Heywood, *Curtaine Lecture*, pp. 99, 100; Bullinger, *Christian State*, p. 23ᵛ; John Sadler, *The Sick Womans Private Looking-Glasse* (London, 1636), p. 108; Carter, *Christian Commonwealth*, p. 142. See also Nicholas Culpeper, *A Dictionary for Midwives* (London, 1671), pp. 70–71.

[12] Vives, *Verie Fruitfull*, R4.

[13] Matthew Griffith, *Bethel, or A Forme for Families* (London, 1633), p. 274. See also Carter, *Christian Commonwealth*, p. 195; Gouge, *Domesticall Duties*, p. 452; Richard Greenham, *Works* (London, 1599), p. 37; Stockwood, *Bartholomew Fairing*, pp. 21, 22–23; Whately, *Care-Cloth*, p. 33.

[14] Gouge, *Domesticall Duties*, pp. 196–197.

[15] Cleaver, *Godly Form*, p. 112 (italics in original text); discussion of voluntary consent continues on pp. 115–118. See also William Harrington, *The Comendacions of Matrymony* (London, 1528), A3; Perkins, *Christian Oeconomie*, pp. 68–69, 76, 85.

At least one work genuinely tries to debate "whether is the affection of the childe to be preferred before the election of the father," giving arguments on both sides.[16] Others acknowledge that parents must not force children "against their willes to bee assured," for without assent of the parties involved, "what is mariage but a binding of people apprentices to a perpetuall thraldome?"[17] Yet the advice offered resistant offspring evokes the image of meek and probably ineffective dissent: "But if notwithstanding all the meanes that they can vse, they still finde their heart altogether auerse, they may in a reuerend manner entreat their parent to forbeare to presse that match, and to thinke of some other."[18]

From the beginning of the Elizabethan period, commentators insist that "the authority of marying young folkes, lieth in the Parentes, and not in them selues."[19] In 1578, John Stockwood wrote his famed sermon *A Bartholomew Fairing* "Shewing that children are not to marie, without the consent of their parentes, in whose power and choice it lyeth to prouide wiues and husbandes for their sonnes and daughters." And his position is affirmed by many subsequent observers.[20] A few even deny the validity of unions not blessed by parental approval, claiming "that whom the Parents ioyne not, God doth not ioyne; and so their marriage is sinfull, and their liuing together very filthinesse and vncleannesse, vntill by submission they haue procured an after-consent, to ratifie that, which ought not to haue been done before the consent."[21] At the very least, there is no obligation to support rebellious offspring financially: "Parents have but small joy to maintaine theeves and traytors with their meanes and estate, it cost them more the getting, then your easie matches cost you."[22] To some,

---

[16] Charles Gibbon, *A Work Worth the Reading* (London, 1591), p. 3; see pp. following for further relevant discussion.

[17] Griffith, *Bethel*, p. 271. See also Agrippa, *Commendation*, C4–C4ᵛ; Thomas Gataker, *A Good Wife Gods Gift: and, A Wife Indeed* (London, 1623), p. 11; Stockwood, *Bartholomew Fairing*, pp. 80–81. For James's views, see Lawrence Stone, *The Crisis of the Aristocracy, 1558–1641* (Oxford: Clarendon Press, 1965), p. 611.

[18] Gouge, *Domesticall Duties*, p. 450; parents are to "vse all manner of faire meanes to moue their children to yeeld" short of absolute force, p. 564. See also Rogers, *Matrimoniall Honour*, p. 81; Stockwood, *Bartholomew Fairing*, p. 78.

[19] Bullinger, *Christian State*, p. 12ᵛ; see also pp. 11ff.

[20] See, e.g., Pierre Ayrault, *A Discourse for Parents Honour, and Authoritie over their Children*, trans. John Budden (London, 1614); Carter, *Christian Commonwealth*, pp. 194–198.

[21] Whately, *Care-Cloth*, p. 34. See also Gouge, *Domesticall Duties*, pp. 212–213, 446, 448–452, 563–565; Griffith, *Bethel*, pp. 274–275; Perkins, *Christian Oeconomie*, pp. 76, 84–86; Stockwood, *Bartholomew Fairing*, pp. 22–23, 28–29.

[22] Rogers, *Matrimoniall Honour*, p. 84.

flouting a father's wishes regarding matrimony represented a heinous offense.

Yet none of the formal advice books or sermons or marriage manuals suggests that mutual affection is insignificant. In fact, the complaints against unauthorized unions would make no sense were there not a certain number of matches made in disregard of parental wishes. But the motives behind defiant behavior are often denigrated as merely carnal desire. A girl might be enticed by "a ryotous wylfull whoorhunter and waster, or such a one as is forsworne, and hath begiled many other," or a boy might simply want "his pretty pussy to huggle withal."[23] It seems scandalous that children would "whollie follow their own will and let out the raines vnto their owne vnbrideled and vnsetled lusts, making matches according to their own sickle fantasies."[24] Because "the desire dieth when it is attained and the affection perisheth when it is satisfied," a young man is advised to "leaue the care of this electiõ to his parentes, ye whiche haue better iudgement & are more free from the agitations and motions of al affections, then they are."[25] Such arguments confirm that emotional attachments could be as fierce in this period as in any other.

At least a few writers, including some supporters of parental authority, strongly affirm the necessity for "a knitting of hearts, before striking of hands."[26] For example, Edmund Tilney says, "Wherfore, let loue be rooted deeply in the mans hart towardes the woman," and George Whetstone insists, "The office of Free choise, is the roote or foundation of Marriage, which consisteth onely in the satisfaction of fancie: for where the fancie is not pleased, all the perfections of the world, cannot force looue, and where the fancie delighteth, many defects are perfected, or tollerated among the Marryed."[27] However, it would be a mistake to overemphasize

[23] Bullinger, *Christian State*, p. 24 (see also p. 13ᵛ); Stubbes, *Anatomie of Abuses*, p. 65.

[24] Stockwood, *Bartholomew Fairing*, pp. 11–12. See also Gouge, *Domesticall Duties*, p. 197; Michel Eyquem de Montaigne, "On Some Verses of Virgil," in *The Complete Works*, trans. Donald M. Frame (Stanford, CA: Stanford University Press, 1948), pp. 645–647.

[25] *Advice to a Son: Precepts of Lord Burghley, Sir Walter Raleigh, and Francis Osborne*, ed. Louis B. Wright (Ithaca, NY: Cornell University Press, 1962), p. 21; Juan Luis Vives, *The Office and Duetie of an Husband*, trans. Thomas Paynell (London, 1553), D4ᵛ. See also Rogers, *Matrimoniall Honour*, p. 65.

[26] Cleaver, *Godly Form*, p. 322.

[27] Edmund Tilney, *A Brief and Pleasant Discourse of Duties in Mariage, Called the Flower of Friendshippe* (London, 1568), B5; Whetstone, *Heptameron*, Y1. See also Bullinger, *Christian State*, p. 15ᵛ; Carter, *Christian Commonwealth*, pp. 10–11; Thomas Gataker, "A Good Wife," in *Two Mariage Sermons* (London, 1620), p. 11; Gouge, *Domesticall Duties*, p. 197; Dorothy Leigh, *The Mother's Blessing* (London, 1616), p. 52; Robert Southwell, S.J., *Two*

the influence of this position or to ignore the fact that not a single work advocates the primacy of personal affection in the face of legitimate parental objections. The veto some allow when children cannot accept their elders' selection has not yet become a right of absolute individual choice. To prevent future regret for an imprudent marriage, the older generation was expected to cool foolish ardors, ensuring that "the Match be . . . made, aswell, by foresight, as free choyce."[28]

In many ways, civil and canon law reinforced parental power in nuptial affairs. The Church of England forbade a priest to marry any minor unless the father or guardian "shall either personally, or by sufficient testimony, signifie to him their consents giuen to the said Marriage."[29] As early as 1559, the Articles of Inquiry sought to discover weddings performed without parents' approval, and subsequent articles in 1584, 1597, and 1604 prescribed suspension for any minister violating these rules.[30] The requirements were especially strict for a license allowing a marriage to be solemnized more rapidly than usual. In these circumstances, for everyone save widows or widowers, regardless of age, *expresso concensu Parentum* had to be established either in person or upon the sworn testimony of an individual of good character well known to the church official granting the license.[31] Thus valid parental objections could not be hidden from the parish by means of a hasty wedding, even if the parties involved were adults. Church courts provided a forum where children could bring complaints if they felt unfairly restrained from marriage by their parents, but prosecutions on this ground were rare and decisions in favor of the offspring rarer still.[32]

For fatherless heirs and heiresses still in their minority, whose marriages were especially subject to abuse, the law protected the rights of the guardian.[33] Only if a binding agreement had been made before his death could

---

Letters and Short Rules of a Good Life, ed. Nancy Pollard Brown (Charlottesville: University Press of Virginia, 1973), p. 51; Vives, *Office and Duetie*, D1; William Whately, *A Bride-Bush, or a Wedding Sermon* (London, 1617), pp. 7–11; John Wing, *The Crowne Conjugall or, The Spouse Royall* (Middleburgh, 1620), pp. 43–47.

[28] Whetstone, *Heptameron*, X3. See also Whately, *Care-Cloth*, A2ᵛ.

[29] *Constitutions and Canons Ecclesiastical 1604* (Oxford: Clarendon Press, 1923), L3ᵛ.

[30] *A Collection of Articles, Injunctions, Canons, Orders, Ordinances, and Canons Ecclesiastical* (London: Stevens and Co., 1846), p. 4; *Constitutions*, L3ᵛ–L4.

[31] *Collection*, pp. 38, 14; *Constitutions*, Q4ᵛ, R1.

[32] Ralph A. Houlbrooke, *The English Family, 1450–1700* (London: Longman, 1984), pp. 68–69.

[33] For the fullest discussions of wardship, see Joel Hurstfield, *The Queen's Wards: Wardship and Marriage under Elizabeth I*, 2d ed. (London: Frank Cass, 1973), esp. pp. 130–156;

a father choose his child's matrimonial partner. After the father's death, the right to manage the life and property of minor offspring passed technically to the crown but in actuality to the Court of Wards, where guardianship often went to the highest bidder. Once assigned to a supervisor, wards could not make any betrothal contract without permission. If they did, all parties involved could be enjoined by stiff recognizances to appear in court, the contract could be set aside, and the audacious minor fined. While a guardian could make no lawful commitments for a female charge until she reached fourteen, if between then and age sixteen he presented a candidate whom she rejected, he not only retained control of her fortune until her majority but was entitled to recoup the value of her marriage. Conversely, if he failed to offer her an alliance before she turned sixteen, he lost the value of the marriage and got only two years' income from her land. Should an heiress manage to marry without a guardian's approval, her husband forfeited control of his wife's inheritance until she became twenty-one, for "no woman heire can be married, but by her Lords disposing and assent."[34] The sole restriction concerned marrying a ward in disparagement, that is, to someone below a dependent's rank in society. Otherwise, all the advantages lay on the guardian's side. Thus the wardship system virtually ensured that those in authority arranged marriages with little interference from the children involved.

In London, where citizens enjoyed certain privileges and immunities not granted to other Englishmen, a curious set of orders was decreed in 1580 for the protection of orphans. The document is worth quoting at some length because it so tellingly reflects the official attitude toward children who married as they pleased. The mayor and aldermen express concern because

> children (Orphanes of the sayd Citie) sometimes in the lyues of their Parents, and sometimes after their deceases, beeing lefte wealthy and rich, doe bestowe themselues in vngodly Mariages, for the most part in their young age, at their owne wills & pleasures, without the consent and against the mindes of their friends, saying & affirming, that the Law & custome of the said Citie giueth vnto them their portions, whether they mary by the assent of their friends or not, & so do daily cast away &. . . . bestow themselues vpon simple & light persōs, hauing neither cūning, knowledge, substance, ne good or honest cōditions.[35]

H. E. Bell, *An Introduction to the History and Records of the Court of Wards and Liveries* (Cambridge: Cambridge University Press, 1953), pp. 104–105, 125–126.

[34] *The Lawes Resolutions of Womens Rights* (London, 1632), pp. 9, 22.

[35] *Orders Taken and Enacted, for Orphans and Their Portions* (London, 1580), A2–A2ᵛ.

The orders go on to specify fines and other penalties for young women under eighteen and young men under twenty-one who marry without their guardians' approval. However, the laws of the time were not entirely one-sided. Civil statutes provided that no one might be compelled into a marriage.[36] Also, as indicated in chapter 2, at ages twelve and fourteen, girls and boys were allowed the right of dissent to any union arranged during their childhood, though the effectiveness of objection from one so young may perhaps be doubted.[37] Even when promised against her will, a woman was presumed to consent to marriage if consummation occurred.[38] Thus the dominance of patriarchal authority over personal affection spelled out theoretically found strong support in the laws of England's church and state.

However, putting into practice the strictures and statutes proved particularly difficult with certain social groups. As adolescents, young adults, or sometimes even as children, large numbers of both sexes left their homes to go into service in other households. Researchers estimate that perhaps 40 percent or more of the population were under twenty and that, among the 10 percent or so of all ages who were servants, the vast majority were between fifteen and twenty-four years old, with the proportion dropping sharply as people got older.[39] Not only were household servants young, but they were rarely married, frequently orphaned, and usually cut off from direct supervision by their parents.[40] The terms of employment

[36] *Lawes*, p. 59.

[37] Martin Ingram, *Church Courts, Sex, and Marriage in England, 1570–1640* (Cambridge: Cambridge University Press, 1987), pp. 173–175, finds only rare instances of such dissent, which could indicate a decline either in this custom or in active opposition by betrothed children.

[38] Henry Swinburne, *A Treatise of Spousals, or Matrimonial Contracts* (London, 1686), p. 225; see also *Lawes*, p. 60.

[39] John Hajnal, "Two Kinds of Pre-Industrial Household Formation System," in *Family Forms in Historic Europe*, ed. Richard Wall, Jean Robin, and Peter Laslett (Cambridge: Cambridge University Press, 1983), pp. 69, 92–95. According to his research, 35 percent of males, 27 percent of females between the ages of 15 and 19 were in service, 30 percent and 40 percent respectively for ages 20–24, 15 percent each for ages 25–29, 6 percent and 7 percent for ages 30–39, 2 percent each for ages 40–49. See also Nigel Goose, "Household Size and Structure in Early-Stuart Cambridge," *Social History* 5 (1980): 371, 374; Ann Kussmaul, *Servants in Husbandry in Early Modern England* (Cambridge: Cambridge University Press, 1981), passim, especially her definition of the term *servant*, App. I; Marjorie K. McIntosh, "Servants and the Household Unit in an Elizabethan English Community," *Journal of Family History* 9 (1984): 11; Lawrence Stone, *The Family, Sex and Marriage in England 1500–1800* (New York: Harper and Row, 1977), p. 167; Keith Wrightson, *English Society, 1580–1680* (London: Hutchinson, 1982), p. 42.

[40] See, e.g., Susan Dwyer Amussen, "Féminin/masculin: le genre dans l'Angleterre de

varied in length, with a year the minimum,[41] thus allowing a mobility that further intensified the problems of control over such persons. Against the practical values of learning skills and saving money before entering marriage[42] stood the temptations to irregular courtship inherent in the relative freedom enjoyed by individuals at this age and social level. Since masters bore responsibility for all in their households—indeed the word *family* denoted everyone under one roof, with no distinction between blood kin and servants—they had to set rules and exercise vigilance.[43] One order bluntly warns, "Item, That none toy with the maids, on paine of 4d."[44] Householders were to bring offenders to church, then if necessary to the magistrate, "and if that serue not, . . . discharge thē from the family, vnlesse they amend."[45]

---

l'epoque moderne," *Annales Économies, Sociétés, Civilisations* 40 (1985): 270; idem, *An Ordered Society: Gender and Class in Early Modern England* (New York: Basil Blackwell, 1988), p. 68; Vivien Brodsky Elliott, "Single Women in the London Marriage Market: Age, Status and Mobility, 1598–1619," in *Marriage and Society: Studies in the Social History of Marriage*, ed. R. B. Outhwaite (New York: St. Martin's Press, 1981), pp. 89–90; Hajnal, "Two Kinds," pp. 72, 95; Houlbrooke, *English Family*, pp. 72–73; Ingram, *Church Courts*, pp. 138–139, 156; Richard Wall, "Introduction," in *Family Forms*, p. 15; Sue Wright, " 'Churmaids, Huswyfes and Hucksters': The Employment of Women in Tudor and Stuart Salisbury," in *Women and Work in Pre-Industrial England*, ed. Lindsey Charles and Lorna Duffin (Dover, NH: Croom Helm, 1985).

[41] Kussmaul, *Servants*, p. 32; Elliott, "Single Women," p. 92, found the average term of service in London was just over four years; Wright, " 'Churmaids,' " p. 104, found provincial serving women worked for one to two years at a time, rarely longer than four years.

[42] Hajnal, "Two Kinds," p. 95; Kussmaul, *Servants*, p. 26; McIntosh, "Servants," pp. 3, 18–19.

[43] On this point see, e.g., Susan Dwyer Amussen, "Gender, Family, and the Social Order, 1560–1725," in *Order and Disorder in Early Modern England*, ed. Anthony Fletcher and John Stevenson (Cambridge: Cambridge University Press, 1985), pp. 196–200; Christopher Hill, "The Spiritualization of the Household," in *Society and Puritanism in Pre-Revolutionary England* (New York: Schocken Books, 1964), pp. 443–447; Kussmaul, *Servants*, pp. 7–8; Peter Laslett, *The World We Have Lost, Further Examined* (London: Methuen, 1983), pp. 1–21; idem, "Introduction: The History of the Family," in *Household and Family in Past Time*, ed. Laslett and Richard Wall (Cambridge: Cambridge University Press, 1972), pp. 26, 80, 82; Gordon J. Schochet, *The Authoritarian Family and Political Attitudes in Seventeenth-Century England: Patriarchalism in Political Thought* (New Brunswick, NJ: Transaction Books, 1988), pp. 70–71.

[44] Sir John Harington, *Nugae Antiquae*, ed. Henry Harington (London: Vernor and Hood, 1804), 1:207; idem, *The Letters and Epigrams of Sir John Harington*, ed. Norman Egbert McClure (Philadelphia: University of Pennsylvania Press, 1930), p. 269. See also Coke's articles requiring "all unlawful games, drunkenness, whoredom and incontinency in private families to be reported, as on their good government the commonwealth depends"; Hill, "Spiritualization," p. 448.

[45] Fenner, *Artes*, B^v.

It was understood that the decisions of superiors prevailed in marital matters, as in other affairs. Hence a will of 1600 leaves five pounds to a maidservant provided she "marry with a man approved of to my good Mistress . . . for his fear of God and honest conversation."[46] Though the very existence of such stipulations implies that strict control of so large and so volatile a group proved impossible, the late age at marriage discussed in chapter 2 indicates that most in service did not rush into wedlock, regardless of the extent to which they could indulge their passions. Ironically, about the only legal advantage for anyone marrying without permission accrued to women servants who "purposely mary to free themselues: because our lawes doe free a maide that is maried from her seruice to master and mistresse."[47] The same gender differentiation applied also to apprenticeship: "If a man prentice in London marry, he shall be forced to serve of his time, and yet loose his freedome [the right to practice his craft in the City]. But yf a woman prentice marry, shee shall onely forfayte hir libertie, but shall not be forced to serve."[48] While this kind of behavior was frowned upon as "vnlawfull libertie,"[49] such regulations reveal that some individuals, even under direct supervision, married without regard for rules or the wishes of their superiors. As for the army of the mobile poor, their exercise of marital freedom was extremely difficult to regulate—or even to record.[50]

In literature, liberty of another kind prevails. Fictive worlds can transgress customs that bind the living. And indeed some of the poetry, prose, and drama of the period would lead one to believe that love alone leads to marriage and that disapproving fathers are just comic figures to be cleverly circumvented. Yet other works, especially those outside the standard canon, often refract a vision strikingly close to that presented in the law and teachings of the period. For example, this rhymed complaint confirms

---

[46] McIntosh, "Servants," p. 21.

[47] Gouge, *Domesticall Duties*, p. 607.

[48] John Manningham, *The Diary of John Manningham of the Middle Temple, 1602–1603*, ed. Robert Parker Sorlien (Hanover, NH: University Press of New England, 1976), p. 42. For another authority who claims a married apprentice must double his years of service, see Richard Jones, *The Passionate Morrice*, ed. F. J. Furnivall, New Shakspere Society, ser. 6, no. 2 (London: N. Trübner, 1876): 87.

[49] Gouge, *Domesticall Duties*, p. 607.

[50] Consult the work of A. L. Beier, *Masterless Men: The Vagrancy Problem in England, 1560–1640* (New York: Methuen, 1985); J. A. Sharpe, *Crime in Early Modern England, 1550–1750* (London: Longman, 1984); David Underdown, *Revel, Riot, and Rebellion: Popular Politics and Culture in England 1603–1660* (Oxford: Clarendon Press, 1985); Keith Wrightson, "Aspects of Social Differentiation in Rural England, c. 1580–1660," *Journal of Peasant Studies* 5 (1977): 33–47.

the existence of matches made with scant concern for the feelings of the partners.

> For 'tis not now as erst in elder daies,
> When marriage was contracted by affection,
> For kindred now so much the matter swaies,
> The parties haue small choice in loues election;
> > But many times, ere one behold the other
> > An vnaduised match the friends do smother;
> > And howsoeuer they two can agree,
> > Their frends haue woo'd, & they must married be.[51]

A fictional father with a riotous son resolves "to marry him before he be starke mad, or a worse mischeefe (if possible) befall him."[52] No consultation with the son, much less the bride, is even suggested. Another piece of paternal counsel reminds a daughter "what a hard fauoured woman she was, and of no louely qualities," but "through the great care that I haue had for thee, I haue procured thee such an husband, as the most courteous and beautifull damsell that is, could not desire a better."[53] Obviously the offspring here have no say in marriage.

Even in tales where individuals lose their hearts, a due respect for their elders' approval often emerges. In Erasmus's dialogue between a suitor and his beloved, she refuses to say she loves him: "I will tell you what were a better way for vs both. You shall treate with your Parentes and myne, and with their will and consent let the matter be concluded."[54] Similarly, a wanton young woman trying to entrap a naive lover into a wedding mimics proper behavior by insisting on "the counsell and consent of my parents."[55] And a maid eager to marry ruefully acknowledges, "Our Parents

---

[51] Nicholas Breton, *Cornu-copiae, Pasquils Night-cap* (London, 1612), p. 17. See also Breton's *An Olde Mans Lesson, and a Young Mans Love* (London, 1605), B3ᵛ.

[52] Francis Lenton, *Characterismi: or, Lentons Leasures* (London, 1631), no. 29. For other instances of fictional fathers who propose to bestow less-than-perfect sons in marriage, see Ester Sowernam, *Ester Hath Hang'd Haman* (London, 1617), p. 24; Swetnam, *Araignment*, p. 6.

[53] Robert Snawsel, *A Looking Glasse for Maried Folkes* (London, 1610), D7. For a formal, rhymed statement of parental authority in general, see *The Uncasing of Machivils Instructions to his Sonne* (London, 1613), F2ᵛ–F3.

[54] Desiderius Erasmus, *A Modest Meane to Mariage* (London, 1568), C2ᵛ. See also Jones, *Passionate Morrice*, pp. 53–54.

[55] Thomas Dekker, "The Batchelors Banquet," in *The Non-Dramatic Works*, ed. Alexander B. Grosart (1884; reprint, New York: Russell and Russell, 1963), 1:252, 253.

willes (you know) must be obay'd."[56] Part of the literary interest in widows, who became standard butts of satire, derives from their freedom to select a husband instead of simply accepting the family's selection. Hence a country widow is described as "her owne woman, and not subiect to the auaricious counsell of peeuish parents."[57] While much literature touts the primacy of love, some writers denounce it in harsh terms. "Loue is the virgins crack; the widowes crosse; the bachelers bane; the maried mans purgatory; the young mans misery; and the ageds consumption: a fained god; an idle fancy; a kind of fury; & in some, a frenzie."[58] In more cynical terms, Nicholas Breton dismisses all talk of love as a charade for seduction, subjugation, and trafficking in the marital market. Love? "there is no such thinge: there is bargaining and selling, looking and telling, lust and folly, commanding &´obeying, marying & getting of Children."[59]

The central issue here, of course, is the extent to which either didactic or fictional literature encodes the thoughts and actions of individuals in the society. Some persons, including some among the wellborn, did marry for love, or at least chose their own spouse. It is reported to Sir Francis Willoughby that his daughter "is so great with Mr. Candish's son that she is fully minded to have him. . . . Whether you like it or not it must go forwards and be a match."[60] Seeking to marry a pretty, propertied young widow, Sir Thomas Barrington was "said to be so much in love with her that he would be willing to accept any conditions she might care to insist on."[61] More restrained indications of love appear in the report that with Lord Berkeley "affection (upon motion formerly made) grewe between him

[56] Samuel Rowlands, *Tis Merrie When Gossips Meete* (London, 1602), D3ᵛ. See also Breton, *Olde Mans Lesson*, E2–E3, for another example of seeking approval from both partners' parents; Angel Day, *The English Secretary* (London, 1607), pp. 139–140, for an enforced marriage.

[57] Lenton, *Characterismi*, no. 7. For other views of widows, see, e.g., Andrew Kingsmill, "A Godly Advise . . . Touching Mariage," in *A Viewe of Man's Estate* (London, 1574), J3ᵛ–J6; Henry Parrott, "A young Nouices new yonger wife," in *Cures for the Itch. Characters, Epigrams, Epitaphs* (London, 1626); Wye Saltonstall, *Picturae Loquentes* (London, 1631), no. 4.

[58] Thomas Gainsford, *The Rich Cabinet Furnished with Varieties of Excellent Descriptions* (London, 1616), p. 87.

[59] Nicholas Breton, *Choice, Chance, and Change* (London, 1606), H2.

[60] Wallace Notestein, "The English Woman, 1580–1650," in *Studies in Social History*, ed. J. H. Plumb (London: Longmans, Green, 1955), p. 75; note, pp. 75–76, the pair's "riding, flawning, roisting, and flirting" while en route to London.

[61] J. T. Cliffe, *The Puritan Gentry: The Great Puritan Families of Early Stuart England* (London: Routledge and Kegan Paul, 1984), p. 65.

. . . and Elizabeth Carey," while the Earl of Bedford's daughter happily prepared to wed the Earl of Bristol's son, "thear being setled a private affection between the yongue couple."[62] Throughout the long search to find husbands for Joan Meux and her cousin Joan Altham, the family qualify their prospective choices with "if it please God to send likeing of boothe sides." They rationalize a failed attempt with the excuse that "if hir affections had stood right at first this could not have directed them." Nonetheless, Joan Meux's mother declares, "I thank God I find hir very wiling to be directed."[63]

Not surprisingly, when an unauthorized attraction developed, difficulties involving parental consent often arose. Speaking of his first wife, Dorothy, Gervase Holles says that "whilst I was yet but a boy and shee an infant I tooke a passionate . . . inclination to marry hir wch every yeare grew up more and more into a resolution." At a considerable financial sacrifice, Gervase's father magnanimously accepted the boy's choice. Nonetheless, the son acknowledges, "Here was a ground (as high as could be from any act y^t was not impious, ungracious, or dishonest) for an angry father's lasting displeasure."[64] While Holles was fortunate enough to obtain indulgent assent to his wishes, others found their elders' cooperation more problematic. Having refused her father's choice of Mr. Hamilton, Mary Rich, the Earl of Cork's daughter, set her heart on a younger son, an "ill and horribly disobedient" decision. After being estranged for some considerable time, "I was at last . . . led into my father's chamber, and there, upon my knees, humbly begged his pardon, which after he had, with great justice severely chid me, he bid me rise, and was . . . reconciled to me, and told me I should suddenly be married."[65] What is noteworthy in the foregoing instances is not so much the child's defiance for the sake of love but more especially the awareness of impropriety in such defiance, together with grateful relief at being allowed to wed the desired spouse. Though the recorded accounts may be motivated by guilt or by a

[62] John Smyth, *The Berkeley Manuscripts. The Lives of the Berkeleys*, ed. Sir John Maclean (Gloucester, 1883), 2:395; Arthur Searle, ed., *Barrington Family Letters, 1628–1632*, Camden Society Publications, 4th ser., 28 (1983): 235.

[63] Searle, *Barrington*, pp. 113, 107, 125.

[64] Gervase Holles, *Memorials of the Holles Family, 1493–1656*, ed. A. C. Wood, Camden Society Publications, 3rd ser., 55 (1937): 228, 204.

[65] Linda A. Pollock, *A Lasting Relationship: Parents and Children over Three Centuries* (Hanover, NH: University Press of New England, 1987), pp. 260, 261. See also Sara Heller Mendelson, *The Mental World of Stuart Women: Three Studies* (Amherst: University of Massachusetts Press, 1987), pp. 66–77.

need to seem less intransigent, only a powerful social ideology could engender rhetoric like this.

While those described above united in marriage, not all lovers did. Susan Ives of Norwich was dissuaded from a union by her mother, and the widowed Elizabeth Cocke was locked up in a brother's house to prevent her wedding to Ralph Thompson.[66] When Thomas Whythorne secretly courted his master's daughter, "þis fier kowld not be kept so klos, but . . . at lenkth þis loov of owrz was detekted . . . wherfor þer waz sekret means fownd not only to hinder owr loovz but also to separat þem." Interestingly, he reports that the girl insisted on obtaining the "*good wi⟨ll⟩ and pleaziur of my parents.*" They subsequently bestowed this young woman on someone else.[67] Occasionally, despite compelling reasons for a union, parents would still withhold consent. For example, a maidservant of Michael Hickes's was denied to the man who got her with child because her family thought he was a "bare fellow . . . [with] nothing but a little money."[68]

The irregular, clandestine courtships of James Whythorne and Hickes's servingwoman point out the relatively lax supervision over the lesser social orders. Sometimes their wooings followed a pattern similar to that of the more privileged, as with the humbly born country girl "sent up to London by her father . . . to marry."[69] But such paternal control was more often entirely absent. Ralph Josselin's courtship proceeded after "my eye fixed with love upon a Mayde"[70] quite without reference to his parents or those of his wife, Jane. While the clergyman Josselin conducted a chastely affectionate suit, not all exercised self-restraint. Simon Forman's servant, John Braddedge, began his sexual career at sixteen, fathered at least one bastard, and at twenty-five finally married a lame Flemish woman.[71] In a female parallel to Braddedge, Dr. Forman treated Margaret Kendall, wife of an actor, who "left her maidenhead at about 13 yers, and had many suters at

[66] Amussen, *Ordered Society*, pp. 105, 106; see also pp. 71–72. Check as well Ingram, *Church Courts*, pp. 201–203, 211.

[67] James Osborn, ed., *The Autobiography of Thomas Whythorne* (Oxford: Clarendon Press, 1961), p. 78 (italics in original text).

[68] Alan G. R. Smith, *Servant of the Cecils: The Life of Sir Michael Hickes, 1543–1612* (Totowa, NJ: Rowman and Littlefield, 1977), p. 166.

[69] Elliott, "Single Women," p. 95.

[70] Alan Macfarlane, ed., *The Diary of Ralph Josselin* (London: Oxford University Press for the British Academy, 1976), p. 7.

[71] A. L. Rowse, *Sex and Society in Shakespeare's Age: Simon Forman the Astrologer* (New York: Charles Scribner's Sons, 1974), p. 52.

15 yers or 16 of age and was in diuers humors and might haue had many good matches / & yet maried non—but in thend was with child by one, and she maried to another, to a player."[72] In an odd cross between seduction and the match arranged by a patriarchal figure, one Elizabeth Purkey claimed in 1595 that her former master, Robert Dey, a rector of Cranwich, had fathered her child and then set up a marriage for her with Robert Bate, a thatcher, before the baby's birth.[73] Where affection or attraction beckoned, ordinary folk were much freer to respond, although courtships might drag on for years before a poor couple could afford to marry.[74]

In many instances the records show that love played no role at all in the contracting of a marriage and that the idea of mutual consent really meant concurrence with family decisions—yielded willingly or unwillingly. Penelope Rich was "married against her will unto one against whom she did protest at the very solemnity and ever after."[75] When Walter Mildmay was asked to wed Grace Sherrington, he resisted, "being then more willinge to travile to get experience of the world, than to mary so soone." However, "his father told him, yf he did not marry me, he should never bring any other woman into his house. Upon which importunitie of his father he was content."[76] The future Lady Mildmay dutifully assented to the match without protest and apparently without ever having seen her prospective husband. Nor was this unusual. Even widows sometimes found themselves strictly immured and entirely subject to others' marital plans. Margaret Devereaux had no voice whatsoever in the selection of her second husband. When the first one died, she was sent by her father "unto my La. of Huntyngdone, and at her fyrst comynge she was brought to her chamber, which she closely kept untyll she was maryed . . . whyther none wer suffered to come, withowte especiall admyttance."[77] No similar record survives for the circumstances of most marriages, but the view of at least one

---

[72] Ashmolean MS 306.349–349ᵛ; reference supplied by Barbara Traister in private correspondence. For further evidence, see, e.g., Ingram, *Church Courts*, pp. 265–268, 285; Michael MacDonald, *Mystical Bedlam: Madness, Anxiety, and Healing in Seventeenth-Century England* (Cambridge: Cambridge University Press, 1981), pp. 89–97.

[73] Amussen, "Gender," p. 215. She brought charges because Dey refused to pay all the dowry he had promised.

[74] Elliott, "Single Women," p. 95, refers to courtships lasting as long as eight years.

[75] Lansdowne MS 885.86, as cited by Sylvia Freedman, *Poor Penelope: Lady Penelope Rich, An Elizabethan Woman* (Bourne End, Bucks.: Kensal Press, 1983), p. 2.

[76] Rachel Weigall, ed., "The Journal of Lady Mildmay, circa 1570–1617," *The Quarterly Review* 215 (1911): 122.

[77] Dorothy M. Meads, ed., *Diary of Lady Margaret Hoby, 1599–1605* (Boston: Houghton Mifflin, 1930), p. 12.

letter writer appears in his praise of a young man "for that you lovingly followed therein your good father's advice and direction, whose assent in such cases is necessary for him to give, and as dutiful for you to crave."[78]

Despite all the emphasis upon parental power, some couples did defy it, often at great cost. John Donne's elopement with the eighteen-year-old daughter of Sir George More deprived him not only of family approval for the marriage but of Anne's dowry, his post as secretary to her uncle, his future advancement, and, during imprisonment, his liberty.[79] Romances especially flourished at court, where seductions and secret weddings occurred between Mary Fitton and the Earl of Pembroke, Elizabeth Vernon and the Earl of Southampton, Dorothy Devereux and Sir Thomas Perrot, to name just a few.[80] However, the relative freedom at Court made circumstances there quite different from those prevailing elsewhere. Then, too, the scandal attached to such matches, not to mention punishments that included beatings and disinheritance and imprisonment, indicates how much these marriages outraged those in authority. If love affairs were truly commonplace among the nobility, they could hardly have created the notoriety they did.

According to contemporary evidence, parents of this period assumed that their wishes should not be transgressed in marital matters. One outraged father writes, "But my daughter, who was the chiefest cause of my care and my greatest hope of comfort, having taken upon her this weighty vow of marriage, directly contrary to my mind, as wilfully bent in the frowardness of her heart to disobey me, and violently as it were, to carry me into my grave with tears, hath contemptuously trodden under foot all humanity and duty, both to God and to me her poor father."[81] In 1579, Sir Richard Cholmley entailed his son's estate because the young man had not "married with his approbation" but had chosen "Mrs. Jane Boulmer, who, though of good family, had no good fame, and was of a humour he liked better for a mistress than a wife for his son."[82] Through several gen-

---

[78] Sir Harris Nicolas, *Memoirs of the Life and Times of Sir Christopher Hatton* (London: Richard Bentley, 1847), p. xlv. See also Allison D. Wall, ed., *Two Elizabethan Women: Correspondence of Joan and Maria Thynne, 1575–1611*, Wiltshire Record Society Publication 38 (1982): 55.

[79] Robert J. Clements and Lorna Levant, eds., *Renaissance Letters: Revelations of a World Reborn* (New York: New York University Press, 1976), pp. 415–416, reprints Donne's letter to Sir George, which pleaded in vain for forgiveness.

[80] See Stone, *Crisis*, pp. 591–610; idem, *Family*, pp. 181–193.

[81] Nicolas, *Memoirs*, pp. xxxiv–xxxv.

[82] Sir Hugh Cholmley, *Memoirs* (London, 1787), pp. 10–11.

erations the wills of the Verney family insisted that daughters accept the matches provided for them.[83] When Sir Walter Aston married without permission, he had to pay his guardian four thousand pounds, and in 1591, Henry Wriothesley, Earl of Southampton, was fined five thousand for refusing to take Elizabeth Vere to wife.[84] Nor did parents and guardians stand alone in upholding their sway over marital decisions. At the age of seventeen, Ralph Josselin felt compelled to support his father by interceding with "my sister Anna in hindring her from marrying a widdow(er), when my father had cast her of, and. in reconciling her unto him agayne."[85] For all these individuals, parental authority was not some theoretical dictum or fictional invention. It assumed genuine power over their lives, regardless of whether offspring assented to or defied that authority.

In the teeth of the evidence—at best merely summarized in the preceding paragraphs—how do modern scholars interpret the degree of external control over people's right to marry as they pleased? On some matters, the methodical work of demographers is helpful. For instance, if premarital sex is regarded as an indication of attraction or affection, then studies on the rates of bastardy and bridal pregnancy become important. Earlier hypotheses that custom sharply limited intercourse before marriage have been challenged by recent findings showing a fairly high incidence of pregnant brides, although the numbers of illegitimate births, which might indicate casual sex, remained low.[86] Those haled into ecclesiastical courts to answer for their conduct frequently mentioned love as a motive and

[83] Frances Parthenope and Margaret M. Verney, *Memoirs of the Verney Family*, 2d ed. (London: Longmans, Green, 1907), 1:38, 40, e.g.

[84] Stone, *Crisis*, p. 602; Kathy Lynn Emerson, *Wives and Daughters: The Women of Sixteenth-Century England* (Troy, NY: Whitston Publishing Company, 1984), p. 234.

[85] MacFarlane, *Diary*, p. 4.

[86] David Levine and Keith Wrightson, "The Social Context of Illegitimacy in Early Modern England," in *Bastardy and Its Comparative History*, ed. Peter Laslett, Karla Oosterveen, and Richard Wall (Cambridge: Harvard University Press, 1980), p. 161, say one woman in three was with child at the altar. See also Richard L. Greaves, *Society and Religion in Elizabethan England* (Minneapolis: University of Minnesota Press, 1981), pp. 204–223; 801n.27; Ingram, *Church Courts*, pp. 157–163, 220; Peter Laslett, "Introduction: Comparing Illegitimacy over Time and between Cultures," in *Bastardy*, pp. 14, 53–59; idem, *World*, pp. 104, 161; McIntosh, "Servants," p. 20; R.A.P. Finlay, "Population and Fertility in London, 1580–1650," *Journal of Family History* 4 (1979): 36–37. P.E.H. Hair, "Bridal Pregnancy in Earlier Rural England Further Examined," *Population Studies* 24 (1970): 61–66, confirms bridal pregnancy but does not support Laslett's view that betrothal was a license to copulate.

generally married their sexual partners.[87] However, lest one picture a kingdom where ardor reigned, it must be recalled that premarital sex, whether subsequently legitimized or not, occurred primarily among the poor and obscure, where supervision was lax and parents either absent or dead.[88]

Thus, while virtually all recent investigators agree that ordinary folk often had considerable freedom, some disagreement persists as to how much freedom those at the upper social levels enjoyed. And there is further disagreement as to the ideological bases for whatever freedom did or did not exist. Lawrence Stone, of course, has steadfastly maintained that among the aristocracy, interest (wealth, rank, power) took precedence over affect (love, companionship, sexual attraction).[89] Both Stone and Peter Laslett dismiss the notion that the "state of perpetual courtship" portrayed in much literature governed the behavior of any save a handful of courtiers.[90] Yet such historians as Keith Wrightson and Christopher Hill insist that the wishes of children regarding marriage prevailed more often than

[87] Keith Wrightson and David Levine, *Poverty and Piety in an English Village: Terling, 1525–1700* (New York: Academic Press, 1979), pp. 128–129. See also P.E.H. Hair, ed., *Before the Bawdy Court* (New York: Paul Elek Books, 1972), pp. 105–106; Ingram, *Church Courts*, pp. 199, 224–230; Sharpe, *Crime*, pp. 81–82.

[88] See, e.g., Ingram, *Church Courts*, pp. 159–163, 269–273; Walter J. King, "Punishment for Bastardy in Early Seventeenth Century England," *Albion* 10 (1978): 132–133; Levine and Wrightson, "Social Context," pp. 166, 170–171; G. R. Quaife, *Wanton Wenches and Wayward Wives: Peasants and Illicit Sex in Early Seventeenth Century England* (New Brunswick, NJ: Rutgers University Press, 1979), pp. 248–249; Sharpe, *Crime*, pp. 100–101, 110; Wrightson and Levine, *Poverty*, pp. 131–132.

[89] This argument extends from "Marriage among the English Nobility in the 16th and 17th Centuries," *Comparative Studies in Society and History* 3 (1960–1961): 182–206, right through *Crisis* and *Family* and "Social Mobility in England, 1500–1700," in *Seventeenth-Century England; Society in an Age of Revolution*, ed. Paul Seaver (New York: New Viewpoints, 1976). Marianne Novy, "Shakespeare and Emotional Distance in the Elizabethan Family," *Theatre Journal* 33 (1981): 316–326, thinks Stone's theory of family coldness more valid than some critics admit, identifying it as essentially a masculine system rather than a feminine one.

[90] Laslett, "Introduction," in *Bastardy*, p. 58. For other representative views, see, e.g., Carroll Camden, *The Elizabethan Woman* (Houston: Elsevier Press, 1952), pp. 65–66, 79–80; Jean Louis Flandrin, *Families in Former Times: Kinship, Household, and Sexuality*, trans. Richard Southern (Cambridge: Cambridge University Press, 1979), pp. 130ff., 166–168; John R. Gillis, *For Better, for Worse: British Marriages, 1600 to the Present* (Oxford: Oxford University Press, 1985), pp. 12–14, 37; Alan Macfarlane, *Marriage and Love in England: Modes of Reproduction 1300–1840* (Oxford: Basil Blackwell, 1986), pp. 119–147, 176–208.

has been supposed.[91] Stone readily admits that by the end of the seventeenth century, sons and daughters were at least permitted a veto of prospective spouses, largely as a result of the Puritan concern for mutual love and concord between husband and wife.[92] However, Richard Greaves's analysis of Protestant, Anglican, and Catholic views reveals a virtually identical range of opinion and behavior in all three groups. What he sees as a growing conflict between "traditional patterns of authority" and "developing individualism," which pervaded the entire society,[93] inevitably emerged at a critical event like marriage.

The debate over the relative extent of parental authority and private affection occupies modern historians quite as much as it did the Elizabethans; however, it flattens out the complexities of rank, gender, and reputation to assert that patriarchy was waning or that love matches were the norm. Even among ordinary folk, who had a good deal of autonomy in marriage, the selection of a spouse publicly demonstrated one's sound or ill judgment. And the crucial importance of well-governed households for community stability brought pressures from neighbors no less than from masters and parents, all of whom acted to curb unwise or immature decisions regarding matrimony. The higher up the social scale, the stronger and more complicated the restraints. Among the privileged, opportunities for interaction between eligible gentlemen and suitable young ladies were relatively restricted, and indulgent fathers or sympathetic guardians decidedly in the minority. No matter what dreams of romantic love stirred the readers of poetry, no matter what recent elopement titillated gossipers, no matter what flirtations transpired, the majority in the upper echelons of society knew that so important a matter as marriage would involve their elders. However valid the claims for some assertion of individual preferences, unions of the gently born were weighted in favor of parental authority, both in theory and in actuality. Though the spectrum of possibil-

[91] Christopher Hill, "Sex, Marriage and Parish Registers," in *The Collected Essays*, vol. 3 (Amherst: University of Massachusetts Press, 1986), pp. 203–204; Wrightson, *English Society*, pp. 72–79. See also Anthony Fletcher, *County Community in Peace and War: Sussex 1600–1900* (London: Longman, 1975), pp. 30–31; Derek Hirst, *Authority and Conflict: England, 1603–1658* (Cambridge: Harvard University Press, 1986), p. 24; Ingram, *Church Courts*, pp. 141–142; Sharpe, *Early Modern England*, pp. 61–76.

[92] Stone, *Crisis*, pp. 611–612; idem, *Family*, pp. 136–138; idem and Jeanne C. Fawtier Stone, *An Open Elite? England 1540–1880* (Oxford: Clarendon Press, 1984), p. 89. For further accounts of the Puritan view of marriage, see chap. 1, n.5.

[93] Greaves, *Society*, p. 204 and passim. For the implications of Greaves's work, see chap. 1, nn. 5 and 6.

ities ranged from complete liberty of personal choice to enforced compliance with the will of others,[94] in most cases an uneasy balance prevailed between individual consent and familial power, with the proportions varying for every match. What Martin Ingram has called *"multilateral* consent"[95] not only could be but undoubtedly was frequently reached with amity on all sides. Yet the degree of property or prestige involved markedly increased the possibility for conflict. With this complex set of marital possibilities in mind, then, theatergoers observed stage courtships.

Though personal affection may have been secondary to parental authority in some segments of Shakespeare's society, it is not so in his plays. In comedy, history, and tragedy alike, love is presented as the primary impetus for wooing. Even in those situations where marriages are entirely arranged by others, the partners still talk of love. Without having so much as seen Margaret, Henry VI professes that her "wondrous rare description" has engendered "love's settled passions in my heart" (*1H6*, V.vii.1, 4).[96] In *King John*, too, when a union is abruptly proposed between the Dauphin of France and Blanche of Spain, the young prince responds ardently, though the two have just met and have as yet exchanged not a word.

> LOUIS. I do protest I never loved myself
>   Till now enfixèd I beheld myself
>   Drawn in the flattering table of her eye.
>
> .   .   .   .
>
> KING JOHN. Speak then, Prince Dauphin, can you love this Lady?
> LOUIS. Nay, ask me if I can refrain from love,
>   For I do love her most unfeignedly.[97]
>
> (II.i.502–504, 525–527)

---

[94] Laurence Lerner, *Love and Marriage: Literature and Its Social Context* (New York: St. Martin's Press, 1979), p. 65, describes the spectrum in slightly different terms, distinguishing between the "marriage of propriety" (in which "the partner is chosen on grounds of personal, social and economic suitability") and the "arranged match" (in which "the decision is not taken by the couple themselves"), against which he sets the "love match" (in which "the young couple take their own decision . . . because they are in love"). Lerner disagrees with Stone about the absence of parental affection, though on the basis of personal opinion rather than historical research.

[95] Ingram, *Church Courts*, p. 136.

[96] Robert B. Pierce, *Shakespeare's History Plays: The Family and the State* (Columbus: Ohio State University Press, 1971), p. 49, finds such speeches "specious."

[97] Allan Lewis, "Shakespeare and the Morality of Money," *Social Research* 36 (1969): 373–388, thinks Blanche's and Louis's words are "hypocritical declarations," p. 382.

Virtually every marriage in Shakespeare is preceded by a protestation of love. Few woo so outrageously as Richard III, when he importunes the grieving Anne over the coffin of Henry VI, and few so irresistibly as Henry V in his halting French, but declarations of affection constitute an indispensable part of courtship, regardless of the context.

Since the consent of parental figures, as well as the assent of the couple, was required for a valid betrothal or marriage, nods to this social reality appear even within wholly political contexts, as when Henry asks Catherine, "Wilt thou have me?" and she dutifully responds, "Dat is as it shall please *de roi mon père*" (*H5*, V.ii.244–245). Similarly, Blanche tells the Dauphin,

> My uncle's will in this respect is mine.
> If he see aught in you that makes him like,
> That anything he sees which moves his liking
> I can with ease translate it to my will;
> Or if you will, to speak more properly,
> I will enforce it easily to my love.
>
> (*Jn.* II.i.511–516)

Since the good son's or daughter's duty was respectful obedience to authority in matters of marriage, dramatic characters also acknowledge this obligation. For example, *Much Ado* shows Antonio counseling Hero, "Well, niece, I trust you will be ruled by your father," while the father himself bids, "Daughter, remember what I told you. If the Prince do solicit you in that kind, you know your answer" (II.i.45–46, 59–61). Beatrice typically makes a joke of the business: "Yes, faith, it is my cousin's duty to make curtsy and say, 'Father, as it please you.' But yet for all that, cousin, let him be a handsome fellow, or else make another curtsy, and say, 'Father, as it please me' " (47–50).[98] However, Hero's silent acquiescence, no matter whether she is to have the prince or Claudio, constitutes the model response of a daughter to her elders' wishes.[99] Her actions in

[98] George R. Hibbard, "Love, Marriage and Money in Shakespeare's Theatre and Shakespeare's England," in *Elizabethan Theatre VI*, ed. Hibbard (Toronto: Macmillan of Canada, 1975), p. 154, almost alone, sees how shocking Beatrice's flippant remark is.

[99] Juliet Dusinberre, *Shakespeare and the Nature of Women* (New York: Barnes and Noble, 1975), p. 96, observes, "Portia, Viola, Beatrice, are women set free from their fathers, and their voice is that of the adult world, where Hero is still a child." Yet Portia is bound by the will of her dead father, Viola passes from the guardianship of her brother to the authority of her master Orsino, and Beatrice's union is engineered by her family and Benedick's prince without the couple's knowledge or permission.

this regard delineate the conventionality that leaves Hero so defenseless when she is faced with slurs on her propriety.

Shakespeare provides few women whose marriages do not require the approval of some masculine figure. Cleopatra and Tamora in the tragedies, widows like Lady Gray and Lady Anne in the histories, the orphaned Olivia and Viola in the comedies represent notable exceptions.[100] However, a remarkable number of men can seek wives according to the bent of their own affections since they are of age and their parents nowhere in evidence. There are ambitious young bachelors like Petruccio, Bassanio, and Fenton. There are the love-struck Demetrius and Lysander, the brothers Orlando and Oliver. Neither Sebastian nor Duke Orsino in *Twelfth Night*, Duke Vincentio nor his subjects Angelo, Claudio, and Lucio in *Measure for Measure* need ask permission in order to marry. And both the County Paris and the general Othello can woo for themselves. The comparative rarity of such freedom at the top of Elizabethan society perhaps accounts in part for the popularity of playgoing among privileged young men in London. Onstage, at least, they could see their wishes enacted, even if offstage they had to defer to the wishes of others in the choice of a mate.

However, in a good many dramatic situations, characters, whether male or female, high or low, are not free to marry without permission. Where the father is not living, a master or a sovereign often wields power over his retainer or subject. Even trusted wellborn companions like Graziano and Nerissa formally ask Bassanio and Portia for permission to marry. Graziano requests that "when your honours mean to solemnize / The bargain of your faith, I do beseech you / Even at that time I may be married too" (*MV*, III.ii.192–194). After Portia inquires whether this is Nerissa's wish also, her waiting gentlewoman replies,

> NERISSA. Madam, it is, so you stand pleased withal.
> BASSANIO. And do you, Graziano, mean good faith?
> GRAZANIO. Yes, faith, my lord.
> BASSANIO. Our feast shall be much honoured in your marriage.

> (209–212)

The effect of the interchange is diminished for a modern audience unaware that Graziano's and Nerissa's request is not mere politeness. They can privately agree to a match, but they may not properly marry without permis-

---

[100] Mark Taylor, *Shakespeare's Darker Purpose: A Question of Incest* (New York: AMS Press, 1982), p. 85, who says Julia in *TGV* has no father, apparently has overlooked I.ii.131.

sion of the lord and lady whom they serve.[101] Working through this familiar obligation, *The Merchant of Venice* juxtaposes courtships at different
social levels with telling effect. While Portia's dead father "Bars me the
right of voluntary choosing" (II.i.16), her attendant has precisely this freedom. Against the greater deference of mistress to parent and the lesser one
of servant to mistress, Shakespeare sets the defiance of Jessica, who neither
asks for nor would receive Shylock's approval of her marriage to Lorenzo.
Graziano, too, can woo Nerissa with none of the strictures imposed on
Bassanio by the casket test or on Lorenzo by the stratagems he must use to
steal a wife from her hostile father. The consent of authority figures affects
all these suits, but it lies less heavily on the retainers than on the other
two pairs of lovers.

In *Timon of Athens*, an old merchant comes to complain that his daughter is being wooed by one of Timon's servants. Disapproving of the suit,
the father appeals to Lucilius's master to exercise his proper control over
"this thy creature": "I prithee, noble lord, / Join with me to forbid him
her resort. / Myself have spoke in vain" (I.i.118, 128–130). Instead of
reprimanding or dismissing Lucilius, as Timon has every right to do, he
uses his power to negotiate a match for his servant:

> OLD ATHENIAN.   Most noble lord,
>   Pawn me to this your honour, she is his.
> TIMON. My hand to thee; mine honour on my promise.
> LUCILIUS. Humbly I thank your lordship.

(150–153)

Quite apart from the questionable judgment Timon displays here, he possesses the same authority as the girl's father. They make the bargain, not
their dependents.

The same situation appears more comically at an even lower rank in *All's
Well That Ends Well*, when Lavatch must request permission to wed "Isbel
the woman" (I.iii.18–19) from the Countess of Roussillon because she
alone can free him from his contract of service. Thus he wants "your lady-
ship's good will to go to the world. . . . Service is no heritage, and I
think I shall never have the blessing of God till I have issue o' my body"

---

[101] Richard A. Levin, *Love and Society in Shakespearean Comedy* (Newark: University of
Delaware Press, 1985), p. 64, misunderstands the dynamics here: "It takes no great stretch
of the imagination to see that regardless of the affection Gratiano and Nerissa presumably
feel for one another, both want marriage only if they can hang onto the coattails of a
wealthy couple."

(18, 23–25). After her questions elicit Lavatch's entirely carnal motives for matrimony, his mistress dismisses both him and his suit: "You'll be gone, sir knave, and do as I command you" (88–89). A good thing, too, for when Lavatch returns from court, he admits, "I have no mind to Isbel since I was at court. Our old lings and our Isbels o'th' country are nothing like your old ling and your Isbels o'th' court. The brains of my Cupid's knocked out, and I begin to love as an old man loves money: with no stomach" (III.ii.12–16). In Lavatch's on-and-off wooing, the playwright sets up a comic counterpart for Bertram's capricious affections, with both characters' marital preferences curbed by one of higher status and power—in Bertram's case the king, his guardian; in Lavatch's his mistress, the countess.[102] Like a parent, the Shakespearean master or mistress is obliged to exercise proper care in approving marriage for a servant who has fallen in love.

When it comes to falling in love, other dramatic situations point up the greater freedom that people of lesser status enjoyed in Elizabethan England. While highborn suitors generally have to contend with the careful supervision of unmarried females, the more humbly born seem to come and go much as they please. As a shepherd's foster daughter, Perdita encounters Prince Florizel by accident when he is out hunting, and thereafter they apparently meet freely and often. At the sheepshearing over which Perdita presides in *The Winter's Tale*, her foster brother, Mopsa, and Dorcas romp and flirt with the same liberty that allows the royal couple to discover and declare their love. Silvius and Phoebe, Audrey and the hapless William wander through the Forest of Arden in *As You Like It* more or less at will, as do the aristocrats. Exiled to raising sheep like peasants or hunting deer like poachers, the nobles pursue an unrestrained courtship whose mimicry of their social inferiors includes a penchant for premarital sex. Hence Celia and Oliver have "made a pair of stairs to marriage, which they will climb incontinent, or else be incontinent before marriage" (V.ii.36–38). Perhaps the most ridiculous and certainly the most detailed description of a lowly love is Lance's milkmaid in *Two Gentlemen of Verona* (III.i.271–355), again an affection he seems to have developed without any of the difficulties that attend his master's suit for the closely guarded

---

[102] For somewhat different views of Lavatch's wooing, see Larry S. Champion, *The Evolution of Shakespeare's Comedy: A Study in Dramatic Perspective* (Cambridge: Harvard University Press, 1970), pp. 110–111; Richard P. Wheeler, *Shakespeare's Development and the Problem Comedies: Turn and Counter-Turn* (Berkeley: University of California Press, 1981), pp. 52–54.

Sylvia. From Lance comes a catalogue of qualities burlesquing individuals at this social level—domestic skills like milking, brewing, scouring, spinning; personal defects like bad breath, toothlessness, and promiscuity. Entirely aside from the humor deriving from this last quality, Shakespeare's plays encode the differing degree of supervision over unmarried individuals at the top and the bottom of society.[103]

In some dramatic situations, marital choices are wholly surrendered to a noble or royal guardian, who exercises his authority and responsibility to make a suitable match for a follower. Thus for Antipholus of Ephesus the duke has provided the wealthy Adriana. When husband and wife confront their ruler at the end of *A Comedy of Errors*, Adriana asks for help with "Antipholus my husband, / Who I made lord of me and all I had / At your important letters" (V.i.137–139). In turn, Antipholus begs, "Justice, sweet prince, against that woman there, / She whom thou gav'st to me to be my wife" (198–199). As the duke confirms, he has arranged the marriage as a reward for valiance:

> Long since, thy husband served me in my wars,
> And I to thee engaged a prince's word,
> When thou didst make him master of thy bed,
> To do him all the grace and good I could.
>
> (162–165)

Almost lost in the denouement's chaos is this vignette of the ruler playing guardian to a fatherless retainer by supplying a good wife with a good fortune as a mark of ducal favor.

Such arrangements were common at every noble or royal court, both fictional and historical. In *Much Ado*, Don Pedro can promise Claudio that "thou shalt have her" and "she shall be thine" (I.i.293, 310), with all the authority of a prince to compel consent from both Leonato and Hero. Of course no compulsion is required for this tractable parent and daughter. Nor does resistance greet Leontes' surprise decision to wed the widowed

---

[103] Marjorie Garber, *Coming of Age in Shakespeare* (New York: Methuen, 1981), p. 140, refers to the frank pursuit of sex by such figures as Costard and Jaquenetta, Bottom and Titania, Touchstone and Audrey, but does not spell out the influence of "lower-class" social rank upon sexual behavior. Carol Thomas Neely, *Broken Nuptials in Shakespeare's Plays* (New Haven: Yale University Press, 1985), p. 203, fills in further details of the Bohemians' "natural, grotesque, or humorous" sexuality, calling chastity "temporary and unnecessary," but she too does not link this activity to status. Nor does Philip Edwards, *Shakespeare: A Writer's Progress* (Oxford: Oxford University Press, 1986), p. 175, in deeming Caliban's behavior less wicked than Cloten's.

Paulina with Camillo: "Thou shouldst a husband take by my consent. . . . I'll not seek far— / For him, I partly know his mind—to find
thee / An honourable husband" (*WT*, V.iii.137, 142–144). Although
Paulina has always displayed remarkable independence and for sixteen
years has governed a household alone, nevertheless this mature courtier is
still subject to her sovereign's command when it comes to matrimony.[104]
The absolute right, even the duty, of a king to make matches for worthy
women is reaffirmed in *Henry VIII*. Upon her deathbed, Queen Katherine
requests for each of "my wretched women, that so long / Have followed
both my fortunes faithfully . . . A right good husband. Let him be a noble, / And sure those men are happy that shall have 'em" (IV.ii.141–142,
147–148). Such arranged matrimony has little appeal now, but the appropriateness of a noble husband or wife in reward for faithful service was not
much questioned then. Nonetheless, the conventionality of this queen's
wish is ironically undercut by the failure of Katherine's own marriage to
Henry, her designated provider of suitable spouses.

The notable dissenter to provisions of this kind is, of course, Bertram.
All's Well That Ends Well completely reverses the situation in other plays
where a sovereign arranges the union of two subjects. Unlike the dutiful
obedience of Camillo and Paulina, Antipholus and Adriana, or the joyful
response of Claudio, Bertram offers the French king sullen resistance. Now
the count is not merely a courtier but is also a royal ward, still lacking the
right to make independent choice of a wife. As the monarch says of all the
candidates he presents to Helen, "Thy frank election make. / Thou hast
power to choose, and they none to forsake" (II.iii.56–57). Such a casual
statement of monarchical authority, combined with the king's subsequent
wrathful threat, shows how thoroughly Shakespeare understands the dark,
tyrannical edge of a guardian's power in these matters:[105]

---

[104] Marianne Novy, *Love's Argument: Gender Relations in Shakespeare* (Chapel Hill: University of North Carolina Press, 1984), p. 177, thinks Paulina's marriage "may seem an
odd attempt to place her back in a patriarchal framework." Williamson, *Patriarchy*, p.
153, observes that "women are once again used to sustain the patriarchy" because Leontes
"still possesses total authority, which absorbs and controls female creativity."

[105] Joseph Westlund, *Shakespeare's Reparative Comedies: A Psychoanalytic View of the Middle
Plays* (Chicago: University of Chicago Press, 1984), p. 130, claims, "No other Shakespearean comedy has so many parental figures who actively support a love match—and no other
match is so inappropriate." I am not convinced the match is inappropriate (see chaps. 3
and 8), and certainly other marriages, notably Hero's and Beatrice's, have at least equal
external support. Neely, *Broken Nuptials*, p. 65, regards each parental figure in the problem
comedies as "dependent on the marriage of youth for its own rejuvenation," though these
figures all "endanger nuptials more by insisting on them than fathers and rulers in earlier

> Check thy contempt;
> Obey our will, which travails in thy good;
> Believe not thy disdain, but presently
> Do thine own fortunes that obedient right
> Which both thy duty owes and our power claims,
> Or I will throw thee from my care for ever
> Into the staggers and the careless lapse
> Of youth and ignorance, both my revenge and hate
> Loosing upon thee in the name of justice
> Without all terms of pity. Speak. Thine answer.

(158–167)

Counterpoising a fearful royal exercise of will against a prideful rebellion in the immature Bertram, *All's Well* explores conflicts inherent in the requirements for mutual consent. Helen has earned the luxury of free choice with the sovereign's full approval, while Bertram is forced into a marriage against his will. Yet she is just as powerless to compel acceptance of her love as he is to compel acceptance of his aversion. Like other parents and guardians, the king may enforce assent to his wishes, but he cannot enforce an affectionate relationship, no matter what he does to make the match more palatable.[106] Perhaps an awareness of the impotence almost all noble wards endured during their minority made Shakespeare's viewers more tolerant of Bertram's response than are present-day critics.[107]

In plays where the father, rather than the ruler or master, exercises au-

---

comedies did by impeding them." Williamson, *Patriarchy*, pp. 73–74, sees Shakespeare as critical of the king in moments when he grows angry or exercises his authority. Virtually alone, Barbara Hodgdon, "The Making of Virgins and Mothers: Sexual Signs, Substitute Scenes and Doubled Presences in *All's Well That Ends Well*," *Philological Quarterly* 66 (1987): 55, notes that the king has supplanted the countess as parent, "granting Helena both a title and a dowry."

[106] As Neely, *Broken Nuptials*, p. 82, points out, Bertram's resistance to the marriage with Helen contrasts with his acquiescence to a match with Lafeu's daughter, Maudlin, which "he agrees to in return for his reconciliation with his elders." She goes on to claim, p. 85, "This is one of the few marriages in Shakespeare that is contracted by parents before the couple even talk to each other," but there are several others. Except for Maudlin's absence from the stage during the betrothal, I find no evidence that the pair have not spoken, especially since Bertram declares he fancied Maudlin before Helen claimed him.

[107] Champion, *Evolution*, p. 108, cautions that we cannot blame the twentieth-century dislike of *All's Well* on a change in views on arranged marriage, because Shakespeare disapproves of such marriages too; Champion cites *Rom.*, *MND*, *TGV*, *WT* as examples. This assertion flattens out the complexities of these plays and ignores the ironic outcome of matches like those in *Shr.*

thority, the situation is much clearer to modern audiences, though they still tend not to realize the full extent of that authority. In some cases consent is so carelessly or capriciously given as to appear a mere formality. For instance, Celia never bothers to consult her father before wedding Oliver, and the disguised Rosalind lightly inquires of Duke Senior, "You say if I bring in your Rosalind / You will bestow her on Orlando here?" He blithely responds, "That would I, had I kingdoms to give with her" (*AYL*, V.iv.6–8).[108] In *Pericles*, King Simonides shows a rare agreement with his daughter's independent selection of an unknown knight to be her husband: "She tells me here she'll wed the stranger knight. . . . I like that well. Nay, how absolute she's in't, / Not minding whether I dislike or no!" (sc. 9, 14, 16–17). Later in the action, the approval of Marina's father is assured even before Lysimachus asks for her in marriage.

> LYSIMACHUS. And when you come ashore I have a suit.
> PERICLES. You shall prevail, were it to woo my daughter,
> For it seems you have been noble towards her.

> (sc. 21, 245–247)

After *The Taming of the Shrew*'s Lucentio and Bianca elope, they kneel, asking "Pardon, sweet father" of Vincentio and "Pardon, dear father" of Baptista, whose responses are amazingly mild.

> BAPTISTA. But do you hear, sir, have you married my daughter without asking my good will?
> VINCENTIO. Fear not, Baptista. We will content you.[109]

> (V.i.103, 105, 124–126)

No wonder Lucentio assures his new wife, "Look not pale, Bianca. Thy father will not frown" (129), for in the next scene the runaway lovers cel-

---

[108] David Sundelson, *Shakespeare's Restorations of the Father* (New Brunswick, NJ: Rutgers University Press, 1983), p. 76, prefers to see here "a father whose unpossessive love is a prelude to other attachment instead of an obstacle." Louis Adrian Montrose, " 'The Place of a Brother' in *As You Like It*: Social Process and Comic Form," *Shakespeare Quarterly* 32 (1981): 40–41, 51–53, thinks the duke, simultaneously lord and brother to his followers, resolves the fraternal and paternal tensions, in this instance bestowing a far greater legacy than Oliver has withheld from Sir Rowland's estate. Erickson, *Patriarchal Structures*, p. 26 (too facilely, I feel), translates Duke Senior's love for Sir Rowland into "family approval of the match."

[109] Irene G. Dash, *Wooing, Wedding and Power: Women in Shakespeare's Plays* (New York: Columbia University Press, 1981), sees the Lucentio-Bianca union as a "marriage based on 'good consent of both' partners," p. 35, ignoring the bypass of advance consent from their parents.

ebrate their wedding with full family acceptance. These casual or arbitrary consents, so seldom noted today when parents' opinions count but little, may well represent instances of unreality or subversion for Shakespeare's audience. Whether sons and daughters did so or not, they were expected to obey their superiors, not simply follow their own wishes.

The plays often delineate a conflict between authority and affection, sometimes at length, sometimes in a brief vignette. Typically, the daughter's heart is fastened upon someone of whom the father disapproves, or else he has a rival candidate of his own. Inevitably, threats and denunciations follow. When they can, parents simply banish unwanted suitors. Sylvia's father, the Duke of Milan, commands Valentine, "Be gone. I will not hear thy vain excuse, / But as thou lov'st thy life, make speed from hence" (*TGV*, III.i.168–169). When he gets to the forest, Valentine meets an outlaw similarly treated: "Myself was from Verona banishèd / For practising to steal away a lady, / An heir, and near allied unto the Duke" (IV.i.45–47). Such duplication emphasizes the appropriateness of the sentence Valentine receives for his offense against a ruler who is both Sylvia's father and his own father-substitute. *Cymbeline*, too, offers an example of the irate king-father-guardian, who exiles Posthumus for marrying Innogen without permission: "Thou basest thing, avoid hence, from my sight! / If after this command thou fraught the court / With thy unworthiness, thou diest. Away" (I.i.126–128). In each of these cases the insult lies not just in the presumed unfitness of the daughter's choice but also in an abrogation of the patriarchal right to approve or disapprove any choice. As Innogen recognizes, her love has "set up / My disobedience 'gainst the King my father" (III.iv.88–89).

The *senex iratus* occurs so often that both critics and playgoers tend to see him only as a barrier figure, a plot device derived from Greek and Roman comedy, without recognizing that the father actually had the legal power to carry out his threatened punishments.[110] Obviously *A Midsummer Night's Dream* exaggerates the situation by setting up death or life in a nunnery as the only alternatives for Hermia if she refuses to marry Deme-

---

[110] For typical views of the *senex iratus* as a weak or marginal figure, see Linda Bamber, *Comic Women, Tragic Men: A Study of Gender and Genre in Shakespeare* (Stanford, CA: Stanford University Press, 1982), p. 114; Champion, *Evolution*, p. 25; Erickson, *Patriarchal Structures*, p. 80; Alfred Harbage, *Shakespeare and the Rival Traditions* (1952; reprint, Bloomington: Indiana University Press, 1970), p. 231; Richard Levin, *New Readings of Old Plays: Recent Trends in the Reinterpretation of English Renaissance Drama* (Chicago: University of Chicago Press, 1979), pp. 151–153; Neely, *Broken Nuptials*, p. 26.

trius.[111] But much of the language in the opening scene reinforces official ideology. "To you your father should be as a god" (I.i.47), counsels Theseus, while Egeus insists, "As she is mine, I may dispose of her" (42), "and all my right of her / I do estate unto Demetrius" (97–98). The words here reflect those in countless writings of the period.[112] Resistant children are most often threatened with disinheritance. The Old Athenian in *Timon* says of his only child,

> If in her marriage my consent be missing,
> I call the gods to witness, I will choose
> Mine heir from forth the beggars of the world,
> And dispossess her all.
>
> (I.i.140–143)

As for Polixenes, whose matrimonial prerogatives have been usurped by his son in *The Winter's Tale*, he promises to disown Florizel. If the young lover "dost but sigh" for Perdita, "we'll bar thee from succession, / Not hold thee of our blood, no, not our kin, / Farre than Deucalion off" (IV.iv.427, 429–431).[113]

---

[111] Susan Wells, *The Dialectics of Representation* (Baltimore: Johns Hopkins University Press, 1985), p. 55, sees this situation not as exaggeration but as "a deviant instance, in which the bonds of marriage—which for us are free, subjective choices, and even for the Elizabethans required for their validity an irreducible minimum of freedom from constraint—appear as simple expressions of unmediated violent force."

[112] As Michael D. Bristol points out, in *Carnival and Theater: Plebeian Culture and the Structure of Authority in Renaissance England* (New York: Methuen, 1985), pp. 177–178, the Pyramus and Thisbe entertainment "seems to warn equally against the dangers of filial disobedience and of arbitrary parental rigidity." He calls it "a substantive admonition as to the dangers concealed by the injunctions surrounding marriage, and most particularly in the effort to reconcile the economic and social purposes of dynastic marriage with the sexual and personal satisfactions of the bride and groom."

[113] Lu Emily Pearson, *Elizabethans at Home* (Stanford, CA: Stanford University Press, 1957), p. 337, thinks the king's anger is aroused by Florizel's boast of his future inheritance—"One being dead" (IV.iv.385). Then, somewhat naively, she says Polixenes "entreats him to trust his father, who will most certainly find the girl pleasing." For dynastic reasons, clearly connected to his threats, the Bohemian ruler cannot look favorably upon a match with a shepherdess; see chaps. 3 and 9. For David Bergeron, *Shakespeare's Romances and the Royal Family* (Lawrence: University Press of Kansas, 1985), p. 163, the key questions in this courtship involve both parental authority and parentage: "Have you a father?" (390) raises the issue of Polixenes' right to "hold some counsel / In such a business" (408–409), and "Is this the daughter of a king?" (V.i.207) raises the issue of Perdita's birth. See also Neely, *Broken Nuptials*, p. 195; Robert Ornstein, *Shakespeare's Comedies: From Roman Farce to Romantic Mystery* (Newark: University of Delaware Press, 1986), p. 229; Williamson, *Patriarchy*, pp. 141, 151.

The longest and most famous passage of this kind belongs to Old Capulet, who rages violently at Juliet's unwillingness to marry Paris:

> God's bread, it makes me mad. Day, night; work, play;
> Alone, in company, still my care hath been
> To have her matched; and having now provided
> A gentleman of noble parentage,
> Of fair demesnes, youthful, and nobly lined,
> Stuffed, as they say, with honourable parts,
> Proportioned as one's thought would wish a man—
> And then to have a wretched puling fool,
> A whining maumet, in her fortune's tender,
> To answer "I'll not wed, I cannot love; . . ."
>
> . . . .
>
> An you be mine, I'll give you to my friend.
> An you be not, hang, beg, starve, die in the streets,
> For, by my soul, I'll ne'er acknowledge thee,
> Nor what is mine shall never do thee good.[114]

(III.v. 176–185, 191–194)

What now seems shocking intransigence would not necessarily have
seemed so to Shakespearean playgoers.[115] Capulet, like Egeus or the Duke
of Milan or the Athenian merchant, is angrily asserting his customary
rights in the marriage of a minor daughter. As her father, he alone has
power to arrange her match. Having done so—and, indeed, having made
an impeccable choice—he feels justifiably outraged at her weak excuses for
refusing his choice. And he is quite within his legal rights to disown her
should she persist in refusing Paris.

---

[114] Brooke's *Romeus and Juliet* increases the father's power and includes a long passage on
parental authority that Shakespeare omits. Painter's version includes Capulet's threat that
"too so close, and to so hard a gaole / I shall thee wed" (lines 1979–1980) if Juliet refuses
to obey; Geoffrey Bullough, *The Narrative and Dramatic Sources of Shakespeare* (London:
Routledge and Kegan Paul, 1957), 1:337. That Bandello has no such passage suggests the
situation's derivation from English ideology. See Leo Salingar, *Shakespeare and the Tradition
of Comedy* (Cambridge: Cambridge University Press, 1974), pp. 313–314.

[115] For a sampling of recent views, all varying from my own, see Dash, *Wooing, Wedding*,
pp. 100, 250; Coppélia Kahn, *Man's Estate: Masculine Identity in Shakespeare* (Berkeley:
University of California Press, 1981), p. 95; Lerner, *Love and Marriage*, p. 79; Kay Stockholder, *Dream Works: Lovers and Families in Shakespeare's Plays* (Toronto: University of Toronto Press, 1987), pp. 30–31.

Theoretically, no one could be forced to marry against his or her will. When first approached, Capulet says,

> But woo her, gentle Paris, get her heart;
> My will to her consent is but a part,
> And, she agreed, within her scope of choice
> Lies my consent and fair-according voice.
>
> (I. ii. 14–17)

In actuality, Juliet's wishes matter so little that Capulet can simply promise her consent in advance and then compel it afterward, if necessary. "Sir Paris, I will make a desperate tender / Of my child's love. I think she will be ruled / In all respects by me. Nay, more, I doubt it not" (III. iv. 12–14). The fact that her father thinks he will rescue Juliet from inconsolable grief prevents him from appearing to be an unfeeling tyrant. Also, because Tybalt's death means that no male of his own house remains alive to assume Juliet's guardianship, Capulet urgently needs to see the girl safely married before he himself dies. By the standards of the day, he acts in his child's best interests. Nevertheless, as with many an Elizabethan match, his authority outweighs her disaffection, and the ultimate weapon for enforcing compliance is a threat of disowning. Possible divorce from one's family carries special weight in a tragedy where house and name bear so much significance.

From time to time a Shakespearean character speaks out against parental tyranny. Sylvia pleads her case in *Two Gentlemen of Verona* with these words to Sir Eglamour:

> Thou art not ignorant what dear good will
> I bear unto the banished Valentine,
> Nor how my father would enforce me marry
> Vain Thurio, whom my very soul abhors.
>
> . . . .
>
> Urge not my father's anger, Eglamour,
> But think upon my grief, a lady's grief,
> And on the justice of my flying hence
> To keep me from a most unholy match,
> Which heaven and fortune still rewards with plagues.
>
> (IV. iii. 14–17, 27–31)

At the end of *The Merry Wives of Windsor*, Fenton expresses the same view of forced matrimony as unholy when he justifies his elopement with Anne Page to her parents.

> Th'offence is holy that she hath committed,
> And this deceit loses the name of craft,
> Of disobedience, or unduteous title,
> Since therein she doth evitate and shun
> A thousand irreligious cursèd hours
> Which forcèd marriage would have brought upon her.
>
> (V.v.217–222)

Yet Shakespeare can take these same sentiments, place them in a different context, and entirely undercut their persuasive power. When Suffolk argues for Margaret to be Henry VI's queen, he calls the ruler "abject, base, and poor" to marry for any reason save "for perfect love" (*1H6*, V.vii.49–50). Insisting that only the woman "whom his grace affects / Must be companion of his nuptial bed" (57–58), Suffolk goes on to contrast the arranged marriage with the love match:

> For what is wedlock forcèd but a hell,
> An age of discord and continual strife,
> Whereas the contrary bringeth bliss,
> And is a pattern of celestial peace.
>
> (62–65)

Ironically, by choosing Margaret out of a personal preference he calls love, Henry enters into an alliance as disastrous for him privately as it is politically.

In a society where partners could be and sometimes were yoked together by those in authority with slim regard for ties of affection, many may have resented "wedlock forcèd." But it is too simple, too facile to say that Shakespeare always supports marriage for love. Instead, his presentations, like the world he shared with his audiences, show multiple perspectives and multiple possibilities. Whereas some spouses selected by father, guardian, or ruler meet with unquestioning acceptance, like Leontes' choice of Camillo for Paulina, other candidates win only eventual approval or encounter outright rejection. Antipholus of Ephesus must ride out the storms stirred up by the possessive Adriana whom the duke has provided for him, and Bertram flees the aggressive love of a bride imposed on him by the King of France. Anne Page avoids the ninnies promoted by her parents to marry Fenton instead. In certain instances, as with Capulet, a near-perfect husband, chosen out of genuine paternal concern, cannot win a heart Juliet has already pledged to Romeo. Sylvia's father will reverse himself and approve of Valentine; Egeus's intent is overborn by Theseus so that Hermia can marry Lysander. Amiable parents like Rosalind's or Bianca's stand alongside angry ones like Cymbeline or Polixenes—a spectrum of response to a child's choice of spouse.

Without diminishing the strength of patriarchal authority, Shakespeare nevertheless challenges it in a variety of ways. Not only do some fathers willingly accede to their offspring's wishes, but some find their power effectively challenged. And throughout a number of plays certain characters follow the dictates of their own affection without interference.[116] If wellborn, they tend to be parentless adults—Sebastian, Bassanio, Othello. If of lesser status, they tend to be servants or country folk—Lance, Audrey, Costard, Maria. While the effective liberty commoners enjoyed in courtship can break through into the more restricted behavior of the privileged, most notably in *As You Like It*, so the restraints imposed by master upon servant can emerge in *All's Well*. Though the pursuit of love, with or without paternal interference, may bring tragedy or spell political disaster, its near-ubiquity in Shakespeare's courtships perhaps marks his most radical departure from accepted social custom. Not all English marriages were loveless; not all children's consents were compelled; not every parent's, guardian's, or master's will prevailed; not every rank exacted identical marital obligations; not every person in a given rank was matched in the same way. But in dealing with the complexities of cultural opinion and activity, Shakespeare invests mutual affection between wooers with greater weight than it carried in much of his society, especially among the privileged. The extent to which he is thereby subversive, critical, or merely conforming to literary conventions is an issue audiences are left to decide for themselves, then as now.

---

[116] In this regard the perceptive work of Lynda Boose falters when she suggests in "The Father's House and the Daughter in It," in *Daughters and Fathers*, ed. Boose and Betty S. Flowers (Baltimore: Johns Hopkins University Press, 1989), that Shakespearean fathers control loss of self by controlling the daughter's choice of husband, pp. 31–32, 40. While such action may characterize some plays, it by no means characterizes all.

Agents and Go-Betweens

A business of this nature is first to be treated of by friends.
—Wallace Notestein, "The English Woman, 1580–1650"

But yet I would my master had Mistress Anne; or I
would Master Slender had her; or, in sooth, I would
Master Fenton had her. I will do what I can for
them all three, for so I have promised.
—*Wiv.*, III.iv. 102–106

B ECAUSE discordances between patriarchal power and personal preference resonate so strongly upon modern sensibilities, there is a ten-
dency to polarize the selection process in these terms rather than see the
collective aspect of making a match. It was rarely so simple as a child's
choice versus a parent's choice. More often, other individuals were also
involved both in searching for an appropriate spouse and in convincing the
parties involved to accept or reject a particular candidate. With a matrimonial system in which the partners could not always exercise autonomy
in picking a mate, the influence of outsiders inevitably assumed greater
importance.[1] Especially in the upper social echelons families sought assistance in locating suitable prospects. And, when located, a prospect still
might require investigation by trusted friends or persuasion by powerful
allies. A crucial decision like marriage could not be left to chance. Always
young folk are admonished to rely upon "the good aduise and direction of
their parents and trustie friendes in this behalfe, who haue better iudge-

---

[1] For a sociological approach to the nexus of obligations to kin, neighbors, and other
associates, see Ronald F. E. Weissman, "Reconstructing Renaissance Sociology," in *Persons
in Groups: Social Behavior as Identity in Medieval and Renaissance Europe*, ed. Richard C. Trex-
ler (Binghamton, NY: Center for Medieval and Early Renaissance Studies, 1985), esp. pp.
40–45. All the historical works on marriage, the family, and the society make this point.
In addition to those cited elsewhere, see David Cressy, "Kinship and Kin Interaction in
Early Modern England," *Past and Present* 113 (1986): 44, 68–69; Margaret J. M. Ezell,
The Patriarch's Wife: Literary Evidence and the History of the Family (Chapel Hill: University
of North Carolina Press, 1987), pp. 21–22; Ralph Houlbrooke, "The Making of Marriage
in Mid-Tudor England: Evidence from the Records of Matrimonial Contract Litigation,"
Journal of Family History 10 (1985): 346–347.

ment, and are more free from the motions of all affections, then they are."[2]
The injunctions for those unencumbered by parents or guardians are the
same: "Yea though the partie be not vnder the gouernment of any, yet it
is very meet that counsell be taken of wise and vnderstanding friends: that
in a matter so weightie as mariage is, there may be the aduice of more
heads then one, for the preuenting of such mischiefes as through rashnesse
might fall out."[3] And in many cases, those "friends" (a term referring to
kin, guardians, and close associates) had strong opinions about a proper
mate.

Inevitably, a process whereby others had a veto or went shopping for
one's future husband or wife was subject to abuse. Some flatly say, "Wooe
not by Ambassador," while references to the "Vexations of friends in the
matches of their *Children*"[4] hint at the problems parents had to face when
they relied upon outside assistance. Discriminating between his heir's supporters and those of prospective wives, William Wentworth counsels,
"Take advice of your wise auncyentt frendes befor yow attempt anie thing
touching that matter. For hir frends woll laie plotts and worke upon yow
and corrupt your seruants and frends all they can to procure such a riche
matche for their daughter or kinswoman."[5] That most cynical of fathers,
Henry Percy, ninth Earl of Northumberland, also cautions his son against
"packs" of unscrupulous agents: "Her modesty, education, good qualytes,
love, poore [power], good disposition of parents, yowr ears will be blowen
full of. . . . Her vices yow shall be sure will be concealed, if yow be not
the more cunning to discover [them] by good scoutes." To ascertain the
truth, Percy recommends generous bribes of a servant or "a false brother
thrust into a house from whence yow are to have a wyfe."[6] And indeed his

[2] Robert Cleaver, *A Godly Form of Householde Government* (London, 1598), p. 149. See
also Thomas Gataker, *A Good Wife Gods Gift: and, A Wife Indeed* (London, 1623), p. 58;
Michel Eyquem de Montaigne, "On Some Verses of Vergil," *The Complete Works*, trans.
Donald Frame (Stanford, CA: Stanford University Press, 1948), p. 646; Daniel Rogers,
Matrimoniall Honour (London, 1642), p. 54; John Wing, *The Crowne Conjugall or, The
Spouse Royall* (Middleburgh, 1620), p. 69.

[3] William Gouge, *Of Domesticall Duties* (London, 1622), p. 197. See also Juan Luis
Vives, *The Office and Duetie of an Husband*, trans. Thomas Paynell (London, 1553), D6.

[4] Alexander Niccholes, *A Discourse of Marriage and Wiving* (London, 1620), p. 48; Matthew Griffith, *Bethel, or A Forme for Families* (London, 1633), p. 271.

[5] *Wentworth Papers, 1597–1628*, ed. J. P. Cooper, Camden Society Publications, 4th
ser., 12 (1973): 20.

[6] Henry Percy, ninth Earl of Northumberland, "Instructions . . . to his Son," *Archaeologia* 27 (1838): 345–346.

assumption that false reports of desirable marriage partners abound is echoed by other authorities. Joseph Swetnam is one of several who suggest,

> And if thy state be good, marry neare home, and at leisure, but if thy state be weake and poore, then to better thy selfe after enquiry made of her wealth & conditions, goe far off & dispatch it quickly, for doubt least tatling speaches which commonly in these cases runns betwixt party and party, and breakes it off euen then when it is come to the up shot.[7]

Here again are the elements of advance inquiry, the wisdom of delay to sift out misrepresentations about the candidate, and the necessity for speed when unflattering information about oneself might be revealed by "tatling speaches."

Fictional treatments routinely present situations where "your frendes with one consent haue offerde you in Mariage a ientlewoman of a good house," or "I myght haue had / Another maner of man, then he is / If I had folowed, my frendes aduyse."[8] Similarly, Bawdyn Bacheler, "being suter to a certeyne Gentle woman for maryag, wryteth to a frende of hers for to haue his helpe and furtheraunce therin." Bawdyn also offers her kinsman forty pounds if he can bring the wooing to a successful conclusion.[9] However, fiction as well as advice literature shows a keen awareness of the problems attendant on involving others in courtship. The potential treachery of the go-between finds cynical expression in this bit of verse:

> If that thy friend doe lacke a little wit,
> And in his humour frame an idle fit,
> To take a wife; and vse thee for his wooing,
> Speake for thy friend, but for thy selfe be doing:
> "If thou find'st her worth the catching take her,
> "If not, let thy friend be sure to haue her.[10]

---

[7] Joseph Swetnam, *The Araignment of Lewde, Idle, Froward, and Unconstant Women* (London, 1615), p. 46. See also *Advice to a Son: Precepts of Lord Burghley, Sir Walter Raleigh, and Francis Osborne*, ed. Louis B. Wright (Ithaca, NY: Cornell University Press, 1962), p. 10; John Norden, *The Fathers Legacie* (London, 1625), A5ᵛ; William Cecil, Lord Burleigh, *Precepts* (London, 1636), p. 2.

[8] Thomas Wilson, *The Arte of Rhetorique* (London, 1553), p. 22; Edward Gosynhyll, *Here Begynneth the Schole House of Women* (London, 1560), B1. See also Nicholas Breton, *Cornu-copiae, Pasquils Night-cap* (London, 1612), p. 17; Swetnam, *Araignment*, p. 6.

[9] *A Lyttle Treatyse Called ye Image of Idlenesse* (London, 1574), B1–B2.

[10] *The Uncasing of Machivils Instructions to his Sonne* (London, 1613), pp. 19–20.

And another short verse speaks of the power of outsiders to prevent a marriage instead of approving it. "Many Matches haue bene broken, / though both Parties were content, / When the Maides good-will is gotten, / then her Friends will not consent."[11]

The presumption that marital negotiations should be a group effort rather than a private decision is solidly based in actual behavior. Repeatedly, contemporary records show the assistance of relatives or other allies in arranging matches. In 1588, Julian Cordwell reluctantly agreed to marry Henry Cordwell "by means of the importunity, suit and earnest soliciting of him unto her friends, viz. her father and mother, her master and her lady and mistress with other of her dear friends, who altogether did so menace and evil intreat her."[12] When Dr. Simon Forman began his search for a wife, he considered several different women but relied on the goodwill of others to forward his suits. After meeting Sara Archdell in company several times, including one visit to the theater, he failed to win her because he could never secure her uncle's assistance. Subsequently, Mrs. Blague, wife of the dean of Rochester and rector of Lambeth, furthered Forman's successful match with Jane Baker.[13] In a similar situation, one John Scacie reported in 1584 that "theare hath beene good will and motion of mariage betweene this respondent and Jane Banister but noe perfett contract because the frendes of this respondent and the same Jane haue not yet concluded."[14]

Higher up the social ladder, Lady Verney asked John Coke to inquire about a union between one of her daughters and the Naunton family. Of matrimonial negotiations, she reported that "it was friends which did all."[15] The suitability of Sir Rowland Hayward's child Joan as wife for Sir John Thynne's son was investigated by Richard Young, who successfully

[11] Hyder Rollins, ed., *A Pepysian Garland* (Cambridge: Cambridge University Press, 1922), p. 232.

[12] Martin Ingram, *Church Courts, Sex, and Marriage in England, 1570–1640* (Cambridge: Cambridge University Press, 1987), p. 182.

[13] A. L. Rowse, *Sex and Society in Shakespeare's Age: Simon Forman the Astrologer* (New York: Charles Scribner's Sons, 1974), pp. 75–77, 92.

[14] E.R.C. Brinkworth, ed., *The Archdeacon's Court*, Oxfordshire Record Society 23 (1942): 53.

[15] Miriam Slater, "The Weightiest Business: Marriage in an Upper-Gentry Family in Seventeenth-Century England," *Past and Present* 72 (1976): 30. See also *The Private Correspondence of Jane Lady Cornwallis, 1613–1644* (London, 1842), p. 227; Sara Heller Mendelson, *The Mental World of Stuart Women: Three Studies* (Amherst: University of Massachusetts Press, 1987), pp. 69–70.

obtained consent from both fathers.[16] The rich widow of Sir William Hatton was approached by Sir Francis Bacon through the Earl of Essex,[17] who exerted considerable energy in matrimonial affairs. He advised Sir William Harvey not to wed the Dowager Countess of Southampton and tried to reconcile her to her new daughter-in-law. Eventually Lord Henry Howard interceded with the earl to secure his agreement to his mother's union with Harvey.[18] Lady Margaret Hoby's three marriages all took place amid an exchange of correspondence and counteroffers supporting various rival candidates. Her first marriage "was effected by the meanes of the sayde Earle of Essex and the late Earle of Huntingdon," as was her second match with Thomas Sidney, nephew to Huntingdon's wife. Though Sidney won out, letters of recommendation for Thomas Hoby included Lord Burghley's assurance that the suitor was "a yonge gentlemane of good byrth, honesty and understandynge, beyng allyed unto me, and of neer kyndred to dyvers my chyldren." When Sidney died in 1595, Hoby finally wed Margaret, again with the backing of Burghley and other prominent supporters. However, the Countess of Essex declined Hoby's request for her help, "not but that I holde you worthe of her you desir, but that in honnor I cannot be for you sens I have promest an othar not to be against him."[19] Thus went deputized courtship for an aristocrat—"his wooing hitherto hath been like himself, a great prince, by proxy."[20]

While it is not surprising that monarchs could scarcely woo in person or that peers used political allies to effect advantageous marriages, the

[16] Allison D. Wall, ed., *Two Elizabethan Women: Correspondence of Joan and Maria Thynne, 1575–1611*, Wiltshire Record Society Publication 38 (1982): 54.

[17] George R. Hibbard, "Love, Marriage and Money in Shakespeare's Theatre and Shakespeare's England," in *Elizabethan Theatre VI*, ed. Hibbard (Toronto: Macmillan of Canada, 1975), p. 136–137.

[18] G.P.V. Akrigg, *Shakespeare and the Earl of Southampton* (Cambridge: Harvard University Press, 1968), pp. 73–74.

[19] Dorothy M. Meads, ed., *Diary of Lady Margaret Hoby, 1599–1605* (Boston: Houghton Mifflin, 1930), pp. 9, 25, 31. Samuel Rawson Gardiner, ed., "Introduction," *The Fortescue Papers*, Camden Society Publications, n.s., 1 (1871), provides more details of Margaret's courtship. The Barrington letters show both kin and acquaintances involved in the search for husbands, including at various times Sir Francis Harris, Sir Gilbert Gerard, Sir Thomas Barrington, and outside advocates such as the Earl of Bedford, Sir Nathaniel Rich, and Oliver St. John; see Arthur Searle, ed., *Barrington Family Letters, 1628–1632*, Camden Society Publications, 4th ser., 28 (1983): 84, 89, 105, 116, 120, 182 for representative instances.

[20] Lawrence Stone, *The Crisis of the Aristocracy, 1558–1641* (Oxford: Clarendon Press, 1965), p. 650.

extent to which matrimonial agents were employed by all the privileged, and perhaps by lesser folk as well, is not generally recognized.[21] An entire marriage market developed in London, where attorneys and others acted as brokers to recommend suitable prospects for their clients.[22] So widespread was the practice that certain laws specified the limitations on various kinds of emissaries. Proxies could be employed at every stage of courtship, from initial inquiries to the nuptial ceremony itself, provided "the Contractors themselues be willing and witting, or that they ratifie it when it is done."[23] As with the issue of parental authority, the question of consent came to the fore. Should either party alter in intent, then a deputy's agreement became void, whether or not such alteration was yet known to the other party or to the agent.[24] However, a "messenger," unlike a "proctor" (or agent), was considered to be the very voice of his sender, whose words carried the presumption of consent to any proposals he delivered. For those with more limited authority, even a simple emissary had to be specifically named as one's agent, could negotiate on behalf of his designator but not for himself, and could not treat with a complete stranger, "for unto those who be utterly *unknown* to us, we cannot yield our Consent."[25] In other words, the intermediary had neither a hunting license nor the right to make binding decisions. Letters, as well as human deputies, could convey consent or dissent, provided they were not forgeries.[26] But the law wrapped careful restrictions around the exercise of authority on behalf of another. However necessary the good offices of reliable friends in courtship, go-betweens were not supposed to contravene the wishes of their clients or overstep the limits of their mandates.[27] Such laws would

[21] Lawrence Stone, *The Family, Sex and Marriage in England 1500–1800* (New York: Harper and Row, 1977), p. 98, extends the practice even to the lower middle classes, as does Miranda Chaytor, "Household and Kinship: Ryton in the Late 16th and Early 17th Centuries," *History Workshop* 10 (1980): 42.

[22] Stone, *Crisis*, pp. 623–624; Hibbard, "Love," p. 142; Lawrence Manley, ed., *London in the Age of Shakespeare* (University Park: Pennsylvania State University Press, 1986), pp. 272–273.

[23] *The Lawes Resolutions of Womens Rights* (London, 1632), p. 62. See also Henry Swinburne, *A Treatise of Spousals, or Matrimonial Contracts* (London, 1686), pp. 154ff.; Alexander W. Renton and George G. Phillimore, *The Comparative Law of Marriage and Divorce*, in *Burge's Commentaries on Colonial and Foreign Laws* (London: Bradbury, Agnew, 1910), 3:18.

[24] William Harrington, *The Comendacions of Matrymony* (London, 1528), A3ᵛ; Swinburne, *Treatise*, pp. 165–166.

[25] Swinburne, *Treatise*, pp. 163, 164, 162.

[26] Ibid., pp. 185–192.

[27] Ibid., pp. 162ff.

hardly have existed were agents not in common use among those arranging marriages—and were abuses not sometimes apparent.

The custom of wooing by proxy or having one's suit backed by friends appears in various ways in Shakespeare, although it has attracted little critical attention. Sometimes geographical separation dictates a match set up by others, as when Gloucester negotiates a marriage between the daughter of the Earl of Armagnac and Henry VI, or Warwick a union between Lady Bona and Edward IV. In still other situations, the secrecy of a wooing necessitates the use of trusted friends. Thus Juliet sends her Nurse with messages to Romeo and Friar Laurence, while the unsavory Paroles goes back and forth between Diana and Bertram. And Richard III urges Queen Elizabeth to win her daughter for his wife: "Be the attorney of my love to her. / Plead what I will be, not what I have been; / Not my deserts, but what I will deserve" (R3, IV.iv.344–346).

Yet courting via others can often be treacherous. While Gloucester pledges Henry VI to the French earl's daughter, Suffolk's candidate, Margaret, is chosen instead—a double betrayal since Suffolk woos Margaret not just to be Henry's queen but also to be his own mistress. Acting as his ruler's agent at the French court, Warwick finds that Edward IV has married Lady Gray, despite the insult to Lady Bona and her brother, the French sovereign. Juliet's trusted Nurse advises her to enter a bigamous marriage with Paris, while Paroles becomes the chief witness against Bertram in Diana's suit before the King of France. And the Yorkist Queen Elizabeth bestows her daughter on Richmond, not Richard. Occasionally a rare man such as Petruccio can gain some advantage from backers, for Gremio, Hortensio, and the disguised Tranio all promise to "be contributors, / And bear his charge of wooing, whatsoe'er" (Shr., I.ii.214–215) because they are so eager to get Kate married. But more often, the assistance of others is used by Shakespeare as a device to complicate courtships in comedy and tragedy alike.

Either actual or suspected treachery always centers on the go-between. While Claudio in *Much Ado* has the good fortune to employ a prince for his spokesman,[28] the early scenes of the play turn on misunderstandings

---

[28] Peter G. Phialas, *Shakespeare's Romantic Comedies: The Development of Their Form and Meaning* (Chapel Hill: University of North Carolina Press, 1966), p. 173, says Claudio "is unwilling to woo her [Hero] and instead enlists Don Pedro." In fact, Don Pedro volunteers. Richard A. Levin, *Love and Society in Shakespearean Comedy* (Newark: University of Delaware Press, 1985), pp. 92–93, contends that "Don Pedro, without explanation, substitutes a new and far less straightforward scheme for helping Claudio to his bride" because the bachelor ruler needs to "find for himself a role on an occasion when his own failure to

about Don Pedro's intent. Although Don John knows the truth of the arrangements, he tells Claudio that the prince plans to marry Hero. Never a bold or confident lover, the young man declares,

> 'Tis certain so, the Prince woos for himself.
> Friendship is constant in all other things
> Save in the office and affairs of love.
> Therefore all hearts in love use their own tongues.
> Let every eye negotiate for itself,
> And trust no agent. . . .

(II.i. 164–169)

Here as in much else he is mistaken, but Claudio speaks more accurately than he knows. Whether the agents be Don John or Borachio and Margaret or the well-intended friends of Beatrice and Benedick, what others say and do cannot be accepted without question. Even if true, words and appearances must be tested by personal experience, or "negotiation," not by a designated proxy.

The complexity of the various testings and trustings in *Much Ado* partly depends upon a whole series of go-betweens, both requested and volunteered, whose motives are hidden more often than open. What Don Pedro freely agrees to do for Claudio's betterment he also proposes for Benedick.

DON PEDRO. I will in the interim undertake one of Hercules' labours, which is to bring Signor Benedick and the Lady Beatrice into a mountain of affection th'one with th'other. I would fain have it a match, and I doubt not but to fashion it, if you three will but minister such assistance as I shall give you direction.

LEONATO. My lord, I am for you, though it cost me ten nights' watchings.

CLAUDIO. And I, my lord.

DON PEDRO. And you too, gentle Hero?

HERO. I will do any modest office, my lord, to help my cousin to a good husband.

DON PEDRO. . . . I will teach you how to humour your cousin that she shall fall in love with Benedick, and I, with your two helps, will so practice on Benedick that, in despite of his quick wit and queasy stomach, he shall fall in love with Beatrice.

(341–352, 355–360)

---

woo would otherwise be noticeable." Levin seems unaware of the cultural precedents for Don Pedro's advocacy.

The methods these matchmakers must use upon their unsuspecting candidates reverse the more conventional wooing of Hero and Claudio. However, the elements of trickery, slander, misperception, secondhand information, suffering, declaration, testing, temporary withdrawal, and a final alliance after proof is produced firmly set the Beatrice-Benedick courtship into the play's dominant patterns. All the characters are surrounded by others acting for or against their interests and manipulating their perceptions of reality. Appropriately, in the end each must see and speak for himself. What happens here offers a telling commentary on the tangled schemes that frequently characterized matrimonial negotiations in Elizabethan England.

A rather different use of go-betweens emerges in *Two Gentlemen of Verona* and the more sophisticated *Twelfth Night*. In the earlier play Shakespeare employs both a false ambassador and a disguised lady who must woo for another. After betraying the secret courtship of Valentine and Sylvia to her father, Proteus agrees to slander his friend and to promote Sir Thurio, the duke's candidate for his daughter. "If I can do it / By aught that I can speak in his dispraise / She shall not long continue love to him" (III.ii.46–48). With multiple duplicity, Proteus woos Sylvia for himself and thus violates his vows to Julia, his friendship with Valentine, the trust of his master the duke, and his promised advocacy of Sir Thurio. In a final twist of unwitting cruelty, he sends the disguised Julia as his own ambassador to Sylvia.

> And now am I, unhappy messenger,
> To plead for that which I would not obtain;
> To carry that which I would have refused;
> To praise his faith, which I would have dispraised.
> I am my master's true-confirmèd love,
> But cannot be true servant to my master
> Unless I prove false traitor to myself.
> Yet will I woo for him, but yet so coldly
> As, heaven it knows, I would not have him speed.
>
> (IV.iv.97–105)

In this speech the swift reversals, the conflict of competing loyalties, the rhetorical parallelism of self-debate, the paradoxical sense of unique dilemma and hoary cliché reflect the motifs shaping both dramatic language and action in *Two Gentlemen of Verona*. These factors find especially acute expression in the falsities of Proteus and Julia, functioning as agents in matters of the heart.

Much of the delight in *Twelfth Night* derives from the games Shakespeare plays with the familiar go-between figure. In the Orsino-Viola-Olivia triangle he both combines and capsizes the Proteus-Julia-Silvia situation. Like Proteus, Viola/Cesario is sent to press a master's unwanted suit.

> VIOLA. Say I do speak with her, my lord, what then?
> ORSINO. O then unfold the passion of my love,
> Surprise her with discourse of my dear faith.
> It shall become thee well to act my woes—
> She will attend it better in thy youth
> Than in a nuncio's of more grave aspect.
>
> (I.iv.23–28)

Like Julia, the disguised Viola loves her lovelorn master: "I'll do my best / To woo your lady—yet a barful strife— / Whoe'er I woo, myself would be his wife" (I.iv.40–42). Unlike Julia, however, she faithfully argues on Orsino's behalf. Nonetheless, he eventually turns his wrath upon the messenger who seems to have betrayed him: "I partly know the instrument / That screws me from my true place in your favour. . . . Him will I tear out of that cruel eye" (V.i.120–121, 125).

What turns this comedy on its ear is Olivia's relentless pursuit of the reluctant go-between. Instead of the devoted Sylvia, scorning Proteus's ignoble courtship, *Twelfth Night* offers an ardent aggressor: "Run after that same peevish messenger" (I.v.290), she commands Malvolio. At their second meeting she declares,

> Cesario, by the roses of the spring,
> By maidhood, honour, truth, and everything,
> I love thee so that, maugre all thy pride,
> Nor wit nor reason can my passion hide.
>
> (III.i.147–150)

Though Olivia admits, "I have said too much unto a heart of stone, / And laid mine honour too unchary out" (III.iv.197–198), she continues to bid Cesario return, urging jewels and pictures upon him, compelling him to her will—"Thou shalt not choose but go. / Do not deny" (IV.i.56–57). When Sebastian/Cesario appears, hers is the proposal, hers the betrothal arrangement. Amid all the other festive holiday reversals pervading

113

Twelfth Night, one should also include this reversal of the false go-between who woos for himself rather than his master, as well as the reversal of the disdainful lady. Instead of the expected character types, the topsy-turvy comedy provides the unwilling but utterly true ambassador, wrongly accused of betrayal, and one of Shakespeare's most relentless heroines. In both instances, the revolution of type involves a revolution of gender roles, Viola overtly playing the man's part via her disguise and Olivia taking the traditionally masculine initiative for pressing a marriage suit. Again, the use of the familiar cultural phenomenon of a courtship conducted by others is subjected to the peculiar aesthetic demands of this comedy, rather than to some independent formula. Whether through its overturn of gender roles or its overturn of stereotypes, *Twelfth Night* upends the device of go-between along with everything else.

Nowhere do suitors' advocates figure more prominently than in *The Merry Wives of Windsor*. The play begins with Justice Shallow and Sir Hugh Evans planning a match for Shallow's cousin, Slender: "It were a goot motion if we leave our pribbles and prabbles, and desire a marriage between Master Abraham and Mistress Anne Page" (I.i.49–52). In a society where so many marital negotiations were handled by others and where so many offers were seconded by powerful friends and relatives, Slender's behavior caricatures the passive cooperation of the model candidate. His sole contribution to the initial discussion is "Mistress Anne Page? She has brown hair, and speaks small like a woman" (I.i.43–44). Later in the scene, when his sponsors break the matter to him directly, he utterly fails to comprehend what they have in mind, despite their desperate efforts at explanation. Nonetheless, he declares himself ready enough to fall in with their plans, a perfect parody of the docility enjoined upon the principals in marriages negotiated by others: "I will marry her, sir, at your request. But if there be no great love in the beginning, yet heaven may decrease it upon better acquaintance, when we are married and have more occasion to know one another. I hope upon familiarity will grow more contempt. But if you say, 'marry her,' I will marry her. That I am freely dissolved, and dissolutely" (I.i.227–233). Not even with Sir Thurio does Shakespeare show more deliciously the idiocy of a match backed by supporters regardless of the fitness of the suitor.

Yet other candidates also seek allies to press their claims upon Anne. Though Master Page prefers Slender, the Host of the Garter Inn pleads for "young Master Fenton. . . . He will carry't, he will carry't; 'tis in his buttons he will carry't" (III.ii.60, 62–64), and eventually the Host pockets one hundred pounds for assisting his protégé with an elopement. Fenton seeks additional help from Mistress Page: "I must advance the colours of my love, / And not retire. Let me have your good will." Though she pledges, "I will not be your friend nor enemy. / My daughter will I question how she loves you, / And as I find her, so am I affected" (III.iv.80–81, 89–91), she actually supports Dr. Caius. As for Mistress Quickly, she is the universal advocate between the besieged girl and her wooers. "Never a woman in Windsor knows more of Anne's mind than I do, nor can do more than I do with her, I thank heaven" (I.iv.124–126), she boasts. Hence Mistress Quickly promises Slender's servant, "I'll do your master what good I can" (88–89), while she vows to her own master, Dr. Caius, "Sir, the maid loves you, and all shall be well" (116–117). Taking money from Fenton to "let me have thy voice in my behalf" (151), she declares, "Master Fenton, I'll be sworn on a book she loves you" (140–141). And all this in less than fifty lines. Beyond even the manifest absurdity of "yon fool" Slender (III.iv.82) and Anne's justifiable aversion to marriage with Caius—"Alas, I had rather be set quick i'th' earth / And bowled to death with turnips" (86–87)—the good-natured dishonesty of Mistress Quickly sharply underlines the nonsense inherent in the whole system of courtship by committee. Moreover, the dramatic action reveals that she does nothing to further the cause of any of her clients.

Still, Shakespeare does not permit his comic critique of the process to end here. The agents suing for Anne on behalf of their aspirants find a parallel in Falstaff's identical suits for Mistress Page and Mistress Ford— no marriage intended, of course. Again the universal "spokesmate, or go-between" (II.ii.253), Mistress Quickly, is employed to deliver Sir John's messages and keep her friends' secrets. To allay or confirm his suspicions, Ford himself crazily hires Falstaff as a substitute seducer of his wife, in effect paying the fat knight to do what all feared an agent might do: steal another's woman for himself.

> There is money. . . . Spend it, spend it; spend more; spend all I have; only give me so much of your time in exchange of it as to lay an amiable siege to the honesty of this Ford's wife. Use your art of wooing, win her to consent to you. If any man may, you may as soon as any.
>
> (223–228)

Passing himself off as a rejected lover, Ford argues that Falstaff's success with the lady will then ensure his own. "Methinks you prescribe to yourself very preposterously" (231), observes Sir John. But in the terms of this play, all the interpositions of substitutes, advocates, messengers, messages, and go-betweens are preposterous prescriptions. Moreover, those who employ such methods receive their punishment in the final act. Falstaff gets pinched, pursued, and humiliated; "a great lubberly boy" is foisted off on Slender (V.v.181); and Dr. Caius protests, "By Gar, I am cozened! I ha' married *un garçon*, a boy; *un paysan*, by Gar" (200–201). Regardless of intercessors, whether well-intentioned or unscrupulous, only honest, straightforward affection guarantees a happy, faithful marriage in this particular comic world. That principle holds as true for Mistress Page and Mistress Ford as for Mistress Fenton, the newest wife of Windsor.

The Janus faces of trust and betrayal that appear when one man relies upon another to forward his courtship find expression not only in comedy but also in one major tragedy. *Othello* sets up two contrasting situations. Roderigo, a would-be suitor who has been rejected by Desdemona's father, is assured by Iago that she will soon tire of her husband and then turn to her former wooer, provided he offers sufficiently rich gifts. The men enter into a classic relationship of presumed advocacy and cynical manipulation.

> RODERIGO. Wilt thou be fast to my hopes if I depend on the issue?
> IAGO. Thou art sure of me. Go, make money. . . .
> RODERIGO. I'll sell all my land.   *Exit*
>
> IAGO. Thus do I ever make my fool my purse—
>   For I mine own gained knowledge should profane
>   If I would time expend with such a snipe
>   But for my sport and profit.
>
>   (I.iii.361–363, 374–378)

Though critics have noted the parallels between Iago's duping of Roderigo and his duping of Othello, they often miss the secondary parallel between Roderigo's trust in Iago as a messenger to Desdemona and Othello's similar reliance upon Cassio. Yet it is precisely this reliance that forms the basis for Iago's initial attack. As Desdemona reveals, it was "Michael Cassio, / That came a-wooing with you, and so many a time / When I have spoke of you dispraisingly / Hath ta'en your part" (III.iii.71–74). Seizing on this piece of information, Iago presses the Moor for confirmation.

> IAGO. Did Michael Cassio, when you wooed my lady,
>   Know of your love?

116

OTHELLO. He did, from first to last. Why dost thou ask?

. . . .

IAGO. I did not think he had been acquainted with her.
OTHELLO. O yes, and went between us very oft.
IAGO. Indeed?

. . . .

OTHELLO.   Thou dost mean something.
 I heard thee say even now thou liked'st not that,
 When Cassio left my wife. What didst not like?
 And when I told thee he was of my counsel
 In my whole course of wooing, thou cried'st "Indeed?"
 And didst contract and purse thy brow together
 As if thou then hadst shut up in thy brain
 Some horrible conceit.

         (96–98, 101–103, 112–119)

With his gift for improvisation, Iago could no doubt inflame Othello's jealousy in countless ways. But the insidious strategy he uses not only echoes his manipulation of Roderigo's wooing but also taps into the general suspicion of go-betweens that pervaded Shakespeare's society.

Cassio has already publicly praised "divine Desdemona" (II.i.74) in the extravagant terms appropriate for a lover: she is "a maid / That paragons description and wild fame, / One that excels the quirks of blazoning pens" (62–64). Before he ever undermines Othello, Iago tells Roderigo that Desdemona and Cassio are lovers. And, privately, the villain convinces himself: "That Cassio loves her, I do well believe it. / That she loves him, 'tis apt and of great credit" (285–286). The further information that Cassio has been the intimate agent for Othello throughout the secret courtship of Desdemona simply strengthens such a possibility. It may also explain how the Moor can claim "That she with Cassio hath the act of shame / A thousand times committed" (V.ii.218–219). The general's trust in his lieutenant arises from their shared military experience; yet a brave soldier is not necessarily a chaste spokesman in his commander's courtship. After all, though Cassio may or may not be "A fellow almost damned in a fair wife" (I.i.20), the courtesan Bianca, who follows him about the streets of Cyprus, appears as testimony to his carnal appetites. Such purely circumstantial evidence would matter little were not the possibility of betrayal inherent in a wooing entrusted partly or wholly to others. Even a gull like Roderigo can eventually—and rightly—tell Iago that "your words and performances are no kin together" (IV.ii.187–188). Because false agents

117

regularly garnered criticism in Elizabethan society, Shakespeare's audience perhaps had less reason than modern playgoers to regard Othello as a fool for suspecting dishonesty, both verbal and sexual, from his lieutenant in love and war or from his wife.

Shakespeare did not invent the conventional attitudes toward go-betweens, nor did his countrymen. The long-standing distrust of the lover's emissary stems in part from such classical figures as Pandarus, who appears in *Troilus and Cressida*. From one point of view, Pandarus is entirely trustworthy, since he neither woos for himself nor fails his client nor accepts competing commissions. "Words, vows, gifts, tears, and love's full sacrifice / He offers in another's enterprise" (I.ii.278–279). Of course, the irony undercutting his exemplary service is the fact that he labors on behalf of a secret seduction rather than lawful matrimony. All Pandarus's enticements are intended to lure Troilus and Cressida into bed but no further. Here, then, appears the final debasement of the Shakespearean agent in courtship. He truly becomes a "bawd," a "broker-lackey," one of the "Good traders in the flesh," the "Brethren and sisters of the hold-door trade" (277; Epi., 2, 6, 14, 19).[29] While his function in the Troilus tales, as well as his frankly lascivious role in this bitter play, are well recognized, the affinities between Pandarus and other "pitiful goers-between" (III.ii.196–197) have not received adequate attention.

If at some level Shakespeare regards all solicitation on behalf of one suitor or another as a form of sexual pandering, he nonetheless makes diversely creative use of the custom in his dramas. He mines the riches of potential betrayal, ranging from the official ambassador's desertion by a Henry VI or an Edward IV to the false promises of a Proteus. In between are emissaries who pocket a fee but do nothing else, like Mistress Quickly or Sir Toby Belch or Iago, and representatives unjustly suspected of disloyalty, like Viola and Cassio. The comically perverse advocacies in *Merry Wives* come to naught, but the promotion of appropriate matches by friends and family at last achieve success in *Much Ado*. Go-betweens may come from any segment of society: the priest Friar Laurence, the bawd-uncle Pandarus, the prince Don Pedro, the corrupt Paroles, the forsaken

---

[29] Harry Berger, Jr., *Second World and Green World: Studies in Renaissance Fiction-Making* (Berkeley: University of California Press, 1988), p. 143, declares Pandarus to be "the paradigm of pure external agency, a communicator of the parts of others with no privacy or privation of his own. . . . He is not a trader 'in the flesh' until Cressida's behavior has made him so." I do not see how the blame can be entirely displaced upon Cressida (what of Troilus's culpability?), especially when Pandarus so blatantly subverts the traditional function of a matrimonial emissary into that of a bawd.

Julia, the manipulative Suffolk, the earthy Nurse. Though Richard III boasts of his wooing for Lady Anne, "I [have] no friends to back my suit withal / But the plain devil" (I.ii.223–234), in his next wooing he expects Queen Elizabeth to intercede for him with her daughter. No consistent pattern or attitude prevails. Even when a comedy like *Twelfth Night* subverts the cluster of ideas attaching to the suitor's spokesman, the intent seems less a matter of criticism than a part of the general frivolity involved in overturning custom. What is important for a modern viewer to understand is both the common nature of outsiders' involvements in courtships and also the responsibilities, strictures, and suspicions surrounding the practice. Without such an awareness, certain features in the plays remain elusive at best, while others are subject to misinterpretation.

{ CHAPTER VI }

Dowries and Jointures

A good portion makes hir the better and manie tymes not the
prouder. . . . For hir ioyncture lett itt nott be too large,
lest your heyre fele the smarte and a second husband the
swe[e]te of that grosse ouersight.
—*Wentworth Papers*

I never read but England's kings have had
Large sums of gold and dowries with their wives.
—*2H6*, I.i.125–126

MONEY can be a troublesome issue in any marriage, but the Elizabethans tried to settle economic arrangements before a wedding took place. Hence today what often appears mercenary simply represented the customary planning for appropriate financial stability.[1] Since husbands and wives were expected to set up an independent household, some kind of reliable support was required even at the bottom of society—a job at journeyman's wages, a shop or a trade, a cottage and field, the basic goods for housekeeping.[2] And because newlywed couples did not share a roof

[1] For further discussion of this point in works not cited below, see Michael D. Bristol, *Carnival and Theater: Plebeian Culture and the Structure of Authority in Renaissance England* (New York: Methuen, 1985), p. 163; Barbara B. Diefendorf, "Family Culture, Renaissance Culture," *Renaissance Quarterly* 40 (1987): 672–676; Joel Hurstfield, *The Queen's Wards: Wardship and Marriage under Elizabeth I*, 2d ed. (London: Frank Cass, 1973), pp. 151–153; Michael MacDonald, *Mystical Bedlam: Madness, Anxiety and Healing in Seventeenth-Century England* (Cambridge: Cambridge University Press, 1981), pp. 94–95; Lawrence Stone, "Social Mobility in England, 1500–1700," in *Seventeenth-Century England: Society in an Age of Revolution*, ed. Paul Seaver (New York: New Viewpoints, 1976), p. 47; Louise A. Tilly and Joan W. Scott, *Women, Work, and Family* (New York: Holt, Rinehart, and Winston, 1978), p. 25; Merry E. Wiesner, "Beyond Women and the Family: Towards a Gender Analysis of the Reformation," *The Sixteenth Century Journal* 18 (1987): 320.

[2] See John Hajnal, "Two Kinds of Pre-Industrial Household Formation System," in *Family Forms in Historic Europe*, ed. Richard Wall, Jean Robin, and Peter Laslett (Cambridge: Cambridge University Press, 1983), pp. 69, 73; Peter Laslett, "Size and Structure of the Household in England over Three Centuries," *Population Studies* 23 (1969): 200; idem, *The World We Have Lost, Further Explored* (London: Methuen, 1983), pp. 92ff.; Alan Macfarlane, *Marriage and Love in England: Modes of Reproduction 1300–1840* (Oxford: Basil Blackwell, 1986), pp. 79–102; idem, "The Myth of the Peasantry; Family and Economy

with parents, except in rare circumstances, the wait for a vacant dwelling or an adequate living often delayed a union, as discussed in chapters 2 and 4. To avoid the burden of maintaining their families, a parish here and there even hindered the marriages of paupers.[3] Further up the social scale, prenuptial arrangements for property commitments played a more critical role. While the privileged ranks included a limited number of professionals and merchants, no gentleman ever worked with his hands. By definition, a gentleman was one who "can liue idely, and without manuall labour, and will beare the Port, charge and countenance of a Gentleman."[4] Obviously, bearing that port, charge, and countenance cost a considerable sum, increasing geometrically from marginal gentility to the dizzying heights of aristocracy and royalty. There the fortunes settled upon betrothed couples were as munificent as they were necessary.

In general, the settlements consisted of two kinds of support. From the bride's family came a dowry, or portion, as it was also called, consisting of money, lands, and valuables like jewels or plate. This portion was payable at the time of the wedding or in installments shortly thereafter. From the groom came agreement to the dower (not to be confused with dowry), or jointure, that his new wife would receive should she be widowed and thus become a dowager. In addition, his family had to specify a living allowance for the couple and the husband's inheritance at his father's demise. Such arrangements thus guaranteed support for each party, providing both income for the male and life insurance for the female. However, certain inequities stemmed from this system. Daughters always represented a drain on the family's disposable assets, and an abundance of daughters could spell disaster, since almost all privileged young women were expected to marry and to bring a portion with them. Sons, on the other hand, could bolster the family fortunes through receipt of a bridal

---

in a Northern Parish," in *Land, Kinship and Life-Cycle*, ed. Richard M. Smith (Cambridge: Cambridge University Press, 1984), pp. 344–345; Keith Wrightson, *English Society, 1580–1680* (London: Hutchinson, 1982), pp. 68–70. Miranda Chaytor, "Household and Kinship: Ryton in the Late 16th and Early 17th Centuries," *History Workshop* 10 (1980): 45–47, points out a few exceptions to this practice.

[3] Alice Clark, *Working Life of Women in the Seventeenth Century* (New York: Harcourt, Brace and Howe, 1920), pp. 81–87; John R. Gillis, *For Better, for Worse: British Marriages, 1600 to the Present* (Oxford: Oxford University Press, 1985), pp. 89–90; Martin Ingram, *Church Courts, Sex, and Marriage in England, 1570–1640* (Cambridge: Cambridge University Press, 1987), pp. 131, 215.

[4] Sir Thomas Smith, *The Common-wealth* (London, 1640), p. 55. Smith is writing during Elizabeth's reign, not in 1640.

dowry, while the payment of dower or jointure could generally be deferred several years or, should the wife die first, be avoided altogether. Though there might not be enough money or land to provide livings for all one's sons, younger brothers (unlike their sisters) always had the option to remain single. For men who could or did wed, a living father who gripped the purse strings sometimes tyrannized marital negotiations. Fortunate indeed were widows, with money of their own, and unmarried sons who had already come into their inheritance. Such individuals could not only make a more independent choice of a mate, as discussed earlier, but could set their own terms for dowry and jointure.

Since a dowry, though customary, was not required for a valid marriage, no laws compelled its payment. Instead, the parties signed a contract, which then could be enforced in the courts. However, English law carefully delineated all women's rights to dower, partly to see that widows did not become a charge upon society and partly to prevent husbands from abrogating those rights out of perversity or anger. Thus, "the Christian custome and Law of the Realme giueth euery good Wife part of her Husbands Lands to liue on when hee is dead, which wee call Dower."[5] Hence came the custom of "endowment" at the church door before a wedding, which still survives in the traditional ceremony as "with all my worldly goods I thee endow."[6] Rents, offices, advowsons, and land could constitute the dower but not services or annuities.[7] At the very least, a widow got a habitation equal to one-third of her husband's house, together with one-third of his dowerable possessions. A London widow not only inherited the usual third if there were children but received half her husband's estate if she were childless.[8] Only a premarital agreement to accept more or less than what the law provided waived dower rights, and even if the widow remarried, a new husband could not dispose of his wife's dower as he could her other property.[9]

Technically, a jointure was different from a dower, though in common parlance the terms were used interchangeably. While the dower vested only at widowhood, the jointure represented a gift made to the wife or the

[5] *The Lawes Resolutions of Womens Rights* (London, 1632), p. 90.

[6] Ibid., pp. 100, 106–108; *The Book of Common Prayer, 1559*, ed. John Booty (Charlottesville: University Press of Virginia, 1976), p. 293.

[7] *Lawes*, pp. 98–99.

[8] Richard L. Greaves, *Society and Religion in Elizabethan England* (Minneapolis: University of Minnesota Press, 1981), pp. 134–135.

[9] *Lawes*, p. 147; Pearl Hogrefe, *Tudor Women: Commoners and Queens* (Ames: Iowa State University Press, 1975), p. 13.

couple, either before or after the wedding, as "a present possession" from the husband or his family.[10] For example, jointure might be an estate made over to the woman during her lifetime, or to the man during his lifetime with a remainder to his widow until her death. Hence, depending on the nature of a husband's possessions and the prenuptial agreements, his wife could have both dower and jointure, either of them, or neither of them. Yet few married women lacked financial protection, for "the greatest part of honest, wise and sober men, are of themselues carefull to purchase somewhat for their Wiues, if they be not, yet they sometimes stand bound by the womans parents to make their Wiues some Joynture." With most wives, "men are faine to assure part or all of such Lands as they haue (in ioynture or otherwise) to them, ere they can win their loue."[11] Should a marriage prove unusually felicitous, of course a husband could give his spouse more than he originally promised, so long as any children had been provided for.[12]

Of more immediate importance than dower or jointure to a newlywed pair were the possessions a bride brought with her. In cases where "the wife bee an Inheritrix and landed, she is to let her husband enioy it during his life and hers: the which afterward descendeth to her eldest sonne, or in defect of sonnes, it is equally parted betweene her daughters."[13] Since at marriage, property came under the husband's control, women with property were highly desirable prospects. Should a female be so foolish as to give away land in order to persuade a man to marry her, she could legally demand its return if he reneged on his promise. To protect orphaned heiresses against unscrupulous fortune hunters, the City of London enacted orders for fines or forfeiture of the bridal portion in instances where consent to marriage with a minor had not been obtained.[14] Some of these fines went to provide dowries for other unmarried orphans, an indication of the importance of a bridal portion for young women.

[10] *Lawes*, p. 182. See also Paul S. Clarkson and Clyde T. Warren, *The Law of Property in Shakespeare* (Baltimore: Johns Hopkins Press, 1942), pp. 81–84. The term *jointure* derives from the legal status of "joint tenancy" that husband and wife enjoy, though property belonging exclusively to the wife still passed into control of the husband during the marriage.

[11] *Lawes*, pp. 182, 90.

[12] Hogrefe, *Tudor Women*, p. 14. See, e.g., Sir Simonds D'Ewes, *The Autobiography and Correspondence*, ed. James Orchard Halliwell (London: Richard Bentley, 1845), 2:152.

[13] William Vaughan, *The Golden-grove* (London, 1600), N3ᵛ. See also *Lawes*, pp. 73, 79–80; Smith, *Common-wealth*, pp. 243–244.

[14] *Orders Taken and Enacted, for Orphans and Their Portions* (London, 1580), A3ᵛ–A6.

Not surprisingly, the debate that swirled around marrying for wealth, referred to in chapter 3, incorporated the technical terms of financial settlements. Whether advocating the superiority of "the dowry of the minde" over worldly possessions or advising that "men at first woeing be not precipitat in there bargains, making iointers overlarge, out of a littel love, as they call it,"[15] writers confirm the pervasive attention given to money in courtship. Those who ignored such practical matters imperiled their future well-being, for "who marries for love without money has good nights and sorry days."[16] Of all the moral treatises and books of fatherly advice, none puts the matter more plainly than does Francis Osborne's:

> The true extent of her estate . . . is first to be surveyed before you entail yourself upon the owner. And in this common fame is not to be trusted, which for the most part dilates a portion or jointure beyond its natural bounds, proving also not seldom litigious and that found given by will questionable. . . .
>
> As the fertility of the ensuing year is guessed at by the height of the river Nile, so by the greatness of a wife's portion may much of the future conjugal happiness be calculated. . . .
>
> The best of husbands are servants, but he that takes a wife wanting money is slave to his affection, doing the basest of drudgery without wages.[17]

Here all the dangers of an inflated report about fortune, the possibility of litigation, the uncertainty of promised inheritance, and the misery attendant on an inadequate dowry are carefully spelled out. Even denunciations of covetous unions confirm the significance of fiscal settlements. "Fie, fie! marriages, for the most part, are at this day so made, as looke how the butcher bies his cattel, so wil men sel their children. He that bids most shal speed soonest; & so he hath money, we care not a fart for his hones-

---

[15] Stefano Guazzo, *The Civile Conversation*, trans. George Pettie (London: Constable, 1925), 2:7; Henry Percy, ninth Earl of Northumberland, "Instructions . . . to his Son," *Archaeologia* 27 (1838): 332.

[16] Morris P. Tilley, *A Dictionary of the Proverbs in England in the Sixteenth and Seventeenth Centuries* (Ann Arbor: University of Michigan Press, 1950), L552; see also H749. Consult further Phillip Stubbes, *The Anatomie of Abuses* (London, 1595), p. 65; L. Wright, *Display of Dutie* (London, 1621), D5.

[17] *Advice to a Son: Precepts of Lord Burghley, Sir Walter Raleigh, and Francis Osborne*, ed. Louis B. Wright (Ithaca, NY: Cornell University Press, 1962), pp. 68–69. See also pp. 9–10 for Burghley's words on this subject, as well as those of Henry, fifth Earl of Huntingdon, in Antonia Fraser, *The Weaker Vessel* (New York: Alfred A. Knopf, 1984), p. 11.

tie."[18] Thus a traditional list of a bride's virtues seems to save the best asset for last. Such a wife should come "of as noble a house as any of theim, a chaiste one, a sobre one, a Godlie one, an excellent fayre one, hauying with her a wonderfull Dowrie."[19]

Much counsel also centers on other aspects of the financial arrangements associated with marriage. For example, parents are routinely advised to "lay vp some stocke, or competent portion for their children" because "in regard of the times wherein we liue, it is needfull for setting vp in a good calling, and for obtaining a fit match."[20] It follows, then, that a father is denounced when his offspring are "vndone by his spending their portions."[21] At the same time, it is acknowledged that not all children have an equal claim on the family estate. "Let the eldest (carrying himselfe well) have a double portion . . . and the rest, a competent allowance."[22] This custom increased the firstborn son's possibilities for a good match even as it diminished those of his younger brothers.[23] Regardless of what parents set aside in the way of marital support, they were urged not to give all until death, thereby retaining control over their own livelihood instead of

[18] Richard Jones, *The Passionate Morrice*, ed. F. J. Furnivall, New Shakspere Society, ser. 6, no. 2 (London: N. Trübner, 1876): 61–62. See also Robert Abbot, *A Wedding Sermon* (London, 1608), p. 63; Heinrich Bullinger, *The Christian State of Matrimony*, trans. Miles Coverdale (London, 1575), 51–52ᵛ; *A Discourse of the Married and Single Life* (London, 1621), pp. 29–30; Sir Geoffrey Fenton, *Monophylo . . . A Philosophicall Discourse and Division of Love* (London, 1572), pp. 17–17ᵛ; Thomas Gataker, "A Good Wife," in *Two Mariage Sermons* (London, 1620), p. 17; idem, *A Good Wife Gods Gift: and, A Wife Indeed* (London, 1623), pp. 16, 24; Matthew Griffith, *Bethel, or A Forme for Families* (London, 1633), pp. 255–256; Dorothy Leigh, *The Mother's Blessing* (London, 1616), p. 51; Daniel Rogers, *Matrimoniall Honour* (London, 1642), p. 33; John Stockwood, *A Bartholomew Fairing for Parentes* (London, 1589), p. 81; Vaughan, *Golden-grove*, M7ᵛ–M8.

[19] Thomas Wilson, *The Arte of Rhetorique* (London, 1553), p. 34.

[20] William Gouge, *Of Domesticall Duties* (London, 1622), p. 565. See also Thomas Carter, *Carters Christian Commonwealth: Domesticall Dutyes Deciphered* (London, 1627), pp. 147ff.; George Whetstone, *An Heptameron of Civill Discourses* (London, 1582), X4ᵛ.

[21] Robert Snawsel, *A Looking Glasse for Maried Folkes* (London, 1610), D4. See also Gouge, *Domesticall Duties*, p. 567.

[22] Rogers, *Matrimoniall Honour*, p. 92. See also Carter, *Christian Commonwealth*, pp. 148, 158.

[23] See, e.g., *Wentworth Papers, 1597–1628*, ed. J. P. Cooper, Camden Society Publications, 4th ser., 12 (1973): 129; Jack Goody, "Inheritance, Property and Women: Some Comparative Considerations," in *Family and Inheritance: Rural Society in Western Europe, 1200–1800*, ed. Goody, Joan Thirsk, and E. P. Thompson (Cambridge: Cambridge University Press, 1976), p. 12; Joan Thirsk, "The European Debate on Customs of Inheritance, 1500–1700," in *Family and Inheritance*.

subjecting themselves as "captives and prisoners" to the authority of married children.[24]

Looking to the final monetary claims, that is, to jointure and dower rights, one finds further advice concerning appropriate settlements for widows, alongside debate on the advisability of marrying a widow.[25] Typically, Sir Walter Raleigh enunciates the most widely accepted position:

> . . . what thou givest after thy death, remember that thou givest it to a stranger and most times to an enemy, for he that shall marry thy wife will despise thee, thy memory, and thine, and shall possess the quiet of thy labors, the fruit which thou hast planted, enjoy thy love, and spend with joy and ease what thou hast spared and gotten with care and travail. Yet always remember that thou leave not thy wife to be a shame unto thee . . . but that she may live according to thy estate. . . . but leave thy estate to thy house and children. . . . [for] wives were ordained to continue the generations of men, not to transfer them and diminish them.[26]

Side by side with fears of a second husband's reaping the bounty of a first husband's wealth go stern warnings about the misery of marriage to a widow, "for if she be rich she will looke to gouerne."[27] Writers of fiction make much sport of widows and their suitors, portraying the attraction in terms ranging from contempt to amused toleration. "To a younger brother shee's a reversion after three lives, for after the death of three husbands, shee commonly helpes to reedifie his ruinous fortunes againe."[28] As for the

---

[24] Rogers, *Matrimoniall Honour*, p. 92. See also Foulke Robartes, *The Revenue of the Gospel Is Tythes* (Cambridge, 1613), pp. 114–115; Keith Thomas, "Age and Authority in Early Modern England," *Proceedings of the British Academy* 62 (1976): 238–239.

[25] For the best study to date of attitudes toward widows and their representation on stage, see Elizabeth Oakes, "Heiress, Beggar, Saint, or Whore: The Widow in the Society and on the Stage in Early Modern England" (Ph.D. diss., Vanderbilt University, 1990).

[26] *Advice*, p. 22.

[27] Joseph Swetnam, *The Araignment of Lewde, Idle, Froward, and Unconstant Women* (London, 1615), p. 59. See also Pierre de la Primaudaye, *The French Academie* (London, 1586), p. 497; John Newnam, *Newnam's Nightcrowe* (London, 1590), p. 37.

[28] Wye Saltonstall, *Picturae Loquentes* (London, 1631), no. 4. See also Jones, *Passionate Morrice*, pp. 67, 70; *Lawes*, p. 331; Francis Lenton, *Characterismi: or, Lentons Leasures* (London, 1631), no. 7; Martin Parker, *The Wiving Age* (ca. 1625), as cited by L. T. Fitz, " 'What Says the Married Woman': Marriage Theory and Feminism in the English Renaissance," *Mosaic* 13 (1980): 9; *The Uncasing of Machivils Instructions to his Sonne* (London, 1613), p. 20.

reedified fortune, "many get it by an olde blinde widow, that haue wit to spend it with [a] sweeter creature."[29]

Throughout the fiction of the period runs a frank acceptance of money as a determining factor in marriage, an acceptance expressed in the technical terminology of the day. For the poor younger son or the spendthrift, "thinking with thy wiues Dowry to pay thy debts,"[30] a rich match offered the only hope of solvency. While "A true Lover" might desire his betrothed "not for wealth or portion, but *per se*," most who take this attitude are soundly rebuked.[31] According to John Harington, "to haue the portion / Well got, and void of strife, fraud or extortion" is one of the four joys of marriage.[32] And even a teenager "woteth, and hath often heard it, the summe or portion which her father giues her, (besides the legacy her Grandsire left her)."[33] Thus in various treatments, some serious, some satirical, some merely in passing, contemporary writers testify to the hardheaded practicalities inherent in the system of dowry and portion, dower and jointure.

But though the literature of the period affirms the significance of this system, it was in the lives of countless individuals that financial agreements were actually worked out. So important were such matters that fathers' wills routinely specified amounts to be set aside as portions for daughters or jointures for wives and daughters-in-law. Even humble villagers made wills if they had unmarried offspring, providing a house or living for the widow and some small sum at marriage or adulthood for each child.[34] Typically, the diarist John Manningham left legacies of £300

---

[29] Nicolas Breton, *An Olde Mans Lesson, and a Young Mans Love* (London, 1605), B4ᵛ.

[30] *Discourse*, p. 103. See also Lenton, *Characterismi*, no. 16; John Donne, "Epithalamion, Made at Lincoln's Inn," in Lawrence Manley, ed., *London in the Age of Shakespeare* (University Park: Pennsylvania State University Press, 1986), p. 280.

[31] Saltonstall, *Picturae*, no. 5. For the opposing view, see Samuel Rowlands, *Tis Merrie When Gossips Meete* (London, 1602), D4ᵛ; *Uncasing*, p. 14.

[32] Sir John Harington, *The Letters and Epigrams of Sir John Harington*, ed. Norman Egbert McClure (Philadelphia: University of Pennsylvania Press, 1930), p. 213.

[33] Henry Parrott, "A young Novices new yonger wife," in *Cures for the Itch. Characters, Epigrams, Epitaphs* (London, 1626).

[34] Susan Dwyer Amussen, *An Ordered Society: Gender and Class in Early Modern England* (New York: Basil Blackwell, 1988), pp. 86–92; J. P. Cooper, "Patterns of Inheritance and Settlement by Great Landowners from the Fifteenth to the Eighteenth Centuries," in *Family and Inheritance*, pp. 209–220, 318–323; Cicely Howell, "Peasant Inheritance Customs in the Midlands, 1280–1700," in *Family and Inheritance*, pp. 145–146; Margaret Spufford, *Contrasting Communities: English Villagers in the Sixteenth and Seventeenth Centuries* (Cam-

and £250, respectively, to his minor children Susan and Elizabeth "to remaine for the increase of their portions." Richard Manningham, his father, also willed £10 to a friend's daughter "at her daye of marriage" and 20 marks to a maidservant for the same purpose.[35] The amounts are not so handsome as the dowries of £1,000 and £666 3s. 4d. that Sir Nicholas Bacon had to pay out as guardian for the two elder daughters of the late Sir William Drury, but the principle is the same.[36]

Not surprisingly, in instances where a lapse occurred between the promise of a sum and its full payment, Englishmen often had to resort to law. Thus one finds Sir Nicholas in court demanding an accounting from Sir Robert Drury for "ane assuranc of the CCCC[li] that he have receyved for his sisters portions."[37] London's Chancery Court was filled with disputes over monetary provisions for marriages, including the Belott-Mountjoy suit in which Shakespeare testified.[38] The dramatist's own son-in-law, Thomas Quiney, failed to produce £100 in land as promised in his settlement with Judith Shakespeare.[39] Not that litigation was always required. As Mary, Lady Peyton, writes to Anne Oxinden in 1632, "I have had so [much] spech with your brother conserning your father's wille and your

bridge: Cambridge University Press, 1974), pp. 85–89, 104–118, 159–164; idem, "Peasant Inheritance Customs and Land Distribution in Cambridgeshire from the Sixteenth to the Eighteenth Century," in *Family and Inheritance*, pp. 158–172; Richard T. Vann, "Wills and the Family in an English Town: Banbury, 1550–1800," *Journal of Family History* 4 (1979): 362–363; Keith Wrightson and David Levine, *Poverty and Piety in an English Village: Terling, 1525–1700* (New York: Academic Press, 1979), pp. 95–99.

[35] John Manningham, *The Diary of John Manningham of the Middle Temple, 1602–1603*, ed. Robert Parker Sorlien (Hanover, NH: University Press of New England, 1976), pp. 289, 285. See also Frank F. Foster, "Politics and Community in Elizabethan England," in *The Rich, the Well Born, and the Powerful*, ed. Frederic Cople Jaher (Urbana: University of Illinois Press, 1973), p. 130.

[36] R. C. Bald, *Donne and the Drurys* (Cambridge: Cambridge University Press, 1959), p. 28.

[37] Ibid., p. 30.

[38] S. Schoenbaum, *William Shakespeare: A Documentary Life* (New York: Oxford University Press, 1975), pp. 210–213. For other examples of bitter family quarrels over marriage portions, see Alice T. Friedman, "Portrait of a Marriage: The Willoughby Letters of 1585–86," *Signs: Journal of Women in Culture and Society* 11 (1986): 546; Anne Clifford, Countess of Pembroke, *The Diary of the Lady Anne Clifford*, intro. V. Sackville-West (New York: George H. Daran, 1923), pp. 78, 104; Allison D. Wall, ed., *Two Elizabethan Women: Correspondence of Joan and Maria Thynne, 1575–1611*, Wiltshire Record Society Publication 38 (1982): 51–53.

[39] W. Nicholas Knight, "Patrimony and Shakespeare's Daughters," *University of Hartford Studies in Literature* 9 (1977): 178, 184.

portion, . . . he is now confirmed in it and says you shall have your dewe as soune as he can."[40] Evidently the terms set down by Anne's father were clear enough to ensure her brother's compliance, but sometimes provisions allowed for interpretation. For example, Michael Wentworth decrees that "if any of my daughters will not be advised by my executors, but of their own fantastical brain bestow themselves lightly upon a light person, then I will that daughter to have only £66 instead of the £100 which was promised to the obedient."[41] Among the aristocracy, the Earl of Northumberland allowed a future "wife of my said sonne Henry a joincture of five hundreth pounds yearlie towards the procuringe of a good match for him," provided that this younger son "shall competentlie dispose of himself in marriage."[42] Both situations leave ample scope for determining that a child has made a poor choice and hence forfeited some or all of the money promised.

A few in the society simply disregarded monetary considerations. Sir Walter Raleigh got no dowry at all when he eloped with Elizabeth Throckmorton, and the advanced pregnancy of an impoverished Elizabeth Vernon forced the Earl of Southampton into a secret marriage at a point when he desperately needed a wealthy heiress to redress his indebtedness.[43] Sometimes a dowry was reduced, as was the case with the Earl of Cork's daughter, who got a smaller portion of £7,000 when she insisted on wedding a younger son.[44] And sometimes a child was denied a dowry, as happened with recusant Anne Bellamy, who gave up her faith while imprisoned in 1592 and then married the servant of her examiner.[45] Gervase Holles clung to his childhood sweetheart, Dorothy, although "hir father was not able

---

[40] Dorothy Gardiner, ed., *The Oxinden Letters, 1607–1642* (London: Constable, 1933), p. 87.

[41] Cited in Lawrence Stone, *The Family, Sex and Marriage in England 1500–1800* (New York: Harper and Row, 1977), p. 182.

[42] G. R. Batho, ed., *The Household Papers of Henry Percy, Ninth Earl of Northumberland (1564–1632)*, Camden Society Publications, 3d ser., 93 (1962): 131.

[43] George R. Hibbard, "Love, Marriage and Money in Shakespeare's Theatre and Shakespeare's England," *Elizabethan Theatre VI*, ed. Hibbard (Toronto: Macmillan of Canada, 1975), p. 136; G.P.V. Akrigg, *Shakespeare and the Earl of Southampton* (Cambridge: Harvard University Press, 1968), pp. 67–71.

[44] Linda A. Pollock, *A Lasting Relationship: Parents and Children over Three Centuries* (Hanover, NH: University Press of New England, 1987), p. 260; Sara Heller Mendelson, *The Mental World of Stuart Women: Three Studies* (Amherst: University of Massachusetts Press, 1987), p. 76.

[45] Kathy Lynn Emerson, *Wives and Daughters: The Women of Sixteenth-Century England* (Troy, NY: Whitston Publishing Company, 1984), pp. 13–14.

to give hir any portion." When Gervase's father asked, "Do you understand that I am endebted and have no hopes to winde myselfe out of that laborinth but by your marriage?"[46] he enunciated the stern realities affecting his son's choice. Not every woman of little or no fortune relinquished desirable prospects. Archbishop Loftus married his daughters "to the sons and heirs of five honest and virtuous English gentlemen. . . . in regard rather of their favour to my religion . . . than of any portion of money, which in respect of the slenderness of my living, I was able to disburse."[47] In one extraordinary instance, Sir Richard Cholmley forfeited £1,000 of his daughter's portion to Lord Lumley when the girl preferred to marry a poor younger brother.[48] Yet such costly decisions do not typify the time's courtship practices.

Far more common is this response to a proposed marriage with a woman who has nothing but her own virtues and the distant possibility of an inheritance: "Those hopes of a large reversion you mention, by a Lady soe accomplisht, are fyne and plausible and sound welle in the eare but they fill not the hand at all."[49] Indeed, alliances at every social level were routinely quashed on economic grounds, as was Jane Whalley's attraction to the poor chaplain Roger Williams.[50] Without adequate resources, no household could survive. Thus local records tell of a girl's suitor who "dyd demaund in marriadg her father's farmehold . . . and went no further" when it was denied.[51] Similarly, when Joane Wilson in 1583 discovered the extent of John Clifford's debts, she broke off their courtship.[52] The profligate Robert Greene confessed, "I married a Gentlemans daughter of good account, with whom I liued for a while: but . . . I cast her off,

---

[46] Gervase Holles, *Memorials of the Holles Family, 1493–1656*, ed. A. C. Wood, Camden Society Publications, 3d ser., 55 (1937): 203.

[47] Sir Harris Nicolas, *Memoirs of the Life and Times of Sir Christopher Hatton* (London: Richard Bentley, 1847), p. 424.

[48] Lawrence Stone, *The Crisis of the Aristocracy, 1558–1641* (Oxford: Clarendon Press, 1965), p. 610.

[49] Gardiner, *Oxinden*, pp. 107–108.

[50] She was later married to another clergyman, William Hook, who eventually became chaplain to Oliver Cromwell, to whom the Whalley family were related by marriage; Arthur Searle, ed., *Barrington Family Letters, 1628–1632*, Camden Society Publications, 4th ser., 28 (1983): 19, 25.

[51] *Depositions and Other Ecclesiastical Proceedings from the Courts of Durham*, Publications of the Surtees Society 21 (1845): 234; Chaytor, "Household and Kinship," p. 41.

[52] Amussen, *Ordered Society*, p. 72. The Barrington letters are replete with details of offers deemed insufficient; see, e.g., Searle, *Barrington*, pp. 103, 104, 119, 120.

hauing spent vp the marriage money which I obtained by her."[53] Greene's desertion may be reprehensible, but his wish to get his hands on a dowry was common at every station in society.

Marriage portions varied tremendously, of course, from the meager allotment of a few shillings by a villager to his daughter right up to the £40,000 James I bestowed upon the Princess Elizabeth.[54] In 1582, Bridget Paston's dowry was £30,000, and in 1599 a settlement of £28,000 was involved in the stormy Spencer-Compton wedding.[55] Lady Anne Clifford not only got a £15,000 portion inherited from her father but also, at the death of her mother and her paternal uncle, all the family's possessions.[56] So customary were these matters that they were reported as idle gossip. Thus Philip Gawdy writes from London, "My Lo. of Sussex and Sr Mihill Stanhop haue agreede of a marriage to be presently solemnysed. My Lo. assureth all his land but ij^c [£200] a yeare to my Lo. Fitzwalter, and Sr Mihill Stanhop gyuethe his daughter vijc^{li} [£700] a yeare in present and viijc^{li} [£800] a yeare more in reuersion."[57] According to Lawrence Stone, the average portion given for peers' daughters was about £2,000 in the 1580s and 1590s but rose to £3,800 by 1603, with wealthier gentry, lawyers, and merchants giving £2,500 to £3,000.[58] For example, Margaret Denton, oldest daughter of a powerful Buckinghamshire family, brought £2,300 to the Verneys when she married the only son, Sir Edmund, in 1612.[59] More modestly, the dowry of £700 that Joan Churchman's father provided at her wedding to Richard Hooker became the core of the couple's financial security and formed a substantial part of the £1,100 estate Hooker left at his death.[60]

[53] Robert Greene, "The Repentance of Robert Greene," in *The Life and Complete Works*, ed. Alexander B. Grosart (1881–1883; reprint, New York: Russell and Russell, 1964), 12:177.

[54] John Cordy Jeaffreson, *Brides and Bridals* (London: Hurst and Blackett, 1872), 1:215.

[55] Catherine Drinker Bowen, *The Lion and the Throne: The Life and Times of Sir Edward Coke (1552–1634)* (Boston: Little, Brown, 1957), p. 71; Lu Emily Pearson, *Elizabethans at Home* (Stanford, CA: Stanford University Press, 1957), pp. 325–326.

[56] George C. Williamson, *Lady Anne Clifford* (Kendal: Titus Wilson, 1922), p. 456.

[57] Philip Gawdy, *Letters of Philip Gawdy*, ed. Isaac Herbert Jeayes (London: J. B. Nichols and Sons, 1906), p. 176. See also Searle, *Barrington*, p. 235, for a similar report.

[58] Stone, *Crisis*, pp. 638–642. Cooper, "Patterns," p. 307, sets the figures slightly higher but indicates that the daughters of knights and London merchants had portions averaging £859 for the years 1551–1600, p. 311.

[59] Miriam Slater, *Family Life in the Seventeenth Century: The Verneys of Claydon House* (London: Routledge and Kegan Paul, 1984), pp. 7, 150n.9.

[60] C. J. Sisson, *The Judicious Marriage of Mr. Hooker and the Birth of The Laws of Ecclesi-*

As those who warned against marriage to widows and against overlarge jointures realized, the death of a husband could mire families in serious problems. On the one hand, some spouses were left with insufficient resources. Lady Mary Wroth, for example, found herself in 1614 with a jointure of £1,200 to defray debts of £23,000 and support an infant son. When the child died in 1616, all his inheritance went to an uncle.[61] Furthermore, some wills stripped a widow of her possessions should she remarry. Richard Hudson allowed "His wife to enjoy his inn aforesaid, with kine, cattle, household stuff, &c., for two years after his decease, provided she remain unmarried and behave herself well."[62] But a far more common complaint than that of inadequate provision or the threat of disinheritance at remarriage was the lament that estates were being impoverished by the drain of jointure or dower rights. At his father's death, Henry Percy had to "pass to yowr grandmouther, for part of her jointer, all the western lands; whereby she receaved more fynes in her lyfe tyme, being but 120[lb] yearely, then I did of all the lands I had in England besides; I paing the rest of her jointer by equall portions yearely."[63] By such means the older generation benefited at the expense of the younger.

Arrangements for dowry and dower inevitably impinged upon crucial aspects of society. Not only did the agreed-on sums enable married couples and widows to live in some degree of comfort, but the amounts also quantified the status of the individuals involved. The payments were nicely calculated to maintain one's position or to move it up or down.[64] It is no accident that 32 percent of the new peers created in James's reign had married heiresses during Elizabeth's reign.[65] Nor is it unusual that mar-

---

astical Polity (Cambridge: Cambridge University Press, 1940), p. 24. For other settlements, see Searle, *Barrington*, pp. 84, 103, 119, 124.n, 171, 181; Cooper, "Patterns," pp. 210, 216, 217, 219, 306–312.

[61] Retha M. Warnicke, *Women of the English Renaissance and Reformation* (Westport, CT: Greenwood Press, 1983), p. 192.

[62] *Calendar of Wills Proved and Enrolled in the Court of Husting, London, 1258–1688*, ed. Reginald R. Sharpe (London: Corporation of the City of London, 1890), 2:698. See also F. G. Emmison, *Elizabethan Life: Home, Work, and Land, from Essex Wills and Sessions and Manorial Records* (Chelmsford: Essex County Council, 1976), p. 101; Howell, "Peasant Inheritance," pp. 141–143; Spufford, *Contrasting Communities*, p. 113.

[63] Percy, "Instructions," p. 321.

[64] See, e.g., the work of Amussen, *Ordered Society*, and David Underdown, *Revel, Riot and Rebellion: Popular Politics and Culture in England 1603–1660* (Oxford: Clarendon Press, 1985), for assessments of the way property and marriage functioned to regulate social status.

[65] Stone, *Crisis*, pp. 176–177, 617, 627. The proportion of the aristocracy who married heiresses, 1600–1629, jumped to 43 percent.

ginal individuals, like impoverished younger sons of good birth, either had to find wives with money or perhaps forgo matrimony altogether. And quite beyond the function of establishing status, marital finances also operated as an index of independence. So long as the terms of the portion or the living allowance or the inheritance or the jointure had not been set, children, regardless of age, remained subject to parental control. At their leisure and pleasure, fathers could determine their offspring's future, the ultimate threat being outright refusal to provide a share of the estate. At the same time, parents had to strike a balance among the rights of their children (especially if there were many), the claims of elders for support, and the need to maintain themselves adequately until they died. The entire system represented a transfer of power between generations that emphasized postmortem rather than premortem distribution.[66] Hence the extraordinary freedom of widows and unmarried adult heirs whose fathers were deceased is rooted in their independent control of possessions that had passed to them through death. For others, the very means of maintaining life could rest with goods and income controlled by others.

Nothing in courtship affronts modern sensibilities quite so much as the insistence that an exchange of money accompany an exchange of vows.[67] Yet an Elizabethan or Jacobean could hardly ignore such matters, fixed as they were into the matrix of existence. The constant references to dowries, portions, jointures, and dowers give ample evidence that Shakespeare's plays recognize the financial basis on which marriages rested. The language ranges from *Love's Labour's Lost*'s designation of Aquitaine as "a dowry for a queen" (II.i.8) to the observation of *Lear*'s Fool that "The codpiece that will house / Before the head has any, / The head and he shall louse, / So beggars marry many" (Q sc. 9 and F III.ii.27–30). Indeed, those instances where courtship onstage proceeds wholly without regard to wealth represent very special cases. In two of the middle comedies, not only is rank taken lightly, but so are practical questions of portions and jointures. When Maria devises the letter that deceives Malvolio, Sir Toby swears, "I could marry this wench for this device. . . . And ask no other dowry with her but such another jest" (*TN*, II.v.175, 177–178). That he later fulfills the oath, despite his admitted improvidence, underlines the carnival freedom of *Twelfth Night*, where both a duke and a countess also

---

[66] See Goody, "Inheritance," p. 25 and passim.

[67] For critics who do consider such matters in their social context, see David Bergeron, *Shakespeare's Romances and the Royal Family* (Lawrence: University Press of Kansas, 1985), pp. 76–77; Fitz, " 'What Says' "; Laurence Lerner, *Love and Marriage: Literature and Its Social Context* (New York: St. Martin's Press, 1979), pp. 61–62.

wed with scant concern for the wealth or status of their spouses. In *As You Like It*, Rosalind jokes about her lover's poverty, saying a snail "carries his house on his head—a better jointure, I think, than you make a woman" (IV.i.52–53). Yet despite Arden's frivolities, at the end of the wedding comes the good news that Rosalind and Orlando will share "a potent dukedom," while the restoration of Oliver's estate brings "your land, and love, and great allies" (V.iv.167, 187). Not even in comic fictions do married folk live on love alone, although the festive worlds of *Twelfth Night* and *As You Like It* downplay the importance of wealth in affairs of the heart.

Other comedies accept the monetary aspects of courtship in ways that can either elude or outrage modern critics. For example, in *A Comedy of Errors*, Luciana advises her supposed brother-in-law, "If you did wed my sister for her wealth, / Then for her wealth's sake use her with more kindness" (III.ii.5–6).[68] And in *A Midsummer Night's Dream*, Theseus compares the delay of his marriage with Hippolyta "to a stepdame or a dowager / Long withering out a young man's revenue" (I.i.5–6), a situation that commonly enforced postponement of matrimony. Conversely, the expectation of inheritance expedites Lysander's proposed elopement with Hermia: "I have a widow aunt, a dowager / Of great revenue, and she hath no child, / And she respects me as her only son" (157–159). Of wealthy widows like Lysander's aunt, who were proverbial targets for matrimony, Shakespeare makes curiously little use. Though several women take a second husband—or even a ninth, as does Mistress Overdone—scant mention of their riches appears. Timon bitterly claims that her gold "makes the wappered widow wed again" (*Tim.*, IV.iii.38). Yet Edward IV marries the impoverished Lady Gray, a "distressèd widow" (*R3*, III.vii.175). Only Hortensio in *The Taming of the Shrew* decides, "I will be married to a wealthy widow / Ere three days pass, which hath . . . long loved me" (IV.ii.37–38)—a decision he will come to regret. Such casual references as those just cited can easily be overlooked, but when Shakespeare offers more obvious examples of wealth's allure for would-be wooers, he provokes a fundamental disjuncture between past and present assumptions. Hence, Claudio, Fenton, Bassanio, and Petruccio have all been denounced as fortune hunters even though their behavior was standard practice among non-fictional gentlemen of similar rank and in similar circumstances.[69]

[68] Peter G. Phialas, *Shakespeare's Romantic Comedies: The Development of Their Form and Meaning* (Chapel Hill: University of North Carolina Press, 1966), p. 12, showing no comprehension of Elizabethan law regarding dowry, contends that Adriana "may still control and even repossess that dowry, that is, take back what she has given."

[69] For example, Richard A. Levin, *Love and Society in Shakespearean Comedy* (Newark:

A courtier, like Claudio in *Much Ado*, cannot expect to maintain the costs of serving as a prince's officer in war or peace, much less assume the expenses for his own household, without considerable wealth. Thus, despite his attraction to Hero, the suitor's first question must be, "Hath Leonato any son, my lord?" Only with the reassuring answer, "No child but Hero. She's his only heir" (I.i.277–278), does he proceed to ask for Don Pedro's approval and the lady's consent.[70] Claudio's entirely conventional wooing, however crass it seems now, receives support from the prince, together with a promise of riches from Leonato: "Count, take of me my daughter, and with her my fortunes" (II.i.283–284). That her betrothed must move to a deeper faith in Hero is clear enough from the ensuing events, but even during his final penance he is not compelled to marry a penniless bride. Instead, Leonato decrees:

> My brother hath a daughter,
> Almost the copy of my child that's dead,
> And she alone is heir to both of us.
> Give her the right you should have giv'n her cousin,
> And so dies my revenge.[71]

(V.i.280–284)

University of Delaware Press, 1985), p. 25, sees the marriages of Bassanio and Claudio as "a betrayal of affection for self-interest." Charles Frey, " 'O sacred, shadowy, cold, and constant queen': Shakespeare's Imperiled and Chastening Daughters of Romance," in *The Woman's Part: Feminist Criticism of Shakespeare*, ed. Carolyn Lenz, Gayle Greene, Carol Thomas Neely (Urbana: University of Illinois Press, 1980), p. 295, does not think highly of " 'lovers' greedy for dowry (suitors of Kate, Portia, and Anne Fenton [*sic*]; Angelo in *MM*; Burgundy in *Lear*)." More charitably, Paul N. Siegel, *Shakespeare in His Time and Ours* (Notre Dame, IN: University of Notre Dame Press, 1968), pp. 166–168, 171, calls characters like Fenton, Bassanio, Orlando, or Sebastian "male Cinderellas."

[70] Robert Ornstein, *Shakespeare's Comedies: From Roman Farce to Romantic Mystery* (Newark: University of Delaware Press, 1986), p. 123, thinks Claudio's inquiry shows "sensible concern" and parallels it with Benedick's soliloquy about the perfect wife, who will be rich—"that's certain." Kenneth Muir, *Shakespeare's Comic Sequence* (New York: Barnes and Noble, 1979), p. 75, points out that only a single line shows Claudio's interest in any dowry, as does Alexander Leggatt, *Shakespeare's Comedy of Love* (London: Methuen, 1974), p. 155. Bertrand Evans, *Shakespeare's Comedies* (Oxford: Clarendon Press, 1960), pp. 80–86, reaches the acme of revulsion for Claudio. See also Levin, *Love and Society*, p. 92; David Omerod, "Faith and Fashion in 'Much Ado About Nothing,' " *Shakespeare Survey* 25 (1972): 102; Margaret Loftus Ranald, " 'As Marriage Binds, and Blood Breaks': English Marriage and Shakespeare," *Shakespeare Quarterly* 30 (1979): 74, and *Shakespeare and His Social Context* (New York: AMS Press, 1987), p. 14.

[71] According to Ranald, " 'As Marriage Binds,' " p. 76, Leonato's reference to money here is a twist of the knife designed to punish Claudio further.

How fitting that Claudio, who has wooed by proxy rather than face-to-face, who has relied on the evidence of his eyes rather than his heart, should have to take a wife sight unseen. At least with Hero, his affection precedes assurances of her wealth. Now, in comic comeuppance, the "substitute" bride's wealth is all he knows of her; he must blindly accept whatever temperament, beauty, or virtue she possesses. Yet many an Elizabethan courtier might gladly have entered such a rich marriage, even without the unexpected resurrection of a lost love.

The Merchant of Venice also offers a couple whose marriage requires money and whose behavior has occasioned severe condemnation.[72] When Lorenzo steals Jessica from Shylock's house, he also takes the "gold and jewels she is furnished with" (II.iv.31). From her window she calls, "Here, catch this casket. It is worth the pains," and before descending she goes to "make fast the doors, and gild myself / With some more ducats" (II.vi.33, 49–50). The word "casket" sets up an obvious affinity between Jessica and Portia, one of whose caskets contains a fortune far greater than the Jew's ducats. While the play firmly establishes Lorenzo's love for Jessica, her theft of gold and jewels distresses many. Yet a young gentleman like Lorenzo (or Bassanio) cannot afford to marry a bride with no dowry. What Jessica takes is some part of the portion that Shylock would unquestionably have denied her for this union. Though one may object to the prodigal use the runaway lovers make of the purloined portion—fourscore ducats spent in a single night, a ring exchanged for a monkey—the need for money in marriage, as in every other aspect of life, is insistently affirmed in this play's language and action. Since Shylock and Antonio both abruptly discover they cannot exist without their riches, why should Jessica and Lorenzo, or Bassanio, be any different? In *The Merchant of Venice* all fortunes are problematical. What the Jew can "Fast bind, fast find"

---

[72] Even defenders of Jessica and Lorenzo have misgivings. Leggatt, *Shakespeare's Comedy*, p. 125, wants to interpret the ducats as symbolic of Jessica's transfer of love from her father to her husband but thinks the casket and the second trip for more money throw "the focus on the literal wealth she is stealing." Joseph Westlund, *Shakespeare's Reparative Comedies: A Psychoanalytic View of the Middle Plays* (Chicago: University of Chicago Press, 1984), p. 25, cannot understand why she takes money and jewels "in a world where Antonio and Portia dispense money so lavishly," unless she "cannot be sure of how to get along once she elopes." The audience would never expect the couple to rely on Antonio and Portia for support, although the former generously obtains an inheritance for them, while the latter offers them hospitality. Ranald, *Shakespeare and His Social Context*, pp. 69–70, almost alone recognizes that these "impulsive, romantic rule-breakers" take the casket in lieu of a dowry, though they are still "guilty of material theft."

(II.v.53) is subject to theft and profligate dispersal. And the immense portion of Portia (her very name echoing her bridal wealth), clutched from beyond the grave by her father, is subject to seizure and dispensation by a son-in-law whom he cannot—and perhaps would not—personally choose.

For Shylock's daughter and son-in-law, a final piece of good fortune comes at the hands of Antonio. At the trial, when the Jew's possessions are confiscated, half to the state and half to his intended victim, Antonio makes this proposal:

> So please my lord the Duke and all the court
> To quit the fine for one half of his goods,
> I am content, so he will let me have
> The other half in use, to render it
> Upon his death unto the gentleman
> That lately stole his daughter.
> Two things provided more: that for this favour
> He presently become a Christian;
> The other, that he do record a gift
> Here in the court of all he dies possessed
> Unto his son, Lorenzo, and his daughter.
>
> (IV.i.377–387)

In the furor over Shylock's enforced conversion, few notice that Antonio is equally concerned to enforce Shylock's paternal obligations. He assures for Jessica the inheritance to which she is entitled, with himself as trustee for half her wealth.[73]

Significantly, the merchant does not convert any of this wealth to a living allowance for the couple—the traditional obligation of the groom or his family. Instead, Antonio will invest the money as he has done in the past, the phrase "in use" again aligning himself and the Jew.[74] Though

---

[73] Among the few who even note what Jessica and Lorenzo get are Philip Edwards, *Shakespeare: A Writer's Progress* (Oxford: Oxford University Press, 1986), p. 102; Joan Ozark Holmer, "Loving Wisely and the Casket Test," *Shakespeare Studies* 11 (1978): 66; Richard P. Wheeler, *Shakespeare's Development and the Problem Comedies: Turn and Counter-Turn* (Berkeley: University of California Press, 1981), p. 173.

[74] Levin, *Love and Society*, p. 76, is convinced that "in use" means Antonio may be charging interest. When Levin subsequently, p. 84, credits Portia with being generous to Jessica and Lorenzo at Shylock's expense, he ignores Antonio's role in the transaction. So do Lynda E. Boose, "The Comic Contract and Portia's Golden Ring," *Shakespeare Studies* 20 (1988): 246; Herbert S. Donow, "Shakespeare's Caskets: Unity in *The Merchant of Venice*," *Shakespeare Studies* 4 (1968): 92; Marvin Felheim and Philip Traci, *Realism in Shake-*

both men will eventually give equal sums to Lorenzo and Jessica, Shylock does not yield his half until death, but her benefactor must hand over his amount whenever that event occurs. So Antonio establishes himself a second time as a father-substitute, just as he has already done in bearing the costs of his kinsman Bassanio's wooing.[75] Like any careful parent at a daughter's marriage, he legally guarantees what should eventually be hers, thereby becoming a co-father with Shylock.[76] Lorenzo has willingly married Jessica without hope of her inheritance. Hence it is truly "manna in the way / Of starvèd people" when Nerissa brings this news to Belmont: "There do I give to you and Jessica / From the rich Jew a special deed of gift, / After his death, of all he dies possessed of" (V.i.294–295, 291–293). Thus are the financial considerations confronting any contract of matrimony appropriately woven into the monetary texture of a play that presses questions about value, risk, commitment, mercy, justice, love, and law.

Unquestionably the comedy confronting the issue of money most directly is *The Taming of the Shrew*.[77] No nonsense here about affection pre-

---

speare's Romantic Comedies: "O Heavenly Mingle" (Washington, DC: University Press of America, 1980), pp. 122–123; David M. Sundelson, *Shakespeare's Restorations of the Father* (New Brunswick, NJ: Rutgers University Press, 1983), p. 85. C. L. Barber, *Shakespeare's Festive Comedy: A Study of Dramatic Form and Its Relation to Social Custom* (1959; reprint, New York: World Publishing Company, 1968), p. 187, gives the credit to the Venetian court; Diane Elizabeth Dreher, *Domination and Defiance: Fathers and Daughters in Shakespeare* (Lexington: University Press of Kentucky, 1986), p. 63, gives it to Venetian law.

[75] Steven Mullaney, "Brothers and Others, or the Art of Alienation," in *Cannibals, Witches, and Divorce*, ed. Marjorie Garber (Baltimore: Johns Hopkins University Press, 1987), p. 79, notes that in the source Antonio is Bassanio's adoptive father. David Sundelson, "The Dynamics of Marriage in *The Merchant of Venice*," *Humanities in Society* 4 (1981): 249, sees Portia transforming Antonio into "a good father, compliant now and rather childlike," to replace her own more intransigent father. Dreher, *Domination*, p. 135, recognizes Antonio's fatherly role but in confused terms: "He has financed Bassanio's courtship, providing, as it were, a dowry." Only women got dowries.

[76] Austin C. Dobbins and Roy W. Battenhouse, "Jessica's Morals: A Theological View," *Shakespeare Studies* 9 (1976): 107, think Jessica's inheritance "implies a hearty approval of the marriage." For dissents, see Shirley Nelson Garner, "Shylock: 'His stones, his daughter, and his ducats,' " *The Upstart Crow* 5 (1984): 45; Jonathan Goldberg, "Shakespearean Inscriptions: The Voicing of Power," in *Shakespeare and the Question of Theory*, ed. Patricia Parker and Geoffrey Hartman (New York: Methuen, 1985), p. 123.

[77] For other monetary analyses of the play's action, see George R. Hibbard, "*The Taming of the Shrew*: A Social Comedy," in *Shakespearean Essays*, ed. Alwin Thaler and Norman Sanders (Knoxville: University of Tennessee Press, 1964); idem, ed., *The Taming of the Shrew* (Baltimore, MD: Penguin Books, 1967), pp. 31–32; Margaret Loftus Ranald, "The

ceding or at least tempering the allure of riches. As Petruccio candidly announces, "I come to wive it wealthily in Padua; / If wealthily, then happily in Padua" (I.ii.74–75). His declaration marks him not as a base fortune hunter but as a man who cuts right through the superficialities to the substance of marriage negotiations.[78] His father being dead, Petruccio can choose any wife he pleases and enjoy unrestricted use of her portion. Some wooers shun Kate "though her father be very rich," because "any man is so very a fool to be married to hell" (I.i.122–124). Nevertheless, "there be good fellows . . . would take her with all her faults, and money enough" (126–129). And such a one is Petruccio. Gremio cynically claims, "Why give him gold enough and marry him to a puppet or an aglet-baby, or an old trot with ne'er a tooth in her head" (I.ii.77–79). Yet it is shortsighted of Hortensio to protest that despite Kate's youth, her beauty, her excellent upbringing, and her fortune, he "would not wed her for a mine of gold" (91). "Thou know'st not gold's effect," sensibly replies Petruccio. "Tell me her father's name and 'tis enough" (92–93).

However mercenary it seems today, Petruccio's courtship follows a highly conventional procedure, exaggerated enough to make it amusing but perilously close to actual experience. Having located, sight unseen, "One rich enough to be Petruccio's wife" (66), the suitor must now negotiate financial terms with Kate's father—who turns out to be a family acquaintance. The unexpected wooer comes straight to the point with Baptista.

> PETRUCCIO. You knew my father well, and in him me,
> Left solely heir to all his lands and goods,
> Which I have bettered rather than decreased.
> Then tell me, if I get your daughter's love,
> What dowry shall I have with her to wife?
> BAPTISTA. After my death the one half of my lands,
> And in possession twenty thousand crowns.
> PETRUCCIO. And for that dowry I'll assure her of
> Her widowhood, be it that she survive me,

Manning of the Haggard; or *The Taming of the Shrew*," *Essays in Literature* 1 (1974): 154; idem, *Shakespeare and His Social Context*, p. 121.

[78] John Weld, *Meaning in Comedy: Studies in Elizabethan Romantic Comedy* (Albany: State University of New York Press, 1975), p. 178, is among those who think "Petruchio, by his own assertion, is led by avarice," though later Weld tries to reverse himself. Hugh Richmond, *Shakespeare's Sexual Comedy: A Mirror for Lovers* (New York: Bobbs-Merrill, 1971), p. 99, refers to Petruccio's "mercenary egotism."

In all my lands and leases whatsoever.
Let specialties be therefore drawn between us,
That covenants may be kept on either hand.
BAPTISTA. Ay, when the special thing is well obtained—
That is her love, for that is all in all.

(II.i.116–129)

Among other things, this conversation reveals Petruccio to be a capable manager of money, having already enlarged his inheritance and now seeking to enlarge his wealth still further with Kate's dowry. If widowed, she can enjoy the income from his property during her lifetime, but the estate itself is secured for his heirs, rather than any subsequent husband or children of Kate's. In return, Petruccio gets a fortune in ready money—twenty thousand crowns amounting to five thousand pounds,[79] more than double the sum most peers offered with their daughters—and the prospect of half Baptista's lands unless he should predecease his father-in-law.[80] Petruccio's call for "specialties" to seal such a splendid bargain refers to a legal instrument usually employed to secure a debt that might otherwise be repudiated.[81] While the word perhaps emphasizes the suitor's awareness of good terms he wants guaranteed before Baptista can reconsider, it may also indicate the wooer's awareness that Kate's father will want to clinch the agreement before Petruccio can renege.

As for getting Kate's love, Baptista seems motivated less by concern for

[79] For the equivalence of crowns to pounds, see Sandra K. Fischer, *Econolingua: A Glossary of Coins and Economic Language in Renaissance Drama* (Newark: University of Delaware Press, 1985), who says a crown equaled 5*s*., a ducat 9*s*. if in gold, and (by 1610) an angel 11*s*., pp. 63, 69, 41.

[80] Coppélia Kahn, "*The Taming of the Shrew*: Shakespeare's Mirror of Marriage," *Modern Language Studies* 5 (1975): 91, claims that, for Baptista, Kate's and Bianca's "marriages provide insurance against having to support his daughters in widowhood, promise grandsons to whom he may pass on the management and possession of his property." However, jointure is a matter of negotiation precisely because widows were the responsibility of the groom's family, not the bride's. Moreover, Baptista leaves half his estate directly to Kate, not her children. Lisa Jardine, *Still Harping on Daughters: Women and Drama in the Age of Shakespeare* (Totowa, NJ: Barnes and Noble, 1983), p. 60, denounces Petruccio as "a fortune-hunting rascal, supported by *her* fine dowry," ignoring his inherited wealth. She wrongly asserts that if the husband died first, his wife's dowry reverted to her family or else could be willed to her children, p. 80. Ranald, *Shakespeare and His Social Context*, p. 121, gratuitously speculates that Kate "might be able to use her jointure to remarry and improve her social position," but Petruccio's health seems sound, his status in no way demeaning.

[81] Stone, *Crisis*, p. 514.

her wishes than by fear of her temper. Of his favorite, Bianca, he says,
" 'Tis deeds must win the prize, and he of both / That can assure my
daughter greatest dower / Shall have my Bianca's love" (338–340). Without regard for the girl's wishes or consent, he treats her love as a possession
that is his to bestow and proceeds to auction her off to the highest bidder.[82]
While Petruccio has bought an apparently flawed "commodity" (324), the
suitors for Bianca drive the price up and up for what appears to be a perfect
piece of wifely merchandise. Incredibly, they ask for no dowry, and Baptista offers none. Though presumably Bianca, like Kate, would get half
his lands at her father's death, he never mentions such an inheritance.[83]
Instead, the auction centers on what each candidate bids as a dower, or
jointure, for Bianca's widowhood. Old Gremio first promises his city
house with all its rich furnishings and many chests filled with crowns,
together with his farm and its six hundred milk cows and six score oxen.
"Myself am struck in years, I must confess, / And if I die tomorrow this is
hers, / If whilst I live she will be only mine" (356–358). The reckless
Tranio, disguised as his master Lucentio, offers three or four houses just
as good, besides two thousand ducats (four hundred pounds) a year in land.
When the desperate Gremio adds his argosy of ships, Tranio throws in
three argosies, "two galliasses / And twelve tight galleys" (374–375),
vowing to double anything Gremio might pledge next. His rival yields:
"Nay, I have offered all. I have no more, / And she can have no more than
all I have" (377–378). Even modern audiences enjoy the auction, reveling
in the joke that Tranio's bid is mere bluff. But what Shakespeare's audience would also have seen is a bankrupting jointure for a bride with no
formal promise of dowry.

A further problem besets the offer of Tranio/Lucentio. Unlike Petruccio, this young man has a father who controls all the family assets. The
careful Baptista therefore insists, "And let your father make her the assurance, / She is your own. Else, you must pardon me, / If you should die
before him, where's her dower?" (383–385). Bianca will be married to

---

[82] Irene G. Dash, *Wooing, Wedding and Power: Women in Shakespeare's Plays* (New York:
Columbia University Press, 1981), p. 53, is among those who flatly call both marriages
an auction of daughters, as is Leggatt, *Shakespeare's Comedy*, p. 47, though he recognizes
its conventionality. Weld, *Meaning*, p. 179, and Dreher, *Domination*, p. 8, find Baptista
"money-loving" and "mercenary," although all profits go to his daughters at considerable
cost to himself.

[83] Petruccio alone says Bianca has a "dowry wealthy" (IV.vi.66). Jardine, *Still Harping*,
p. 100n.39, claims Baptista "has already promised Bianca a handsome dowry" before the
auction.

Lucentio only "if you make this assurance; / If not, to Signior Gremio" (392–393). At these words Gremio takes heart: "Sirrah, young gamester, your father were a fool / To give thee all, and in his waning age / Set foot under thy table" (396–398). And he is right. No father, whether Italian or English, would have affirmed the settlement Tranio proposes, nor would he (like Lear) have relinquished his estate before death. But then the scheming Tranio simply supplies a bogus parent with no such sensible scruples: "And he shall be Vincentio of Pisa, / And make assurance here in Padua / Of greater sums than I have promisèd" (III.iii.6–8). In the scene between the substitute father and Baptista, the two men do not even discuss specific terms, as does Petruccio. The pseudo-parent asks for no portion, makes no inquiry into Bianca's inheritance, and agrees to "a sufficient dower" (IV.iv.44) without questioning what Tranio has pledged. Instead, the fathers simply send for a scrivener and Bianca so that the agreement can be signed "privately and well" (56).[84]

Shakespeare's merry but merciless exposure of the matrimonial market takes a different turn when Bianca elopes with no thought for the fortune Baptista is so keen to obtain for her.[85] By omitting altogether the stage of financial negotiations, she and Lucentio risk their future security. Legally, Vincentio is not obliged to make the couple a living allowance, to designate his son as his heir, or to provide a jointure for Bianca should she be widowed. Nor does Baptista have to supply a dowry. In this comedy the bride and groom simply kneel to obtain pardon. But certainly, while Shakespeare may be laughing at marriage-for-money-and-never-mind-love, he is also laughing at marriage-for-love-and-never-mind-money.[86]

---

[84] Ernest Pettet, *Shakespeare and the Romance Tradition* (New York: Staples Press, 1949), pp. 72–74, though recognizing the economic and social priorities of marriage here and seeing Lucentio as "quite regardless of fortunes and marriage contracts," nonetheless thinks the Pedant (the stand-in Vincentio) and the contract are pointless.

[85] Among those who see the Bianca-Lucentio elopement as a triumph of romantic love over commercial haggling are Carol F. Heffernan, "*The Taming of the Shrew*: The Bourgeoisie in Love," *Essays in Literature* 12 (1985): 8–9; Phialas, *Shakespeare's Romantic Comedies*, pp. 28–30. Leggatt, *Shakespeare's Comedy*, p. 48, thinks Lucentio "has won a conventional sweetheart in a conventional way" but feels that "when the prize turns out to have been a baited trap, not merely the character but the convention he has operated under are mocked." Dreher, *Domination*, p. 109, apparently accepting Tranio's boasts at face value, claims that Bianca rejects Hortensio for Lucentio, "the wealthiest suitor."

[86] According to Juliet Dusinberre, *Shakespeare and the Nature of Women* (New York: Barnes and Noble, 1975), p. 123, "When dramatists uphold the love match against the mercenary marriage, *as they unfailingly do* [italics mine], they uphold women's values

After all, in the final scene the lovesick Lucentio literally loses money on his bride, while the hardheaded Petruccio wins his bet and more. In language consistent with the monetary-marital fabric of the play, Baptista observes:

> The wager thou hast won, and I will add
> Unto their losses twenty thousand crowns,
> Another dowry to another daughter,
> For she is changed as she had never been.
>
> (V.ii.117–120)

Kate's triumph—and her superior value as woman, wife, daughter—is expressed in the terms most appropriate to the comic action.

No other play explores the implications of dowries and dowers so bluntly as *The Taming of the Shrew*. However, these financial issues often function in other significant ways. For example, the plot of *Measure for Measure* revolves around the status of two portions. Claudio and Juliet keep secret their sexual union

> Only for propagation of a dower
> Remaining in the coffer of her friends,
> From whom we thought it meet to hide our love
> Till time had made them for us.
>
> (I.ii.138–141)

The control of her portion by "friends" means that Juliet's parents are dead and that matrimonial decisions thus lie with her guardians. Claudio too is obviously parentless, since he has only his sister to plead his case and he has made a match for himself. His wife's dowry thus assumes increased importance because it would come directly to him rather than to his father. No matter how much he loves his intended bride, Claudio would be foolish to sacrifice one of the chief advantages of his marriage, though his financial prudence certainly does not excuse his sexual imprudence.[87] Mariana and Angelo present a rather different situation. After her portion had been agreed on,

---

against men's." I find her generalization impossible to reconcile with Shakespeare's subtlety in treating this issue, especially in *Shr.*'s reversals of expectation.

[87] Westlund, *Shakespeare's Reparative Comedies*, p. 161, considers the liaison the lovers' ability "to adjust their wishes to the demands of reality (the need for a dowry, the hope that her 'friends' will drop their opposition, and the quasi-legal status of their secret marriage)." Alan Sinfield, *Literature in Protestant England, 1560–1660* (London: Croom Helm, 1983), p. 72, recognizes the "friends" of Juliet as her kinsmen.

her brother Frederick was wrecked at sea, having in that perished vessel the dowry of his sister. . . . There she lost a noble and renowned brother, . . . with him, the portion and sinew of her fortune, her marriage dowry; with both, her combinate husband. . . . [Angelo] swallowed his vows whole, pretending in her discoveries of dishonour; in few, bestowed her on her own lamentation, which she yet wears for his sake. (III.i.217–224, 227–231)

Money, or rather the lack of money, is the critical issue in both these situations. Neither Claudio nor Angelo wants a bride who brings less than her full price, yet each winds up accepting a wife "devalued" through his sexual involvement with her. In the process, each man experiences public humiliation and very nearly loses his life. When Juliet's pregnancy becomes obvious, Claudio goes to prison and is sentenced to die, saved only by the duke's secret intervention and his providential substitution of Ragusine's head for Claudio's. Because of the duke's secret intervention and his providential substitution of Mariana's maidenhead for Isabella's, Angelo too faces public exposure and a death sentence but is reprieved. Yet his lust, like Claudio's, finally earns him a wife bereft of dowry. The duke offers Mariana a better chance in the marriage market with Angelo's estate: "For his possessions, / Although by confiscation they are ours, / We do enstate and widow you with all, / To buy you a better husband" (V.i.419–422). However, while the proffered fortune, representing both a widow's dower and a new dowry, is more generous than her original portion, Mariana refuses to buy a second husband with the life of the first.

The buying and selling of lives, wives, and female bodies stands at the core of *Measure for Measure*.[88] The pimps, whores, and bawds in the subplot merely engage more blatantly in the same business as do Angelo and Claudio.[89] This flesh trade inevitably cheapens and degrades the women involved: "The stealth of our most mutual entertainment / With character too gross is writ on Juliet" (I.ii.142–143); Mariana, already stained by "discoveries of dishonour," is instantly married at the duke's orders "else imputation, / For that he knew you, might reproach your life" (V.i.417–

---

[88] Among others, Marc Shell, *The End of Kinship: "Measure for Measure," Incest, and the Ideal of Universal Siblinghood* (Stanford, CA: Stanford University Press, 1988), p. 125, also makes this point. For further discussion of the play's monetary language, see R. J. Kaufman, "Bond Slaves and Counterfeits: Shakespeare's *Measure for Measure*," *Shakespeare Studies* 3 (1967): 89–96; Arthur C. Kirsch, "The Integrity of 'Measure for Measure,' " *Shakespeare Survey* 28 (1975): 99–100.

[89] For a broader discussion of this issue, see Gayle Rubin, "The Traffic in Women: Notes on the 'Political Economy' of Sex," in *Towards an Anthropology of Women*, ed. R. Rayna Reiter (New York: Monthly Review Press, 1975).

418). But the trafficking cheapens and degrades the men involved too, leading them to deceive and connive, generally with indifference toward the suffering of their female partners. In the final bargains, every husband gets less than he hoped for but more than he deserves, while the wives all move upward both financially and socially.[90] Lucio takes a destitute whore and a bastard son, Claudio a dowryless wife he has made pregnant, Angelo the deflowered dowryless bride he has scorned, and the duke a dowryless virgin who has yet to accept him. Though Lucio, Claudio, and Angelo may have to settle for blemished if ethically superior wives, they all escape death sentences. And while the duke may not have an immediate assent to his proposal of marriage, he at least escapes a blunt refusal from the abused Isabella. He has shed his guise as trickster-friar, and if she sheds hers as overstrict nun, they may both become responsible citizens in Vienna, observing the laws, setting a moral example, embracing legal marriage, and producing legitimate children—precisely what is demanded of the other couples. In the fulfillment of these obligations, money is a secondary matter.

Occasionally a Shakespearean play will use a matrimonial settlement to bribe agreement to a proposed match. For instance, when King John persuades Louis, the Dauphin of France, to marry his niece, Blanche of Spain, he makes an incredible offer:[91]

> Her dowry shall weigh equal with a queen;
> For Anjou and fair Touraine, Maine, Poitou,
> And all that we upon this side the sea—
> Except this city now by us besieged—
> Find liable to our crown and dignity,
> Shall gild her bridal bed. . . .
>
> *(Jn.*, II.i.487–492)

Besides England's five French provinces, John also promises "thirty thousand marks of English coin" (531), so eager is he to seal this match and thus subvert Arthur's claims to the throne. In a comparable gesture, Timon of Athens assists his servant, Lucilius, to wed an heiress. Discovering

---

[90] Only John D. Cox, *Shakespeare and the Dramaturgy of Power* (Princeton: Princeton University Press, 1989), p. 155, reminds one not to overlook Kate Keepdown's "material improvement" by focusing on Lucio's punishment, though he does not note the similar improvement of the other female characters.

[91] Allan Lewis, "Shakespeare and the Morality of Money," *Social Research* 36 (1969): 382, says that "love is sold for real estate" in this transaction, though it is hard to see anything like genuine love here.

that the Athenian merchant will endow his child with "Three talents on the present; in future, all" (I.i.145), Timon responds, "Give him thy daughter. / What you bestow in him I'll counterpoise, / And make him weigh with her" (148–150). In effect, he pledges the equivalent of the father's lifetime of hard-won profits, a largesse pressing even Timon to confess that "To build his fortune I will *strain* a little" (147; italics mine).[92] However, excessive generosity, amounting to outright bribery, can provoke unpleasant results. In *King John*, the Bastard revolts when the spoils of England's conquests are so recklessly given away, and the marriage is no sooner solemnized than Philip breaks the peace to battle against the English once more. Nor does Lucilius show much lasting gratitude, though he vows, "Never may / That state or fortune fall into my keeping / Which is not owed to you" (I.i.153–155). When profligacy brings ruin, his favored servant, like everyone else, deserts Timon. It would seem that property settlements in marriage, regardless of the size, cannot alone buy allegiance or love or gratitude.

In a far more profound way, Shakespeare explores the reverse situation in *King Lear*. Here the denial of a marriage portion represents a break with family, custom, and society.[93] Lear's awful words, "Thy truth then be thy dower" (Q sc. 1, 101; F I.i.108), lose their force with modern audiences, who do not perceive the practical and symbolic value of the dowry. The king's subsequent curse of "my sometime daughter" seems clear enough:

> Here I disclaim all my paternal care,
> Propinquity, and property of blood,
> And as a stranger to my heart and me
> Hold thee from this for ever.
>
> (Q 113, 106–109; F 119, 113–116)

Yet the "dower," which Lear denies, defines Cordelia's identity as princess, daughter, woman. By erasing that, her father seeks to erase her very being, both as his child and as another man's wife. The problem is not just that the king's infantile desire to quantify everything leads him to withhold her promised portion, as if he can punish through subtracting sums of money or acres of land. It is also that the nuptial settlement extends the

---

[92] David Cook, "Timon of Athens," *Shakespeare Survey* 16 (1963): 88, believes that Timon's "brief replies to the Old Man . . . show immediate right feeling." H. J. Oliver, ed., *Timon of Athens*, Arden Shakespeare (London: Methuen, 1959), p. xliii, thinks the father "mercenary" and sees in Timon's action "nothing that is even open to criticism."

[93] For a very different interpretation of the significance of a dowryless Cordelia, see Dusinberre, *Shakespeare and the Nature of Women*, p. 125.

tangible evidence of any parent's existence from his own generation to the next, with a first payment due at the wedding and the remainder at his death. Because Cordelia's dowry is her share of the kingdom, its bestowal conflates the two points—her marriage and his mortality—at which a father should formally indicate paternity, approval, responsibility, and the passage of what he possesses to what he has begotten. By dis-owning a daughter, Lear denies that she belongs to him as well as that she is entitled to anything which does belong to him.[94]

In any family of means, the abrupt withdrawal of a daughter's rightful portion and inheritance would be shocking. But it is infinitely more outrageous to greet another sovereign as Lear does Burgundy, asking "what in the least / Will you require in present dower with her / Or cease your quest of love?" (Q 181–183; F 190–192). Confused but still polite, Burgundy responds, "Most royal Majesty, / I crave no more than hath your highness offered; / Nor will you tender less" (Q 183–185; F 192–194). Still, Lear continues his public humiliation of Cordelia before the court and both her royal suitors, stating bluntly that "her price is fallen" (Q 187; F 196), for she brings to marriage herself alone. "Will you, . . . Dowered with our curse and strangered with our oath / Take her or leave her?" (Q 192, 194–195: 194 reads "covered" for "dowered"; F 201, 203–204). In this most bizarre of all the matrimonial negotiations Shakespeare portrays, he distinctly spells out the position of each interested party, leaving no doubt as to the monetary terms of choice or refusal. Having assured himself that Cordelia bears "no vicious blot" (Q 219; F 227), France addresses his rival:

> Will you have her?
>
> She is herself a dowry.
>
> BURGUNDY. (*to Lear*)   Royal King,
> Give but that portion which yourself proposed,
> And here I take Cordelia by the hand,
> Duchess of Burgundy.

[94] Lynda E. Boose, "An Approach through Theme: Marriage and the Family," in *Approaches to Teaching Shakespeare's "King Lear,"* ed. Robert H. Ray (New York: Modern Language Association, 1986), p. 65, says that the dowry is "the material sign of a daughter's separateness from her family." However, here Lear's denial of dowry relegates her to solitary existence, rather than continued inclusion in his family. Since it passes directly from father to husband, the dowry is more properly a sign of the woman's separation from one family and incorporation into another, rather than a sign of independent status. Note Boose's landmark analysis of the ritual aspects of this scene in "The Father and Bride in Shakespeare," *PMLA* 97 (1982): 325–347.

LEAR. Nothing. I have sworn. I am firm.

BURGUNDY. (*to Cordelia*) I am sorry then you have so lost a father
That you must lose a husband.

CORDELIA.   Peace be with Burgundy;
Since that respect and fortunes are his love,
I shall not be his wife.

FRANCE. Fairest Cordelia, that art most rich, being poor;
Most choice, forsaken; and most loved, despised:
Thee and thy virtues here I seize upon.
Be it lawful, I take up what's cast away.
Gods, gods! 'Tis strange that from their cold'st neglect
My love should kindle to inflamed respect.—
Thy dowerless daughter, King, thrown to my chance,
Is queen of us, of ours, and our fair France.

(F 240–257; minimal differences in Q)

Considered in light of traditional marriage settlements among royalty, what happens here violates the accepted order quite as much as does Lear's premature disposal of his kingdom. Burgundy behaves like a prudent ruler, insisting upon the promised portion for his duchess. France's action more closely mirrors Lear's, in that he rashly takes Cordelia with nothing but her apparent virtues, just as Lear rashly dowers her with nothing but her apparent faults.[95] By giving away all his possessions on the one hand and on the other by claiming a queen with no possessions, each sovereign takes steps with serious political consequences, regardless of how noble or ignoble his decision may be. Ironically, the high-minded France, who marries for naught but "inflamed respect," soon sends out "servants . . . Which are to France the spies and speculations / Intelligent of our state" (F III.i.14–16).[96] On the basis of their reports, he dispatches troops to

[95] For opposing views of France's choice, see Stanley Cavell, *Disowning Knowledge: In Six Plays of Shakespeare* (New York: Cambridge University Press, 1987), p. 65; Ranald, *Shakespeare and His Social Context*, p. 216; Irving Singer, *The Nature of Love: Courtly and Romantic* (Chicago: University of Chicago Press, 1984), 2:232. Marjorie Garber, *Coming of Age in Shakespeare* (New York: Methuen, 1981), p. 121, agrees with my contention that France's decision "remains a most untypical point of view for an Elizabethan monarch," though she cautions about Shakespeare's ability to depart from convention, especially in matters of romantic love.

[96] The longer Q reading specifies:

> From France there comes a power
> Into this scattered kingdom, who already,
> Wise in our negligence, have secret feet

seize the kingdom on behalf of Cordelia even before Lear is cast out by Goneril and Regan. Hence that initial acceptance of a dowryless consort does not prevent the French king from claiming his rights as husband any more than the English king's resignation of his lands prevents him from insisting upon his privileges as ruler. Wars both civil and foreign, alienation, exile, and death all stem in part from the fateful denial of Cordelia's dowry.

No one in Shakespeare's world ever lived on love alone. From beggar or husbandman to merchant or prince, money provided all with the means of existence. And at those social levels where gentlemen did not work with their hands for a living, wealth in some form was necessary to continue living. Thus the arrangements for dowries and dowers, future inheritance and present income formed a critical part of courtship, for they determined one's standing in family and community. The plays of Shakespeare offer a wide range of approaches to the issue of money in marriage. Sometimes bridal portions are fancifully ignored, sometimes disastrously rejected; for some suitors, riches take precedence over love, while for others love outweighs fortune; some lovers get more wealth than they deserve, yet others are punished with less than they seek. And in the process Shakespeare explores a host of corollary issues—the price of a woman's body, the value of virtue, the calculation of a father's love, the worth of royal position, the cost of commitment. Thus the measurable sums of dowries and jointures are transformed to represent human relationships that can never be measured. It may be, too, that the uneasiness, even the contempt, some feel for a Bassanio or a Petruccio results not only from the modern aversion to marrying for money but also from a genuine ambivalence in the texts toward the Elizabethans' linkage of the matrimonial with the monetary. Nonetheless, viewing a concern for financial security negatively comes more easily to present-day society, where freedom (including the choice of a mate), personal happiness (especially in the guise of love), and prosperity (with remunerative labor readily available to the vast majority) are taken for granted—or at least idealized. Contemporary assumptions in this regard differ markedly from those familiar to Shakespeare. Steeped in his culture's presuppositions, he probes the complications attendant upon the

---

In some of our best ports, and are at point
To show their open banner.

(sc. 7, 21–25)

The Folio not only minimizes the French invasion but suppresses references to it in acts IV and V.

economics of courtship, adhering to no single position. Even when a plot hinges upon a technicality of portion or jointure, the effect is as likely to be critical as conventional. Merciless exposure in one play becomes blithe acceptance in the next. But without a grasp of the social codes involved, it is impossible to see the subtleties in Shakespeare's treatment of this vital aspect of wooing.

Formal Proposals, Public Contracts, and Proper Weddings

Newyears day: at night invited to supper to Goodman Gaynes: I
went in to call Goodwife shepheard, and their my Jane being I
stayed with her, which was our first proposall of the match to
one another, which wrought a mutuall promise one to another
Jan: 23: and by all our consents a Contract: Sept. 28 1640:
and our marriage. October 28. following.
                    —*The Diary of Ralph Josselin*

KING PHILIP. It likes us well.—Young princes, close your hands.
AUSTRIA. And your lips too, for I am well assured
    That I did so when I was first assured.
                    —*Jn.*, II.i.534–536

W HILE financial arrangements required particular attention, they
formed only one part of the courtship ritual. In the usual sequence
of events, the prospective couple met under properly supervised circumstances to see whether or not each could tolerate the other as husband or
wife. Upon reaching an accord, they then entered into a spousal pact, duly
witnessed, in which both parents and children gave formal consent to the
match upon mutually agreeable terms. The binding pledge to marry was
usually accompanied by an exchange of rings or other tokens and often by
the signing of a legal document specifying the financial commitments.
After a reading of the banns in the parish churches of the contracted couple
or the purchase of a license to dispense with banns, the wedding itself was
celebrated by a priest with others present. The formal ceremony then gave
way to feasting and celebration, highlighted by bedding the bride and
groom. At each stage of the mating dance, however, a complex set of
customs came into play.[1]

At the stage of acquaintanceship between the man and woman, for in-

---

[1] For discussions of these customs in works not cited elsewhere, see Gellert Spencer
Alleman, *Matrimonial Law and the Materials of Restoration Comedy* (Philadelphia: University
of Pennsylvania Press, 1942), pp. 5–35; Cumberland Clark, *Shakespeare and Home Life*
(London: Williams and Norgate, 1935), pp. 210–217.

stance, circumstances could range from a lifetime of familiarity to an exchange of letters or messages sent by proxy between persons who had never met. A thicket of restrictions hedged about any proposal not made face-to-face,[2] but, except for royal alliances, most affianced couples had at least seen one another to determine whether or not they felt "a mutuall liking."[3] Hence, John Stanhope, contemplating a union between one of his daughters and Lord Scrope's son, wrote of "a progress which he intendeth into Lancashire, where the young couples [*sic*] may see one another, and, after a little acquaintance, may resolve accordingly."[4] And one of Joan Meux's prospective suitors wanted "to have a sight of her privatly, with out any notice till approbation."[5] The literary tradition of love at first sight may have received cultural reinforcement in those social ranks where introduction to one's future spouse was sometimes restricted to a single visit. Love, or at least liking, had to be determined at first glance.

In certain instances, encounters seemed more than a mere formality. Sir Simonds D'Ewes, for example, visited a prospective candidate, "but finding her face rough and unpleasant, I could upon no terms affect her." Deep into negotiations for the hand of Anne Barnardiston, he recognized that the one remaining requirement for "an happy conclusion of the business" is "our mutual consents and likings upon an interview," and soon he was permitted "the full liberty of seeing and speaking with the young gentlewoman." Once she had accepted him, D'Ewes gave her a diamond necklace accompanied by an ardent letter, the only one he ever sent her "during my wooing-time."[6] At a lesser social level, when music master Thomas Why-

---

[2] Henry Swinburne, *A Treatise of Spousals, or Matrimonial Contracts* (London, 1686), pp. 162–166, 185–192.

[3] William Gouge, *Of Domesticall Duties* (London, 1622), p. 196.

[4] Sir Harris Nicolas, *Memoirs of the Life and Times of Sir Christopher Hatton* (London: Richard Bentley, 1847), p. 78; Lu Emily Pearson, *Elizabethans at Home* (Stanford, CA: Stanford University Press, 1957), p. 282. See also Steven W. May, "*A Midsummer Night's Dream* and the Carey-Berkeley Wedding," *Renaissance Papers 1983* (Raleigh, NC: Southeastern Renaissance Conference, 1984), p. 49.

[5] Arthur Searle, ed., *Barrington Family Letters, 1628–1632*, Camden Society Publications, 4th ser., 28 (1983): 181. See also Dorothy M. Meads, ed., *Diary of Lady Margaret Hoby, 1599–1605* (Boston: Houghton Mifflin, 1930), p. 28.

[6] Sir Simonds D'Ewes, *The Autobiography and Correspondence*, ed. James Orchard Halliwell (London: Richard Bentley, 1845), 1:311, 309, 313, 316. See also Linda A. Pollock, *A Lasting Relationship: Parents and Children over Three Centuries* (Hanover, NH: University Press of New England, 1987), p. 260; Allison D. Wall, ed., *Two Elizabethan Women: Correspondence of Joan and Maria Thynne, 1575–1611*, Wiltshire Record Society Publication 38 (1982): xix.

thorne courted a youthful heiress-pupil, he "furnished my self ⟨with⟩ kon-
venient apparrell and ʒiuels so well az I kowld (with þe gloriouz she⟨w⟩ of
þe which emong oþer things, A yoong mayden must be woed)." He also
sang "ij or iij prety ditties mạd of loov" to the accompaniment of virginal
or lute. Years later, again playing the role of a devoted suitor, Whythorne
made several visits to a widow, increasing their frequency when she complained "bekawz I kạm but ons in three daiez." He wrote her a sonnet,
professed love, shared a breakfast, and even had a ring engraved with "Ðe
eie doth fýnd, Ðe hart doth chooz And loov doth býnd. Til death doth
looz."[7] Nonetheless, the woman professed dissatisfaction with the ring and
rejected her wooer.

Such gifts and such behavior apparently formed the stock-in-trade of
hopeful candidates allowed access to eligible women. The literature of the
period refers to "Sutors with gifts" such as "Garters Kames, Purses, Gir-
dles, store of Rings, / And many a hundred daintie pretie things."[8] The
more severe frowned with suspicion on "pleasant wordes, with such smil-
yng and secret countenances, with such signes, tokens, wagers, purposed
to be lost, before they were purposed to be made, with bargaines of wearing colours, floures, and herbes, to breede occasion of after meeting of him
and her, and bolder talking of this and that &c."[9] Nonetheless, at least a
few suits proceeded quite openly with visits, letters, and presents. Among
country folk, once parental approval was obtained,

> the younge man goeth perhapps twice, to see howe the mayd standeth af-
> feckted; then if hee see that shee bee tractable, and that her inclination is
> towards him, then the third time that hee visiteth, hee perhapps giveth her
> a tenne shillinge peece of gold, or a ringe of that price; or perhapps a twenty
> shillinge peece, or a ringe of that price; then the next time, or next after that,
> a payre of gloves of 6s. 8d. or 10s. a payre; and after that, each other time,
> some conceited toy or novelty of less value. They visite usually every three

[7] James Osborn, ed., *The Autobiography of Thomas Whythorne* (Oxford: Clarendon Press,
1961), pp. 76–77, 187–188, 195.

[8] Samuel Rowlands, *Tis Merrie When Gossips Meete* (London, 1602), C3; idem, *A Whole
Crew of Kind Gossips, All Met to be Merry* (London, 1609), A4. See also Nicholas Breton, *An
Olde Mans Lesson, and a Young Mans Love* (London, 1605), E2; Angel Day, *The English
Secretary* (London, 1607), pp. 143–148; Thomas Dekker, "The Batchelors Banquet," in
The Non-Dramatic Works, ed. Alexander B. Grosart (1884; reprint, New York: Russell and
Russell, 1963), 1:248, 250; Henry Willoby, *Willobie his Avisa, or the True Picture of a
Modest Maid, and a Chast and Constant Wife* (London, 1594), p. 21. For a full discussion of
lovers' tokens, see Pearson, *Elizabethans*, pp. 333–334.

[9] Roger Ascham, *The Scholemaster* (London, 1570), p. 29ᵛ.

weekes or a moneth, and are usually half a yeare, or very neare, from the first goinge to the conclusion. [10]

Not all courtships lasted so long as six months or allowed so much visitation between a couple or came to so successful a conclusion. Nevertheless, after agreement was reached, the next stage was a formal contract, "which is also called espousing, affiancing, betrothing, or handfasting," "sponsion" or "sponsalia" or simply *"Making themselves sure."* [11] As all the authorities concurred, "Spousals are a mutual Promise of future Marriage, being duly made between those Persons, to whom it is lawful." [12] Distinctions prevailed, however, between spousals *de praesenti* and spousals *de futuro*. Using the present tense, as in "I take thee for my husband," *de praesenti* vows bound a couple immediately and irrevocably as marital partners. Using the future tense, as in "Wilt thou have this woman," *de futuro* vows were an exclusive pledge to marry at some later date. [13] Both kinds of spousals required a church ceremony before the conferral of any matrimonial rights, including sexual intercourse, dower, inheritance, the husband's control of the wife's property, or legitimization of children. However, if any betrothed partners consummated their union before the religious rites, they were indissolubly—if irregularly—joined for life. [14] For modern au-

[10] Henry Best, *Farming and Account Books*, ed. C. B. Robinson, Surtees Society Publications 33 (1857): 116. See also John R. Gillis, *For Better, for Worse: British Marriages, 1600 to the Present* (Oxford: Oxford University Press, 1985), pp. 30–34.

[11] Robert Cleaver, *A Godly Form of Householde Government* (London, 1598), p. 107; William Whately, *A Care-Cloth, or a Treatise of the Cumbers and Troubles of Marriage* (London, 1624), p. 31; Swinburne, *Treatise*, p. 1; Matthew Griffith, *Bethel, or A Forme for Families* (London, 1633), p. 269.

[12] Swinburne, *Treatise*, p. 5. See also Cleaver, *Godly Form*, pp. 106, 112ff.; Gouge, *Domesticall Duties*, p. 198; Griffith, *Bethel*, p. 269; *The Lawes Resolutions of Womens Rights* (London, 1632), pp. 52–53.

[13] Griffith, *Bethel*, p. 270; William Harrington, *The Comendacions of Matrymony* (London, 1528), A3; Steven Ozment, *When Fathers Ruled: Family Life in Reformation Europe* (Cambridge: Harvard University Press, 1983), pp. 26–27; Pearson, *Elizabethans*, pp. 312–320; Chilton Latham Powell, *English Domestic Relations, 1487–1653* (New York: Columbia University Press, 1917), pp. 3–4; Margaret Loftus Ranald, " 'As Marriage Binds, and Blood Breaks': English Marriage and Shakespeare," *Shakespeare Quarterly* 30 (1979): 71; idem, "The Betrothals of *All's Well That Ends Well*," *Huntington Library Quarterly* 26 (1963): 180; Daniel Rogers, *Matrimoniall Honour* (London, 1642), pp. 96–126; Ernest Schanzer, "The Marriage Contracts in *Measure for Measure*," *Shakespeare Survey* 13 (1960): 81–89; idem, *The Problem Plays of Shakespeare* (New York: Schocken Books, 1963), pp. 75–77, 109–110; Swinburne, *Treatise*, "To the Reader" and pp. 8–9, 11–13, 223.

[14] Jean Bodin, *The Six Bookes of a Commonweale*, trans. Richard Knolles (London, 1606), p. 15; Swinburne, *Treatise*, pp. 15, 108, 121, 218–221, 223–224, 227.

diences, the situation seems further complicated by the fact that, after making their preliminary pledges, the affianced pair were entitled to call each other "husband" and "wife" and to regard each other's parents as their own.[15] The anomalous, often confusing status of this stage of courtship emerges in rather fuzzy explanations that "spousage, although it bee a degree vnder mariage, yet it is more then a determined purpose, yea more then a simple promise."[16]

While nothing but the bare promise, mutually made (*consensus nuptialis*), was required for a valid contract, the customary procedure involved the presence of witnesses, the joining of hands (if possible by the bride's father), oral vows or other signs of assent, the gift of a ring or another appropriate token, a spousal kiss, and the signing of legal documents. The law further distinguished among contracts pure and simple and those with conditions, between vows made face-to-face and those made by proxy, between public pledges and private ones, between promises sworn and unsworn, between betrothals by words and by tokens.[17] Almost every variation for indicating consent was duly considered. For example, if one party asked the other to show a willingness to marry by giving a kiss or a hand or by accepting a ring or a cup of wine, then the specified response constituted assent. Alternatively, when a third party bade the pair to join hands or kiss or embrace if they wished to wed, then their doing so signified an engagement.[18]

Typically, however, "*Subarration*, that is the giving and receiving of a *Ring*, is a Sign of all others, most usual in Spousals and Matrimonial Contracts."[19] Though Henry Swinburne, the great legal authority in these matters, says the kind of metal is irrelevant, he grows uncharacteristically poetic in explaining that the ring,

> round, and without end, importeth thus much, that their mutual love and hearty affection should roundly flow from the one to the other, as in a Circle, and that continually, and forever . . . ; The Finger on which this Ring is to be worn is the fourth Finger of the left hand . . . there is a Vein of Blood

[15] Gillis, *For Better*, p. 17. See also Griffith, *Bethel*, p. 270.

[16] Richard Greenham, *Works* (London, 1599), p. 289. See also Cleaver, *Godly Form*, pp. 107, 112ff.; Gouge, *Domesticall Duties*, p. 199; Griffith, *Bethel*, p. 270; Swinburne, *Treatise*, p. 3.

[17] Swinburne, *Treatise*, pp. 10–11.

[18] Ibid., pp. 203–207. See also William Ames, *Conscience, with the Power and Cases Thereof* (London, 1639), p. 227.

[19] Swinburne, *Treatise*, p. 207.

which passeth from that fourth Finger unto the Heart, called *Vena amoris*, Loves Vein.[20]

One popular token of betrothal was the gimmal ring, or joint ring (*Oth.*, IV.iii.72–73), consisting of two or more linked bands that interlocked (see illustration). At the formal engagement, the sections were separated, with the upper and lower segments going to the future bride and groom. Witnesses kept any other circlets until all the parts, sometimes as many as nine, were rejoined at the wedding.[21] Quite frequently a spousal ring was engraved with a "posy," or saying, such as "Our contract / Was Heaven's act" or "God above / Encrease our love."[22] The other common symbols of

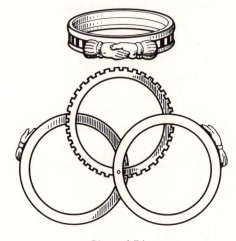

Gimmal Ring

[20] Ibid., p. 208. Swinburne dislikes the fashion of wearing a ring for any other purpose but admits that this token presented merely as a gift or in jest cannot represent spousals, pp. 208–209.

[21] Robert Chambers, ed., *The Book of Days: A Miscellany of Popular Antiquities* (Philadelphia: Lippincott, 1869), 1:220; John Cordy Jeaffreson, *Brides and Bridals* (London: Hurst and Blackett, 1872), 1:162–164; T. F. Thistleton-Dyer, *Folk Lore of Shakespeare* (London: Griffith and Farrar, ca. 1883), pp. 347–348; Edward J. Wood, *The Wedding Day in All Ages and Countries* (New York: Harper's, 1869), 2:137–139.

[22] Chambers, *Book of Days*, 1:221. See also *Love's Garland; or Posies for Rings, Handke(r)chers, and Gloves* (London, 1624); W. Miles Barnes, "The Diary of William Whiteway," *Proceedings of the Dorset Natural History and Antiquarian Field Club* 13 (1892): 59; Edward I. Berry, *Shakespeare's Comic Rites* (Cambridge: Cambridge University Press, 1984), p. 164; Pearson, *Elizabethans*, pp. 332–333; Rachel Weigall, ed., "The Journal of Lady Mildmay, circa 1570–1617," *The Quarterly Review* 215 (1911): 122; Wood, *Wedding Day*, 2:139, 149–152.

betrothal were the joined hands and the kiss.[23] The very term *handfasting* graphically evokes this mode of making a fast, or binding, pledge to marry. In a standard form of contracting, the parties joined hands and then vowed, "I *R*. doe promise to thee. *F*. that I will be thine husband, which I will confirme by publike mariage, in pledge whereof I give thee mine hand. In like manner doth the woman to the man."[24]

Increasingly, however, propertied families demanded security more reliable than a ring or a kiss or a handclasp. While a priest or minister could serve as an ideal corroborator of the spousals,[25] a written agreement was even better. Often running to many pages, marriage documents spelled out in legally enforceable terms just what was agreed to on each side. Duly signed and witnessed, these contracts provided fees for the lawyers who specialized in their drafting, cases for the Chancery Courts that had jurisdiction over them, and cause for endless bitterness between parties who had to sue for fulfillment of conditions.[26] Although "dower, pledges, solemnity, written instruments," and the like were merely the "Accidents of Marriage,"[27] few entered into that state without them—and almost none at the highest social levels. Even among yeomen, "Soe soone as the younge folkes are agreed and contracted, then the father of the mayd carryeth her over to the younge mans howse to see howe they like of all, and there doth the younge mans father meete them to treate of a dower, and likewise of a joynture or foeffment for the woman; and then doe they allsoe appointe and sette downe the day of marriage, which may perhapps bee aboute a fortnight or three weekes after."[28] This account accords well with the experience of William Whiteway, who won consent to his proposal from Eleanor Parkins on 6 April 1620, was betrothed before family and friends on 4 May, and married on 14 June "in the presence of the greatest part of the town."[29]

During the engagement period, reading the banns was particularly important, because certain circumstances, explained in the next chapter,

[23] For the history of the kiss as an emblem of union, see Berry, *Shakespeare's Comic Rites*, pp. 184–185; Nicolas James Perella, *The Kiss Sacred and Profane* (Berkeley: University of California Press, 1969), pp. 158–243.

[24] Greenham, *Works*, p. 299. See also Gouge, *Domesticall Duties*, p. 198.

[25] Thomas Cartwright, *A Dictionary of Church-Government* (London, 1644), B3; Powell, *English Domestic Relations*, p. 19.

[26] Pearson, *Elizabethans*, p. 324; Lawrence Stone, *The Crisis of the Aristocracy, 1558–1641* (Oxford: Clarendon Press, 1965), p. 637.

[27] *Lawes*, p. 62.

[28] Best, *Farming*, pp. 116–117.

[29] Barnes, "Diary," p. 59.

could invalidate a contract. Thus it was essential to discover any impediments before a man and woman were married.[30] The church canons decreed, "No Minister vpon paine of suspension *per triennium ipso facto*, shall celebrate Matrimonie betweene any persons . . . except the Bannes of Matrimonie haue bene first published three seuerall Sundaies or Holy dayes in the time of diuine Seruice in the Parish Churches and Chappels where the saide parties dwel."[31] Since it took a minimum of two weeks for three Sundays to elapse, betrothals usually lasted about a month or so.[32] However, the time could be greatly shortened by the purchase of a special license from the consistory court, which required not only a substantial bond but also oaths from reliable witnesses that no legal or religious barriers existed.[33] The fees for such a license usually ranged from 3s. 8d. to 10s. 4d., though the bond for Shakespeare's own dispensation was £40, a very considerable sum.[34] When the banns proceeded in the usual way, the fee for their reading varied from 1s. to 4s. It was also customary to recompense the clergyman and church employees for the wedding service, the Book of Common Prayer specifying that the ring be laid "upon the book with the accustomed duty to the priest and clerk."[35] Yet paying these costs doubtless seemed preferable to excommunication for marrying irregularly without banns or license or priest.

Regardless of whether the preliminary stages were long or short, the fees modest or dear, the appointed nuptial day duly arrived. With it came another series of customs and regulations, some of which were mandated

[30] For further discussion of the period between betrothal and wedding, see Robert Abbot, *A Wedding Sermon* (London, 1608), p. 62; Cleaver, *Godly Form*, pp. 133–138; Gouge, *Domesticall Duties*, pp. 200–202; Rogers, *Matrimoniall Honour*, p. 118.

[31] *Constitutions and Canons Ecclesiastical 1604* (Oxford: Clarendon Press, 1923), L3–L3ᵛ. See also *A Collection of Articles, Injunctions, Canons, Orders, Ordinances, and Canons Ecclesiastical* (London: Stevens and Co., 1846), p. 4; Edmund Gibson, *Codex Juris Ecclesiastici Anglicani* (Oxford: Clarendon Press, 1761), 1:424–427; Harrington, *Comendacions*, A4ᵛ.

[32] See Best, *Farming*, p. 116, where two or three weeks is normal in Yorkshire. Gillis, *For Better*, p. 12, says it took "several months," but he may include the stages before formal betrothal.

[33] *Collection*, p. 38; *Constitutions*, L3, Q3–R1ᵛ; Gibson, *Codex*, 1:428–429.

[34] S. Schoenbaum, *William Shakespeare: A Documentary Life* (New York: Oxford University Press, 1975), pp. 62–63; Richard L. Greaves, *Society and Religion in Elizabethan England* (Minneapolis: University of Minnesota Press, 1981), p. 180.

[35] *The Book of Common Prayer, 1559*, ed. John Booty (Charlottesville: University Press of Virginia, 1976), p. 292. Simon Forman's outlay was 8s. 2d.; see A. L. Rowse, *Sex and Society in Shakespeare's Age: Simon Forman the Astrologer* (New York: Charles Scribner's Sons, 1974), p. 93.

by the church. In order to ensure a Christian union, at some point before the ceremony the priest had to hear the couple recite the catechism; he also had to give them communion, and he had to enter in the parish register before witnesses each wedding he performed.[36] At certain times of the canonical year—Advent, Christmas, part of Lent, and from Rogation Sunday to Trinity—marriages were not supposed to be solemnized. As a bit of doggerel in a Cambridgeshire parish register puts it,

> Advent marriage doth thee deny,
> But Hilary gives thee liberty.
> Septuagesima says thee nay,
> Eight days from Easter says you may.
> Rogation bids thee to contain,
> But Trinity sets thee free again.[37]

Nor could ministers "vnder any pretence whatsoeuer, ioyne any persons . . . at any vnseasonable times, but onely betweene the houres of eight and twelue in the forenoone, nor in any priuate place, but either in the said Churches or Chappels where one of them dwelleth, and likewise in time of Diuine Seruice."[38] As with the banns, a license could set aside interdicted seasons or hours or places. Evening weddings in great homes, for example, or dawn weddings in the spring were legitimized by this device.[39] Puritans often preferred to be married on Sundays during regular services. No Puritan by any standard, Simon Forman had a Sunday morning nuptial at seven o'clock, while both the sister and father of Sir Simonds D'Ewes married in London churches on Wednesday mornings in February and March, respectively.[40] No one knows where or when Shakespeare wed

---

[36] *Constitutions*, M2ᵛ–M3ᵛ; Greaves, *Society*, p. 180; Reginald Haw, *The State of Matrimony* (London: S.P.C.K., 1952), p. 64.

[37] F. G. Emmison, *Elizabethan Life: Morals and the Church Courts* (Chelmsford: Essex County Council, 1973), p. 158. Ursula M. Cowgill, "The People of York, 1583–1812," *Scientific American*, n.s., 222 (1970): 107, substantiates the decline of marriages in Lent, as does Haw, *State of Matrimony*, p. 61. However, P.E.H. Hair, "Bridal Pregnancy in Earlier Rural England Further Examined," *Population Studies* 24 (1970): 67, says that by 1610 the Advent restrictions were virtually disregarded. Probably it is not coincidental that the Puritans' 1603 "Millenary Petition" complains of "the restraint of marriage at certain times"; see G. E. Howard, *A History of Matrimonial Institutions* (Chicago: University of Chicago Press, 1904), 1:415.

[38] *Constitutions*, L3ᵛ, M2ᵛ, Q4ᵛ. See also Emmison, *Elizabethan Life*, pp. 155–157; Gibson, *Codex*, 1:429–430; Pearson, *Elizabethans*, p. 342.

[39] Powell, *English Domestic Relations*, p. 6n; Greaves, *Society*, p. 183.

[40] Rowse, *Sex*, p. 92; D'Ewes, *Autobiography*, 1:174, 229.

Anne Hathaway, but the bond for their license was posted on Wednesday, 28 November 1582. The single bann required may have been read immediately before a ceremony on St. Andrew's Day, Friday the 30th.[41]

Once the time and place of a wedding had been set, the couple, together with family and friends, made what preparations their means and other circumstances allowed, for "on ye day of mariage, there is made good cheere, the Bride is fresh and new, and all nouelties are pleasaunt."[42] Clothing could be as elaborate as Princess Elizabeth's gown, with its cloth-of-silver train alone costing £130 and its sleeves embroidered with diamonds. She wore "a crown of refined golde, made Imperiall by the pearles and diamonds thereupon placed, which were so thicke beset that they stood like shining pinnacles upon her amber-coloured haire dependantly hanging, playted down over her shoulders to her waiste, between every plaight a roll or liste of gold-spangles, pearles, rich stones and diamonds."[43] From this giddy height of extravagance, marriage finery ranged downward to the humble bride's crown of flowers and the ribbons adorning her own and her groom's clothing.[44] In 1601, a Staffordshire father spent 31s. for his daughter's dress, 7s. 6d. for bones to line it, 16s. for trimming, 8s. 6d. for a hat.[45] If time and money did not permit new attire,[46] the couple wore garments from their existing wardrobes.

Yet apparel perhaps accounted for the least of the wedding expenses, since the celebration could involve feasting and entertainment for several days. James I spent an astronomical £53,294 on Princess Elizabeth's wedding, and Lord Hunsdon complained in 1584 that when his two daughters

[41] Schoenbaum, *William Shakespeare*, pp. 62–65.

[42] Pierre Boaistuau, *Theatrum Mundi* (London, 1581), p. 136.

[43] Ann Monsarrat, *And the Bride Wore . . . . : The Story of the White Wedding* (London: Gentry Books, 1973), p. 42; Alexander Niccholes, *A Discourse of Marriage and Wiving* (London, 1620), 2:542–543; David Bergeron, *Shakespeare's Romances and the Royal Family* (Lawrence: University Press of Kansas, 1985), p. 207; Phyllis Cunnington and Catherine Lucas, *Costume for Births, Marriages, and Deaths* (New York: Barnes and Noble, 1972), p. 93; Pearson, *Elizabethans*, p. 346. See also Roland Mushat Frye, *The Renaissance Hamlet* (Princeton: Princeton University Press, 1984), pp. 88–94, for accounts of expensive dresses at royal weddings.

[44] Monsarrat, *And the Bride*, pp. 22–26; Pearson, *Elizabethans*, p. 343; John Stephens, *Essayes and Characters* (London, 1615), pp. 353, 357; Wood, *Wedding Day*, 2:170, 186–187.

[45] Greaves, *Society*, p. 188; Keith Wrightson, *English Society 1580–1680* (London: Hutchinson, 1982), p. 89.

[46] Best, *Farming*, p. 117; D'Ewes, *Autobiography*, 1:322.

married, he "was att as grete chargys with the tyme of theyr maryagys, as theyr maryage-money [portions] came unto."[47] As is often the case today, the bride's family bore the principal costs for the festivities. On the wedding day, events began early in the morning when attendants came to dress the bride, attaching ribbons and other souvenir favors to various parts of her gown.[48] Next arrived friends to escort her from home, with the groom either in their midst or awaiting the party at the church.[49] Sir Dudley Carleton describes the procession at the Whitehall marriage of Sir Philip Herbert and Lady Susan Vere: "The Court was great and for that day put on the best bravery. The Prince [James I] and Duke of Holst led the Bride to Church, the Queen followed him from thence."[50] Music, eating, and drinking could accompany this stage of the day's schedule. Thus, besides objecting to the "pompe and pride, and gorgiousnes of raimēt and Jewels" of wedding guests, Heinrich Bullinger dislikes the "great noyse of basens and drooms," preferring "comly honest raiment, without pride, without dromming & piping." Worse, in his view, is the fact that "earely in the morning the wedding people begin to exceede in superfluous eating and drinking. . . . And when they come to the preaching, they are halfe dronken, some altogether."[51]

The ceremony itself had to be performed by an ordained clergyman[52] *in facie ecclesiae*, literally "in the face of the church." While the term refers to the medieval custom of marrying on the porch at the church door, most weddings in Shakespeare's day took place inside before the altar.[53] The

[47] Jeaffreson, *Brides*, p. 215; Monsarrat, *And the Bride*, p. 42; Robert Cary, *Memoirs of Robert Cary, Earl of Monmouth* (Edinburgh: Archibald Constable, 1808), p. 165.

[48] Monsarrat, *And the Bride*, p. 22; Pearson, *Elizabethans*, p. 343; Wood, *Wedding Day*, pp. 186–187.

[49] Best, *Farming*, p. 117; Pearson, *Elizabethans*, p. 342; Samuel Rowlands, *The Bride* (London, 1617), A4ᵛ; Wood, *Wedding Day*, 2:184–185.

[50] Monsarrat, *And the Bride*, p. 39. See also Gouge, *Domesticall Duties*, p. 206; John Stow, *The Annales or Generall Chronicle of England*, continued . . . by Edmond Howes (London, 1615), p. 928.

[51] Heinrich Bullinger, *The Christian State of Matrimony*, trans. Miles Coverdale (London, 1575), pp. 58ᵛ–59. On the use of music, see Pearson, *Elizabethans*, pp. 344, 352. For a simpler wedding breakfast, see Nicholas Breton, *Choice, Chance, and Change* (London, 1606), H1ᵛ, where "a bride cake and a messe of cream, with the helpe of a cold pie, staied our stomackes well."

[52] William Perkins, *Christian Oeconomie*, trans. Thomas Pickering (London, 1609), p. 94.

[53] Gillis, *For Better*, p. 18; Pearson, *Elizabethans*, p. 341.

form prescribed in the Book of Common Prayer calls for the presence of "friends and neighbors," for without witnesses the marriage was not valid.[54] The ensuing ritual began with one final opportunity for either the couple or the congregation to reveal any impediment to the union. Then, using verbs of the future tense, the priest bade bride and groom to join right hands (gloved for a maiden, ungloved for a widow) and repeat their betrothal promises, while the woman's father also had to confirm his willingness to give her "unto this man." At last, in verbs of the present tense, the pair bound themselves forever, their commitment symbolized in the placing of a ring on the third finger of the wife's left hand.[55] Finally the officiant could pronounce the couple duly married in the eyes of God and man. Kneeling under a "care-cloth" (unless either party had been previously married) the newlyweds received a blessing from the priest, who also bestowed a benediction kiss upon the groom for him to give in turn to the bride. Customarily, prayers and a sermon accompanied the rite of matrimony, and often the sacrament of communion.[56] Wine, bread, sweetmeats, and bride cake were blessed and distributed to the congregation.[57] Sometimes little pieces of cakes or buns were squeezed through a wedding ring and thrown over the bride's head, while any leftover refreshments went to the poor.[58]

Once the church ceremonies came to an end, the wedding party typically made its way back to the home of the bride's father for further cele-

[54] *Book of Common Prayer*, p. 290; Harrington, *Comendacions*, A5ᵛ–A6; Richard Hooker, "The Celebration of Matrimonie," in *Of the Laws of Ecclesiastical Polity*, ed. W. Speed Hill (Cambridge: Harvard University Press, 1977), 2:401–406; Sir Thomas Smith, *The Commonwealth* (London, 1640), p. 241; William Vaughan, *The Golden-grove* (London, 1600), N3. As Ozment notes, *When Fathers Ruled*, p. 26, Erasmus was among the reformers who urged validity only for public marriages. Some Puritans, while affirming the public character of weddings, rejected use of the prayer book ceremony; see, e.g., Monsarrat, *And the Bride*, p. 31. The very word *weds* refers to the Anglo-Saxon sureties given to the bride's family, with the offering and receiving held in a public *beweddung* that made the couple "wyf" and "husband" thereafter; see Gillis, *For Better*, p. 17.

[55] *Book of Common Prayer*, p. 292. See also Gouge, *Domesticall Duties*, pp. 203–205; Griffith, *Bethel*, p. 275.

[56] Gibson, *Codex*, 1:431–432; Pearson, *Elizabethans*, pp. 349–350; Powell, *English Domestic Relations*, p. 22. For some surviving examples of wedding sermons, see William Bradshaw, "A Mariage Feast," and Thomas Gataker, "A Good Wife," in *Two Mariage Sermons* (London, 1620); Samuel Hieron, *The Bridegroome* (London, 1617); William Whately, *A Bride-Bush, or a Wedding Sermon* (London, 1617).

[57] Pearson, *Elizabethans*, p. 351.

[58] Jeaffreson, *Brides*, p. 204.

bration.[59] At the least, festivities included a fine meal.[60] Even when Sir Thomas Hoby married Margaret Sidney, still in mourning for her second husband, he thought it fitting "to please the Beholders with a Sermon and a Dinner."[61] At the bride-ales of common folk, "it is incredible to tell what meat is consumed and spent, each one bringing such a dish. . . . [so] that the goodman of the house is not charged with anything saving bread, drink, sauce, houseroom, and fire."[62] Relatively simple fare consisted of "Capons, Chickins, Geese, Lambes, pigs, yea and some Bullocks, brought in by the tennants, with malt and meale, beside Apples plummes and plumm cakes."[63] At "beggar weddings" of the poor, guests also brought gifts of money and household goods.[64] However, contributions at country nuptials paled by comparison with the lavish presents at noble weddings. More than £1,000 in plate and jewels went to Lord Herbert and Anne Russell, while gifts worth £2,500 were showered upon Sir Philip Herbert and Lady Susan Vere.[65] In return, guests expected mementos of the occasion—sometimes just ribbons or pins from the bride's gown but often gloves, knives, slippers, and more costly tokens.[66]

Moreover, the company counted on celebration, as much as the family could afford, ranging from simple songs, dances, toasts, and jests to elaborate masques and days of festivity. Clerics allow "a lawfulnesse of feasting, and mutuall rejoycing at mariage solemnities,"[67] though they frown

[59] Details of the painting *A Fete at Bermondsey* suggest such an occasion. Erna Auerbach and C. Kingsley Adams, *Paintings and Sculpture at Hatfield House* (London: Constable, 1971), p. 54, think the black garment on the supposed bride means it cannot be a wedding, but brides wore dresses of various colors, including black.

[60] See, e.g., D'Ewes, *Autobiography*, 1:175, 229; Rowse, *Sex*, p. 93; Best, *Farming*, p. 117.

[61] Meads, *Diary*, p. 32.

[62] William Harrison, *The Description of England*, ed. Georges Edelen (Ithaca, NY: Cornell University Press, 1968), p. 131.

[63] Breton, *Choice*, D3ᵛ.

[64] Vaughan, *Golden-grove*, N3ᵛ, refers to gifts for those "which stande in neede," as well as to the "bason, dish, or cup" for receipt of such gifts, M8. See also Susan Dwyer Amussen, *An Ordered Society: Gender and Class in Early Modern England* (New York: Basil Blackwell, 1988), p. 157; Gillis, *For Better*, pp. 87–88; Wrightson, *English Society*, p. 62.

[65] Pearson, *Elizabethans*, p. 163; Monsarrat, *And the Bride*, p. 39. See also Sylvia Freedman, *Poor Penelope: Lady Penelope Rich, An Elizabethan Woman* (Bourne End, Bucks.: Kensal Press, 1983), p. 48; Greaves, *Society*, p. 187; Searle, *Barrington*, p. 19.

[66] Best, *Farming*, p. 117; Cunnington and Lucas, *Costume*, p. 67; Alan Macfarlane, ed., *The Diary of Ralph Josselin* (London: Oxford University Press for the British Academy, 1976), p. 29; Pearson, *Elizabethans*, p. 352; Wood, *Wedding Day*, 2:188–190.

[67] Griffith, *Bethel*, p. 277. See also Bullinger, *Christian State*, 60ᵛ; Gouge, *Domesticall*

upon "the prophaner sort," who suppose weddings "neuer well seasoned, or aright celebrated, vnlesse filthy discourse and obscene songs be as common as any ordinarie seruice . . . making a Brothel-house of a Bridehouse."[68] Actually, these celebrations often consisted of nothing more exceptionable than a "variety of sports, as hunting, hawking Musicke and dauncing, courting, and kissing, and what not,"[69] but in some villages the rowdy, bawdy physicality of "rough music" could verge on the riotous.[70] Even among the privileged, weddings served as entertaining diversion. In her diary Grace Mildmay records that "some great personages, ladies of myne acquaintance, would persuade me to go with them to the Court, to feastes, marryages, and plays."[71] Without question, the most expensive nuptial production was the masque.[72] The one Francis Bacon devised for Frances Howard's second wedding cost £2,000.[73] No wonder

---

Duties, p. 206; Hieron, *Bridegroome*, p. 28; Pierre de la Primaudaye, *The French Academie* (London, 1586), p. 497.

[68] Bradshaw, "Mariage Feast," E2ᵛ; see also E3, F2ᵛ. Others echoing such sentiments include Gouge, *Domesticall Duties*, pp. 206–207; Griffith, *Bethel*, pp. 278–279; Hieron, *Bridegroome*, pp. 28ff. Bullinger, *Christian State*, pp. 59ᵛ–60, delivers an especially ferocious blast.

[69] Breton, *Choice*, D3ᵛ; see also H2ᵛ. For other descriptions of wedding entertainments, see Desiderius Erasmus, "The Unequal Marriage," in *Colloquies* (London: Gibbings and Company, 1900), 3:62; Robert Langham, *A Letter*, ed. R. J. P. Kuin (Leiden: E. J. Brill, 1983), pp. 49ff.; Sir John Suckling, "76. A Ballade. Upon a Wedding," in *The Works of Sir John Suckling*, ed. Thomas Clayton (Oxford: Clarendon Press, 1971), 1:79–84; Margaret Baker, *Folklore and Customs of Rural England* (Totowa, NJ: Rowman and Littlefield, 1974), pp. 137–146; Charles Read Baskervill, *The Elizabethan Jig* (Chicago: University of Chicago Press, 1929), p. 13; Gillis, *For Better*, pp. 55, 63–73; Jeaffreson, *Brides*, pp. 242–247; Powell, *English Domestic Relations*, p. 26.

[70] For "rough music" analyses, see Michael D. Bristol, *Carnival and Theater: Plebeian Culture and the Structure of Authority in Renaissance England* (New York: Methuen, 1985), chap. 10; Natalie Zemon Davis, "The Reasons of Misrule: Youth Groups and Charivaris in Sixteenth-Century France," *Past and Present* 50 (1971): 41–75; Martin Ingram, "Le charivari dans l'Angleterre du XVIᵉ et du XVIIᵉ siècle. Aperçu historique," in *Le Charivari*, ed. Jacques Le Goff and J. C. Schmitt (Paris: Mouton, 1981); idem, "Ridings, Rough Music and the 'Reform of Popular Culture' in Early Modern England," *Past and Present* 105 (1984): 79–113; Jean-Claude Margolin, "Charivari et mariage ridicule au temps de la Renaissance," in *Les Fêtes de la Renaissance*, ed. Jean Jacquot et Elie Konigson (Paris: Centre National de la Recherche Scientifique, 1975), 3:579–601; Henri Rey-Flaud, *Le Charivari: Les Rituels Fondamentaux de la Sexualité* (Paris: Payot, 1985); E. P. Thompson, "Rough music: Le Charivari anglais," *Annales Économies, Sociétés, Civilisations* 27 (1972): 285–312.

[71] Weigall, "Journal," p. 125. Grace refused such offers.

[72] Greaves, *Society*, pp. 186–188; Pearson, *Elizabethans*, pp. 359–361.

[73] Monsarrat, *And the Bride*, p. 41.

that when "It was motion'd to the Innes of Court to praesent a maske at this mariadge, . . . it was deny'd."[74] However, that union eventually featured two court masques (one of which "pleased the king so well, that he caused them to performe it againe"), along with an entertainment at the Merchant Taylors Hall that included "a Wassaile, 2. seuerall pleasant maskes, & a play, & . . . dances," followed by a second "princely banquet" lasting until "about 3 a clock in the morning."[75]

Regardless of how many days the festivities lasted, the most important event occurred when the marriage was sexually consummated, customarily on the wedding night. From a legal standpoint, for dower and other rights, the union had to be "of fact consumat, by the mutuall couiunction [conjunction] of their bodies"—had to be transformed, in other words, from *matrimonium initiatum* into *matrimonium ratum*.[76] Hence a lawyer pragmatically recommends that "when supper is done dance a while, leaue out the long measures till you be in bed, get you there quickly, and pay the Minstrels to morrow."[77] Around this final stage of courtship clustered a host of customs. When escorts led the couple to the flower-strewn bed, they superstitiously removed all pins from the wife's dress to avoid bad luck. Even among aristocrats, "at night there was sewing into the sheet, casting off the bride's left hose, with many other pretty sorcerie."[78] And James's penchant for visiting the nuptial chamber of newlyweds, including his own daughter, is well known.[79] However private or public its circumstances, the act of intercourse made permanent the transfer of identity and property between husband and wife. Not only a change of name occurred—"She that in the Morning was faire weather, is at night perhaps Rainebow or Goodwife Foule, Sweet heart going to Church, and Hoist-

---

[74] *Wentworth Papers, 1597–1628*, ed. J. P. Cooper, Camden Society Publications, 4th ser., 12 (1973): 57.

[75] Stow, *Annales*, p. 928. See also Monsarrat, *And the Bride*, pp. 34, 42.

[76] Bodin, *Six Bookes*, p. 15; Margaret Loftus Ranald, *Shakespeare and His Social Context* (New York: AMS Press, 1987), p. 37. See also Harrington, *Comendacions*, A6ᵛ; *Lawes*, p. 52; Whately, *Care-Cloth*, p. 31. Lynda E. Boose, "Othello's Handkerchief: 'The Recognizance and Pledge of Love,' " *English Literary Renaissance* 5 (1975): 364, notes that bloody wedding sheets figured in the evidence at Henry VIII's divorce case.

[77] *Lawes*, p. 118.

[78] Monsarrat, *And the Bride*, p. 39. See also Jeaffreson, *Brides*, pp. 249–250; Pearson, *Elizabethans*, pp. 356–359; Wood, *Wedding Day*, 2:214–224.

[79] Pearson, *Elizabethans*, p. 359; Lawrence Stone, "Marriage among the English Nobility in the 16th and 17th Centuries," *Comparative Studies in Society and History* 3 (1960–1961): 198; Antonia Fraser, *The Weaker Vessel* (New York: Alfred A. Knopf, 1984), p. 16.

brick comming home."[80] But, as the law bluntly put it, *"That which the Husband hath is his owne,"* while *"That which the Wife hath is the Husbands."*[81] At the end of the wedding day, the woman yielded up her body, her name, and her worldly goods.

There are ample instances of proper formal wooings, public contracts, and weddings in Shakespeare. From the initial approach of a hopeful suitor to the first bedding of a newly married couple, the plays teem with minute details of the familiar rituals. Prospective partners meet during masked entertainments in *Much Ado about Nothing*, *Love's Labour's Lost*, and *Romeo and Juliet*. Coached by his uncle Shallow, Slender stumbles ineptly through a tête-à-tête with Anne Page. Orlando and Biron write limping verses, while Don Armado and Hamlet send love letters of dubious literary merit. Lovers as disparate as Lysander and Othello, Gremio and Valentine present gifts intended to attract the favor of their chosen ladies. Olivia sends a ring as a token of favor to Viola/Cesario and gives a pearl to Sebastian/Cesario. Proteus begs a picture of Sylvia; Shylock has had a turquoise of Leah when he was a bachelor; the French princess and her ladies receive pearls, diamonds, and gloves from their admirers. As for Autolycus, he brings a whole bag of trinkets for country lasses like Mopsa and Dorcas:

> Lawn as white as driven snow,
> Cyprus black as e'er was crow,
> Gloves as sweet as damask roses,
> Masks for faces, and for noses;
> Bugle-bracelet, necklace amber,
> Perfume for a lady's chamber;
> Golden coifs and stomachers
> For my lads to give their dears.
>
> (*WT*, IV.iv.219–226)

For couples already espoused, says Rosalind, time "trots hard with a young maid between the contract of her marriage and the day it is solemnized. If the interim be but a se'nnight, time's pace is so hard that it seems the length of seven year" (*AYL*, III.ii.306–309). At their betrothals, Portia and Nerissa each give their new husbands a ring, Graziano's engraved

[80] *Lawes*, pp. 125, 129, 130. See also Rowlands, *Bride*, A3ᵛ; Smith, *Common-wealth*, pp. 236–240. Curiously, in her chapter on "Nomination and Election," pp. 52–79, Marjorie Garber, *Coming of Age in Shakespeare* (New York: Methuen, 1981), does not connect the significance of one's affirmation or change of name with the marriage ceremony's alteration of a wife's name.

[81] *Lawes*, pp. 129, 130.

with the posy "Love me and leave me not" (*MV*, V.i.150). In *The Tempest* Prospero produces an elaborate masque to celebrate the "contract of true love" (IV.i.84) between Miranda and Ferdinand following their espousal,[82] which the prince's father subsequently ratifies with "Give me your hands" (V.i.217). Falstaff impresses into his troops "contracted bachelors, such as had been asked twice on the banns" (*1H4*, IV.ii.17–18), who will pay him bribes to be released from service rather than cancel their impending weddings. And Don Armado concludes his hapless pursuit of Jaquenetta in *Love's Labour's Lost* by declaring, "The catastrophe is a nuptial" (IV.i.76). Saturninus refers to "priest and holy water" (*Tit.*, I.ii.318), while the father of Joan la Pucelle recalls, "I gave a noble to the priest / The morn that I was wedded to her mother" (*1H6*, V.i.23–24). Drenched in the crimson of blood, Macbeth is "Bellona's bridegroom" (I.ii.54); Portia pressures Brutus with reminders of "that great vow / Which did incorporate and make us one" (*JC*, II.i.271–272). Such a myriad of specific allusions suffuse the canon that the experiences common to courtship leap vividly to life, at least when one understands the experiences to which they refer.

Only twice does Shakespeare show the complete pattern of conventional courtship—an appropriate property agreement submitted for approval on both sides, followed by a private meeting between the future spouses, a declaration of love by the man, an eventual consent by the woman, then the public betrothal ceremony, to be confirmed by a marriage in church. At the conclusion of *Henry V*, the young English ruler presents his treaty of peace with France. Sending his counselors to discuss the various articles with the French king and queen, Henry asks, "Yet leave our cousin Catherine here with us. / She is our capital demand, comprised / Within the fore-rank of our articles" (V.ii.95–97). With her attendant Alice discreetly chaperoning, the princess entertains a model wooing. Ignoring the

[82] Linda Bamber, *Comic Women, Tragic Men: A Study of Gender and Genre in Shakespeare* (Stanford, CA: Stanford University Press, 1982), p. 191, erroneously calls this a "wedding masque." So do Paul Brown, " 'This thing of darkness I acknowledge mine': *The Tempest* and the Discourse of Colonialism," in *Political Shakespeare: New Essays in Cultural Materialism*, ed. Jonathan Dollimore and Alan Sinfield (Ithaca, NY: Cornell University Press, 1985), p. 67; Stephen Greenblatt, *Shakespearean Negotiations: The Circulation of Social Energy in Renaissance England* (Oxford: Clarendon Press, 1988), pp. 144, 159; Carol Thomas Neely, *Broken Nuptials in Shakespeare's Plays* (New Haven: Yale University Press, 1985), p. 198; Ruth Nevo, *Shakespeare's Other Language* (London: Methuen, 1987), pp. 136, 147; Kay Stockholder, *Dream Works: Lovers and Families in Shakespeare's Plays* (Toronto: University of Toronto Press, 1987), p. 230; Marilyn L. Williamson, *The Patriarchy of Shakespeare's Comedies* (Detroit: Wayne State University Press, 1986), p. 114.

fact that he has already demanded Catherine's hand and the French lands as her dowry, Hal moves through a brilliant dialogue.[83] The king shifts from blank verse to prose when the princess protests her inadequate command of English. He compliments her beauty and deprecates his own skill as a speaker. He angles for an early conclusion to his suit with, "I know no ways to mince it in love, but directly to say, 'I love you.' . . . Give me your answer, i'faith do, and so clap hands and a bargain" (127–131), the handclasp of course to signify her consent. When Catherine sidesteps a direct answer, he launches into a long, charming speech about his defects as a lover and a man, admitting disingenuously that "if thou canst love me for this, take me. If not, to say to thee that I shall die, is true—but for thy love, by the Lord, no. Yet I love thee, too" (150–153). Five more times he essays for her assent, while she parries him with questions and evasions. Through 140 lines Henry pursues his elusive bride-to-be in English interspersed with French. Even in the foreign tongue, says Catherine, "Your *majesté* 'ave *faux* French enough to deceive de most sage *demoiselle* dat is *en France*" (216–217). Inevitably, she comes to the agreement already ratified for her: "Den it sall also content me" (248). When Catherine still resists the customary gift of her hand that would seal an English bargain, Henry takes the more intimate symbol of compliance—a kiss from her lips.

Victorious in private, he now moves through the public ratification of his betrothal. First, the king turns to Catherine's father for formal approval of the match and agreement to the terms of their treaty-contract.

KING HARRY. Shall Kate be my wife?
KING CHARLES. So please you.
KING HARRY. I am content, so the maiden cities you talk of may wait on
    her.

(320–323)

When it turns out that France has not agreed to designate his son-in-law as "*Notre très cher fils Henri, Roi d'Angleterre, Héritier de France*" (334–335), the English ruler insists upon this requirement also as a condition of the espousal. "Let that one article rank with the rest, / And thereupon give

---

[83] Peter Erickson, *Patriarchal Structures in Shakespeare's Drama* (Berkeley: University of California Press, 1985), p. 10, finds this wooing "a mechanical final step in the completion of an all-around man." Lance Wilcox, "Katherine of France as Victim and Bride," *Shakespeare Studies* 17 (1985): 66, sees Hal, "the king of rapists," redeemed here by the willingness of the victim, by becoming husband rather than predator. These attitudes typify the uneasiness evoked by this courtship.

me your daughter" (341–342) represents his final declaration on the matter. The lords' "Amen" (351) is not just a perfunctory sign of approval but rather the legal witnessing of a marriage contract. The procedure ends with Henry's formal acknowledgment of Catherine as wife and consort: "Now welcome, Kate, and bear me witness all / That here I kiss her as my sovereign Queen" (352–353).[84] Point for point, the espousal of these two follows the customary rituals of courtship. Only the solemnities of a wedding now remain, as Henry recognizes, saying, "Prepare we for our marriage" (365). The very model of a king at war is the very model of a king at wooing, though in both enterprises hard political necessities subvert the nobility of his actions. Were Catherine a hunchbacked hag, Hal would still be obliged to establish his sovereignty over France by marrying her. The delightful courtship scene simply sweetens both the policies and the personalities involved in this bargain of state diplomacy.

Nothing could contrast more with the decorum of *Henry V* than the burlesque wooing in *The Taming of the Shrew*.[85] Yet, like Hal, Petruccio selects, sight unseen, a suitable wife (also named Katherine), negotiates finances with her father, and then gets a private meeting in which to win her consent. Kate's salty refusal to accept her lover's compliments, his courtship, or his proposal are really as much beside the point as are the princess's feelings about her marriage. In his characteristic way, Petruccio slashes to the heart of things, exposing the necessities that lie behind the niceties of the mating rite:

> And therefore setting all this chat aside,
> Thus in plain terms: your father hath consented
> That you shall be my wife, your dowry 'greed on,
> And will you, nill you, I will marry you.
>
> (II.i.262–265)

Kate publicly protests the arrangements made for her and rejects her wooer. To Baptista she storms, "You have shown a tender fatherly regard,

---

[84] It is difficult to see why Wilcox, "Katherine of France," p. 71, says of this kiss that "Katherine has again been cornered into public behavior bound to establish her in everyone's eyes as Henry's wife and lover," when she has already kissed in private and when the other essentials of the spousal are already set.

[85] For other analyses of the courtship protocols here, see George R. Hibbard, *"The Taming of the Shrew*: A Social Comedy," in *Shakespearean Essays*, ed. Alwin Thaler and Norman Sanders (Knoxville: University of Tennessee Press, 1964); Margaret Loftus Ranald, "The Manning of the Haggard; or *The Taming of the Shrew*," *Essays in Literature* 1 (1974): 149–165.

/ To wish me wed to one half-lunatic, / A madcap ruffian and a swearing Jack" (281–283). To her suitor's designation of a Sunday wedding she responds, "I'll see thee hanged on Sunday first" (294). Petruccio blithely dismisses these objections as mere pretense, continuing to portray Kate other than she actually is. According to him, she has responded privately with ardent affection: "She hung about my neck" and gave "kiss on kiss" (304)—just what a lover hopes for.

At this point, Petruccio wins his first battle in a way that would have been much clearer to Elizabethans than it is to modern spectators. Kate must agree to the betrothal for it to be valid, and her uncharacteristic silence—however obtained—marks her consent during the crucial moments of espousal. Petruccio first bids, "Give me thy hand, Kate," and then they formally receive Baptista's blessing, which symbolically transfers his daughter to her approved husband: "I know not what to say, but give me your hands. / God send you joy, Petruccio! 'Tis a match" (310, 314–315). The delighted Gremio and Tranio, now free to pursue Bianca, immediately seal the bargain with "Amen, say we. We will be witnesses" (316), just like the courtiers at Hal's betrothal. Wickedly comic, the contracting ceremony even includes Petruccio's acknowledgment of his new status as Baptista's son and of Kate's as his affianced wife, a reconfirmation of the wedding date with its jewels and finery, and the spousal kiss:

> Father, and wife, and gentlemen, adieu.
> I will to Venice. Sunday comes apace.
> We will have rings, and things, and fine array;
> And kiss me, Kate. We will be married o' Sunday.
>
> (317–320)

Though caricature, this scene still follows the prescribed steps for wooing as faithfully as does the final scene of *Henry V*.

Additionally, *The Taming of the Shrew* follows the bridal path all the way to the altar and beyond. Petruccio has already referred to Baptista's obligations: "Provide the feast, father, and bid the guests" (312). On the appointed Sunday morning, when all stands in readiness—the bride in her best attire, the priest in attendance, and the company assembled—the groom is nowhere to be seen. Belatedly, Petruccio arrives to make as full a mock of the marriage ceremony as he has made of the other courtship rituals. Instead of the usual escort of friends, the groom is attended only by his lackey. Instead of his finest garments, "Why, Petruccio is coming in a new hat and an old jerkin, a pair of old breeches thrice-turned, a pair of boots that have been candle-cases, one buckled, another laced, an old rusty sword ta'en out of the town armoury with a broken hilt, and chapeless, with two broken points" (III.ii.43–48). The servant Grumio is no better, "with a linen stock on one leg and a kersey boot-hose on the other, gartered with a red and blue list; an old hat, and the humour of forty fancies pricked in't for a feather—a monster, a very monster in apparel" (64–68). As for the bridegroom's horse, it beggars description. Despite all pleas to "doff this habit, shame to your estate, / An eyesore to our solemn festival" (100–101), Petruccio stands firm. Not only does such outrageous behavior fit into his plans for taming Kate, but he implicitly recognizes that the essentials of any betrothal or wedding, as well as any marriage, lie not in the decorations of external appearance but in the legal, religious, and emotional bonds at the heart of the marital relationship: "To me she's married, not unto my clothes" (117).

Having conformed to every technical requirement of the wooing while flouting its romantic conventions, Petruccio now conforms to every technical requirement of the church ceremony while flouting its solemnity. Concerned lest the hour slip past the noon deadline for weddings, he observes, "The morning wears, 'tis time we were at church" (111). As Gremio reports of the religious service, the groom consents to take Katherine as his wife but makes the vows in outrageous fashion:

> "Ay, by Gogs-woun's," quoth he, and swore so loud
> That all amazed the priest let fall the book,
> And as he stooped to take it up
> This mad-brained bridegroom took him such a cuff
> That down fell priest, and book, and book, and priest.
>
> (III.iii.33–37)

Petruccio further "took the bride about the neck / And kissed her lips with such a clamorous smack / That at the parting all the church did echo" (50–52). Still, nothing in the prayer book invalidates a marriage or even compels the officiant to stop the nuptials because of such behavior. Nor does Petruccio's final carousal "after many ceremonies done" (42), when he throws the dregs of his wine into the sexton's face, negate the fact that both parties are duly joined for life. All the peripheral customs are irrelevant, including the wedding feast.[86] "I know you think to dine with me

---

[86] As Carol F. Heffernan analyzes the situation, "*The Taming of the Shrew*: The Bourgeoisie in Love," *Essays in Literature* 12 (1985): 10–11, Petruccio wins Kate "flying in the face of middle class formalities"; she adds that his "failure to attend the reception is an abuse

today, / And have prepared great store of wedding cheer. / But so it is my haste doth call me hence" (58–60). The revelry following the marriage rites has no real power in authorizing the union.

After cutting through to the meaning of the prenuptial agreements, Petruccio now cuts through to the hard facts implied by the binding vows he has just exchanged with Kate:

> I will be master of what is mine own.
> She is my goods, my chattels. She is my house,
> My household-stuff, my field, my barn,
> My horse, my ox, my ass, my anything.[87]

(101–104)

With or without a proper feast, with or without proper decorum, with or without proper attire, the spousal has been ratified by a wedding, and Kate is Petruccio's forever. The marriage remains unconsummated for a week, nightly lectures on chastity substituting for a proper bedding. However, at Bianca's wedding celebration, Kate takes the honors from both her sister and Hortensio's bride, departing early with acclaim and a second dowry for the final step to lawful matrimony: "Come, Kate, we'll to bed" (V.ii.189).[88] Thus from the initial inquiry about a bride to a triumphant sexual union, *The Taming of the Shrew* keeps to all the essential requirements for conventional courtship while violating all its proprieties. Espe-

---

of bourgeois convention," as if such matters were important only at this social level. Heffernan's anachronistic use of the terms "middle class," "bourgeois," and "reception" typify the interpretations of ahistorical critics. Marion D. Perret, "Petruchio: The Model Wife," *Studies in English Literature* 23 (1983): 230, finds Kate disobedient for inviting guests to the feast "contrary to her husband's wishes" but shows no awareness that such entertainment was customary. Petruccio's refusal to attend is peculiar, not Kate's invitation.

[87] Michael W. Kaufman, "Spare Ribs: The Conception of Women in the Middle Ages and the Renaissance," *Soundings* 56 (1973): 157, points out that anthropologists call this ritual that confers ownership a "purchase of the right" and consider it the "foundation of the patriarchal family."

[88] With ahistorical aplomb, Irene G. Dash, *Wooing, Wedding and Power: Women in Shakespeare's Plays* (New York: Columbia University Press, 1981), p. 36, says Petruccio's postponement of consummation shows that "Shakespeare was more sensitive than his interpreters have been to the reactions of a woman at such a moment." Lynda E. Boose, "The Comic Contract and Portia's Golden Ring," *Shakespeare Studies* 20 (1988): 245, claims that Kate's offer of her hand under Petruccio's foot enacts the Rite of Sarum in which the bride prostrated herself before the groom after he endowed her and gave her a ring. Even though the endowment and the ring-giving do not accompany Kate's actions here, Boose nonetheless claims the 1596 audience "would almost certainly have recognized" a rite discontinued forty-five years earlier.

cially when set alongside the other matches in the play, Shakespeare's technique both affirms and brutally exposes the approved methods for making a match.

Understanding the various steps required for a betrothal and a wedding soon makes it clear that Shakespeare routinely informs his audience about the status of the various unions he presents onstage. In *Much Ado*, for instance, Leonato presides over the espousal of his daughter Hero and Count Claudio, an engagement that she ratifies before witnesses with an inaudible whisper.

> LEONATO. Count, take of me my daughter, and with her my fortunes. His grace hath made the match, and all grace say amen to it.
> BEATRICE. Speak, Count, 'tis your cue.
> CLAUDIO. . . . Lady, as you are mine, I am yours. I give away myself for you, and dote on the exchange.
> BEATRICE. (*to Hero*) Speak, cousin. Or, if you cannot, stop his mouth with a kiss, and let not him speak, neither. . . . My cousin tells him in his ear that he is in her heart.
> CLAUDIO. And so she doth, cousin.
>
> (II.i.283–286, 288–291, 295–297)

When Claudio rejects Hero, supposedly causing her death, he goes through the same public betrothal ritual again with Leonato's mysterious "niece," even acknowledging her right of refusal:

> CLAUDIO. Which is the lady I must seize upon?
> ANTONIO. This same is she, and I do give you her.
> CLAUDIO. Why then, she's mine. Sweet, let me see your face.
> LEONATO. No, that you shall not till you take her hand
>   Before this Friar and swear to marry her.
> CLAUDIO. (*to Hero*) Give me your hand before this holy friar.
>   I am your husband if you like of me.
> HERO. (*unmasking*) And when I lived I was your other wife;
>   And when you loved, you were my other husband.[89]
>
> (V.iv.53–61)

In this comedy of to-have-or-not-to-have, the two spousals designate the

---

[89] Garber, *Coming of Age*, p. 226, says that Claudio's "acceptance of a bride sight unseen reverses the dangerous and misleading demand for ocular proof." Ranald, " 'As Marriage Binds,' " pp. 75–76, and *Shakespeare and His Social Context*, pp. 18–19, points out that this spousal is *de praesenti* and thus virtually indissoluble, as is the first betrothal.

points where the lovers formally agree to have each other. But the counterpoints set up in the action make it seem first to Hero's father and then to Claudio that she will have the prince instead. Between the two formal commitments lie the bride's apparent entertainment of another man, the groom's disavowal of his pledges, the injured young woman's withdrawal from him into "death," and his reconciliation with her in a graveside penance. Hence the formal betrothals form only part of the ping-pong movements from acceptance to rejection that characterize *Much Ado*—and only the last blind trothplight represents a permanent union.

Similarly, Beatrice and Benedick also initiate and then abort straightforward vows of commitment. In the past they too have pledged and unpledged a heart: "He lent it me a while, and I gave him use for it, a double heart for his single one. Marry, once before he won it of me, with false dice. Therefore your grace may well say I have lost it" (II.i.260–263). As matters stand, each is at first determined not to have the other, indeed not to marry at all. Next the pendulum swings to desperate mutual desire and then to the inevitable stage of formally witnessed betrothal vows that will end their vacillation. Benedick has already broached the question of marriage through the friar, receiving the approval of both Leonato and the prince. Yet when he confronts Beatrice, she balks, her response consistent with the history of their relationship and also with the basic movements of the comic action.

> BEATRICE.   . . . what is your will?
> BENEDICK. Do not you love me?
> BEATRICE.   Why no, no more than reason.
>
> . . . .
>
>   Do not you love me?
> BENEDICK.   Troth no, no more than reason.
>
> (V.iv.73–74, 77)

Yet, with the further assistance of their friends and the written evidence of their own hands, they too proceed teasingly through the required public declaration of their willingness to marry, including the usual kiss.[90]

> BENEDICK. Come, I will have thee, but by this light, I take thee for pity.

---

[90] See also Ranald, " 'As Marriage Binds,' " p. 77. Neely, *Broken Nuptials*, p. 56, does not note the spousal represented by the kiss but sees it "manifesting their mutual desire, . . . a truce in their merry wars," which "silences Beatrice for the rest of the play" and allows Benedick to control the nuptials.

BEATRICE. I would not deny you, but by this good day, I yield upon great persuasion, and partly to save your life, for I was told you were in a consumption.

BENEDICK. (*kissing her*) Peace, I will stop your mouth.

(92–97)

What remains one of the most charming proposals in the canon is also the familiar espousal ritual that customarily preceded a wedding ceremony, marking a conclusion to the play, to the alteration of intent, and to the unmarried condition.

Twelfth Night presents another pair of betrothals, one formally ratified, the other more irregularly contracted, but both equally valid. Rather than let Cesario/Sebastian further elude her, Olivia bids him, "Plight me the full assurance of your faith" in "the chantry by" (IV.iii.26, 24) before a cleric whom she has summoned. Sebastian vows, "I'll follow this good man, and go with you, / And having sworn truth, ever will be true" (32–33). When called to testify about the rite he has witnessed, the priest describes a classic espousal:[91]

> A contract of eternal bond of love,
> Confirmed by mutual joinder of your hands,
> Attested by the holy close of lips,
> Strengthened by interchangement of your rings,
> And all the ceremony of this compact
> Sealed in my function, by my testimony.

(V.i.154–159)

As a result, Olivia is fully entitled to call Cesario/Sebastian her "husband" (141, 142), even though the wedding has yet to be performed. A few lines

---

[91] Karl P. Wentersdorf, "The Time Problem in *Othello*: A Reconsideration," *Jahrbuch, Deutsche Shakespeare-Gesellschaft West* (1985): 70, says the spousal is probably *de futuro*; but Garber, *Coming of Age*, p. 119, and Pearson, *Elizabethans*, p. 334, say it is probably *de praesenti*. I think the text indicates only that it is a spousal. Among the few who recognize the ceremony to be a betrothal are Jorg Hasler, *Shakespeare's Theatrical Notation: The Comedies* (Bern: Francke Verlag, 1974), p. 164; William G. Meader, *Courtship in Shakespeare; Its Relation to the Tradition of Courtly Love* (New York: Columbia University, King's Crown Press, 1954), p. 155; Ernest Pettett, *Shakespeare and the Romance Tradition* (New York: Staples Press, 1949), p. 82; Ranald, *Shakespeare and His Social Context*, pp. 103–104. Those mistaking it for a wedding are too numerous even to list.

later, Sebastian further clarifies their vows by using the terms "contracted" and "betrothed" (259, 261).

When the sex and identity of Cesario/Viola are finally revealed, Orsino leads her too through the ritual declaration of love, clasp of hands, and promise of marriage.

> ORSINO. Boy, thou hast said to me a thousand times
>   Thou never shouldst love woman like to me.
> VIOLA. And all those sayings will I overswear,
>   And all those swearings keep as true in soul
>   As doth that orbèd continent the fire
>   That severs day from night.
> ORSINO.   Give me thy hand,
>   And let me see thee in thy woman's weeds.
>
> . . . .
>
>   Here is my hand. You shall from this time be
>   Your master's mistress.
>
>   (265–271, 322–323)

Eventually their handfasting will also be ratified with a wedding. Now the contracted wife of Viola's brother-guardian, Olivia properly offers to host the occasion:

> OLIVIA. My lord, so please you—these things further thought on—
>   To think me as well a sister as a wife,
>   One day shall crown th'alliance on't, so please you,
>   Here at my house and at my proper cost.
> ORSINO. Madam, I am most apt t'embrace your offer.
>
>   (313–317)

In *Twelfth Night*, the betrothals do not primarily halt a pattern of vacillation, as in *Much Ado*. Instead, these pledges order the chaos that has provided the comic impetus for the play. In a sense, the handfastings place the future into fast, or firm, hands that will curb the excesses and irregularities of Illyria. And they do so by strict adherence to the protocol required for entering such a commitment.[92]

---

[92] For other plays that enact a betrothal ceremony, see *WT*, IV.iv.358–417, V.iii.107–109, 137–139, 142–147; *Per.*, sc. 9, 103–113; *Jn.*, II.i.485–540; *Tit.*, I.i.238–245, 312–334; *Tmp.*, IV.i.7–14, 32; and *MV*, III.ii.135–148, 163–174. Only this last spousal has been subject to critical dispute. Diane Elizabeth Dreher, *Domination and Defiance: Fa-*

Perhaps the most intriguing use of nuptial customs occurs in *Richard II*, when the dethroned king parts from his wife. Step by step, backward through the oath, the kiss, the joined hands, Richard reverses the process by which they were united.

> RICHARD. Doubly divorced! Bad men, you violate
> A twofold marriage: 'twixt my crown and me,
> And then betwixt me and my married wife.
> (*To the Queen*) Let me unkiss the oath 'twixt thee and me—
> And yet not so, for with a kiss 'twas made.
> Part us, Northumberland: I towards the north,
> Where shivering cold and sickness pines the clime;
> My queen to France, from whence set forth in pomp
> She came adornèd hither like sweet May,
> Sent back like Hallowmas or short'st of day.
> QUEEN. And must we be divided? Must we part?
> RICHARD. Ay, hand from hand, my love, and heart from heart.
>
> . . . .
>
> Come, come, in wooing sorrow let's be brief,
> Since, wedding it, there is such length in grief.
> One kiss shall stop our mouths, and dumbly part.
> Thus give I mine, and thus take I thy heart.
> *They kiss*
> QUEEN. Give me mine own again. 'Twere no good part
> To take on me to keep and kill thy heart.
> *They kiss*
> So now I have mine own again, be gone,

thers and Daughters in Shakespeare (Lexington: University Press of Kentucky, 1986), pp. 132–133, mistakenly thinks a spousal precedes the casket test. Lisa Jardine, "Cultural Confusion and Shakespeare's Learned Heroines: 'These are old paradoxes,'" *Shakespeare Quarterly* 38 (1987): 13, claims that if Bassanio parts with the ring, Portia can break their betrothal. However, since their vows are solemnized in church before this happens, she cannot use such grounds for a dissolution. Jardine places Nerissa's ring in a different category, "a pledge of *sexual* fidelity, in another social class." Legally, both rings have exactly the same status. For other aspects of Portia's transfer of wealth and status to Bassanio, see Jonathan Goldberg, "Shakespearean Inscriptions: The Voicing of Power," in *Shakespeare and the Question of Theory*, ed. Patricia Parker and Geoffrey Hartman (New York: Methuen, 1985), pp. 123–124; Karen Newman, "Portia's Ring: Unruly Women and Structures of Exchange in *The Merchant of Venice*," *Shakespeare Quarterly* 38 (1987): 19–33; Ranald, *Shakespeare and His Social Context*, p. 67.

That I may strive to kill it with a groan.

RICHARD. We make woe wanton with this fond delay.

Once more, adieu. The rest let sorrow say.

(V.i.71–82, 93–102)

This brilliant inversion of wedding protocol images Richard's enforced separation from the English crown, to which he has also been married. It extends as well the other inverted ceremonies where Richard both presides and participates—the aborted tournament, the surrender to Bolingbroke, the uncrowning.[93] The language also perpetuates the king's characteristic ambivalence. First he is divorced, then wed, the oath unkissed, then not unkissed, the hearts exchanged, then reexchanged. In the bitter reversal of their royal union, Northumberland serves not as a priest to marry them nor a groomsman to attend their marriage nor an ambassador to deliver a bride-queen to Richard but rather as the authority who parts them, the official witness to their severance, the escort to the divorced king's solitary, celibate prison. The queen, too, exchanges the pomp and springtime adornment of her wedding journey to England for the tears of a dark autumnal return to the compelled chastity of exile in a French convent. Replacing dalliance in a bridal bed, woe alone is wanton. And though the wooing stage of their new status is brief, the sorrow of separation into which they enter will, like marriage, last until death.[94]

Through references in other works, Shakespeare offers glimpses of the kind of celebrations that usually attended the wedding day. Brides in two plays discuss their nuptial attire. When Juliet pretends to accede to the marriage with Paris, she asks the Nurse to "go with me into my closet / To help me sort such needful ornaments / As you think fit to furnish me tomorrow" (IV.ii.33–35). Fittingly, Juliet is dressed, "as the custom is, / All in her best array" (IV.iv.107–108)—presumably her wedding finery— when she goes to meet her husband, Romeo, for their final union in the Capulet tomb. A less fatal preparation, but one with obvious correspondences to *Romeo and Juliet*, occurs when Hero selects clothes for the aborted

[93] Walter Pater, "Shakespeare's English Kings," *Appreciations, With an Essay on Style* (London: Macmillan, 1918), p. 198, is perhaps the first to note the inverted rite of the deposition. So far as I know, no one else has noted this particular inversion.

[94] Robert B. Pierce, *Shakespeare's History Plays: The Family and the State* (Columbus: Ohio State University Press, 1971), p. 164, feels, "The figure of marriage to the crown is not quite conventional and so loses the power of the orthodox commonplace, and it lacks the startling inevitability of Shakespeare's richer metaphors." Within the context of traditional courtship, however, the passage does show a "startling inevitability."

wedding that causes her presumed death. Like Juliet, she chooses the best garments from her existing wardrobe, debating the merits of one rebato (ornamental collar) over another. To a compliment on the "most rare fashion" of her gown, she responds, "God give me joy to wear it, for my heart is exceeding heavy" (*Ado*, III.iv.13–14, 23–24). On its own terms this premarital chatter is inconsequential. However, when set into the play's motifs of disguise and deceit, the focus on the bride's dress assumes considerable importance. Well might her heart be heavy, since Hero adorns herself for a shameful "death" and, worse, the loss of a husband. Regardless of what she wears, she will appear either faithless or stainless depending upon the faith of the beholder. The masks at the betrothal party, Margaret's use of Hero's clothing in the midnight rendezvous with Borachio, and the veiled figures in the final spousal scene all testify to the irrelevance of external garments in the issues of love and trust that lie at the heart of marriage and of *Much Ado*—precisely the point a madly dressed Petruccio makes more farcically at the wedding in *The Taming of the Shrew*.

Not only the bride but the bridegroom too was expected to wear grand attire, as the outcry over Petruccio's appearance indicates. Moreover, the husband-to-be was usually accompanied by friends, who escorted the bride from her home to the church. Thus at "almost five o'clock," Ursula urges Hero, "Madam, withdraw. The Prince, the Count, Signor Benedick, Don John, and all the gallants of the town are come to fetch you to church" (47, 89–91). An early arrival, the sign of an impatient lover, is referred to by *Romeo and Juliet*'s Friar Laurence—"the bridegroom in the morning comes / To rouse thee from thy bed" (IV.i.107–108). Hence a nervous Capulet greets the dawning with,

> Good faith, 'tis day,
> The County will be here with music straight,
> For so he said he would.
> *Music plays within*
> I hear him near.
>
> . . . .
>
> Go waken Juliet; go and trim her up.
> I'll go and chat with Paris. Hie, make haste.
>
> (IV.iv.21–23, 26–27)

The obvious irony here is that Paris comes to fetch his bride to her tomb. There she will join in death with the man she has married in life, and there her would-be bridegroom will also die. Similarly, Claudio and his friends, intending a public disgrace instead of a nuptial, will find they have escorted Hero to the church for apparent burial.

After the religious ceremony came appropriate feasting, usually at the bride's home, with the newly married couple presiding over the festivities. Several plays refer to this part of the wedding day, including Hamlet's dark comment that his father's "funeral baked meats / Did coldly furnish forth the marriage tables" (I.ii.179–180) of Gertrude and Claudius. Saturninus grudgingly invites his brother and Lavinia, who "left me like a churl" (*Tit.*, I.i.482), to share the revelry of his own marriage: "Come, if the Emperor's court can feast two brides / You are my guest, Lavinia, and your friends. / This day shall be a love-day, Tamora" (485–487). The presence of friends, the role of host taken by the elder brother as head of the family and of the state, even the mention of "day" in an era when weddings were held between dawn and noon, all inhere in an Englished Rome. In a military setting, the marriage banquet of Desdemona and Othello merges with the jubilee of victory over the Turkish fleet. Given the absence of the bride's father and kinsmen, the Moor presides, combining a host's function with his roles as general and bridegroom, proclaiming "sport and revels" for the "triumph" and "the celebration of his nuptial" (II.ii.5, 4, 7).

Not that every wedding is immediately followed with a great feast. Though insisting that the marriage of Helen and Bertram shall "be performed tonight," the King of France postpones the banqueting: "The solemn feast / Shall more attend upon the coming space, / Expecting absent friends" (*AWW*, II.iii.181–183). And for Juliet's hasty wedding to Paris, which Shakespeare adds to his sources, Capulet decrees:

> We'll keep no great ado—a friend or two.
> For hark you, Tybalt being slain so late,
> It may be thought we held him carelessly,
> Being our kinsman, if we revel much.
> Therefore we'll have some half a dozen friends,
> And there an end.
>
> (III.iv.23–28)

Nevertheless, even for so small a celebration, Capulet hires "twenty cunning cooks" (IV.ii.2–3), sets the household on its ear, and keeps servants up all night making preparations. If so much effort goes into a modest feast, one can well imagine the party prepared by Baptista for Kate's wedding, where "there wants no junkets" (*Shr.*, III.iii.120), and then for Bianca's the next week. In *The Taming of the Shrew* the audience actually sees *"the servingmen with Tranio bringing in a banquet"* (V.ii.s.d.).

Whether wagering on the obedience of wives ever formed a part of nuptial festivities is doubtful. However, certain other forms of entertainment were common enough in both Shakespeare and his society. The musicians brought for Juliet's wedding with Paris, as well as the dances that conclude *As You Like It* and *Much Ado*, usually formed part of the "triumphs, mirth, and rare solemnity" (*TGV*, V.iv.159). At the highest social levels the celebration might go on for days—indeed Theseus promises, "A fortnight hold we this solemnity / In nightly revels and new jollity" (*MND*, V.i.362–363). In any case, some diversion is necessary to fill the time between the feast after the morning wedding and the onset of night when the bride could be brought to bed. As Theseus inquires of Philostrate, "Come now, what masques, what dances shall we have / To wear away this long age of three hours / Between our after-supper and bed-time?" (32–34). Here the guests see the "tedious brief scene of young Pyramus / And his love Thisbe: very tragical mirth" (56–57), improbably performed by Bottom and his company of rude mechanicals.[95] However, English royalty and nobility enjoyed far more elaborate productions on such occasions.[96]

For bride and groom, the end of the wedding day came at bedtime. When " 'tis not yet ten o'th' clock," Othello leaves his feast to make "wanton the night" with Desdemona (II.iii.13, 16). Theseus notes, "The iron tongue of midnight hath told twelve. / Lovers, to bed" (*MND*, V.i.356–357). Thus "when our nuptial day was done, / And tapers burnt to bedward" (*Cor.*, I.vii.31–32), then "Hymen's torch" (*Tmp.*, IV.i.97), "the happy wedding torch" (*1H6*, III.iii.9), lit the bride and groom to their chamber. Gertrude's wistful lament at Ophelia's grave, "I thought thy bride-bed to have decked, sweet maid" (*Ham.*, V.i.242), refers to the custom of strewing flowers upon the linens to perfume the night's pleasures. As for the guests, carousing long after the bedding, toasting "happiness to their sheets!" (*Oth.*, II.iii.26), eventually they too left off celebrating for slumber.

[95] Bristol, *Carnival*, pp. 172–178, says that this performance intrudes the "rough music" of village charivari into an aristocratic celebration, making "a mockery, not only of the harmony of the wedding feast, but more generally of the contradictions of aristocratic marriage, where the pattern of conflicting imperatives is as likely to result in violence as in harmony," p. 177.

[96] Marion Colthorpe, "Queen Elizabeth I and *A Midsummer Night's Dream*," *Notes and Queries*, n.s., 34 (1987): 207, finds no evidence that a professional company ever performed at any wedding before 1614.

Now sleep y-slackèd hath the rout,
No din but snores the house about,
Made louder by the o'erfèd breast
Of this most pompous marriage feast.

(Per., sc. 10, 1–4)

And so ended the road from the unwedded to the wedded state.[97]

Shakespeare makes relatively little use of the experiences that followed the nuptial night, except in *The Taming of the Shrew*, where Petruccio tames Kate during the interval between wedding and bedding. On the morning after her marriage feast, musicians come to entertain Desdemona.[98] Ironically, they are hired by Cassio, familiar with such traditions, and dismissed by the alien Othello because "to hear music the general does not greatly care" (III.i.16–17). Whatever her response to the conventional serenade, before the day is out, this new wife will lament that she cannot "look for such observancy / As fits the bridal" (III.iv.147–148). In a similarly grim postlude to a wedding, Titus Andronicus proposes a hunt on the morning after the marriages of his daughter and his emperor. Since Lavinia and Bassianus will turn out to be the prey, he murdered, she ravished and mutilated, this choice of amusement is macabrely fitting. Fitting too that, instead of the customary music, baying dogs greet the doomed pair, together with the savage Tamora and Saturninus, who will hunt down the house of the Andronici: "Uncouple here, and let us make a bay / And wake the Emperor and his lovely bride" (II.ii.3–4). Jokes about the hour's being "too early for new-married ladies" (15) juxtapose the pleasures of the wedding night with the horrors of the daylight rape to which one bride will abandon the other.

Eschewing horror, though certainly not irony, a brief passage related to courtship appears in *Coriolanus*. When the banished Roman warrior offers himself to his former Volscian rival, Aufidius embraces him warmly, uttering these words of welcome: "But that I see thee here, / Thou noble thing, more dances my rapt heart / Than when I first my wedded mistress

---

[97] Garber, *Coming of Age*, pp. 143–148, discusses the consummation itself, with aubades in *Rom.* and *Tro.* (a modified one in *AWW* she misses), together with such emblems of defloration as a spotted handkerchief in *Oth.*, Thisbe's bloody mantle in *MND*, Cloten's body in *Cym.*, and the bloody napkin in *AYL*.

[98] François Laroque, "An Archaeology of the Dramatic Text: *Othello* and Popular Traditions," *Cahiers Élisabethains* 32 (1987): 19–21, sees both this scene and the opening scene as a perverted form of mattinata, charivari, or rough music, sometimes used to "protest against ill-assorted marriages or against strangers who married local women," p. 20. See above, n.70.

saw / Bestride my threshold" (IV.v.116–119). This speech moves beyond the wedding celebration to the very end of the bridal path. As a rule, marriage festivities took place in the home of the bride's father or some other relative or friend. Not until the new wife crossed her husband's threshold did she become mistress of his house, fully subject to his rule, wholly his own. The advent of Coriolanus into Aufidius's household, appropriately enough during a feast, marks his movement from the Roman family into which he was born to the Volscian one he freely "marries." Already he and his new "spouse" have had encounters intensifying their mutual admiration: "He is a lion / That I am proud to hunt" (I.i.29–30). Already Caius Marcius has adopted his new surname, derived from the Volscians' principal city of Corioles. Now, in the loving clasp of his chosen partner—"Let me twine / Mine arms about that body" (IV.v.107–108)— he enters a relationship from which only death will sever him. In a parallel to the sealing of a betrothal with parental approval, he is asked to "take our friendly senators by th' hands" (133).[99] Afterward, Aufidius and Coriolanus pursue their goals together, while ever vying to see who will head this masculine military marriage. That so unnatural a wedding of one's enemy, involving divorce of wife, child, mother, and nation, cannot be sustained is tragically borne out by the play's subsequent action.

What seems most striking about Shakespeare's uses of the traditional forms of betrothal and marriage is the density with which they appear in widely varied texts. While an occasional comedy, like *The Taming of the Shrew*, will provide a full, if parodic, treatment of the step-by-step mating dance, most plays rely on compression, a kind of shorthand, to signify the precise status of a couple at any given point. Signals like letters, gifts, joined hands, kisses, rings, witnesses, even the casual mention of a wedding torch link up with a whole set of assumptions that were the ordinary furnishings of an Elizabethan mentality. Domestic touches, like the quinces for festal pies or the bride's preference of one rebato over another, bring to instant life the experiences anticipated by almost every affianced couple and their families. Grander allusions to masques and triumphs speak of realms where marriage brought not just an exchange of vows but untold wealth and power. However, the inevitable alterations of the courtship experience wrought by time's passage necessitate a relearning of Renaissance codes to enable the modern audience to appreciate fully what

[99] Alexander Leggatt, *Shakespeare's Political Drama: The History Plays and the Roman Plays* (London: Routledge, 1988), p. 205, also recognizes this encounter as a parody of a marriage bond, which will eventually break, as the one with his Roman wife will not.

Shakespeare is doing in any play. He may provoke discomfort by exposing the harsh realities underlying the protocols of etiquette. He may pair conventional and unconventional enactments of the same ritual in mutually devastating commentary. While adhering to the aesthetic demands of each dramatic context, he may ease tensions, shatter illusions, point to some wider social implication, or clarify an otherwise ambiguous relationship. Whether conforming to, reversing, burlesquing, or attacking a given situation, he works through culturally shared expectations about the proper way to proceed from first acquaintance to consummated matrimony. But his effects quite lose their power over those who do not know how English subjects once made their matches.

Secret Promises and Elopements, Broken Contracts and Divorces

Errour, condition, parentage, and vow,
Adultery (the law will not allow
Disparitie in divine worship) and
Violence or force, or where we understand;
In priesthood, there's profaneness, or else where,
False faiths profest, wee likewise must forebeare,
When there is precontract, for honesty,
Affinitie, and disability:
These twelve from present marriage us disswade,
Or can retract from wedlock when 'tis made.
—Thomas Heywood, *A Curtaine Lecture*

Quoth she, "Before you tumbled me,
You promised me to wed."
So would I 'a' done by yonder sun,
An thou hadst not come to my bed.
—*Ham.*, IV.v.62–65

THOUGH the conventional steps leading to an indissoluble marriage seemed clear enough to English subjects, there were also shortcuts, detours, and journeys abandoned altogether. In some cases, lovers made private rather than public promises to marry. And whatever the nature of their espousals, couples could and did consummate unions without waiting for a religious ceremony. Legally binding contracts, whether *de futuro* or *de praesenti*, might be set aside if any of several impediments existed. Elopements and secret weddings sometimes occurred. Under certain circumstances marriages were annulled, and on a few grounds even a form of divorce was possible. But because such situations represented a departure from prescribed behavior, a plethora of opinion, advice, legal restrictions, social stigma, and economic punishments converged upon those who strayed from the more conventional ways of making a match.

Of particular concern was the danger of clandestine meetings between an unmarried man and woman lest they lead to sexual intercourse. The Elizabethans' great fear of seduction derived from the ensuing stain on the female's reputation, the likelihood of pregnancy, and the possibility of her subsequent abandonment. At every level, the social structure required a child to be supported by his parents so he would not become a charge on the general public. Hence, church courts prosecuted with vigor cases of bastardy, fornication, prenuptial pregnancy, and adultery.[1] The homily *Against Whoredom and Uncleanness* was read in every parish, there were legal penalties for harboring unwed mothers, pregnancy meant dismissal for unwed servants, and midwives were instructed to use extreme means during labor for determining the fathers of illegitimate children. After 1610 "Euery lewd woman which shall haue any bastard which may be chargeable to the parish" was to be committed "to the house of correction, to be punished and set on work, during the term of one whole year."[2] Not surprisingly, the records show a low incidence of illegitimacy—about 3 percent or less, though a small upsurge around the turn of the century has not been fully explained.[3]

[1] In addition to evidence in the works cited below, see Susan Dwyer Amussen, "Féminin/masculin: le genre dans l'Angleterre de l'epoque moderne," *Annales Économies, Sociétés, Civilisations* 40 (1985): 271–276; E.R.C. Brinkworth, ed., *The Archdeacon's Court*, Oxfordshire Record Society 23 (1942): passim; R. H. Helmholz, *Canon Law and the Law of England* (London: Hambledon Press, 1987), pp. 184–185. I am also indebted to unpublished work on London by R. Mark Benbow.

[2] Alan Macfarlane, "Illegitimacy and Illegitimates in English History," in *Bastardy and Its Comparative History*, ed. Peter Laslett, Karla Oosterveen, and Richard M. Smith (Cambridge: Harvard University Press, 1980), p. 73. See also Susan Dwyer Amussen, "Gender, Family and the Social Order, 1560–1725," in *Order and Disorder in Early Modern England*, ed. Anthony Fletcher and John Stevenson (Cambridge: Cambridge University Press, 1985), pp. 200, 207; E.R.C. Brinkworth, *Shakespeare and the Bawdy Court of Stratford* (London: Phillimore, 1972), pp. 73, 80–91; F. G. Emmison, *Elizabethan Life: Morals and the Church Courts* (Chelmsford: Essex County Council, 1973), pp. 25–30; Martin Ingram, *Church Courts, Sex, and Marriage in England, 1570–1640* (Cambridge: Cambridge University Press, 1987), pp. 237, 282, 285–291. Walter J. King, "Punishment for Bastardy in Early Seventeenth-Century England," *Albion* 10 (1978): 151, thinks that women were punished more harshly because removing males from productivity would have damaged the economy. However, since the mother could scarcely avoid detection and was also victimized by the lower status of her gender, a masculine system of justice inevitably placed the greater onus on her. See, e.g., Susan Dwyer Amussen, *An Ordered Society: Gender and Class in Early Modern England* (New York: Basil Blackwell, 1988), pp. 111–117.

[3] Peter Laslett, "Introduction: Comparing Illegitimacy over Time and between Cultures," in *Bastardy*, pp. 14, 22; David Levine and Keith Wrightson, "The Social Context of Illegitimacy in Early Modern England," in *Bastardy*, pp. 159, 164, 170–171; Karla Oosterveen and Richard M. Smith, "Bastardy and the Family Reconstitution Studies of

Aside from the activities of prostitutes and habitually wanton women, casual illicit sex seems to have been relatively common among the poor and the obscure.[4] Social historians account for differences in behavior between the upper and lower ranks in a variety of ways. They point to the opportunities for interaction provided by fairs or village festivities, by the movements of seasonal laborers, and by the employment of unmarried young adults as household servants.[5] Under such circumstances, a great deal more promiscuity might have occurred had it not been for strict formal and informal controls, particularly in the village or neighborhood, where all actions were matters of common knowledge. Yet advice routinely given to masters, together with the proceedings of the church's so-called bawdy courts and the tenor of much popular literature, confirms the existence of premarital and extramarital sexual activity. Philip Stubbes doubtless exaggerates in his complaint against festivals that "of fourtie, threescore, or a hundred Maides, going to the wood ouernight, there haue scarcely the third part of them returned home againe undefiled."[6] Nonetheless, illicit encounters did occur. In a suit for defamation it was alleged that one Isobel Lombye

---

Colyton, Aldenham, Alcester and Hawkshead," in *Bastardy*, pp. 100–101; G. R. Quaife, *Wanton Wenches and Wayward Wives: Peasants and Illicit Sex in Early Seventeenth Century England* (New Brunswick, NJ: Rutgers University Press, 1979), pp. 225–242; Edward Shorter, *The Making of the Modern Family* (New York: Basic Books, 1975), pp. 80–85; Keith Wrightson and David Levine, *Poverty and Piety in an English Village: Terling, 1525–1700* (New York: Academic Press, 1979), pp. 126–127, 132.

[4] Emmison, *Elizabethan Life*, pp. 20–24; Ingram, *Church Courts*, pp. 158–163, 269–273; Laslett, "Introduction," pp. 54–59; idem, "The Bastardy Prone Sub-Society," in *Bastardy*, pp. 217–246; Levine and Wrightson, "Social Context," 164, 166, 168–171; Quaife, *Wanton Wenches*, pp. 229–230; J. A. Sharpe, *Crime in Early Modern England 1550–1750* (London: Longman, 1984), pp. 100, 110; Keith Wrightson, *English Society, 1580–1680* (London: Hutchinson, 1982), pp. 84–86; Wrightson and Levine, *Poverty*, pp. 128, 131–132.

[5] John R. Gillis, *For Better, for Worse: British Marriages, 1600 to the Present* (Oxford: Oxford University Press, 1985), pp. 23ff.; Ralph A. Houlbrooke, *Church Courts and the People during the English Reformation, 1520–1570* (Oxford: Oxford University Press, 1979), p. 58; Ingram, *Church Courts*, pp. 156–157, 225–226, 240–241; Ann Kussmaul, *Servants in Husbandry in Early Modern England* (Cambridge: Cambridge University Press, 1981), pp. 79–83; Alan Macfarlane, *Marriage and Love in England: Modes of Reproduction 1300–1840* (Oxford: Basil Blackwell, 1986), p. 296; David Underdown, *Revel, Riot, and Rebellion: Popular Politics and Culture in England 1603–1660* (Oxford: Clarendon Press, 1985), pp. 46, 49–52, 59–63; Wrightson, *English Society*, pp. 74–79.

[6] Phillip Stubbes, *The Anatomie of Abuses* (London, 1595), p. 109; see also pp. 57–58, 64.

appoynted one Lancelot Osward her father's man a place wheare he shold come and have his pleasure of her and occupye her and seide further that he the saide Lancelot came and his prick would not stand and so came the second and third time to th'appoynted place and afforsaide and saide that yt . . . would not stand, and that the fourth tyme had his pleasure of her and occupyed her meanyng that the saide Lancelot Osward had carnell knowledge of the body of the said Isobel Lombye and that she was a whore.[7]

Understandably, a clever couplet counsels: "And for thy seruants let no *Belly* swell, / A baudy house is but an earthlie hell."[8]

This is not to suggest that seduction, or even bastardy, never occurred among the elite. Mary Fitton got pregnant by William Earl of Pembroke, while Penelope Rich bore five illegitimate offspring to her lover, Lord Mountjoy.[9] But these scandals did not typify the behavior of the privileged. Quite the opposite. Grace Mildmay recalls careful warnings from her governess: "Also, she advised me to avoyd such companye by all means possible, and to take heede of whom I received gifts, as a book wherein might be some fine words whereby I might betray myself unawares, or gloves or apples or such like, for that wicked companions would ever presente treacherous attempts."[10] All the advice books affirm Lady Grace's upbringing and caution against clandestine encounters. The household

---

[7] J. A. Sharpe, *Defamation and Sexual Slander in Early Modern England: The Church Courts at York*, Borthwick Papers 58 (1980): 21. For other examples see, e.g., Amussen, *Ordered Society*, pp. 71, 159, 167; Brinkworth, *Shakespeare and the Bawdy Court*, p. 75; Christopher Hill, "The Spiritualization of the Household," in *Society and Puritanism in Pre-Revolutionary England* (New York: Schocken Books, 1964), p. 448; A. L. Rowse, *Sex and Society in Shakespeare's Age: Simon Forman the Astrologer* (New York: Charles Scribner's Sons, 1974), pp. 52, 78–82; Alan G. R. Smith, *Servant of the Cecils: The Life of Sir Michael Hickes, 1543–1612* (Totowa, NJ: Rowman and Littlefield, 1977), pp. 165–166; Ashmolean MSS 306.349–349ᵛ and 206.426 (references supplied by Barbara Traister in private correspondence).

[8] *The Uncasing of Machivils Instructions to his Sonne* (London, 1613), F3ᵛ. See also Sir John Harington, *Nugae Antiquae*, ed. Henry Harington (London: Vernor and Hood, 1804), 1:107; idem, *The Letters and Epigrams of Sir John Harington*, ed. Norman Egbert McClure (Philadelphia: University of Pennsylvania Press, 1930), p. 269.

[9] Robert V. Schnucker, "Elizabethan Birth Control and Puritan Attitudes," *Journal of Interdisciplinary History* 5 (1975): 655; Katherine Usher Henderson and Barbara F. McManus, eds., *Half Humankind: Contexts and Texts of the Controversy about Women in England, 1540–1640* (Urbana: University of Illinois Press, 1985), p. 74. See also Lawrence Stone, *The Crisis of the Aristocracy, 1558–1641* (Oxford: Clarendon Press, 1965), pp. 609–610, 663–668.

[10] Rachel Weigall, ed., "The Journal of Lady Mildmay, circa 1570–1617," *The Quarterly Review* 215 (1911): 121.

master declares, "I must take special heed of any secret meetings, messages, or more than ordinary liking between the men and women of my family. I must see that the men have no haunt of women to their chambers, lest lewdness be cloaked under some other pretense."[11] As for the fine declarations of lovers, "Their fawning is but flattery: their faith falshoode: their faire wordes allurements to destruction: and their large promises tokens of death, or of euils worse then death."[12]

For a woman, sexual seduction was the evil worse than death. Among ordinary folk, chastity might or might not matter, but the importance of guaranteeing correct lines of inheritance and descent increased the significance of virginity for wealthy and titled females.[13] Stern are the warnings against even the appearance of impropriety: "She ought also to be more circumspect and to take better heed that she give no occasion to be yll reported of, and so to beehave her selfe, that she be not onlye not spotted wyth anye fault, but not so much as with suspicion."[14] The maidenhead is regarded as "brittle ware, which vnlesse your care be the greater for the preseruation, may get a cracke that no Art of man can make whole againe, and a blow, that no herbe is of sufficient efficacy to cure."[15] Writers graphically portray the techniques of unscrupulous wooers:

They know the flexible disposition of Women and the sooner to ouerreach them, some will pretend they are so plunged in loue that except they obtaine

[11] Robert Southwell, S.J., *Two Letters and Short Rules of a Good Life*, ed. Nancy Pollard Brown (Charlottesville: University Press of Virginia, 1973), p. 49.

[12] *Jane Anger, her Protection for Women* (London, 1589), C3ᵛ. See also *A Lyttle Treatyse Called ye Image of Idlenesse* (London, 1574), B6; Isabella Whitney, *The Copy of a Letter . . . to her Unconstant Lover* (London, ca. 1567).

[13] See, e.g., Dorothy Leigh, *The Mother's Blessing* (London, 1616), pp. 33–43; Lu Emily Pearson, *Elizabethans at Home* (Stanford, CA: Stanford University Press, 1957), p. 282; Mary Beth Rose, "Moral Conceptions of Sexual Love in Elizabethan Comedy," *Renaissance Drama*, n.s., 15 (1984): 6–7; Keith Thomas, "The Double Standard," *Journal of the History of Ideas* 20 (1959): 195–216. Quaife, *Wanton Wenches*, pp. 244–249, argues that chastity was not particularly important to most people.

[14] Baldassare Castiglione, *The Courtier*, trans. Sir Thomas Hoby (London: David Nutt, 1900), p. 215. See also Giovanni M. Bruto, *The Necessarie, Fit, and Convenient Education of a Yong Gentlewoman*, trans. W. P. (London, 1598), I6ff.; Heinrich Bullinger, *The Christian State of Matrimony*, trans. Miles Coverdale (London, 1575), 91ᵛ–92; Jacques DuBosc, *The Compleat Woman* (London, 1639), pp. 49, 62; Thomas Gainsford, *The Rich Cabinet Furnished with Varieties of Excellent Descriptions* (London, 1616), p. 163ᵛ; Henry Willoby, *Willobie his Avisa, or the True Picture of a Modest Maid, and a Chast and Constant Wife* (London, 1594), pp. 5–9.

[15] Nicholas Breton, *A Poste with a Packet of Mad Letters* (London, 1633), p. 2.

their desire they will seeme to drown'd, hang, stab, poyson, or banish them-selues from friends and countrie. . . . Some will pretend marriage, another offer continuall maintenance, but when they haue obtained their purpose, what shall a woman finde, iust that which is her euerlasting shame and griefe.[16]

Those who lose their virginity are denounced as "Monsters," "more vile then filthy channell durt fit to be swept out of the heart and suburbes of your Countrey."[17]

Because seduction could so easily masquerade as an intention to marry, secret betrothals came under particular criticism and suspicion. As part of their regular duties, parish priests were to report "Whether you know any to have made privy contracts of Matrimony, not calling two or more wit-nesses thereunto, nor having thereto the consent of their Parents."[18] These "privy contracts" were thought to derive from "knauery, falshood, and deceite. . . . wherby yong ignoraunt people are vtterly begiled and des-troied."[19] Although a private handfasting or "besponsation" roughly fol-lowed the form of a public spousal, with *de futuro* or *de praesenti* vows, the clasp of hands, the kiss, and usually a ring or other token, its validity was difficult to prove.[20] Indeed, "it is so little esteemed of, (vnlesse it be very

---

[16] Ester Sowernam, *Ester Hath Hang'd Haman* (London, 1617), p. 45. See also Roger Ascham, *The Scholemaster* (London, 1570), pp. 29ᵛ–30; Thomas Dekker, "The Batchelors Banquet," in *The Non-Dramatic Works*, ed. Alexander B. Grosart (1884; reprint, New York: Russell and Russell, 1963), 1:245–246; John Downame, *Foure Treatises* (London, 1609), pp. 177ff.; Richard Jones, *The Passionate Morrice*, ed. F. J. Furnivall, New Shak-spere Society, ser. 6, no. 2 (London: N. Trübner, 1876): 95–96; *The Lawes Resolutions of Womens Rights* (London, 1632), p. 377; Samuel Rowlands, *The Bride* (London, 1617), D3; Willoby, *Willobie his Avisa*, pp. 12, 21; Linda Woodbridge, *Women and the English Renais-sance: Literature and the Nature of Womankind, 1540–1620* (Urbana: University of Illinois Press, 1984), p. 84.

[17] DuBosc, *Compleat Woman*, p. 64; Joseph Swetnam, *The Araignment of Lewde, Idle, Froward, and Unconstant Women* (London, 1615), p. 27. See also *The Mothers Counsell* (Lon-don, 1631), p. 3; Sowernam, *Ester*, p. 25.

[18] *A Collection of Articles, Injunctions, Canons, Orders, Ordinances, and Canons Ecclesiastical* (London: Stevens and Co., 1846), p. 4. See also Emmison, *Elizabethan Life*, p. 144; Pear-son, *Elizabethans*, p. 24.

[19] Bullinger, *Christian State*, 11ᵛ–12, 13ᵛ. See also Robert Cleaver, *A Godly Form of Householde Government* (London, 1598), p. 136; Thomas Dekker, "The Seven Deadly Sinnes of London," in *The Non-Dramatic Works*, ed. Alexander B. Grosart (1885; reprint, New York: Russell and Russell, 1963), pp. 46–47; Downame, *Foure Treatises*, pp. 177ff.; Wil-liam Gouge, *Of Domesticall Duties* (London, 1622), p. 632; Juan Luis Vives, *The Office and Duetie of an Husband*, trans. Thomas Paynell (London, 1553), D5.

[20] *Lawes*, p. 54; Martin Ingram, "Spousals Litigation in the English Ecclesiastical Courts

manifest) that another promise publique made after it, shall be preferred and preuaile against it."[21] Not even a ring could unequivocally demonstrate a betrothal, especially if it were made of rush or some other perishable substance.[22] Unless acknowledged by both parties or by witnesses, a private pledge had no legal standing, and it could be set aside if either partner were a minor.[23] Still, some lovers did make clandestine commitments. The dangerous consequences of believing a secret promise to marry appear in this contemporary report of a duel:

> My Lo. of Dunkelly fought in the feilde withe S[r] Calistines Brooke vppon Wednesday last and . . . thrust him quight throughe the hande vp into the arme. The cause breifly was S[r] Cal: had promysed hys syster mariage, and gott her withe chylde and then refusing her my Lo. her Brother vndertooke her iust quarrell, whiche god iustly reuenged.[24]

With less peril than a duel might pose, an abandoned partner could sue for fulfillment of vows. Records of such suits appear in every ecclesiastical court, where the parties and those vouching for them sought to establish the credit of their testimony. For judges, as for society, factors of status or reputation or family influence heavily affected the verdicts.[25]

With either secret or public spousals, matters grew still more complicated if a couple indulged in sexual intercourse before being married *in facie ecclesiae*. This act translated the espoused condition into a binding union. Regardless of whether or not parents had consented, whether either partner had been forced into betrothal, whether contractual conditions had been fulfilled, whether fornication with someone else had previously occurred, or whether "the Man were constrained, through *fear of death* to know the woman," nonetheless "Spousals do become Matrimony by carnal

---

c. 1350–c. 1640," in *Marriage and Society: Studies in the Social History of Marriage*, ed. R. B. Outhwaite (New York: St. Martin's Press, 1981), pp. 46–47; idem, *Church Courts*, pp. 196–198, 208–209; Chilton Latham Powell, *English Domestic Relations, 1487–1653* (New York: Columbia University Press, 1917), p. 17.

[21] *Lawes*, pp. 53–54. See also Matthew Griffith, *Bethel, or A Forme for Families* (London, 1633), p. 272; William Harrington, *The Comendacions of Matrymony* (London, 1528), A4–A4[v]; Henry Swinburne, *A Treatise of Spousals, or Matrimonial Contracts* (London, 1686), pp. 193–202.

[22] Pearson, *Elizabethans*, p. 333.

[23] Swinburne, *Treatise*, pp. 193–202.

[24] Philip Gawdy, *Letters of Philip Gawdy*, ed. Isaac Herbert Jeayes (London: J. B. Nichols and Sons, 1906), p. 103.

[25] Amussen, *Ordered Society*, pp. 106–107, 152–155; Emmison, *Elizabethan Life*, pp. 144–153; Houlbrooke, *Church Courts*, pp. 60–62; Ingram, *Church Courts*, pp. 191–218.

knowledge."[26] There is some disagreement about a man's right to compel his intended bride to have intercourse, but even forcible rape could become matrimony if the woman wished.[27] The transformation of spousals into wedlock provided special protection for the female involved because it prevented her partner from breaking a contract on the grounds of unchastity. Such a manipulation of betrothal in order to seduce would otherwise have left the man free to marry while damaging the woman's chances for a respectable mate. Any difficulty in enforcing a permanent match centered solely on the problem of proving that a valid promise had actually existed. Unfortunately, while premarital consummation joined an espoused couple for life, it conveyed none of the legal benefits that accrued to properly wedded husbands and wives. According to one authority, "they which dare play man and wife onely in view of heauen, and closet of Conscience, let them be aduised . . . for on earth if the Priest see no celebrated Marriage, the Judge saith no legitimate issue, nor the Law any reasonable or constituted Dower."[28] Besides risking her property rights and the legitimacy of her children, the woman also risked prosecution by the church courts if she became pregnant and could not persuade her partner to marry her, while both offenders could be required to do public penance if found guilty of incontinence.[29]

Despite these serious consequences, some took betrothal as a license for sexual intimacy, equating it with matrimony itself. "Many make it a very mariage, and thereupon haue a greater solemnitie at their contract, then at their mariage: yea many take libertie after a contract to know their spouse, as if they were maried: an unwarrantable and dishonest practice."[30] Though moralists denounced "hādfasted persons brought and layd together: yea, certaine weekes afore they go to the church" for their "wicked lust,"[31] the existing evidence shows a good deal of premarital intercourse

[26] Swinburne, *Treatise*, p. 226; see also pp. 30, 73, 150, 218, 224, 225. Further references include Jean Bodin, *The Six Bookes of a Commonweale*, trans. Richard Knolles (London, 1606), p. 15; *Lawes*, p. 54; William Perkins, *Christian Oeconomie*, trans. Thomas Pickering (London, 1609), pp. 23, 55.

[27] Bodin, *Six Bookes*, p. 15; *Lawes*, p. 60.

[28] *Lawes*, p. 117; see also p. 69. Other authorities are Henricus Cornelius Agrippa, *The Commendation of Matrimony* (London, 1540), B3; Harrington, *Comendacions*, A4, A6; Swinburne, *Treatise*, pp. 233ff.

[29] See, e.g., Brinkworth, *Shakespeare and the Bawdy Court*, pp. 14–18, 75, 80, 87.

[30] Gouge, *Domesticall Duties*, p. 202.

[31] Bullinger, *Christian State*, p. 57. See also Downame, *Foure Treatises*, pp. 177ff.; Richard Greenham, *Works* (London, 1599), p. 299; Robert Snawsel, *A Looking Glasse for Maried Folkes* (London, 1610), E3ᵛ.

between engaged couples, mostly at the lower social levels.[32] According to one proverb, "Courting and wooing bring dallying and doing."[33] In some parishes as many as a third of the brides were, like Anne Hathaway, pregnant at their weddings.[34] But when a pregnancy did not lead to a wedding, the ensuing stigma was so great that some women invented promises of marriage, while some men either bribed a partner's silence or paid someone else to marry her.[35] Frequently, however, the ecclesiastical court records show that an unmarried mother was truly espoused to her baby's father. For instance, Grace Burles told the religious officials in 1602 that Edward Shipman "myndeth shortlye to marye her" but "was prest for a soldier in the last presse." And in fact, upon Edward's return six months after their child was born, he and Grace became husband and wife.[36]

As with seduction, however, sexual consummation of public or private spousals only infrequently characterized the behavior of the privileged. Unchaperoned encounters came more easily to ordinary individuals than to the daughters of elite families. Dalliances certainly occurred, but they were both scandalous and risky.[37] For example, Lady Sheffield tried for years to prove that she and the Earl of Leicester had made a secret contract in 1571 that was ratified one winter night in 1574 before the birth of their son in August. Though the child eventually sued for legitimization and his father's title, the case was first dismissed, then permanently es-

[32] See n.4 above.

[33] Morris P. Tilley, *A Dictionary of the Proverbs in England in the Sixteenth and Seventeenth Centuries* (Ann Arbor: University of Michigan Press, 1950), C739.

[34] Richard L. Greaves, *Society and Religion in Elizabethan England* (Minneapolis: University of Minnesota Press, 1981), pp. 204–213; P.E.H. Hair, "Bridal Pregnancy in Rural England in Earlier Centuries," *Population Studies* 20 (1966): 233–237; idem, "Bridal Pregnancy in Early Modern England Further Examined," *Population Studies* 24 (1970): 61, 65; Ingram, *Church Courts*, p. 220; Laslett, "Introduction," pp. 53–54; David Levine, *Family Formation in an Age of Nascent Capitalism* (New York: Academic Press, 1977), pp. 127–145; Levine and Wrightson, "Social Context," p. 161; Oosterveen and Smith, "Bastardy," p. 109; Keith Wrightson, "The Nadir of English Illegitimacy in the Seventeenth Century," in *Bastardy*, p. 189; Wrightson and Levine, *Poverty*, p. 131.

[35] Amussen, *Ordered Society*, pp. 71, 112–115, 159, 167; Ingram, *Church Courts*, pp. 199, 282–283. For fictional treatments of these situations, see Edward Gosynhyll, *Here Begynneth the Schole House of Women* (London, 1560), A3–A3ᵛ; Dekker, "Batchelors Banquet," pp. 244–254; Thomas Heywood, *A Curtaine Lecture* (London, 1637), pp. 235–236.

[36] Wrightson and Levine, *Poverty*, pp. 128, 130. See also Emmison, *Elizabethan Life*, p. 3; Houlbrooke, *Church Courts*, pp. 60, 65; Ingram, *Church Courts*, pp. 267–268; Sharpe, *Crime*, pp. 81–82.

[37] Stone, *Crisis*, pp. 606, 663–666.

topped.[38] In desperate circumstances, lovers could resort to an elopement or a secret wedding, but such behavior invariably fueled gossip and criticism.[39] Everyone at court was shocked when Sir Thomas Perrot and Dorothy Devereux broke into a church and were married by a strange clergyman over the strenuous protests of the local parish priest, an action that provoked a Privy Council inquiry.[40] Denying the validity of his daughter Elizabeth's elopement with William Lord Compton, Sir John Spencer locked her up, beat her, and had to be imprisoned before the newlyweds could live together.[41] To ensure the legality of an irregular ceremony, a public wedding sometimes followed a covert one. Thus, when the widowed Lady Essex secretly wed the Earl of Leicester in 1578, her father later held a service attended by other nobles.[42] Similarly, Elizabeth Cecil and Edward Coke, married in 1598 without banns, with no special license, at night, and in a private house, repeated their vows at St. Andrew's Church after they were called before the archbishop.[43]

In instances of surreptitious ceremonies, officiating clerics were subject to censure and offenders to punishment by the church courts.[44] Moreover, the parties involved risked forfeiting the financial support guaranteed by spousal contracts, not to mention incurring parental wrath. Predictably, there was severe disapproval for "clandestine mariages," in part because they led to "*Alienation of parents affection from their children, Disinheriting Heires, Enmity betwixt the friends of each party so married, Litigious suits in Law, Ruine of families.*"[45] A statute of 1597, designed to redress abductions

[38] Elizabeth Jenkins, *Elizabeth and Leicester* (New York: Coward-McCann, 1962), pp. 186–187.

[39] The word *elopement* is here used in its modern sense, but in the Elizabethan period it also meant leaving one's spouse to live with another partner, an offense for which a woman forfeited her dower rights. See *Lawes*, p. 144.

[40] Pearson, *Elizabethans*, pp. 321–322; Greaves, *Society*, p. 133; Kathy Lynn Emerson, *Wives and Daughters: The Women of Sixteenth-Century England* (Troy, NY: Whitston Publishing Company, 1984), p. 69.

[41] Greaves, *Society*, p. 133.

[42] Pearson, *Elizabethans*, p. 341.

[43] Catherine Drinker Bowen, *The Lion and the Throne: The Life and Times of Sir Edward Coke (1552–1634)* (Boston: Little, Brown, 1957), pp. 123–125; Emerson, *Wives*, p. 47; Pearson, *Elizabethans*, pp. 321–322.

[44] *Constitutions and Canons Ecclesiastical 1604* (Oxford: Clarendon Press, 1923), L3–L4; Emmison, *Elizabethan Life*, pp. 155–158; Gillis, *For Better*, p. 90; Greaves, *Society*, p. 181.

[45] Gouge, *Domesticall Duties*, pp. 205, 452; see also pp. 452–453, 212–213. Other authorities include Cleaver, *Godly Form*, p. 136; John Stockwood, *A Bartholomew Fairing for Parentes* (London, 1589), pp. 76–77; John Wing, *The Crowne Conjugall or, The Spouse Royall* (Middleburgh, 1620), pp. 125–126.

of heiresses as a means of forcing marriages, sentenced offenders to death without a priest in attendance.[46] In virtually all quarters, an elopement represented a serious breach of propriety. Nonetheless, some couples did manage to wed in an irregular fashion, and certain members of the clergy connived at the rules.[47] In London such ceremonies were performed at several churches, including the Tower, Holy Trinity (Minories), St. James (Duke Place), and the chapels at the Mint and Newgate prison.[48] Whether private matrimony represented religious dissent, an evasion of impediments, or the assertion of personal choice, it was regarded as a subversion of the protocols surrounding more conventional marriage.

In contrast with impetuous lovers who copulated prematurely or married covertly, other espoused couples found reasons to break off their engagements. Certain penalties fell upon a fiancé who willfully reneged on his promise of marriage.

> By the Civil Law, whosoever having contracted Spousals *de futuro*, doth, without just Cause, refuse to deduce the same Spousals into Matrimony, doth not only lose the token (which is commonly a Ring) given to the other Party in pledge, and earnest of the Contract . . . together, with all other gifts whatsoever simply bestowed in hope of future Marriage . . . ; but is bound to make two-fold Restitution for the tokens and pledges received in Confirmation of the said Contract . . . whether they be Rings, Braceletts, Jewels, or other things.[49]

But there were legitimate grounds for dissolution. As discussed in chapter 2, those contracted in childhood could dissent when they came to years of discretion and thus cancel a parental agreement. However, to be valid, the

---

[46] 39 Eliz. c. 9; Thomas, "Double Standard," p. 211. Roger Fulwood was arraigned on this charge in 1637 after abducting Sara Cox, but the marriage was annulled, Sara declared a virgin, and Roger pardoned; see Antonia Fraser, *The Weaker Vessel* (New York: Alfred A. Knopf, 1984), pp. 22–25.

[47] Brinkworth, *Shakespeare and the Bawdy Court*, p. 108; Paul Hair, ed., *Before the Bawdy Court* (London: Paul Elek Books, 1972), nos. 250, 449; Ralph A. Houlbrooke, *The English Family, 1450–1700* (London: Longman, 1984), pp. 311–312; G. E. Howard, *A History of Matrimonial Institutions* (Chicago: University of Chicago Press, 1904), 1:415; Ingram, *Church Courts*, pp. 214–218; Lawrence Manley, ed., *London in the Age of Shakespeare* (Philadelphia: Pennsylvania State University Press, 1986), pp. 272–273.

[48] Gillis, *For Better*, pp. 92–96; Edward J. Wood, *The Wedding Day in All Ages and Countries* (New York: Harper's, 1869), 2:235.

[49] Swinburne, *Treatise*, p. 229; see also p. 231. Refer as well to Houlbrooke, *Church Courts*, p. 61; *Lawes*, p. 72.

dissent had to be made before a bishop, his chancellor, or a priest and other witnesses.[50] Betrothed partners could also dissolve their commitment by mutual consent, provided no sexual consummation had taken place, though a penance or reprimand was imposed for breaking a *de praesenti* vow.[51] Not living up to the stated conditions of the spousal contract also invalidated it—unless the conditions were manifestly impossible to fulfill, in which case the contract had been void all along. For example, if the agreement called for a wedding within a certain length of time or payment of sums of money or approval of another party, then the failure to meet such prerequisites provided grounds for ending the engagement.[52] The primary requirement for those under twenty-one, of course, was parental consent, as clerics were repeatedly warned.[53] Yet, for espoused minors, as with any betrothed pair, sexual intercourse canceled all contractual conditions and established an indissoluble union.[54]

Theoretically, more complicated causes for nullifying spousal agreements were supposed to emerge during the time it took to read the banns. These included the existence of a prior contract or marriage, a pending marital suit in an ecclesiastical court, fornication with another party, a foul disease or notable mutilation, consanguinity, extreme cruelty, notorious reputation, criminality, impotence, mistaken identity, holy orders, false religious faith, violence, threats, fraud, infancy, judicial dissolution, or "whensoever there is just and reasonable Cause."[55] Hence, authorities

[50] Swinburne, *Treatise*, pp. 18–28, 43–44, 237. Ingram, *Church Courts*, pp. 173–174, found such dissents extremely rare.

[51] Swinburne, *Treatise*, pp. 165, 213–216, 236; William Whately, *A Care-Cloth, or a Treatise of the Cumbers and Troubles of Marriage* (London, 1624), p. 31; Pearson, *Elizabethans*, p. 319.

[52] Swinburne, *Treatise*, pp. 109–153, 223; *Lawes*, p. 54; Houlbrooke, *Church Courts*, pp. 56–67.

[53] See chaps. 2 and 4; Cleaver, *Godly Form*, p. 129; *Collection*, p. 4; *Constitutions*, L3ᵛ–L4, Q3ᵛ, Q4ᵛ; Stockwood, *Bartholomew Fairing*, p. 18.

[54] See above, n.26.

[55] Swinburne, *Treatise*, p. 239, and pp. 5–7, 16, 223–224, 236–240. See also William Ames, *Conscience, with the Power and Cases Thereof* (London, 1639), pp. 198–202, 204; Bullinger, *Christian State*, 17ᵛ; Cleaver, *Godly Form*, pp. 96, 127; *Constitutions*, Q3ᵛ–Q4; Gouge, *Domesticall Duties*, pp. 181–186; Griffith, *Bethel*, pp. 270, 272; Harrington, *Comendacions*, B1–D2; *Lawes*, pp. 57–62; Pearson, *Elizabethans*, pp. 299–301; Perkins, *Christian Oeconomie*, pp. 24ff., 48ff.; Daniel Rogers, *Matrimoniall Honour* (London, 1642), pp. 96–120; Whately, *Care-Cloth*, pp. 30–31. *Epicoene*, in *Ben Jonson*, ed. C. H. Herford and Percy Simpson (Oxford: Clarendon Press, 1937), 5:264–268, ends with an amusing but technically accurate analysis of the legal grounds that nullify Morose's marriage.

urged that during their espousal "both parties should disclose the one to the other, such imperfections, infirmities, and wants, in either of their bodies, as also the mediocritie & meannesse of their goods and substance, as in trueth it is: yea though it should be with the perill and losse one of the other."[56] Otherwise, the belated revelation of impediments could lead to embarrassing or intolerable situations, many of which are documented in the ecclesiastical court records.[57] If impediments were alleged during the wedding ceremony, the rite had to be deferred until the truth or falsity of the charges could be determined.[58]

Distinctions existed even among impediments. Some (prohibitive) prevailed only before a church wedding and/or consummation, while others (diriment) rendered the marriage invalid from its inception, abrogating both dower rights and legitimacy of offspring.[59] A state of annulment existed, for instance, when partners wed within the interdicted degrees of kinship, which after 1603 were posted in every parish church.[60] These comprised not only in-laws, such as the brother or sister of a deceased spouse, but also godparents and adopted relatives.[61] When anybody killed

[56] Cleaver, *Godly Form*, p. 95. See also Bullinger, *Christian State*, p. 56.

[57] See, e.g., Emmison, *Elizabethan Life*, p. 152. Ingram, *Church Courts*, pp. 174–211, 218, indicates that suits instituted on technical grounds were never numerous.

[58] Edmund Gibson, *Codex Juris Ecclesiastici Anglicani* (Oxford: Clarendon Press, 1761), 1:431.

[59] *Constitutions*, Q3–R1ᵛ; Gellert Spencer Alleman, *Matrimonial Law and the Materials of Restoration Comedy* (Philadelphia: University of Pennsylvania Press, 1942), pp. 125–126; Harrington, *Comendacions*, A2, C4ᵛ–D1; Houlbrooke, *Church Courts*, pp. 71–75; Ingram, *Church Courts*, p. 145; *Lawes*, pp. 65–66; Pearson, *Elizabethans*, pp. 300, 308, 325; Powell, *English Domestic Relations*, pp. 8–10; Margaret Loftus Ranald, *Shakespeare and His Social Context* (New York: AMS Press, 1987), p. 6; Alexander W. Renton and George G. Phillimore, *The Comparative Law of Marriage and Divorce*, in *Burge's Commentaries on Colonial and Foreign Laws* (London: Bradbury, Agnew, 1910), 3:19–24, 136–137; Swinburne, *Treatise*, pp. 223–228; Whately, *Care-Cloth*, p. 30.

[60] "Kindred and Affinity," *Time* (19 August 1940), p. 52; Naseeb Shaheen, "The Incest Theme in *Hamlet*," *Notes and Queries*, n.s., 32 (1985): 51; Oscar D. Watkins, *Holy Matrimony: A Treatise on the Divine Laws of Marriage* (New York: Macmillan, 1895), pp. 646, 708.

[61] *Constitutions*, Q3; William Clerke, *The Triall of Bastardie* (London, 1594), M3–O3ᵛ and passim; Jean Louis Flandrin, *Families in Former Times: Kinship, Household and Sexuality*, trans. Richard Southern (Cambridge: Cambridge University Press, 1979), pp. 19, 24; Gibson, *Codex*, 1:412–415; Harrington, *Comendacions*, B1ᵛff.; *Lawes*, pp. 58, 61, 71; Pearson, *Elizabethans*, p. 300; *Depositions and Other Ecclesiastical Proceedings from the Courts of Durham*, Publications of the Surtees Society 21 (1845): 59; Swinburne, *Treatise*, p. 228.

a spouse in order to marry someone else or made a promise of matrimony contingent upon the death of a spouse, the ensuing union was considered void. So were bigamous marriages (felonious after 1604) or those that followed a prior *de praesenti* promise to another party or those that could not be consummated.[62] Other grounds for nullification included an absence of two years (three years if outside England) with no consummation, as well as compulsion (again not involving sexual intercourse): "Matrimonie holdeth not when it is extorted by force, or by such a feare as may *cadere in constantem virum; quia matrimonia debent esse libera* [befall a strong man, because marriages ought to be uncompelled]."[63] Besides these limited conditions for annulment, a few situations could justify separation, or divorce *a mensa et thoro* (from bed and board), though such circumstances were rare indeed.[64] Adultery, heresy, idolatry, extreme cruelty, or an absence of five years with the presumption of death all provided grounds for a hearing before an ecclesiastical judge.[65] But even if the plaintiff won, a subsequent marriage was almost always prohibited.[66] Not only did all divorce petitions have to be substantiated by the testimony of independent witnesses in open court, but none would be granted without the oath of husband and wife not to wed again during their spouse's lifetime.[67]

One correspondent of the period reports: "The marriage of Sir G. Allington is pronounced voyde in the High Commission and he fined 10,000[li] for his incestuous match [with his niece] and bound in 20,000[li] never heear[a]fter to accompany her againe; an excellent example"; Arthur Searle, ed., *Barrington Family Letters, 1628–1632*, Camden Society Publications, 4th ser., 28 (1983): 190.

[62] Harrington, *Comendacions*, C2[v]; *Lawes*, p. 59; Renton and Phillimore, *Comparative Law*, p. 23. In cases of bigamy, desertion was often involved, with the abandoned spouse sincerely convinced of the missing partner's death; see, e.g., Amussen, *Ordered Society*, pp. 124–126; Ingram, *Church Courts*, pp. 177–180. The most notorious example of annulment based on inability to consummate was that of the Earl of Essex and Frances Howard; see chap. 2, n.20.

[63] *Lawes*, p. 59; Perkins, *Christian Oeconomie*, p. 69.

[64] Alleman, *Matrimonial Law*, pp. 107, 113–114; Emmison, *Elizabethan Life*, pp. 164–170; Reginald Haw, *The State of Matrimony* (London: S.P.C.K., 1952), pp. 91–95; Houlbrooke, *Church Courts*, p. 68; Watkins, *Holy Matrimony*, pp. 9, 427–429.

[65] Gibson, *Codex*, 1:444–447; *Lawes*, pp. 64–67.

[66] William Vaughan, *The Golden-grove* (London, 1600), N6–N6[v]. For Lady Rich's experience when she fruitlessly tried to marry Lord Mountjoy after her divorce, see Fraser, *Weaker Vessel*, p. 295; Pearl Hogrefe, *Tudor Women: Commoners and Queens* (Ames: Iowa State University, 1975), pp. 88–89.

[67] Thomas Carter, *Carters Christian Commonwealth: Domesticall Dutyes Deciphered* (London, 1627), pp. 29–30; *Constitutions*, R1[v]–R2[v]. Some theologians argued that the innocent

Unfortunately, however irregular the circumstances of trothplight or matrimony, marriage was for life. Legal grounds for annulment or divorce from bed and board so seldom existed that the impatient were sternly warned not to expect rescue from the folly of a precipitate liaison:

> Whether therefore thou be married already, or art hereafter to enter into it, keepe vnitie now, and make thy choice so well as thou canst: and I, for my part, would never wish thee to conceiue any hope at all, that whē once that knot is rightly knit, thou canst afterward haue any vndoubted or certaine warrant, that for the adultery of thy wife (if it should fall out, that thy case should bee so hard) thou maist be at liberty to marry againe.[68]

Echoing that awareness, John Harington offers in verse a wry acknowledgment of the indissolubility of marriage.[69]

> A fond yong couple, making haste to marry,
> Without their parents will, or friends consent,
> After one month their marriage did repent,
> And su'd vnto the Bishops Ordinary
> That this their act so vndiscreetly done,
> Might by his more discretion be vndone.
> Vpon which motion he awhile did pause:
> At length, he for their comforts to them said,
> It had beene better (friends) that you had staid:
> But now you are so hampered in the Lawes,
> That I this knot may not vntye (my sonne)
> Yet I will grant you both shall be vndone.[69]

---

party should be allowed to remarry. See Ames, *Conscience*, pp. 210–211; Gouge, *Domesticall Duties*, p. 215; William Perkins, *Workes* (Cambridge, 1618), 3:69–71; John Rainolds, *A Defence of the Judgement of the Reformed Churches* (London, 1609); William Whately, *A Bride-Bush, or a Wedding Sermon* (London, 1617), p. 5. After being called before the Court of High Commission (see Fraser, *Weaker Vessel*, p. 295), Whately recanted his earlier position in *Care-Cloth*, "Advertisement," p. 80. Edmund Bunny's *Of Divorce for Adulterie, and Marrying Againe* (Oxford, 1610) is the best known polemic against remarriage of divorced persons. See also Catherine Belsey, "Alice Arden's Crime," *Renaissance Drama* 13 (1983): 83–102.

[68] Bunny, *Of Divorce*, p. 2. See also Bartholomaeus Batty, *The Christian Man's Closet*, trans. William Lowth (London, 1581), p. 101; Harington, *Letters*, p. 200; Samuel Rowlands, *Tis Merrie When Gossips Meete* (London, 1602), D3ᵛ.

[69] Harington, *Letters*, p. 284. For a couple forced to remain married despite the best efforts of the groom's family to have their union annulled, see Allison D. Wall, *Two Eliz-*

Even in the most influential social circles, the law afforded little escape.[70] Marriage was *"Dura Servitus*, a hard Servitude, because it is for ever indissoluble . . . , how hard soever the Match be; whereas every other Servitude, may at any time be dissolved, the Lord or Master being pleased."[71]

A far higher proportion of defective courtships appear in Shakespeare's plays than seem to have occurred in his society, for the problems attendant upon unsanctioned love—then as now—form the very stuff of dramatic action. Yet in even the most improbable plots, signals as to the implications of irregular behavior appear. With characters of lowly status, such irregularity generally takes the form of sexual promiscuity, sometimes winked at, sometimes punished, sometimes insultingly referred to as "country matters" (*Ham.*, III.ii.111) or "country forms" (*Oth.*, III.iii.242). Such behavior unites elements as diverse as the profligacy of Joan la Pucelle, the fickleness of Lavatch, the attempted rape by Caliban, and the boast of Jack Cade: "There shall not a maid be married but she shall pay to me her maidenhead" (*2H6*, IV.vii.118–120).[72]

The Old Shepherd in *The Winter's Tale* laments that young swains are concerned with nothing "but getting wenches with child, wronging the ancientry, stealing, fighting" (III.iii.60–62). When he stumbles on an abandoned baby, he assumes there must be some " 'waiting-gentlewoman' in the scape. This has been some stair-work, some trunk-work, some behind-door-work. They were warmer that got this than the poor thing is here" (71–74). The infant's supposed bastardy does not prevent the old man from taking it in "for pity" (73) even before he discovers its fardel of gold, any more than his grumbling about youthful liberty affects his kindly tolerance of it at the sheepshearing—at least until the dance of hairy men becomes obscene. Similarly, so long as Polixenes and Camillo presume Prince Florizel is merely amusing himself with a shepherdess, they admire her poised beauty. But when the pair begin moving through the stages of a formal betrothal, the mood changes. A public declaration of love, joined hands, the promise of dowry, the approval of the girl's

---

abethan Women: Correspondence of Joan and Maria Thynne, 1575–1611, Wiltshire Record Society 38 (1982): xxvi, 8–12.

[70] Lawrence Stone, "Marriage among the English Nobility in the 16th and 17th Centuries," *Comparative Studies in Society and History* 3 (1960–1961): 202–203; idem, *Crisis*, pp. 660–662. Though Stone finds forty-nine instances of annulment or separation among the peerage between 1570 and 1659, he includes "notorious marital quarrels" in that figure instead of restricting it to legally sanctioned estrangements.

[71] Swinburne, *Treatise*, pp. 184–185; *Lawes*, p. 69.

[72] See chap. 4, n.103.

father, everything but consent of Florizel's father, who "must not / Mark our contract" (IV.iv.416–417), push the couple right to the edge of a binding spousal before the outraged Polixenes declares, "Mark your divorce, young sir" (417).[73] Only at the point where dalliance threatens to become alliance, lawful and enforceable, does the violence of royal displeasure intervene. The king's view of Perdita's sexual hold over his son appears in the assumption that she might "These rural latches to his entrance open, / Or hoop his body more with thy embraces" (438–439). Though casual coupling can be expected from country folk, matrimony with their betters seems out of the question.

Thus in *The Merchant of Venice*, Jessica charges Lancelot Gobbo with "the getting up of the Negro's belly. The Moor is with child by you, Lancelot" (III.v.36–37).[74] The servant's retort that "if she be less than an honest woman, she is indeed more than I took her for" (39–40) implies the pair's mutual looseness, but this backstairs peccadillo is never even mentioned again, much less ratified by a wedding. A good deal more is made of carnality in *Love's Labour's Lost*. Navarre imposes stiff penalties for fornication: "a year's imprisonment to be taken with a wench" (I.i.276–277). Don Armado's apprehension and custody of Costard for toying with Jaquenetta—his sentence reduced to "fast a week with bran and water" (288–289)—provide comic sport. So does the Spanish knight's infatuation with this wench, this "hobby-horse," this "hackney" (III.i.28–31), who has "sorted and consorted" (I.i.251) with him too. In the final shambles of the Pageant of Nine Worthies, Costard announces, "She's quick. The child brags in her belly already. 'Tis yours" (V.ii.670–671). Though which man has gotten the girl pregnant remains in doubt,[75] Don Armado completes the deflation of his own gentlemanly pretensions by confessing, "I have vowed to Jaquenetta to hold the plow for her sweet love three year"

---

[73] See also David Bevington, *Action Is Eloquence: Shakespeare's Language of Gesture* (Cambridge: Harvard University Press, 1984), pp. 140–141; Pearson, *Elizabethans*, pp. 336–337. Confused about what constitutes valid matrimony (which would be indissoluble), Alan Powers believes that Florizel and Perdita "are really married for a minute or so—the shortest marriage in the opus. After all, Polixenes ends with, 'Mark your divorce, young sir.' " See " 'Meaner Parties': Spousal Conventions and Oral Culture in *Measure for Measure* and *All's Well That Ends Well*," *The Upstart Crow* 8 (1988): 38.

[74] Horst Breuer presumes a sexual liberality in Shakespeare's time but does not discriminate along class lines in his analysis, "Shakespeares Mädchen und Frauen in Familiengeschichtlichen Kontext," *Anglia* 105 (1987): 69–93.

[75] Robert Ornstein, e.g., *Shakespeare's Comedies: From Roman Farce to Romantic Mystery* (Newark: University of Delaware Press, 1986), p. 39, thinks the baby is Costard's.

(870–871). Underscored by the obscene double entendre of his pledge, their sexuality and what may be a limited term of commitment counterpoint the chaster pursuits of the courtly figures, whose declarations and penances are also imperfectly or ambiguously observed. Rather consistently, however, in Shakespeare it is characters of low social status who fornicate with scant regard for the nicer restrictions of betrothal or marriage.

Though all acknowledged the existence of fleshly desires and many pursued them, such liberty seemed particularly threatening to those most bound by the protocols of courtship. Secret wooings and betrothals thus garner special attention because they can so easily disguise an intent to satisfy lust rather than to marry. Such circumstances appear in *Hamlet*, where Laertes and Polonius fear for Ophelia's virtue.[76] After all, the prince has "very oft of late / Given private time to you, and you yourself / Have of your audience been most free and bounteous" (I.iii.91–93). Though Hamlet has made no formal request to court her, "he hath importuned me with love" (110). Laertes advises Ophelia to regard the prince's interest as "The perfume and suppliance of a minute. / No more" (9–10), warning,

> Then weigh what loss your honour may sustain
> If with too credent ear you list his songs,
> Or lose your heart, or your chaste treasure open
> To his unmastered importunity.
>
> (29–32)

Polonius calls Hamlet's vows "mere imploratators of unholy suits, / Breathing like sanctified and pious bawds, / The better to beguile" (129–131). Obediently, Ophelia breaks off all further contact with the prince. No matter how much one may dislike Polonius, he is not simply thwarting a bona fide courtship here but, given the customs of the period, has good reason to fear seduction. In retrospect, he admits, "I feared he did but trifle / And meant to wreck thee," for "it is common for the younger sort / To lack discretion" (II.i.113–114, 117–118).[77]

---

[76] Kenneth Muir, *Shakespeare's Tragic Sequence* (New York: Barnes and Noble, 1979), p. 75, feels their suspicion "is a better index to their own minds than it is to Hamlet's intentions or to Ophelia's frailty." Mark Taylor, *Shakespeare's Darker Purpose: A Question of Incest* (New York: AMS Press, 1982), p. 114, concurs. Angela Pitt, *Shakespeare's Women* (London: David and Charles, 1981), p. 53, is one of the few who note that Ophelia has seen Hamlet "unchaperoned and without her father's approval."

[77] Diane Elizabeth Dreher, *Domination and Defiance: Fathers and Daughters in Shakespeare* (Lexington: University Press of Kentucky, 1986), p. 78, believes Ophelia is sacrificed to

Though, as will be noted in chapter 9, Hamlet's rank makes his conduct especially open to suspicion, a certain stigma attaches to any unsanctioned courtship. Seeing Bianca's shameless flirtation with her presumed tutor, Tranio and Hortensio abruptly reject the young "haggard" for "her lightness." "Fie on her, see how beastly she doth court him" (*Shr.*, IV.ii.39, 24, 34).

> See how they kiss and court. Signor Lucentio,
> Here is my hand, and here I firmly vow
> Never to woo her more, but do forswear her
> As one unworthy all the former favors
> That I have fondly flattered her withal.
>
> (27–31)

While Hortensio's criticism may represent the sour grapes of an unsuccessful suitor, Bianca still violates the rules of discreet feminine conduct, a further indication of her subsequent unruliness as a wife. And certainly the bawdy innuendo of Margaret in *Much Ado* marks her as a careless young woman fully capable of receiving her lover, Borachio, at Hero's chamber window. Though excused by Leonato—"I believe [she] was packed in all this wrong, / Hired to it by your brother" (V.i.291–292)—the waiting woman's behavior contrasts sharply with that of the modest Hero and the forthright Beatrice.[78]

Sometimes a secret wooing leads to a secret betrothal. However, without proof, this kind of pledge can always be broken. For example, in *A Midsummer Night's Dream*, Lysander charges, "Demetrius—I'll avouch it to his head— / Made love to Nedar's daughter, Helena, / And won her soul" (I.i.106–108). According to her, he "hailed down oaths that he was only mine" (243). Even Theseus admits, "I have heard so much, / And with Demetrius thought to have spoke thereof" (111–112). After his night in the woods, this lover confesses, "To her, my lord, / Was I be-

---

"that static and oppressive female virtue: chastity," and, p. 52, she objects to Polonius's "blatant disregard for their [his children's] privacy," both wholly modern judgments. Lisa Jardine, *Still Harping on Daughters: Women and Drama in the Age of Shakespeare* (Totowa, NJ: Barnes and Noble, 1983), p. 72, and William G. Meader, *Courtship in Shakespeare; Its Relation to the Tradition of Courtly Love* (New York: Columbia University, King's Crown Press, 1954), p. 207, claim that Ophelia's return of Hamlet's gifts represents a broken engagement, but the text shows no promise of marriage.

[78] See, e.g., Allen H. Gilbert, "Two Margarets: The Composition of *Much Ado About Nothing*," *Philological Quarterly* 41 (1962): 61–71; Richard A. Levin, *Love and Society in Shakespearean Comedy* (Newark: University of Delaware Press, 1985), pp. 113–115.

trothed ere I see Hermia" (IV.i.170–171). His acknowledgment, along with Theseus's earlier negligence and the fact that the pair have spent a night together unchaperoned, helps to explain why the duke overrules the wishes of Hermia's father.[79] Demetrius is precontracted to Helena, as Hermia is to Lysander, when Egeus demands that his child "here before your grace / Consent to marry with Demetrius" (I.i.39–40). However, when Theseus asks, "What say you, Hermia?" (46), she cleverly avoids any direct answer, which would constitute a public espousal, thus preserving her prior vow to Lysander intact, in contrast with the forsworn Demetrius. During the first part of *Two Gentlemen of Verona*, Proteus also enters into a secret spousal, complete with the offer of "my hand for my true constancy," "a holy kiss" to "seal the bargain," and an exchange of rings (II.ii.8, 7).[80] When Julia produces not one but two rings given by her faithless suitor, such replicative nonsense provides yet another instance of that mockery of courtship conventions which typifies this comedy. As a practical matter rings commonly demonstrate the validity of a private betrothal. However, even with such a token, even when clandestine vows are honored, a certain uneasiness attends most concealed wooings because of an uncertainty as to the motives and the morality involved. And the uneasiness derives in part from the cultural ambiguity attached to an activity both forbidden and indulged in.

Of no play is this so true as *Othello*. Though Desdemona does not even appear until some 450 lines into the action, her elopement with the Moor provides the chief subject for discussion during all the opening dialogue. Has she been bewitched, as her distraught father claims, or is she a willing partner in "making the beast with two backs" (I.i.118–119)? While explaining their courtship before the Venetian senate council, Othello—wittingly or unwittingly—reveals considerable impropriety of behavior. A frequent visitor to Brabanzio's home, the Moor has taken "a pliant hour," without her father's knowledge or permission, "and found good means / To draw from her a prayer of earnest heart / That I would all my pilgrimage

---

[79] Laurence Lerner, *Love and Marriage: Literature and Its Social Context* (New York: St. Martin's Press, 1979), p. 20, is among those who find the duke's decision totally capricious. However, Leonard Tennenhouse, *Power on Display: The Politics of Shakespeare's Genres* (London: Methuen, 1986), p. 74, thinks Theseus ready "to generously forgive where Egeus . . . would be penurious and harsh." Shirley Nelson Garner, "*A Midsummer Night's Dream*: 'Jack shall have Jill; / Nought shall go ill,' " *Women's Studies* 9 (1981): 55, recognizes the betrothal but does not connect it with Theseus's decision.

[80] Powers, " 'Meaner Parties,' " pp. 30, 32, calls this a *de futuro* contract but reveals an imperfect understanding of the status of spousals in law.

dilate" (I.iii.150–152). Their subsequent conversations, kept secret from Brabanzio, take on a questionable nature, especially in view of Desdemona's response to Othello's stories. The Quarto text says, "She gave me for my pains a world of sighs," but the Folio specifies a far more shameless "world of kisses" (158). After that,

> She wished she had not heard it, yet she wished
> That heaven had made her such a man. She thankèd me,
> And bade me, if I had a friend that loved her,
> I should but teach him how to tell my story,
> And that would woo her. Upon this hint I spake.
>
> (161–165)

Now the alien Othello may not recognize any misconduct here, but a contemporary audience almost certainly would have.[81] Brabanzio himself declares, "If she confess that she was half the wooer, / Destruction light on my head if my bad blame / Light on the man!" (175–177), not because he approves of the match but because his daughter would be at fault to encourage Othello so blatantly. Moreover, Desdemona's subsequent actions heighten the initial suspicion regarding her character. She keeps her betrothal hidden from her father yet continues to see Othello privately and, as the play later reveals, to receive Cassio frequently as a go-between.[82] To

---

[81] Marianne Novy, *Love's Argument: Gender Relations in Shakespeare* (Chapel Hill: University of North Carolina Press, 1984), p. 85, disagrees, claiming that Desdemona "resourcefully finds a way to initiate courtship while seeming to him to be merely hinting." However, Peter Stallybrass, "Patriarchal Territories: The Body Enclosed," in *Rewriting the Renaissance*, ed. Margaret W. Ferguson, Maureen Quilligan, Nancy J. Vickers (Chicago: University of Chicago Press, 1986), p. 136, feels that the "untamed" Desdemona is indeed "half the wooer." More typically, A. J. Smith, *Literary Love: The Role of Passion in English Poems and Plays of the Seventeenth Century* (London: Edward Arnold, 1983), p. 38, claims, "Othello's tale of how he wooed her comes as an idyll in the midst of tumult."

[82] Wayne Holmes, "Othello: Is't Possible?" *The Upstart Crow* 1 (1978): 1–23, argues that Cassio and Desdemona have become lovers before Othello marries her. Stanley Cavell, *Disowning Knowledge: In Six Plays of Shakespeare* (New York: Cambridge University Press, 1987), pp. 131–132, is uncertain about the marriage's consummation. T.G.A. Nelson and Charles Haines, "Othello's Unconsummated Marriage," *Essays in Criticism* 33 (1983): 1–18, say Desdemona dies a virgin. Lynda E. Boose, "Othello's Handkerchief: 'The Recognizance and Pledge of Love,' " *English Literary Renaissance* 5 (1975): 362–363, sees the handkerchief with its strawberries (emblem of purity) as a miniature of blood-stained wedding sheets, suggesting that those sheets may be either a test or a proof of her virginity. Karl P. Wentersdorf, "The Time Problem in *Othello*: A Reconsideration," *Jahrbuch, Deutsche Shakespeare-Gesellschaft West* (1985): 73–74, speculates about premarital inter-

elope, she slips away from her home by night, "Transported, with no worse nor better guard / But with a knave of common hire, a gondolier" (I.i.126–127).

Even after the stress of an elopement, the abrupt departure of her new husband from the Sagittary inn, and her predawn summons before the senate council, Desdemona speaks with remarkable composure to her distraught father and the other males assembled. Eliding altogether the fact that she has concealed Othello's courtship from Brabanzio, she facetiously compares herself to her mother in setting the obedience due a husband above that due a father. Rhetorically she sounds correct, but she falsely equates her mother's marriage with her own, which lacks either parental knowledge or approval.[83] With no alternative, since his daughter has confirmed Othello's claims, Brabanzio abandons his charges, bitterly presiding over a postnuptial betrothal: "Come hither, Moor. / I here do give thee that with all my heart / Which, but thou hast already, with all my heart / I would keep from thee" (I.iii.191–194). However, he offers no dowry and refuses Desdemona houseroom during Othello's impending absence. In response, she defends "My downright violence and storm of fortunes" (249), frankly asking to accompany her husband to war, else "The rites for why I love him are bereft me" (257).[84] Where is the young woman her father describes as "A maiden never bold, / Of spirit so still and quiet that her motion / Blushed at herself" (94–96)? The question of whether she is "a super-subtle Venetian" (355) or the "virtuous Desdemona" (III.i.33)

course between Othello and Desdemona, a sexual union she then may have violated with Cassio. The text provides no evidence for any of these notions.

[83] Novy, *Love's Argument*, p. 128, claims that Desdemona "is trying to reassure Brabantio by putting her marriage into an orderly continuity of marriages, trying to remind him that his marriage too was won at the cost of a separation from a father," but Novy ignores the irregular circumstances under which the daughter's match is made. Others who support the orthodoxy of Desdemona's response include Dreher, *Domination*, p. 44–45; Juliet Dusinberre, *Shakespeare and the Nature of Women* (New York: Barnes and Noble, 1975), p. 97; Marjorie Garber, *Coming of Age in Shakespeare* (New York: Methuen, 1981), p. 43; Gayle Greene, " 'This That You Call Love': Sexual and Social Tragedy in *Othello*," *Journal of Women's Studies in Literature* 1 (1979): 26.

[84] Stephen Greenblatt, *Renaissance Self-Fashioning: From More to Shakespeare* (Chicago: University of Chicago Press, 1980), p. 250, says it is this frank declaration that "awakens the deep current of sexual anxiety in Othello." Among those defending Desdemona's statement are Irene G. Dash, *Wooing, Wedding and Power: Women in Shakespeare's Plays* (New York: Columbia University Press, 1981), p. 108; Arthur Kirsch, *Shakespeare and the Experience of Love* (Cambridge: Cambridge University Press, 1981), p. 15. When other characters, like Juliet, express a desire for consummation, the circumstances are never so public as a senate council.

lies at the heart of Othello's agony. But long before the hero's doubts are ever raised, the play thrusts its viewers into a similar doubt regarding this irregular courtship. What kind of young woman would behave as Desdemona does, violating all the proprieties? Is she chaste or prodigal? Is she inherently deceitful or just unconventionally independent? Is her love a lust for the bizarre or a noble spiritual union? At the midpoint of the dramatic action, uncertainties regarding the heroine's morality begin to be resolved for the audience precisely when they are raised for Othello. Yet to see the courtship solely in modern terms, missing entirely its questionable aspects, results in a simplistic view of both Desdemona and Othello.[85]

While this tragedy opens after a secret wooing and an elopement have already occurred, other plots turn on the attempts to sanction a clandestine relationship with matrimony. In some cases, practical problems such as finding a priest to perform the ceremony without the necessary banns or parental consent are either minimized or ignored, with a corresponding emphasis on the means of eloping. Lysander and Hermia simply plan to decamp to another venue where "the sharp Athenian law / Cannot pursue us" (*MND*, I.i. 162–163). Other lovers are similarly vague about the marriage ceremony but full of elaborate plans for getting away. When asked if Silvia loves him, Valentine admits,

> Ay, and we are betrothed. Nay more, our marriage hour,
> With all the cunning manner of our flight,
> Determined of: how I must climb her window,
> The ladder made of cords, and all the means
> Plotted and 'greed on for my happiness.
>
> (*TGV*, II.iv. 177–181)

No fewer than three priests wait secretly to marry Anne Page—one at the deanery for Dr. Caius, one at Eton for Slender, and one at the church for Fenton. All the ceremonies would be considered irregular since they are performed at night " 'twixt twelve and one" (*Wiv.*, IV.vi.48), but the marriage to Fenton would be "so sure that nothing can dissolve" it because he and Anne are "long since contracted" (V.v.215–216). A similar irregularity attaches to the secret wedding of Lucentio and Bianca, which also

---

[85] The list of contemporary critics who either rebuke or idealize Desdemona is far too long to include here. Some few, like Stallybrass, "Patriarchal Territories," p. 141, see two Desdemonas—the "maiden never bold" and the woman of "downright violence." As I have argued in "The Design of Desdemona: Doubt Raised and Resolved," *Shakespeare Studies* 13 (1980): 187–196, the apparent contradictions in this character are a matter of external perception, for both the audience and Othello, rather than of internal inconsistency.

takes place at night. Biondello has arranged a clandestine wedding that will satisfy any legal requirement: "The old priest at Saint Luke's church is at your command at all hours. . . . Take you assurance of her, *cum privilegio ad imprimendum solum*—to th' church take the priest, clerk, and some sufficient honest witnesses" (IV.v.15–16, 19–21). The precise nature of the information in *The Taming of the Shrew* and *The Merry Wives of Windsor* is of course consistent with the realistic details provided for the entire courtship process by these comedies. However, in a society where eligible women of privilege were chaperoned with some care, stratagems for carrying off their stage counterparts may have attracted particular interest. Not only did seemingly gratuitous descriptions of corded ladders and pliant priests answer practical questions, but they appealed to the imagination of anyone who might wish, however fruitlessly, to pursue a similar course.

In quite a different vein Shakespeare is especially careful about what he does and does not present in *Romeo and Juliet*. With two minors whose parents would violently oppose any alliance, it is essential to show how and why the young couple are truly married. Hence, the spectator sees, step by step, the movement from the lovers' first encounter to their indissoluble union. In the balcony scene, Juliet repeatedly urges Romeo (and the audience) not to misjudge her morality: "In truth, fair Montague, I am too fond, / And therefore thou mayst think my 'havior light." "Therefore pardon me, / And not impute this yielding to light love" (II.i.140–141, 146–147). She assumes that with their mutual declarations of love, Romeo has made a private promise to marry her. Despite the physical impossibility of a handfasting, she even uses the correct legal term for their vows: "I have no joy of this *contract* tonight. / It is too rash, too unadvised, too sudden" (159–160; italics mine). By voicing the same misgivings that prudent adults might feel concerning her relationship with Romeo, Juliet establishes her purity as well as her passion. Though the only satisfaction Romeo asks that night is "Th'exchange of thy love's faithful vow for mine" (169), she proposes that he prove his sincerity in the only ethical way possible:

> If that thy bent of love be honourable,
> Thy purpose marriage, send me word tomorrow,
> By one that I'll procure to come to thee,
> Where and what time thou wilt perform the rite,
> And all my fortunes at thy foot I'll lay,
> And follow thee, my lord, throughout the world.
>
> (185–190)

Yet she can still see the alternative interpretation of her wooer's behavior: "But if thou mean'st not well, / I do beseech thee. . . . / To cease thy strife and leave me to my grief" (192–193, 196). In no other play do we get so clear a delineation of honorable intent in an unsanctioned courtship, for the dynamics of *Romeo and Juliet* require a firm belief in the lovers' integrity from first to last.

Further difficulties surround the wedding itself. First, a plausible explanation must be offered for any priest's willingness to officiate in such obviously irregular circumstances. Though chiding young Romeo for his impetuous commitment, Friar Laurence consents on reasonable grounds: "I'll thy assistant be; / For this alliance may so happy prove / To turn your households' rancour to pure love" (II.ii.90–92). A second problem, common to most elopements, arises from the restricted movements of unmarried girls beyond their own households. Since Romeo has no direct access to Juliet such as Lucentio has to Bianca, the Nurse becomes the essential agent between the lovers. She utters the usual warning against seduction in the guise of courtship: "If ye should lead her in a fool's paradise, as they say, it were a very gross kind of behaviour, . . . truly it were an ill thing to be offered to any gentlewoman" (II.iii.155–159). However, what the hero has in mind is a lawful marriage. In sending the following message to Juliet via the Nurse, he clarifies the strategy that will effect an almost impossible union and its consummation.

> Bid her devise
> Some means to come to shrift this afternoon,
> And there she shall at Friar Laurence' cell
> Be shrived and married. . . .[86]
>
> . . . .
>
> Within this hour my man shall be with thee
> And bring thee cords made like a tackled stair,
> Which to the high topgallant of my joy
> Must be my convoy in the secret night.

(169–172, 177–180)

The excuse of going to confession is especially clever, for it offers Juliet a plausible reason to leave the Capulet house, it reasserts the lovers' virtue,

---

[86] Garber, *Coming of Age*, p. 120, mistakenly says the marriage was at 9:30 A.M.; however, Juliet goes to confession in the afternoon. Germaine Greer, "Juliet's Wedding," *Listener* (7 December 1978): 751, casts doubt on the validity of the ceremony because the audience does not see it, yet except for Hymen's rites in *AYL* and the aborted rites in *Ado*, no wedding occurs onstage. Certainly all the principals—Romeo, Juliet, and Friar Laurence—accept its validity, as eventually the parents do.

and it satisfies the requirement for absolution before marriage. During the brief scene at Friar Laurence's cell, the same insistence upon the sanctity of the union appears, with Romeo's request to "close our hands with holy words" (II.v.6) and the friar's directive, "Come, come with me, and we will make short work, / For, by your leaves, you shall not stay alone / Till Holy Church incorporate two in one" (35–37).

Here is no transitory dalliance or secret promise of love, rashly consummated, but rather a religious consecration of private vows between a virgin and her betrothed husband. Nor is it a questionable nighttime affair but rather one inaugurated in the broad light of day, though not before the canonical deadline of noon. While the union might still be annulled at this point, especially in view of Romeo's subsequent killing of Tybalt, Juliet reconfirms her commitment, vowing to "die maiden-widowèd" (III.ii.135) if necessary and sending her bridegroom a ring as token of her fidelity. "O, find him! Give this ring to my true knight, / And bid him come to take his last farewell" (142–143). That same night a sexual consummation makes Romeo and Juliet husband and wife forever. In a final touch of pathos, their fathers tender belated offers of dower and dowry over the bodies of two dead children.[87]

> CAPULET. O brother Montague, give me thy hand.
>   This is my daughter's jointure, for no more
>   Can I demand.
> MONTAGUE.   But I can give thee more,
>   For I will raise her statue in pure gold.
>
>   .   .   .   .
>
> CAPULET. As rich shall Romeo's by his lady's lie,
>   Poor sacrifices of our enmity.
>
>   (V.iii.295–298, 302–303)

With equal offers and clasped hands, the parents enact the spousal agreement between families that should have preceded the marriage of the young lovers, were it not for the feud. As the momentarily widowed wife of Romeo, Juliet will have from the Montagues a golden jointure equal to the golden dowry she brings from the Capulets.

---

[87] Bevington, *Action*, p. 145, to some extent devalues this interchange by saying Capulet is reduced to "bargaining with Montague over a bridal portion for the young woman who is now married to her deathbed." So does Northrop Frye, *Northrop Frye on Shakespeare* (New Haven: Yale University Press, 1986), pp. 31–32, charging that the offer of statues indicates that "two miserable, defeated old men who have lost everything . . . simply cannot look their own responsibility for what they have done straight in the face."

The secret wedding in the tragedy raises other generally unrecognized issues concerning Paris's courtship of Juliet. Though in the play's immediate source he does not appear until after Romeo's banishment, from the first act Shakespeare shows this suitor following the route of conventional wooing. However, when Capulet agrees to the match, he abrogates the requirement for obtaining his daughter's consent, not even allowing a perfunctory interview between the couple. Juliet protests the breach of custom: "I wonder at this haste, that I must wed / Ere he that should be husband comes to woo" (III.v.118–119). During the following scene, Friar Laurence expresses reservations to Paris about the girl's free assent, observing, "You say you do not know the lady's mind? / Uneven is the course. I like it not" (IV.i.4–5). Juliet's possible coercion, which would constitute an impediment to the marriage, is precisely the problem Paris addresses when she arrives at the friar's cell. Before a clerical witness, he tries to elicit her consent.

> PARIS. Happily met, my lady and my wife.
> JULIET. That may be, sir, when I may be a wife.
> PARIS. That "may be" must be, love, on Thursday next.
> JULIET. What must be shall be.
> FRIAR LAURENCE.   That's a certain text.
> PARIS. Come you to make confession to this father?
> JULIET. To answer that, I should confess to you.
> PARIS. Do not deny to him that you love me.
> JULIET. I will confess to you that I love him.
> PARIS. So will ye, I am sure, that you love me.
>
> . . . .
>
> Juliet, on Thursday early will I rouse ye.
> (*Kissing her*) Till then, adieu, and keep this holy kiss.[88]
>
> (18–26, 42–43)

Though she has deftly parried each statement, Juliet's parting kiss means, to Paris, an acceptance of their betrothal. Instead, as both she and Friar Laurence well know, the spousal is not valid because of her prior marriage to Romeo. The Nurse may rationalize, "Your first is dead, or 'twere as good he were / As living hence and you no use of him," and advise, "I think it best you married with the County" (III.v.224–225, 217). But any such union would be bigamy. This dilemma, which provokes Juliet's

---

[88] Novy, *Love's Argument*, p. 108, contrasts the stiff stichomythia of this interchange with the spontaneously lyrical poetry between Juliet and Romeo.

desperate solution, stems from the fact that Shakespeare has taken care to delineate a secret marriage satisfying religious and civil law in every respect.

However, the playwright is equally capable of presenting situations that spell out the ugliest dangers implicit in irregular courtship, as he does in *Measure for Measure*. In the most reprehensible case, a gentleman has debauched one Kate Keepdown, who in turn has brought charges before the Duke that Lucio fathered her child. Privately he admits the deed, but publicly "I was fain to forswear it. They would else have married me to the rotten medlar" (IV.iii.166–167). According to Mistress Overdone, who has cared for the infant and its mother, Lucio "promised her marriage" (III.i.459–460). However, without evidence, that promise is impossible to prove, so the woman can be casually discarded, the bastard left to the charity of a bawd. A similar taint mars the relationship between Claudio and the pregnant Juliet.[89] Though he readily admits to a secret handfasting, this young man has been unwilling to wait for its public ratification before consummation: "Upon a true contract, / I got possession of Julietta's bed" (I.ii.133–134).[90] In neither of these situations, both involving private vows, does Shakespeare provide the scenes of unsullied wooing that lend such sympathy to the plight of Romeo and Juliet. Instead, the women here are treated like criminal bearers of bastards, Kate denied marriage by her despoiler, Juliet by the pious hypocrite Angelo, who decrees that the "fornicatress" merely "have needful but not lavish means" (II.ii.23, 24) for her imminent delivery.[91] Rather than legitimize

[89] Leo Salingar, *Shakespeare and the Traditions of Comedy* (Cambridge: Cambridge University Press, 1974), p. 319, observes Shakespeare's borrowing of names from earlier plays— "a second Juliet, secretly married, appears, and a second Claudio, whose 'headstrong' conduct in marrying without a dowry or a church ceremony . . . makes him the exact opposite of the suspicious, conventional Claudio in *Much Ado*."

[90] See Marc Eccles, ed., *A New Variorum Edition of "Measure for Measure"* (New York: Modern Language Association of America, 1980), p. 35, for notes on "true contract." Marc Shell, *The End of Kinship: "Measure for Measure," Incest, and the Ideal of Universal Siblinghood* (Stanford, CA: Stanford University Press, 1988), p. 110, erroneously equates this contract with the private unions of Romeo and Juliet, Henry VIII and Anne Boleyn, perhaps even Shakespeare and Anne Hathaway, even though Claudio's spousal is not lawfully solemnized as are the other marriages.

[91] E. Pearlman, "Historical Demography for Shakespeareans," *Shakespearean Research Opportunities* 7–8 (1972–1974): 71, thinks that, with one-fifth of Elizabethan brides pregnant, "the utter ordinariness of the situation renders Angelo's response additionally fierce and puritanical." However, the women Pearlman refers to not only marry before the child is born but are rarely gentlewomen like Juliet.

the union and thus the unborn infant, Angelo focuses solely upon the sexual sin and thereby creates, as surely as Lucio does, a nameless child with no means of support. Both women are finally wed to their seducers at the public command of the Duke. His directive, "She, Claudio, that you wronged, look you restore" (V.i.524), meets with silent acquiescence, but Lucio fruitlessly protests, "I beseech your highness, do not marry me to a whore" (513–514).

Yet these are not the only instances of sexual abuse or aborted matrimony. When the loss of Mariana's dowry at sea leads Angelo to break their *de futuro* spousal agreement, he is squarely within his legal rights to refuse a bride when the provisions of the prenuptial contract have not been fulfilled.[92] But he also invents a charge of unchastity as grounds for deserting her[93] and adds to his offense by repeating the lie in public before the Duke.

> My lord, I must confess I know this woman;
> And five years since there was some speech of marriage
> Betwixt myself and her, which was broke off,
> Partly for that her promisèd proportions
> Came short of composition, but in chief
> For that her reputation was disvalued
> In levity.
>
> (214–220)

Amid all the critical focus upon *de praesenti* versus *de futuro* spousals in relation to the bed trick,[94] it is easy to lose sight of the ironic justice by

[92] Meader, *Courtship*, p. 215, is wrong in claiming that an abrogation of the contract requires mutual consent. Without the dowry, its terms remain unfulfilled, but so long as no other contract intervenes, the spousal can be translated into matrimony by sexual intercourse.

[93] Carol Thomas Neely, *Broken Nuptials in Shakespeare's Plays* (Yale University Press, 1985), p. 93, mentions the slander in her analysis of this play but ignores the legitimate ground of the dowry's loss. Among others who discuss the technical aspects of this contract are J. Birje-Patil, "Marriage Contracts in *Measure for Measure*," *Shakespeare Studies* 5 (1969): 111; W. W. Lawrence, *Shakespeare's Problem Comedies*, 2d ed. (1931; reprint, New York: Frederick Ungar, 1960), pp. 95–97; Margaret Loftus Ranald, " 'As Marriage Binds and Blood Breaks': English Marriage and Shakespeare," *Shakespeare Quarterly* 30 (1979): 77–79.

[94] Ernest Schanzer, "The Marriage Contracts in *Measure for Measure*," *Shakespeare Survey* 13 (1960): 81–89, says the Angelo-Mariana spousal was *de futuro*, the Claudio-Juliet spousal *de praesenti*. S. Nagarajan, "*Measure for Measure* and Elizabethan Betrothals," *Shakespeare Quarterly* 14 (1963): 115–119, thinks they were the reverse. Harriet Hawkins, "What Kind of Pre-contract Had Angelo? A Note on Some Non-problems in Elizabethan Drama,"

which Angelo's carnal desire to "disvalue" Isabella "in levity" makes him the instrument for fulfilling his earlier slander against Mariana—and at the same time his act will "fulfill an old contracting" (III.i.538).

> This is the hand which, with a vowed contract,
> Was fast belocked in thine. This is the body
> That took away the match from Isabel,
> And did supply thee at thy garden-house
> In her imagined person.
>
> . . . .
>
> I am affianced this man's wife, as strongly
> As words could make up vows. And, my good lord,
> But Tuesday night last gone, in's garden-house
> He knew me as a wife.[95]
>
> (205–209, 225–228)

Now kin to Claudio as seducer and to Lucio as both seducer and liar, Angelo is swiftly ordered by the Duke to their same marital fate—and for the same reason: "I thought your marriage fit," because the bride's unchastity might "choke your good to come" (417, 419).[96] A hard look at the period's legal penalties for bearing bastards, as well as the social stigma on debauched women, explains why this tough sentence is imposed, no matter how unpalatable it appears in today's very different world.

College English 36 (1974): 173–179, considers the whole matter irrelevant. Powers, " 'Meaner Parties,' " minimizes the entire affair, speculating that "Shakespeare himself and Anne may have—and Claudio and Juliet definitely had—lived together as if married without witnesses" and thus "were married all along, that the only lack was a matter of form," pp. 33, 35. I cannot concur with his suppositions.

[95] Darryl J. Gless, *"Measure for Measure," the Law, and the Convent* (Princeton: Princeton University Press, 1979), p. 201, points out Mariana's use of specific references to a betrothal ceremony in her public accusation—"This is the hand which, with a vowed contract, / Was fast belocked in thine." He might also have mentioned "swor'st," "match," "affianced," "vows," "wife."

[96] Leah Marcus, *Puzzling Shakespeare: Local Reading and Its Discontents* (Berkeley: University of California Press, 1988), pp. 179–183, 194–195, sees the Duke's command entwined with a complicated set of historical associations, including abrogation of the requirement for an episcopal license, abuse of sexual standards through the unlawful bed tricks, coercive marriage, and aversion to special waivers such as papal indulgences. Neely, *Broken Nuptials*, p. 98, incorrectly calls the Claudio-Juliet wedding a "restored marriage." Moreover, she claims, p. 99, that women "have the potential to confer social respectability on men by marrying them and bearing their children, as Juliet and Kate Keepdown do." In the play's action, however, it would seem to be men who bestow respectability on women by marrying them and legitimizing their children.

The matrimonial impediment of sexual dishonor finds its fullest and falsest expression in *Much Ado about Nothing*. There poor Hero is the victim of Don John's plot to make her appear unchaste, to poison the happiness of his brother's friend Claudio, and to embarrass Don Pedro for arranging the match. The enormity of the fault looms even before it is proven.[97]

> DON JOHN. . . . Go but with me tonight, you shall see her chamber window entered, even the night before her wedding day. If you love her then, tomorrow wed her. But it would better fit your honour to change your mind.
>
> . . . .
>
> CLAUDIO. If I see anything tonight why I should not marry her, tomorrow, in the congregation where I should wed, there will I shame her.
>
> DON PEDRO. And as I wooed for thee to obtain her, I will join with thee to disgrace her.
>
> (III.ii.102–106, 113–116)

Much sentimental protest has been expressed against the heartlessness of Claudio's public accusation, but at this level of society, a charge of so serious a transgression must be made openly and affirmed by witnesses.[98] A private conversation with Hero's father might prevent the wedding but would not prevent speculation that perhaps Claudio, not Hero, is at fault—nor would it prevent Hero's being affianced to some other unsuspecting suitor. Equally important, the high drama of the accusation sustains the play's energy at this point.

The scene begins with an enactment of the nuptial ceremony that, except for a mock ritual in *As You Like It*, is the only such Christian ceremony to appear onstage in Shakespeare.[99] Impatient, Leonato calls for an

---

[97] For another full discussion of the marital technicalities in *Ado*, see Ranald, " 'As Marriage Binds,' " pp. 73–77, and idem, *Shakespeare and His Social Context*, pp. 11–32. Marilyn French, *Shakespeare's Division of Experience* (New York: Summit Books, 1981), p. 130, feels that Hero "is already suspect" because she has "been wooed and won by a great nobleman prior to this betrothal." However, the proxy wooing never figures into the accusation at the wedding, though Claudio's false suspicion of Don Pedro obviously presages his false suspicion of Hero.

[98] Among those objecting to Claudio's conduct are Levin, *Love and Society*, p. 86; Ornstein, *Shakespeare's Comedies*, p. 132; John Traugott, "Creating a Rational Rinaldo: A Study in the Mixture of the Genres of Comedy and Romance in *Much Ado about Nothing*," *Genre* 15 (1982): 157. Significantly, Shakespeare's source has the groom send a message instead of denouncing the bride at the wedding; see Geoffrey Bullough, *The Narrative and Dramatic Sources of Shakespeare* (London: Routledge and Kegan Paul, 1958), 2:118.

[99] Bevington, *Action*, p. 142, suggests that government policies against abuse of the

abridged version of the rites—"Only to the plain form of marriage, and you shall recount their particular duties afterwards" (IV.i. 1–3). Amid interruptions, evasions, and promptings from Claudio and Leonato, the priest asks for the couple's required reaffirmation of spousal vows, the anticipated denial of impediments to the marriage, and the father's consent to the match. And then Claudio commences his denunciation, vowing "Not to be married, / Not to knit my soul to an approvèd wanton" (43–44). At first her father raises a logical question as to whether the groom has deflowered Hero, an unethical but understandable act that would have translated their spousals into matrimony.

> I know what you would say. If I have known her,
> You will say she did embrace me as a husband,
> And so extenuate the forehand sin.
> No, Leonato,
> I never tempted her with word too large,
> But as a brother to his sister showed
> Bashful sincerity and comely love.
>
> (48–54)

After general charges of unchastity, confirmed by Don John and Don Pedro, Claudio faces Hero with the damning question: "What man was he talked with you yesternight / Out at your window betwixt twelve and one?" (83–84). Though the bewildered bride denies having talked with any man at such a time, the prince himself steps forward with eyewitness testimony. Moreover, he cites the admission of the "ruffian" to "the vile encounters they have had / A thousand times in secret" (92, 94–95). Amid the theatrics of these interrupted rites, it should not be forgotten that the angry bridegroom has, he thinks, the best of all possible reasons for backing out of marriage to a "rotten orange" who "knows the heat of a luxurious bed" (32, 41), especially since "she was charged with nothing / But what was true, and very full of proof" (V.i. 106–107). The thrust of sympathy for Hero and the condemnation of Claudio arise not from the legal justification for his action but from the audience's awareness that the charge is false. However, the seriousness of the fault, at least by the standards of the time, is intensified by the dramatic buildup to the accusation, by the groom's outrage, by the bride's swoon, and by her father's sense of

---

prayer book may account for the absence of these rites onstage, as may their inherent lack of theatricality. This particular scene he terms "a central visual picture of inverted order," p. 144.

shame. No matter how much one criticizes Hero's accusers, it is unfair to attack them for being horrified at wantonness masquerading as innocence. To say that Claudio and Leonato, like Beatrice or Friar Francis, should have more faith in the virtue of one they love is not to condone sexual liberality. [100] Throughout *Much Ado*, Shakespeare explores the understandable responses of those who proceed sincerely upon incorrect assumptions just as skillfully as he explores their responses when the assumptions are correct. But if the dynamics of perception are being questioned, the desirability of virginity is not.

Though fornication is certainly the most spectacular ground for breaking a spousal agreement, other conditions can also nullify a contract or even a marriage in Shakespeare. By marrying Pistol, Nell Quickly reneges on her engagement to Nim, "and certainly she did you wrong, for you were troth-plight to her" (*H5*, II.i.17–18). When Bassianus seizes Lavinia because she is his "lawful promised love," his "true betrothèd love" (*Tit.*, I.i.294, 403), their prior spousal negates the one Titus Andronicus makes with Saturninus. [101] Legally, the emperor cannot marry Lavinia. Nor can Jessica marry Lorenzo without agreeing to "Become a Christian and thy loving wife" (*MV*, II.iii.21), for any union with a non-Christian would be considered invalid. So would the bigamous marriage proposed for Innogen and Cloten. If King Cymbeline and his queen do not recognize the princess as Posthumus's spouse, the courtiers declare, "She's wedded, / Her husband banished" (*Cym.*, I.i.7–8), and she herself calls her stepbrother "A foolish suitor to a wedded lady" (I.vi.2). [102] Athough the couple have

[100] Robert G. Hunter, *Shakespeare and the Comedy of Forgiveness* (New York: Columbia University Press, 1965), pp. 100–101, points out that Claudio's outburst stems not only from his sense that the proprieties have been violated but also from deep feelings of love for Hero. See also Janice Hays, "Those 'soft and delicate desires': *Much Ado* and the Distrust of Women," in *The Woman's Part: Feminist Criticism of Shakespeare*, ed. Carolyn Lenz, Gayle Greene, Carol Thomas Neely (Urbana: University of Illinois Press, 1980), p. 87. By contrast, Ornstein, *Shakespeare's Comedies*, p. 119, says this scene "discloses something about conventional attitudes that we would prefer never to have known." But Nadine Page, "The Public Repudiation of Hero," *PMLA* 50 (1935): 739–744, long ago insisted that audiences would have demanded public humiliation as a matter of justice.

[101] David M. Sundelson, *Shakespeare's Restorations of the Father* (New Brunswick, NJ: Rutgers University Press, 1983), p. 122, misses the betrothed status of Lavinia and Bassianus, calling him her "lover." Eugene M. Waith, *Patterns and Perspectives in English Renaissance Drama* (Newark: University of Delaware Press, 1988), p. 141, says that Bassianus "seizes his brother's bride."

[102] Dreher, *Domination*, pp. 47–48, first acknowledges this match as bigamy and yet seems to brush aside that insuperable barrier: "Neglecting her welfare, he [Cymbeline]

been separated, perhaps a step toward annulment, and although Cloten claims theirs "is no contract, none" (II.iii.112), this husband has consummated his marriage, for he has intimate knowledge of his wife's body and bedchamber. Like Juliet, Innogen would commit bigamy were she to marry again.

For very different reasons the alliances between Gertrude and her husband's brother, Claudius, as well as the one Richard III proposes to enter with his niece, Elizabeth, are also invalid. In both cases, the unions violate the interdicted degrees of kinship between spouses. The Ghost in *Hamlet* thus specifically refers to Claudius as "that incestuous, that adulterate beast" and charges, "Let not the royal bed of Denmark be / A couch for luxury and damnèd incest" (I.v.42, 82–83).[103] Similarly, in *Richard III*, Princess Elizabeth's mother poses the moral and legal objections to Richard's suit when she asks,

> What were I best to say? Her father's brother
> Would be her lord? Or shall I say her uncle?
> Or he that slew her brothers and her uncles?
> Under what title shall I woo for thee,
> That God, the law, my honour, and her love
> Can make seem pleasing to her tender years?
>
> (*R3*, lines 50–55 after IV.iv.273; see p. 251)

Besides the sin of incest, Queen Elizabeth alludes to another nullifying impediment, criminality, which also applies to the Gertrude-Claudius marriage. Richard must make "quick conveyance with her good aunt Anne" (269), his wife, in order to marry the York princess. In describing his second courtship, the villain himself says that "sin will pluck on sin"

---

matches her with a man she cannot love, simply to please his queen," p. 46. David Bergeron, *Shakespeare's Romances and the Royal Family* (Lawrence: University Press of Kansas, 1985), p. 145, claims that Cloten does not recognize the validity of Innogen's contract because of Posthumus's lesser rank. But even in his rage Cymbeline seems to acknowledge a marriage: "Thou took'st a beggar, wouldst have made my throne / A seat for baseness" (I.i.142–143).

[103] The definitive analyses of this marriage as incest are those of Roland Mushat Frye, *The Renaissance Hamlet* (Princeton: Princeton University Press, 1984), pp. 76–82; Jason P. Rosenblatt, "Aspects of the Incest Problem in *Hamlet*," *Shakespeare Quarterly* 29 (1978): 349–364; Lawrence Rosinger, "Hamlet and the Homilies," *Shakespeare Quarterly* 26 (1975): 299–301; John Dover Wilson, *What Happens in Hamlet?* (Cambridge: Cambridge University Press, 1935), pp. 39–44. Shaheen, "Incest," p. 51, points out that the incest derives from *Hamlet*'s sources. Tennenhouse, *Power*, p. 89, deems the murder itself "incestuous in that it allows one member of the king's family to marry another."

(IV.ii.66). Since English law invalidated any matrimony achieved by the murder of a living spouse—or even a contract to wed upon a spouse's demise—the proposal to Elizabeth takes on a particularly sinister aura. Ironically, the same aura surrounds his grotesque wooing over the casket of Henry VI, when Richard swears he has killed Anne's husband and father-in-law to win her love. [104] Though he is lying about his motives for those killings, the audacious confession of so heinous an impediment adds to the macabre effect of Anne's entertaining his suit. In *Hamlet*, the audience is led to believe that, while Claudius obviously knows of the criminality nullifying his marriage, Gertrude may not. When Hamlet spells out their sin to her with "A bloody deed—almost as bad, good mother, / As kill a king and marry with his brother," she seems baffled: "As kill a king?" (III.iv.27–29). The prince expresses the legal implications of her condition in near-technical terms. This invalid union "makes marriage vows / As false as dicers' oaths" and is "such a deed / As from the body of contraction plucks / The very soul, and sweet religion makes / A rhapsody of words" (43–47). The matrimonial contract, the vows, the religious ceremony are all rendered empty words, devoid of authority. Hence, Hamlet later speaks of "a mother stain'd" (IV.iv.48; p. 777) and says Claudius "whored my mother" (V.ii.65). Quite aside from all the psychological and aesthetic reasons for Hamlet's plea that Gertrude not return to his uncle's bed, he recognizes the unlawfulness of the union. [105] To continue a sexual relationship is indeed "to live / In the rank sweat of an enseamèd bed, / Stewed in corruption, honeying and making love / Over the nasty sty" (III.iv.81–84). However offensively exaggerated his language, [106] Hamlet's position

---

[104] Richard P. Wheeler, "History, Character and Conscience in *Richard III*," *Comparative Drama* 5 (1971–1972): 316, notes Richard's awareness of the sin involved in wooing Princess Elizabeth but does not specify the nature of the sin.

[105] Neely, *Broken Nuptials*, p. 63, says that "Hamlet urges abstinence upon Gertrude even in marriage." Similarly, Tennenhouse, *Power*, p. 114, says the prince "insists upon shifting the crime from the fact of regicide to the act of 'incest,' namely the sexual relations between Claudius and his brother's wife which Hamlet *considers* illicit" (italics mine). Neither seems aware that, besides consanguinity, criminality invalidates the union. Ranald, " 'As Marriage Binds,' " p. 73, and *Shakespeare and His Social Context*, p. 7, is virtually the only one who mentions this impediment. In *Historiae Danicae* the queen knows she has married her husband's murderer, a circumstance Shakespeare alters; see Bullough, *Narrative and Dramatic Sources*, vol. 7 (1973), 62.

[106] On this point see, e.g., C. L. Barber and Richard P. Wheeler, *The Whole Journey: Shakespeare's Power of Development* (Berkeley: University of California Press, 1986), pp. 277–280; Kay Stockholder, *Dream Works: Lovers and Families in Shakespeare's Plays* (Toronto: University of Toronto Press, 1987), p. 55.

regarding an illicit liaison passing for matrimony echoes Elizabethan views.

To a certain extent, Edmund's relationships with Goneril and Regan present an even more interesting twist on the issue of criminality, since the impediment of a prior contract also affects his commitments to the sister queens. Though married to Albany, Goneril offers herself to Edmund, awards him a favor—"Wear this"—and gives him "This kiss," to which he responds, "Yours in the ranks of death" (Q sc. 16 and F IV.ii.21, 22, 25). The proceeding is an ominous enactment of private spousals, duly witnessed by Oswald. Spelling out the crime that lies between their pledges and a marriage, Goneril sends a letter to her lover on the battle-field:

> "Let our reciprocal vows be remembered. You have many opportunities to cut him off. . . . There is nothing if he return the conqueror; then am I the prisoner, and his bed my jail, from the loathed warmth whereof, deliver me, and supply the place for your labour.
>
> Your—wife, so I would say,—affectionate servant, and for you her own for venture, Goneril."
>
> (Q sc. 20, 254–263; F IV.v.262–270)

Having in the meantime also promised himself to the widowed Regan, Edmund acknowledges his dilemma, "To both these sisters have I sworn my love," and he cynically decides, "Let her who would be rid of him devise / His speedy taking off" (Q sc. 22, 59, 68–69; F V.i.46, 55–56).

Unfortunately for his ambitious interest in both sisters' thrones, Edmund and Regan are arrested for treason by Albany, who delineates the illegalities nullifying the bastard's pledges.[107] Addressing Regan, he says,

> For your claim, fair sister,
> I bar it in the interest of my wife.
> 'Tis she is subcontracted to this lord,
> And I, her husband, contradict your banns.
> If you will marry, make your loves to me.
> My lady is bespoke.
>
> (Q sc. 24, 82–87; F V.iii.77–82)

All the terms of courtship—"subcontracted" (precontracted), "banns," "bespoke" (betrothed)—culminate in the bitterly logical conclusion that

---

[107] Garber, *Coming of Age*, p. 118, is one of the few who even notice the complexity of this situation.

if Regan wishes to subsume her independent identity into Edmund's as his wife, then because he was first pledged to Goneril and she in turn is subsumed into her husband as his wife, both plaintiffs must make suit to Albany in order to marry. As the dying bastard concludes of his relationship to the now-dead sisters, "I was contracted to them both; all three / Now marry in an instant" (Q 223–224; F 203–204). It hardly seems necessary to point out how even these minor details of *Lear* mirror the larger issues of rightful and wrongful claims, familial fragmentation and incorporation, love sought and denied and granted, marital alliances proffered and retracted.

Elsewhere in Shakespeare, the attention shifts from impediments to improperly performed ceremonies. *As You Like It* is replete with absurdly mangled rites of various kinds, perhaps reminders not to take any of the improbable matches or events too seriously. In one defective ritual Touchstone brings Audrey before Sir Oliver Martext, his very name indicative of the curate's incompetence. Though her wooer would gladly avoid matrimony altogether, this country wench stoutly insists that she is "not a slut" (III.iii.33). "Sluttishness may come hereafter" (36), observes Touchstone dryly. Initially, the jester-bridegroom suggests the possibility of an irregular wedding outdoors: "Will you dispatch us here under this tree, or shall we go with you to your chapel?" (59–60). Even a bumbler like Sir Oliver seizes on another irregularity with "Is there none here to give the woman? . . . Truly she must be given, or the marriage is not lawful" (61, 63–64). Jaques says, "I'll give her" (65), but then he lectures Touchstone on the impropriety of a beggar wedding performed by a hedge priest.

And will you, being a man of your breeding, be married under a bush, like a beggar? Get you to church, and have a good priest that can tell you what marriage is. This fellow will but join you together as they join wainscot; then one of you will prove a shrunk panel and, like green timber, warp, warp.

(75–80)

Touchstone agrees with Jaques's final conclusion, but for his own reasons: "I am not in the mind but I were better to be married of him than of another, for he is not like to marry me well, and not being well married, it will be a good excuse for me hereafter to leave my wife" (81–84). When the misyoked pair, who "must be married, or . . . live in bawdry" (87) join "the rest of the country copulatives, to swear, and to forswear, according as marriage binds and blood breaks" (V.iv.55–57), Jaques predicts their "loving voyage / Is but for two months victualled" (189–190). The carnality underlying this precarious union tends to characterize lesser social ranks, as discussed elsewhere.

Though in Rosalind and Orlando carnal motivations are more sublimated, they too go through ceremonies that parody both marriages and betrothals. Reversing the usual order, Rosalind commands a mock wedding before there has been any spousal.[108]

ROSALIND. Come, sister, you shall be the priest and marry us.—Give me
    your hand, Orlando.—What do you say, sister?
ORLANDO. (*to Celia*) Pray thee, marry us.
CELIA. I cannot say the words.
ROSALIND. You must begin, "Will you, Orlando"—
CELIA. Go to. Will you, Orlando, have to wife this Rosalind?
ORLANDO. I will.
ROSALIND. Ay, but when?
ORLANDO. Why now, as fast as she can marry us.
ROSALIND. Then you must say, "I take thee, Rosalind, for wife."
ORLANDO. I take thee, Rosalind, for wife.
ROSALIND. I might ask you for your commission; but I do take thee, Orlando, for my husband.

(IV.i.116–131)

While this interchange comes perilously close to the prayer book's form, it cannot constitute a valid marriage because Celia, a woman, is even less qualified to be a priest than Sir Oliver Martext. Moreover, the impediment of mistaken identity might apply, since Orlando thinks his bride is Ganymede, although he calls her Rosalind.[109] By asking for his commission, as if he were an agent for another, she underscores the proxy nature of the ceremony, in which both Celia and herself appear as substitutes.

[108] Peter Erickson, *Patriarchal Structures in Shakespeare's Drama* (Berkeley: University of California Press, 1985), p. 23, calls this a "wedding rehearsal"; Meader, *Courtship*, p. 205, calls it a "spousal." It is neither.

[109] Germaine Greer, "Love and the Law," in *Politics, Power, and Shakespeare*, ed. Frances McNeely Leonard (Arlington: Texas Humanities Resource Center, 1981), p. 124, says that Rosalind here corrects Celia in order to change the vows to present tense. However, the prayer book also begins with a repetition of the betrothal vows in the future tense before shifting to matrimonial vows in the present tense, just as in this mock ceremony; see chap. 7. Agnes Latham, ed., *As You Like It*, Arden Shakespeare (London: Methuen, 1975), pp. 134–135, thinks this a valid espousal, with Ganymede the surrogate for Rosalind (who in fact speaks in her own person). Yet in their bargain Orlando accepts Ganymede as a curative substitute, not an officially designated agent; see chap. 5.

Before the actual wedding occurs, Silvius leads Phoebe, Orlando, and
Rosalind through another ritual in act V, scene ii, where the litany mocks
a recital of the catechism required before a nuptial. The shepherd intones
each quality of a true lover, which the other characters affirm in turn. For
example,

SILVIUS. It is to be all made of faith and service. And so am I for Phoebe.
PHOEBE. And I for Ganymede.
ORLANDO. And I for Rosalind.
ROSALIND. And I for no woman.

(84–88)

Situated between the earlier parody of the prayer book rite and Hymen's
rite yet to come, substituting for Christian theology a theology of love
duly subscribed to by all the parties, this scene prepares spectators for the
wholly pagan ceremony at the play's conclusion. At the same time, these
preliminary vows, neither truly private nor truly public, converge with
another quasi-spousal contrapuntal litany involving accusations of blame
and conditional promises of fulfillment—"If this be so, why blame you me
to love you?" and "I will marry you if ever I marry woman, and I'll be
married tomorrow" (98ff., 107–109ff.). Next, before the duke and his
court as witnesses, Rosalind obtains her father's required consent to marriage, and then the lovers publicly repeat their *de futuro* pledges. At last,
with Hymen presiding, the only wedding Shakespeare ever completes onstage marks the apex of unreality, as far removed from the world of betrothal contracts, impediments, and the like as possible.[110] The skewed
nature of all the rituals, none of which follows the prescribed forms, intensifies the nature of the final ceremony toward which all the action inevitably leads.

In a radically different fashion, the deformation of solemn rites—and
the subsequent violation of those rites—appears in *Troilus and Cressida*.
When Pandarus, like some perverse combination of the Nurse and Friar
Laurence, a pimp-parent-priest, brings Troilus to Cressida's chambers, the
lovers' wooing leads not to the altar but to bed. Though they kiss and
promise to be ever true in love, such crucial words as "contract" and "marriage" are missing. Ironically, in the council chamber, Troilus's arguments

[110] Alexander Leggatt, *Shakespeare's Comedy of Love* (London: Methuen, 1974), pp. 190–
191, notes the contrast between Sir Oliver Martext and Hymen as wedding officiants. He
also observes, p. 212, that "the litany of the four lovers in V.ii. marks the transition" to
"Hymen's entrance . . . the high point of miracle in the play," p. 213.

to continue the war liken the Trojan military commitment to a husband's marital commitment: "How may I avoid— / Although my will distaste what it elected— / The wife I chose?" (II.ii.64–66). Yet he enters no such binding union with Cressida (although his appetite will soon enough "distaste what it elected"). Instead, Pandarus presides over them thus:

> PANDARUS. Go to, a bargain made. Seal it, seal it. I'll be the witness. Here I hold your hand; here, my cousin's. If ever you prove false one to another, since I have taken such pain to bring you together, let all pitiful goers-between be called to the world' end after my name: call them all panders. Let all constant men be Troiluses, all false women Cressids, and all brokers-between panders! Say "Amen."
>
> TROILUS. Amen.
>
> CRESSIDA. Amen.
>
> PANDARUS. Amen. Whereupon I will show you a chamber with a bed—which bed, because it shall not speak of your pretty encounters, press it to death. Away!
>
> (III.ii.193–205)

Here is a butchered form of both the betrothal and the wedding ceremonies.[111] The couple's living fathers neither know of nor confirm their secret bargain, no financial provision is made for the future, and no more sanctity attaches to their coupling than to the adulterous affair between Paris and Helen. It is not even clear from these lines that Pandarus actually joins Cressida's hand with Troilus's; in any case, this "bargain" he witnesses is no handfasting, the "pretty encounters" he blesses no consummation of marriage. Fittingly, Troilus gives as token of his love, not a ring or any other symbol of permanence and perfection, but a sleeve—external, perishable, decorative, a remnant of chivalric ritual. Unlike Juliet, Cressida is legally, if not morally, free to enter into another match at her father's bidding, though the second relationship with Diomedes will be just as degradingly sensual as the first one with Troilus. It is even symbolized by the same sleeve, passed like Cressida from one partner to another when she reenacts the earlier pledging rites and violates her prior "contract."

Shakespeare handles his other great union between unmarried partners quite differently. With Antony and Cleopatra there is no courtship, no betrothal, no wedding, but rather a state of flagrant adultery. At the play's

---

[111] Meader, *Courtship*, p. 225, says that this rite parodies the spousal in everything but confirmation of dowry; he appears to be unaware of the many points at which the ceremony is defective.

opening, Antony is married to Fulvia and shortly thereafter to Octavia. During his brief term as widower, no one ever mentions a marriage to Cleopatra. Yet their relationship, always conducted on a heroic public scale quite unlike the cheap bedroom stealth of Troilus and Cressida, is appropriately solemnized at the play's end. At his suicide, Antony declares, "I will be / A bridegroom in my death, and run into't / As to a lover's bed" (IV.xv.99–101). When Cleopatra resolves to join him in death, she adorns herself not just as a queen but also as a bride: "Give me my robe. Put on my crown. I have / Immortal longings in me" (V.ii.275–276). For the first time she calls Antony "husband," making explicit the fact that her death ceremony is also their nuptial rite: "Husband, I come. / Now to that name my courage prove my title" (282–283). [112] When Iras dies, Cleopatra refers to the kiss that the groom traditionally bestows upon his bride: "If she first meet the curlèd Antony, / He'll make demand of her, and spend that kiss / Which is my heaven to have" (296–298)—the word "demand" perhaps an oblique allusion to marriage vows. Seeming to hear the groom's wedding promise, she responds with her last words, "O Antony! Nay. I will take thee too" (307), and thus echoes the *de futuro* pledges in the prayer book. [113] Their union, never conventional, never consistent with ordinary forms of spousals and weddings, is nonetheless officially ratified by Octavius when he decrees, "She shall be buried by her Antony. / No grave upon the earth shall clip in it / A pair so famous" (352–354). Customarily, only as husband and wife would they be interred in the same tomb.

Though history allows Shakespeare not to marry Antony and Cleopatra

---

[112] Martha Tuck Rozett, "The Comic Structures of Tragic Endings: The Suicide Scenes in *Romeo and Juliet* and *Antony and Cleopatra*," *Shakespeare Quarterly* 36 (1985): 162, acknowledges here a fusion of marriage, consummation, and maternity. Cavell, *Disowning Knowledge*, p. 18, also sees in the conclusion of *Ant.*, as in *WT*, "a new ceremony (or new sacrament) of marriage." Yet when he describes the ceremony, p. 28, he does not seem to recognize the signals to Jacobean audiences that would identify it as a wedding, rather than a "hallucinated, . . . more than half mad" rite. See also Howard Felperin, *Shakespearean Romance* (Princeton: Princeton University Press, 1972), p. 139; Alexander Leggatt, *Shakespeare's Political Drama: The History Plays and the Roman Plays* (London: Routledge, 1988), p. 187; Stockholder, *Dream Works*, p. 226.

[113] Most editors, including the Oxford editors, interpolate here a stage direction for Cleopatra to apply another asp, despite the absence of such a direction in the Folio text and the other indications that only a single serpent is used. I am indebted to a paper read by Edward Snow at the 1989 meeting of the Shakespeare Association of America for pointing out this misleading editorial practice.

in any legal way,[114] history dictates that the dramatist unmarry Henry VIII in an entirely legal way. The only divorce or, more properly, dissolution of marriage in the canon threads its way through a labyrinth of political, religious, and aesthetic issues. This union is no casual promise to be lightly repudiated, no secret ceremony of questionable validity. Instead, the play must deal with matrimony of many years' standing. While the action makes restrained use of the ironies involved—Henry's meeting Anne before he considers divorce, his desperate need for a male heir, the juxtaposition of Anne's coronation against Katherine's death, that death making the subsequent birth of Elizabeth legitimate—the text also sets forth the legal grounds for Henry's action in great detail. Dramaturgically, it is important that the audience accept the validity of the annulment, despite the ambiguities of the king's motives and the sympathy Katherine elicits for her plight. According to Henry, questions as to "Whether our daughter were legitimate, / Respecting this our marriage with the dowager, / Sometimes our brother's wife," gave his conscience "a tenderness, / Scruple, and prick" (II.iv.176–178, 167–168). Katherine protests that her father and Henry's "gathered a wise council to them / Of every realm, that did debate this business, / Who deemed our marriage lawful" (49–51). The crucial point, historically, whether Katherine consummated her earlier union with Henry's brother, is never mentioned. Such evasion makes it seem easier for the marriage to be annulled, at least by English judges, who override the queen's refusal to accept any jurisdiction save the pope's. According to their decree, "for non-appearance, and / The King's late scruple, by the main assent / Of all these learnèd men, she was divorced, / And the late marriage made of none effect" (IV.i.30–33). Though vowing, "My lord, I dare not make myself so guilty / To give up willingly that noble title / Your master wed me to" (III.i.138–140), she is nevertheless set aside. "Katherine no more / Shall be called 'Queen,' but 'Princess Dowager,' / And 'widow to Prince Arthur' " (III.ii.69–71). For an audience more accustomed to marital unions than to the rare marital dissolution, Shakespeare does a masterful job of presenting the technical grounds for England's most famous divorce decree—without really touch-

---

[114] For a historical account of Antony's five marriages, see Eleanor Huzar, "Mark Antony: Marriages vs. Careers," *Classical Journal* 81 (1986): 97–111. In Egypt, Cleopatra and Antony did go through a marriage ceremony, but the union was not recognized in Rome, where Octavia was still his wife, p. 107. Nevertheless, as in Shakespeare, the couple were buried together in Egypt in a royal tomb, p. 110. Neely, *Broken Nuptials*, p. 243n.13, notes that this pair are often married in other versions of the story. However, she does not see the last scene as a wedding rite, except in symbolic terms, pp. 161–162.

ing on the disputed consummation or the disputed authority of the English courts in this matter.

Virtually all the problems associated with secret promises, illicit unions, broken betrothals, and even annulments of marriage appear in *All's Well That Ends Well*, a counterpart, in its way, to the farcical presentation of conventional courtship in *The Taming of the Shrew*.[115] As Margaret Ranald has shown, when the King of France enforces a marriage between Helen and the reluctant Bertram, the young man immediately sets up several bases for voiding the match: disparagement, coercion, nonconsummation, lengthy separation, and failure to comply with a conditional contract.[116] The first two grounds he can but glance at in the king's presence, especially when threatened with permanent royal displeasure. He yields with "Pardon, my gracious lord, for I submit / My fancy to your eyes" (II.iii.168–169). However, when commanded, "Take her by the hand / And tell her she is thine" (174–175), he replies merely, "I take her hand" (177), but does not say Helen will be his, thus not fully agreeing to what the king declares a "contract" (179). Later in private he is more definite about his enforced condition, wailing, "O my Paroles, *they have married me!*" (269; italics mine). As for consummating this marriage and thus making it permanently binding, Bertram immediately pledges, "Although before the solemn priest I have sworn, / I will not bed her" (266–267). He writes to his mother, " 'I have wedded her, not bedded her, and sworn to make the "not" eternal' " (III.ii.21–22). Determined to avoid his bride, the young count vows, "I'll to the Tuscan wars and never bed her" (II.iii.270), callously financing his flight with Helen's dowry. Besides reversing the king's denial of his earlier wish to serve in Florence, this expedition sets up a separation that, if sufficiently prolonged, provides another ground for nullifying the marriage.

---

[115] Susan Bassnett-McGuire, "An Ill Marriage," *Shakespeare Jahrbuch Weimar* 120 (1984): 102, calls *AWW* an "analysis of the complexities of post-Reformation views of the marriage contract and . . . a warning to a class that has grown too complacent in its demands for absolute power."

[116] Margaret Loftus Ranald, "The Betrothals of *All's Well That Ends Well*," *Huntington Library Quarterly* 26 (1963): 179–192, and *Shakespeare and His Social Context*, pp. 33–49. Powers, " 'Meaner Parties,' " p. 37, notes coercion as a grounds for annulment but mistakenly claims that the bed trick would not have betokened consent. See also Joel Hurstfield, *The Queen's Wards: Wardship and Marriage under Elizabeth I*, 2d ed. (London: Frank Cass, 1973), pp. 139–141, for a discussion of disparagement. For other analyses of the nature of the contract, see G. K. Hunter, ed., *All's Well That Ends Well*, Arden Shakespeare (London: Methuen, 1959), pp. 53, 60.

In a message Paroles delivers to Helen, Bertram expresses his intent, though in ambiguous terms:

> Madam, my lord will go away tonight.
> A very serious business calls on him.
> The great prerogative and rite of love,
> Which as your due time claims, he does acknowledge,
> But puts it off to a compelled restraint.

(II.iv.39–43)

The phrases "compelled restraint," "rite of love," and "time claims" at least hint at the technical impediments involved in this situation—enforcement, nonconsummation, lengthy separation. Moreover, the terms "madam" and "my lord" avoid acknowledging the two as husband and wife. The final hurdle Bertram spells out in a letter to Helen: " 'When thou canst get the ring upon my finger, which never shall come off, and show me a child begotten of thy body that I am father to, then call me husband; but in such a "then" I write a "never" ' " (III.ii.57–60). Though difficult, the condition is not patently impossible to fulfill and thus forms yet another legitimate basis for annulment. That a dissolution of this marriage is his firm intent appears in the final words of Bertram's letter: " 'Till I have no wife, I have nothing in France' " (74). It is at least worth noting that Helen's schemes to legitimize the union, which have made her appear unattractively aggressive to some critics, are equaled by Bertram's stratagems to invalidate the union. As a first response to his intention, she gives him "no wife . . . in France." By leaving, she can also avoid any legal prosecution so long as her whereabouts remain unknown.

Through the bed trick, of course, Helen fulfills Bertram's requirements and at last receives his unforced, unconditional consent to their marriage. Significantly, he accepts her immediately, with no proof at all. When she finally appears, claiming, " 'Tis but the shadow of a wife you see, / The name and not the thing," Bertram instantly repeals her anomalous status with "Both, both. O, pardon!" (V.iii.309–310). Though this statement, uttered before witnesses, fully legitimizes her marital position, unreservedly ratifies their bond, and wholly acknowledges his faults, Helen goes on to show that she has also met all her husband's specific requirements.

> HELEN.   There is your ring.
> And, look you, here's your letter. This it says:
> "When from my finger you can get this ring,
> And are by me with child," et cetera. This is done.

Will you be mine, now you are doubly won?

BERTRAM. (*to the King*) If she, my liege, can make me know this clearly
I'll love her dearly, ever ever dearly.

HELEN. If it appear not plain and prove untrue,
Deadly divorce step between me and you.

(312–320)

With a play whose action centers on the satisfaction of legal technicalities, it is appropriate that the principals' final speeches begin with "if" clauses demanding proof.[117] Ironically, each now offers to fulfill what has hitherto been the deepest wish of the other's heart: Bertram to love Helen "dearly, ever ever dearly" and she to grant him "deadly divorce."[118] A modern audience may not like the conditionality of these pledges, but they fit the mode of the play. The double acknowledgment of the match, both in Bertram's first instinctive outburst and in the formal presentation of irrefutable evidence, unites the passionate desire and the legal rationality that underlie not only the dramatic action but, ideally, marriage itself.

That passionate desire, so obvious and yet so restrained in Helen, shows up more grossly in a variety of ways. Lavatch's lusty pursuit of "Isbel the woman" (see chapter 4), combined with Paroles's discourse against virginity in the very first scene, emphasize the sexuality permeating the play. There is more than a hint of physical decadence in the king's "fistula" and its miraculous cure by the virgin he then favors so extravagantly. Debasing to their lowest levels both degree and desire, the central dramatic concerns, Paroles slanders the aristocratic Captain Dumaine by claiming that he "was a botcher's prentice in Paris, from whence he was whipped for getting the sheriff's fool with child—a dumb innocent that could not say him nay" and that "for rapes and ravishments he parallels Nessus" (IV.iii.190–193, 255–256). Such intermingling of mean with noble characterizes the language, action, and structure of *All's Well*. Chief in this regard is Bertram's wooing of Diana. While Helen's behavior is a licit way to bed Bertram, his behavior is an illicit way to bed Diana. Here protes-

---

[117] Neely, *Broken Nuptials*, p. 87, interprets the "if" anaphora as an indication of the conditional nature of all human relationships.

[118] Bassnett-McGuire, "Ill Marriage," bases her analysis of this play on the ambiguity surrounding the concept of divorce as stated in Canon 107 of 1604, which codified the ban on remarriage of divorced persons. However, such a ban had long existed, and in any case Helen here acknowledges death as the only condition that will now divorce her from Bertram. Peggy Muñoz Simonds, "Sacred and Sexual Motifs in *All's Well That Ends Well*," *Renaissance Quarterly* 42 (1989): 58, trivializes Helen's statement by asserting that she "mischievously threatens him with 'deadly divorce.'"

tations of love mask little more than lust, as Mariana warns in the familiar terms of Elizabethan advice literature: "Beware of them, Diana; their promises, enticements, oaths, tokens, and all their engines of lust, are not the things they go under. Many a maid hath been seduced by them" (III.v.18–21).

In this courtship, the antithesis of the lawful marriage to which Bertram was compelled, two points are repeatedly stressed: first, that Diana in no way encourages or reciprocates his passion, and second, that the count does indeed enter into a betrothal contract with her. Again, desire both combines and collides with legality. "Derivèd from the ancient Capilet" (V.iii.161) and rightly named for the goddess of chastity, this young woman is "wondrous cold" when Bertram first speaks with her, and all his "Tokens and letters . . . she did re-send" (III.vi.114, 116). Diana terms her virginity "the jewel of our house, / Bequeathèd down from many ancestors, / Which were the greatest obloquy i'th' world / In me to lose" (IV.ii.48–51). Moreover, she declares, "Marry that will; I live and die a maid" (76). In order to assault such icy resistance, as he thinks successfully, Bertram will promise anything. Helen accurately predicts the course of his "wanton siege":[119] "This ring he holds / In most rich choice; yet in his idle fire / To buy his will it would not seem too dear, / Howe'er repented after" (III.vii.18, 25–28). When oaths fail to assure Diana of his steadfastness, Bertram concedes, "Here, take my ring. / My house, mine honour, yea my life be thine, / And I'll be bid by thee" (IV.ii.53–55). Ironically, the ring will in fact go to one rightly responsible for safeguarding his house, his honor, his very life, to one with a right to bid him obey—to his wife, Helen.

While Shakespeare emphasizes the perversion of using such a symbol to satisfy Bertram's "sick desires" (37), the ring's practical function is to provide undeniable testimony about the kind of relationship he has entered into. Thus, when he slanders Diana as "a common gamester to the camp," the token witnesses, "This is his wife. / That ring's a thousand proofs" (V.iii.191, 201–202). He has indeed promised marriage, with exchange of his own ancestral signet for his bed partner's ring the outward symbol of this promise. In receiving it, Diana riddles, "You have won / A wife of me" (IV.ii.66–67). Though the officers say Bertram merely "fleshes his will in the spoil of her honour" (IV.iii.17), Paroles testifies more damn-

---

[119] This term reinforces R. B. Parker's contention, "War and Sex in *All's Well That Ends Well*," *Shakespeare Survey* 37 (1984): 102, 105, that in this play sex is a spoil of war and war an evasion of sexuality.

ingly: "I knew of their going to bed and of other motions, as promising her marriage" (V.iii.265–267). Potentially, there are two impediments to a match with Diana—Bertram's prior contract with Helen and his pledge, "He had sworn to marry me / When his wife's dead" (IV.ii.73–74), which is nullified by criminality—the premise of a living spouse's death. However, because the count receives word of Helen's demise before he deflowers the presumed Diana, he knows that apparently these barriers to matrimony no longer exist. Were his wife truly dead, as Bertram supposes, then he has made a secret *de futuro* contract of marriage which, when consummated, becomes wedlock, precisely as Diana claims.

Yet the shameful seduction of Diana and the despised match with Helen are not the only knots in this tangled marital skein. Even before Bertram returns from Florence to France, Lafeu and the king plan another alliance, which is presented to the Countess of Roussillon for her approval. [120]

> LAFEU. . . . I moved the King my master to speak in the behalf of my daughter; which, in the minority of them both, his majesty out of a self-gracious remembrance did first propose. His highness hath promised me to do it; and to stop up the displeasure he hath conceived against your son, there is no fitter matter. How does your ladyship like it?
> COUNTESS. With very much content, my lord, and I wish it happily effected.
>
> (IV.v.70–79)

When the last scene opens, Bertram, presumably a widower, stands ready to marry Maudlin (whom the audience never sees). Quite conventionally, the king, still acting as Bertram's guardian, ascertains each party's assent and decrees, "Then shall we have a match" (V.iii.30). Thus the young count will wed, not the "poor maid" (148) he has seduced nor the physician's daughter he has scorned, but the heiress of a nobleman, his first "choice" (46)—and his social equal. [121]

Yet in a comedy where no courtship proceeds in quite the usual way, this one too goes awry. First the "amorous token" (69) he produces for

---

[120] Neely, *Broken Nuptials*, p. 85, compares this arrangement to Octavia's in *Ant.* and Claudio's second match in *Ado.*

[121] Ornstein, *Shakespeare's Comedies*, p. 174, attributes Bertram's willingness to marry Maudlin solely to the fact that the alliance "will redeem him in the eyes of the King, his mother, and Lafew." He calls Bertram's "avowed love of the fair Maudlin" "a rehearsed artificiality," pp. 189–190. Neely, *Broken Nuptials*, pp. 82, 84, agrees. However, the king and Lafeu have thought this match fitting before Helen ever comes to court and may be responding to Bertram's earlier interest in the girl.

betrothal to Maudlin turns out to be Helen's gift from the king, arousing suspicion that Bertram might have murdered his unwanted wife. And then Diana appears, charging him with both seduction and a prior contract. In the face of these formidable impediments, Lafeu breaks off negotiations, declaring contemptuously, "Your reputation comes too short for my daughter, you are no husband for her" (178–179). Just at the point when it seems Bertram must acknowledge as spouse a woman with no fortune, with status inferior to Helen's, and with a presumed stain on her virginity, Helen herself appears to rescue him. The final disposition of Diana comes at the king's hands: "If thou be'st yet a fresh uncroppèd flower, / Choose thou thy husband and I'll pay thy dower" (328–329). Ironically, once again royal beneficence is expressed in allowing an impoverished gentlewoman free choice of her mate, together with a generous portion. The action has come full circle. Yet within its orb Shakespeare has packed virtually every irregularity that might attend upon courtship— enforced marriage, nonconsummation, desertion, seduction, secret betrothal, a bed trick, and such impediments as duress, disparagement, unfulfilled conditions, criminality, and precontract. While many plays touch on aspects of irregular unions, *All's Well That Ends Well* explores these difficult, sensitive problems at length, making dramatic capital out of the loopholes in the fabric of matrimonial regulations.

Irregular or invalid courtship allows Shakespeare his fullest opportunity to explore the rules governing "nuptial breaches" (*Lr.*, Q sc. 2, 143) in the culture that he shared with his audiences. Crossing the boundaries between the licit and the illicit, he can both damn and justify premarital intercourse in *Measure for Measure*, ennoble a secret love in *Romeo and Juliet*, surround it with ambiguity in *Othello*, debase it in *Troilus and Cressida*. The frank sexuality of common folk can rebuke the perversions of a Sicilian king, lead to foolish unions in Arden or Navarre, amuse at Belmont, meet reproof in Roussillon. The whole panoply of impediments to marriage find their way into dramatic action: bigamy, consanguinity, criminality, precontract, false identity, unchastity, disparagement, compulsion, religious disparity. From blatant seduction to royal annulments, the canon treats the complexities of heterosexual commitments with great subtlety. No easy answers emerge, no facile generalizations apply, whether it be to genre or to gender, to rank or to race. Instead, there is at work a sophisticated detachment, which interlaces the requirements of source, character, and action with the technicalities determining one's precise marital status. And the ensuing judgments, whether aesthetic or ethical, can be manipulated into almost any configuration, depending upon each play's structure and textual signals. It finally becomes impossible to say whether Shakespearean drama affirms secret betrothals, runaway lovers, fornication, or any other irregular courtship practice. Instead, the fascination lies in the artistry with which the language, rituals, and symbols related to deviant matrimonial possibilities align themselves against the more conventional route to marriage.

{ CHAPTER IX }

Courtship and Politics

Mariage is a kind of publike action: the well or ill ordering
therof much tendeth to the good or hurt of family,
Church, and common-wealth.
—William Gouge, *Of Domesticall Duties*

And though it be allowed in meaner parties
. . . to knit their souls
(On whom there is no more dependency
But brats and beggary) in self-figur'd knot,
Yet you are curb'd from that enlargement by
The consequence o'th crown.
—*Cym.*, II.iii.116–121

IN A CERTAIN sense, all Elizabethan marriages were political affairs. As
contemporary theorists put it, "Mariage is a Politique action. . . . the
Seminary, not only of the Common-wealth, but of the Church too," for "by
mariage a man encreaseth his friends, allies, kinsfolks & neighbors. . . .
Peace is many times procured between monarchs & princes by mariages,
and infinit quarels & dissentions appeased."[1] Both civil and canon law
guarded matrimony with restrictions, because the welfare of the entire
realm depended upon peaceful transfer of property, stability of household
governance, order in the community, and responsible care of children,
orphans, and widows.[2] Even the "rough music" that attended some wed-

[1] Matthew Griffith, *Bethel, or a Forme for Families* (London, 1633), p. 276. See also Jean
Bodin, *The Six Bookes of a Commonweale*, trans. Richard Knolles (London, 1606), pp. 8ff.;
Pierre de la Primaudaye, *The French Academie* (London, 1586), p. 488.

[2] For others who make this point in quite different contexts, see Michael D. Bristol,
Carnival and Theater: Plebeian Culture and the Structure of Authority in Renaissance England
(New York: Methuen, 1985), p. 164 and passim; Jonathan Goldberg, *James I and the
Politics of Literature: Jonson, Shakespeare, Donne, and Their Contemporaries* (Baltimore: Johns
Hopkins University Press, 1983), p. 86 and passim; Christopher Hill, "The Spiritualiza-
tion of the Household," in *Society and Puritanism in Pre-Revolutionary England* (New York:
Schocken Books, 1964); Leah Marcus, *Puzzling Shakespeare: Local Reading and Its Discontents*
(Berkeley: University of California Press, 1988), p. 215; Louis A. Montrose, " 'Shaping

dings could either provide a safety valve for potential disruption or else serve to shame partners in irregular unions.[3] Doubtless, the ubiquity of formal and informal controls upon courtship helped restrain unruly elements that always seemed ready to burst into chaos.[4] But the higher one stood in the society, the more one's selection of a mate affected the exercise of national and international power. Whereas local gentry might aim at a profitable conjunction of estates, courtiers looked for advancement on a grander scale, and princes sought to influence continents through marital alliances. Unwise choices by the "great and noble" could lead to *"Disturbance of whole townes, cities, and nations."*[5]

For a sovereign, marriage was considered essential, since he served as exemplar for his people "to liue honest, and temperate, the which cannot welbe done, vnlesse they bee maryed." Moreover, "The Prince that hath no wyfe nor children shall haue in hys realme, much grudginge and dyspleasure."[6] James I himself affirmed the duty to marry and beget heirs in order to ensure the well-being of his subjects: "Especiallie a King must . . . Marie for the weale of his people. Neither Marie ye, for any accessory cause or worldly respectes, a woman, vn-able, either / through age, nature, or accident, for procreation of children: for in a king that were a double faulte, aswell against his owne weale, as against the weale of his people."[7] Whatever his personal sexual preferences, James followed his own advice, and so did his children.[8] His wife, Anne of Denmark, not only bore him

---

Fantasies': Figurations of Gender and Power in Elizabethan Culture," *Representations* 2 (1983): 79, 85.

[3] See chap. 7, n.70, as well as Susan Dwyer Amussen, "Féminin/masculin: le genre dans l'Angleterre de l'epoque moderne," *Annales Économies, Sociétés, Civilisations* 40 (1985): 272; idem, *An Ordered Society: Gender and Class in Early Modern England* (New York: Basil Blackwell, 1988), pp. 118, 131; Martin Ingram, *Church Courts, Sex, and Marriage in England 1570–1640* (Cambridge: Cambridge University Press, 1987), pp. 163–164.

[4] See esp. the work of David Underdown, *Revel, Riot, and Rebellion: Popular Politics and Culture in England 1603–1660* (Oxford: Clarendon Press, 1985), pp. 40–41 and passim; J. A. Sharpe, *Crime in Early Modern England 1550–1750* (London: Longman, 1984), pp. 86ff., 100ff.

[5] William Gouge, *Of Domesticall Duties* (London, 1622), p. 452. See also Robert Abbot, *A Wedding Sermon* (London, 1608), pp. 50, 66; John Stockwood, *A Bartholomew Fairing for Parentes* (London, 1589), A2ᵛ, p. 75.

[6] Antony Guerara, *The Dial of Princes*, trans. Sir Thomas North (London, 1557), p. 82ᵛ. See also John Owen, *Certaine Epigrams* (London, 1619), C3ᵛ; W. H., *The True Picture and Relation of Prince Henry* (Leyden, 1634), p. 24.

[7] James I, *Basilicon Doron*, ed. James Cragie (Edinburgh: William Blackwood and Sons, 1944), 1:127.

[8] For the impact of James and his family upon Shakespearean drama, see David Berge-

two sons and a daughter but cemented an alliance among the Protestant realms of Denmark, Scotland, and England. Princess Elizabeth strengthened the country's ties to the German Protestant states by wedding Frederick, Elector of the Palatinate. Following a course of rapprochement with the Catholics, James flirted with the possibility of choosing the Spanish Infanta as a bride for his son Charles, who eventually wed the French Princess Henrietta Maria by proxy at Notre Dame.[9] Ideally, concerns of state rather than personal preference dictated the choice of royal brides and grooms.

No ruler managed to exploit the political possibilities of matrimony or defy convention more shrewdly than Elizabeth I. In her view, the coronation ring married her to her country: "Behold (said she, which I marvell ye have forgotten,) the Pledge of this my Wedlock and Marriage with my Kingdom. . . . And do not (saith she) upbraide me with miserable lack of Children: for every one of you, and as many as are English-men, are Children and Kinsmen to me."[10] Everyone knows how she dangled the prospect of marriage before a long series of suitors while steadfastly remaining the Virgin Queen, to avoid either sharing power with a foreigner or unduly elevating an English nobleman. Though she enjoyed being courted, "she knew well, that they desired hir for hir kingdome, and not of any good wil they bare vnto hir: as it is the custome of Princes to respect onely their alliance and profite, marying often-times by substitutes and proxies those whome they neuer saw but by picture."[11] Elizabeth was quite

---

ron, *Shakespeare's Romances and the Royal Family* (Lawrence: University Press of Kansas, 1985). For a political analysis of the literature of the Caroline period, see Kevin Sharpe, *Criticism and Compliment: The Politics of Literature in the England of Charles I* (Cambridge: Cambridge University Press, 1987).

[9] Ann Monsarrat, *And the Bride Wore . . . . : The Story of the White Wedding* (London: Gentry Books, 1973), pp. 42–43, includes descriptions of Charles's and Elizabeth's weddings.

[10] William Camden, *Annals of the Reign of Queen Elizabeth*, as cited by Alison Plowden, *Marriage with My Kingdom: The Courtships of Elizabeth I* (New York: Stein and Day, 1977), p. 82. See also Allison Heisch, "Queen Elizabeth I and the Persistence of Patriarchy," *Feminist Review* 4 (1980): 47–52. As Jonathan Goldberg points out, James also viewed his relationship to his kingdom as a marriage between husband and wife; "Fatherly Authority: The Politics of Stuart Family Images," in *Rewriting the Renaissance: The Discourses of Sexual Difference in Early Modern Europe*, ed. Margaret W. Ferguson, Maureen Quilligan, Nancy J. Vickers (Chicago: University of Chicago Press, 1986), p. 3.

[11] Primaudaye, *French Academie*, p. 495. For analyses of Elizabeth's position on courtship as it affected her courtiers, see Arthur F. Marotti, " 'Love Is Not Love': Elizabethan Sonnet Sequences and the Social Order," *ELH* 49 (1982): 396–428; Louis A. Montrose, "Celebration and Insinuation: Sir Philip Sidney and the Motives of Elizabethan Courtship," *Renais-*

willing to correspond with Czar Boris Godunov about a possible marriage between his son and one of her subjects,[12] but she was hostile toward matches for her ladies-in-waiting, her courtiers, and the clergy. In the hothouse atmosphere of the royal entourage, where eligible aristocrats enjoyed a rare freedom of association, romantic attachments were bound to flourish. To the extent that the Queen's displeasure curbed imprudent unions, her policy was doubtless a wise one, though she was also defending her vanity and authority. Thus in private conversation, "She did oft aske the ladies around hir chamber, If they lovede to thinke of marriage? And the wise ones did conceal well their liking hereto; as knowing the Queene's judgment in this matter."[13]

However, Elizabeth's antipathy to marriage extended well beyond a proper concern for her attendants' propriety. She insisted that any cleric with a wife lodge her away from his official quarters.[14] When the widowed Richard Fletcher, Bishop of London, married Lady Baker, a member of the royal household, the Queen suspended him for six months, refused to see him for a year, and never again favored him.[15] Understandably, the flirtatious behavior of Mary Howard so concerned her friends that they advised, "She must not entertaine my lorde the earle, in any conversation, but shunne his companye; and moreover be less carefull in attiringe her own person, for this seemethe as done more to win the earl, than her mistresse good will."[16] Blunt refusals or beatings awaited ladies who dared ask Eliz-

---

sance Drama, n.s., 8 (1977): 3–35; Ann Rosalind Jones and Peter Stallybrass, "The Politics of *Astrophil and Stella*," *Studies in English Literature* 24 (1984): 53–68; Maureen Quilligan, "Sidney and His Queen," in *The Historical Renaissance*, ed. Heather Dubrow and Richard Strier (Chicago: University of Chicago Press, 1988).

[12] Robert J. Clements and Lorna Levant, eds., *Renaissance Letters: Revelations of a World Reborn* (New York: New York University Press, 1976), pp. 413–415.

[13] Sir John Harington, *Nugae Antiquae*, ed. Henry Harington (London: Vernor and Hood, 1804), 1:359. Leonard Tennenhouse, *Power on Display: The Politics of Shakespeare's Genres* (London: Methuen, 1986), p. 28, interprets this account as "pure gossip," "folk narrative which has been told and retold many times over." Its cultural force, however, does not rely upon its factual accuracy. Tennenhouse presents a superb analysis of the way courtship figured into Elizabeth's political milieu, though he applies his analysis in a way different from my own.

[14] Monsarrat, *And the Bride*, p. 35; G. E. Howard, *A History of Matrimonial Institutions* (Chicago: University of Chicago Press, 1904), 1:396–398. Joel Berlatsky, "Marriage and Family in a Tudor Elite: Familial Patterns of Elizabethan Bishops," *Journal of Family History* 3 (1978): 7, claims that Elizabeth's objection was supported by "the landed classes, which did not want competition for land and jobs from prelatical progeny."

[15] Berlatsky, "Marriage," p. 10.

[16] Harington, *Nugae Antiquae*, 1:233, 234. See also Tennenhouse, *Power*, pp. 29–30.

abeth's permission to marry, and worse punishments lay in store for those who wed without that permission. From her reaction to the clandestine marriage of the Earl of Southampton emerges a powerful sense of royal fury: "I find her grievously offended," writes Cecil; "her patience was so much moved that she came not to the chapel. She threateneth them all to the Tower, not only the parties but all that are partakers of the practice."[17] For their audacity in marrying without Elizabeth's knowledge, her wrath fell upon the Earl of Leicester and the Countess of Essex, the Earl of Hertford and Frances Howard, John Wingfield and the Countess of Kent, Sir Philip Sidney and Frances Walsingham, the Earl of Essex and Lady Sidney.[18] Besides disgrace, legal means could also be used to prevent or punish unauthorized unions. The Queen sent an order forbidding Sir Robert Sidney to wed Barbara Gamage in 1584, but it arrived a few scant hours after the ceremony.[19] More ominously, prison awaited the likes of Robert Tyrwhit, Elizabeth Throckmorton, and Sir Walter Raleigh.[20]

When it came to those with a claim to the throne, however distant, all matches had serious political repercussions. To marry without the sovereign's permission constituted treason, since it could be a ploy for usurpation or a disparagement of royal blood. No one, least of all Elizabeth, had forgotten the Northumberlands' efforts in 1553 to unite Lady Jane Grey with the Northumberland son, Lord Guilford Dudley, and then enthrone her.[21] Lady Jane's kinswoman, Mary Grey, obtained release from prison only after the death of the husband she had covertly married, yet still the Grey legacy of suspicious matrimonial alliances continued.[22] By Eliza-

[17] G.P.V. Akrigg, *Shakespeare and the Earl of Southampton* (Cambridge: Harvard University Press, 1968), p. 71.

[18] Lawrence Stone, *The Crisis of the Aristocracy, 1558–1641* (Oxford: Clarendon Press, 1965), p. 606.

[19] Michael Brennan, *Literary Patronage in the English Renaissance: The Pembroke Family* (London: Routledge and Kegan Paul, 1988), p. 49; Tennenhouse, *Power*, pp. 27–28; Frances Berkeley Young, *Mary Sidney, Countess of Pembroke* (London: David Nutt, 1912), p. 51.

[20] Stone, *Crisis*, p. 66; Stephen Greenblatt, *Sir Walter Ralegh: The Renaissance Man and His Roles* (New Haven: Yale University Press, 1973), pp. 25, 55, 76, 79.

[21] D'Orsay W. Pearson, "Renaissance Adolescent Marriage: Another Look at Hymen," *Cithara* 23 (1983): 19, notes that besides Lady Jane and Lord Dudley, two other young aristocrats married possible claimants to the throne at this time: Katherine Grey and Lord Henry Herbert, Katherine Dudley and Lord Henry Hastings.

[22] Retha M. Warnicke, *Women of the English Renaissance and Reformation* (Westport, CT: Greenwood Press, 1983), p. 130. See also Doris Mary Stenton, *The English Woman in History* (New York: Macmillan, 1957), p. 59.

beth's decree, the clandestine union of Katherine Grey to the Earl of Hertford was ruled invalid and their children declared bastards. When their son, William Seymour, secretly wed Arabella Stuart, another distant claimant to the crown, James I imprisoned them both. After an aborted attempt to flee to Europe, the unfortunate bride ended her days in the Tower.[23] Regardless of individual wishes, a subject with some trace of royal blood could not marry without facing public consequences.

Nor did aristocrats enjoy much more freedom. Despite the occasional couple who insisted on following their hearts, most children entered into alliances that furthered family interests. A parent like Robert Cary (perhaps regretting his own modest choice of a wife) candidly states, "I married my daughter to my Lord Wharton's son and heir" and "I married my eldest son, to the eldest daughter of Sir Lionell Cranfield, afterwards Earl of Middlesex, and Lord Treasurer of England."[24] In a sermon at the 1607 nuptials of Lord and Lady Hay at Whitehall before King James, the preacher avers that "simply to marie ioynes sex and sex, to marie at home ioynes house and house, but your marriage ioyneth land and land, earth and earth, onely Christ goes beyond it, who ioynes heauen and earth."[25] A shrewd union brought relief from indebtedness, powerful friends, advancement at court, titles, and estates. While not everyone succeeded so brilliantly as Bess of Hardwicke, who parlayed the fortunes of four husbands into vast wealth and a countess's rank,[26] all great families understood the use of matrimony as a tool of dynastic power. As a result of coercion, manipulation, and negotiation, a complicated structure of interlocking family connections developed among the nobility.

Sometimes disastrous abuse resulted. In 1617, when Sir Edward Coke tried to repair his political reverses by wedding his daughter to Buckingham's mentally defective brother, John Villiers, the girl was hidden, then

---

[23] Warnicke, *Women*, pp. 130–131; Lu Emily Pearson, *Elizabethans at Home* (Stanford, CA: Stanford University Press, 1957), pp. 322–323. For further accounts of Arabella (or Arbella), see Bergeron, *Shakespeare's Romances*, pp. 68–69; Pearl Hogrefe, *Women of Action in Tudor England* (Ames: Iowa State University Press, 1977), pp. 74–75; David N. Durant, *Arbella Stuart: A Rival to the Queen* (London: Weidenfeld and Nicholson, 1978); P. M. Handover, *Arbella Stuart* (London: Eyre and Spottiswood, 1957); Ian McInnes, *Arabella: The Life and Times of Lady Arabella Seymour, 1575–1615* (London: Allen, 1968).

[24] Robert Cary, *Memoirs of Robert Cary, Earl of Monmouth* (Edinburgh: Archibald Constable, 1808), pp. 154, 155. Cary had married Elizabeth Trevannion, a widow with "but five hundred pounds a year jointure, and . . . between five and six hundred pounds in her purse," p. 51.

[25] Robert Wilkinson, *The Merchant Royall* (London, 1607), pp. 35–36.

[26] See, e.g., Hogrefe, *Women of Action*, pp. 60–65.

kidnapped, and finally whipped to force her into the match. Throughout, the affair preoccupied everyone "from the King to the favoritt, and from him to the ferriman of Putney, and a women that sells chickens who have been examined for some scandalous words of Sir Jhon Villars soar legg."[27] At the most sordid level, wards of the crown were bought, sold, and married off solely to further the interests of their guardians.[28] With wards, natural offspring, and adult suitors alike, the aid of influential courtiers furthered the consolidation of power. Support from men like Burghley and Essex was actively sought in arranging advantageous unions.[29] Eventually, when straitened finances demanded it, Queen Elizabeth began to substitute her advocacy of marriage suits for cash gifts in the 1590s.[30] As for her successor, James willingly busied himself in promoting politically desirable alliances for his favorites and their kin. A title and a lucrative patent from him bribed the reluctant consent of Lord Denny to his wealthy daughter Honoria's match with the spendthrift Lord Hay.[31] Obviously, not all liaisons derived from the priority of public over personal motives. But one ignores political motivations at the risk of misunderstanding the aristocratic marital system in Renaissance England.

The significance of matrimony to social institutions like the family, the community, the church, and the government is assumed throughout Shakespeare's plays. The involvement of parents and friends in arranging matches, the making of contracts, the witnesses to declarations between betrothed couples, the formal marriage ceremony, the celebratory feasts shared with invited guests—all these extensions of the mating game into the wider world permeate the dramatizations of courtship. Even secret loves ultimately move into the public arena for either confirmation or denunciation. Marriage as a purely private affair simply does not exist. And certainly at the social apex a nuptial often becomes a political tool, manipulated for the interests of the state, controlled at the pleasure of the ruler,

[27] Peter Seddon, ed., *The Letters of John Holles*, Thoroton Society Record Series 35 (1983): 180–181; Stone, *Crisis*, p. 596; G. R. Hibbard, "Love, Marriage and Money in Shakespeare's Theatre and Shakespeare's England," in *Elizabethan Theatre VI*, ed. Hibbard (Toronto: Macmillan of Canada, 1975), pp. 139–141; Antonia Fraser, *The Weaker Vessel* (New York: Alfred A. Knopf, 1984), pp. 12–16.

[28] Stone, *Crisis*, p. 604; Joel Hurstfield, *The Queen's Wards: Wardship and Marriage under Elizabeth I*, 2d ed. (London: Frank Cass, 1973), pp. 58–95.

[29] See, e.g., Dorothy M. Meads, ed., *Diary of Lady Margaret Hoby, 1599–1605* (Boston: Houghton Mifflin, 1930), p. 21.

[30] Stone, *Crisis*, p. 607.

[31] Fraser, *Weaker Vessel*, p. 9.

or contracted for personal advancement. After her death, Cymbeline receives the chilling report that his queen "never loved you, only / Affected greatness got by you, not you; / Married your royalty, was wife to your place, / Abhorred your person" (V.vi.38–41). Though not so brutally ambitious as this one, a number of marriages in Shakespeare are arranged as rewards for notable service. Instances in such plays as *A Comedy of Errors*, *Much Ado*, *All's Well*, *Winter's Tale*, and *Henry VIII* have already been discussed in the preceding chapters. The discomfort sometimes expressed in criticism of these peremptory couplings shows how far present customs have departed from those familiar to Shakespeare's audiences.

Nonetheless, those same discomforts over lesser unions decreed with scant regard for love or even free consent tend to disappear when the plays deal with the highest social levels, with princes and kings and emperors. There the use of marriage as an instrument of state seems fair enough, even to modern observers. Inconsistently, though understandably, critics approve of royal alliances that bring peace, enhance power, swell a treasury, or perpetuate a dynasty but withhold approval for such motives in less exalted individuals. As might be expected, Shakespeare's political marriages range from cynical alliances of convenience to full-blown courtship with declarations of mutual love. Thus, alongside the lyrical wooing of Miranda and Ferdinand in *The Tempest*, the dramatist provides brief glimpses of a less happy royal alliance. When the storm brings Alonso's ship to Prospero's island, the vessel is returning from "the marriage of the King's fair daughter Claribel to the King of Tunis" (II.i.74–76). Typically cruel, Sebastian blames Alonso for the supposed death of Prince Ferdinand in the shipwreck.

> Sir, you may thank yourself for this great loss,
> That would not bless our Europe with your daughter,
> But rather loose her to an African,
>
> . . . .
>
> You were kneeled to and importuned otherwise
> By all of us, and the fair soul herself
> Weighed between loathness and obedience at
> Which end o'th' beam should bow.
>
> (129–131, 134–137)

Beneath the talk of "a sweet marriage," thanks to which "Tunis was never graced before with such a paragon to their queen" (77, 79–80), lies a harsher picture. Against her wishes and against the pleas of friends, a royal

241

child has been escorted to marry a stranger in a move that extends the growing power of Naples to the Tunisian coast.[32]

However advantageous when made, this alliance has a bitter taste after the heir seems lost and Claribel, next in line for Alonso's throne, "is so far from Italy removed / I ne'er again shall see her" (116–117). More ominous still, the distance of the new heir apparent leads Antonio to prompt the king's brother toward assassination and usurpation: " 'How shall that Claribel / Measure us back to Naples? Keep in Tunis, / And let Sebastian wake' " (263–265).[33] Though these dangers never materialize, the strategic maneuvers involved in the Miranda-Ferdinand union brilliantly fulfill the aims of Prospero. When he says of their courtship, "It goes on, I see, / As my soul prompts it" (I.ii.423–424), Miranda's father speaks from a history of betrayal and intrigue. Through her nuptials with the Neapolitan prince, Prospero can redress the injuries done to his dukedom as well as to himself. To seize Milan from his brother, Antonio leagued himself,

> So dry he was for sway, wi'th' King of Naples
> To give him annual tribute, do him homage,
> Subject his coronet to his crown, and bend
> The dukedom yet unbowed—alas, poor Milan—
> To most ignoble stooping.

(112–116)

The return of Prospero to Milan, combined with the marriage of his daughter to Ferdinand, not only restores the rightful ruler and the rightful line of succession but also replaces political subjection with an alliance of

---

[32] Joan Hartwig, *Shakespeare's Tragicomic Vision* (Baton Rouge: Louisiana State University Press, 1972), p. 154, simply contrasts Alonso's rigor with Prospero's more indulgent treatment of Miranda. Stephen Orgel, "Shakespeare and the Cannibals," in *Cannibals, Witches, and Divorce*, ed. Marjorie Garber (Baltimore: Johns Hopkins University Press, 1987), pp. 55–56, notes that the King of Tunis would be both Moslem and black and that Caliban, born of an Algerian mother, would also be Tunisian. Mark Taylor, *Shakespeare's Darker Purpose: A Question of Incest* (New York: AMS Press, 1982), p. 135, says Caliban's name echoes Claribel's, and he sees her marriage as a "callous disposal," p. 128, by a father who, unable to possess her himself, wants her sent as far away as possible. Harry Berger, Jr., *Second World and Green World: Studies in Renaissance Fiction-Making* (Berkeley: University of California Press, 1988), p. 168, views the match as "the civilized European soul compromising with darkness, surrendering its clear beautiful ideals for the sake of expediency."

[33] Bergeron, *Shakespeare's Romances*, pp. 186–189, points out the political implications of Claribel's distance from Naples and also sees parallels between her marriage and Princess Elizabeth's in 1612.

equals.[34] Underlying all the magic power of *The Tempest* is a sophisticated nexus of worldly power, all of it mirrored in the inept usurpation attempted by Caliban, Trinculo, and Stephano, which also involves marrying Miranda to a prospective ruler.

Nothing could be more antithetical to the mood of young love in this romance than the machinations of *Antony and Cleopatra*. Against a background of erotic adultery, the tragedy bluntly presents Antony's match with Octavia as a device to hold him and Octavius "in perpetual amity, / To make you brothers, and to knit your hearts / With an unslipping knot" (II.ii.131–133).[35] While these two great rivals see the advantages of remaining allies rather than enemies, their inherent distrust appears in the response to Agrippa's proposal of the marriage. Neither man wants to commit himself first, and their nervous fencing contrasts sharply with the negotiations of a declared suitor.

> ANTONY.   Will Caesar speak?
> CAESAR. Not till he hears how Antony is touched
>   With what is spoke already.
> ANTONY. What power is in Agrippa,
>   If I would say "Agrippa, be it so,"
>   To make this good?
> CAESAR.   The power of Caesar,
>   And his power unto Octavia.
> ANTONY.   May I never
>   To this good purpose, that so fairly shows,
>   Dream of impediment! Let me have thy hand.
>   Further this act of grace, and from this hour
>   The heart of brothers govern in our loves
>   And sway our great designs.
> CAESAR.   There's my hand.
>   *Antony and Caesar clasp hands*

[34] See also Paul A. Cantor, "Prospero's Republic: The Politics of Shakespeare's *The Tempest*," in *Shakespeare as Political Thinker*, ed. John Alvis and Thomas G. West (Durham, NC: Carolina Academic Press, 1981), p. 249; Philip Edwards, *Shakespeare: A Writer's Progress* (Oxford: Oxford University Press, 1986), p. 174. Stephen Orgel, "Prospero's Wife," in *Rewriting the Renaissance*, p. 63, argues that while this marriage will effectively exclude the usurping Antonio from a future claim to the throne, Milan will still be subjugated to Naples because of a wife's surrender of property to her husband. Orgel need look no further than the marriages of Mary Tudor or Mary Queen of Scots to see his error.

[35] See Marjorie Garber, *Coming of Age in Shakespeare* (New York: Methuen, 1981), pp. 143–144, 156, for a perceptive analysis of this alliance.

A sister I bequeath you whom no brother
Did ever love so dearly. Let her live
To join our kingdoms and our hearts; and never
Fly off our loves again.

LEPIDUS.   Happily, amen.

(145–160)

Despite the denial of impediment, the ritual clasp of hands to signify agreement, the affirmation of kinship, and Lepidus's witnessing of the contract—all the trappings of formal negotiations for betrothal—this is a military and political bargain. Moreover, Octavia is mentioned by name only once in the proceeding. Caesar, Antony, Agrippa—these male figures cement "our loves," "our kingdom," "our great designs." Not even present at her peremptory bestowal, the woman involved merely serves the empire's masculine interests.[36]

Throughout the ensuing speeches and action, the struggles for power surrounding the marriage continue to be emphasized, its emotive qualities either minimized or entirely absent. Maecenas predicts, "If beauty, wisdom, modesty can settle / The heart of Antony, Octavia is / A blessèd lottery to him" (247–249), a prediction that her appearance at the spousal confirms. With references to division rather than union, to worldly affairs, to prayers and rules, this cold match is confirmed by both parties and by a brother-guardian.

ANTONY. The world and my great office will sometimes
    Divide me from your bosom.
OCTAVIA.   All which time
    Before the gods my knee shall bow my prayers
    To them for you.
ANTONY.   Good night, sir. My Octavia,
    Read not my blemishes in the world's report.
    I have not kept my square, but that to come
    Shall all be done by th' rule. Good night, dear lady.
    Good night, sir.
CAESAR. Good night.

(II.iii.1–9)

[36] Jonathan Dollimore, *Radical Tragedy: Religion, Ideology and Power in the Drama of Shakespeare and His Contemporaries* (Chicago: University of Chicago Press, 1984), pp. 213–214, says, "Octavia has of course been coerced into marriage with Antony to heal the rift . . . between him and Caesar, her brother." In fact, she is not even accorded the dignity of coercion but is bestowed without being consulted.

After the tepid politeness of "your bosom," "My Octavia," "dear lady," and the frigid "sir" to Caesar, Antony ends the scene by brutally exposing in private his union's expedient nature. "I will to Egypt; / And though I make this marriage for my peace, / I'th' East my pleasure lies" (36–38).

Over and over, the alliance is described, not with the sensuality lavished upon Cleopatra, but in terms of rapprochement between political rivals: "Caesar and he are greater friends than ever" (II.v.48); "Then is Caesar and he for ever knit together" (II.vi.115); "He married but his occasion here" (130–131). At the same time, there are warnings that "the band that seems to tie their friendship together will be the very strangler of their amity" (120–122). As Octavius cautions, "Let not the piece of virtue which is set / Betwixt us as the cement of our love / To keep it builded, be the ram to batter / The fortress of it" (III.ii.28–31). Again there is an emphasis on "our love" between males, rather than between husband and wife, combined with inanimate references like "piece of virtue," "cement," "builded," and the phallic war imagery of the battering ram. When Octavia is sent back to Rome, she comes ostensibly as a peace emissary but actually as a declaration of armed hostility—symbolically, a peace treaty rejected in favor of a new alliance. On so titanic a canvas, every marital relationship finds martial expression, whether it be a Fulvia in arms to summon back her husband by opposing Caesar, an Octavia avenged by her insulted brother, or a Cleopatra exercising self-proclaimed rights as consort and general. For Antony, each nuptial commitment moves him closer to political and military disaster.

Precisely at the center of the play stands act III, scene vi, whose language most extensively pairs war with marriage. It opens with Octavius's description of Antony and Cleopatra, "publicly enthroned" like a royal family, with "Caesarion, whom they call my father's son, / And all the unlawful issue that their lust / Since then hath made between them" (5, 6–8). By contrast, Octavia arrives, not similarly displayed "I'th' market place," but "come / A marketmaid to Rome" (3, 50–51). The love and respect due the wife and sister of the world's two rulers can only be demonstrated by martial panoply. "You come not / Like Caesar's sister. The wife of Antony / Should have an army for an usher, and / The neighs of horse to tell of her approach." Octavius continues, "Nay, the dust / Should have ascended to the roof of heaven, / Raised by your populous troops" (42–45, 48–50). Lacking such trappings of power, the only kind of power that ultimately prevails in the political arena, Octavia inevitably seems "unloved" (53). In the same association of matrimony and warfare, he tells his "wrongèd sister" her husband "hath given his empire / Up to a whore;

who now are levying / The kings o'th' earth for war" (65, 66–68). Her tame words "heart" and "afflict" (77, 78) palely echo the central motifs here. But Caesar far more crudely characterizes the military-matrimonial infidelity that will doom his foe: "Only th'adulterous Antony, most large / In his abominations, turns you off, / And gives his potent regiment to a trull" (93–95).

As a means to bring peace by cementing political alliances, marriage fails more often than it succeeds in Shakespeare. Thus when King John of England and King Philip of France mass their troops before Angers, a city both claim, the impasse—and the impending slaughter—are averted by a proposed match between Louis and Blanche.[37] "This union shall do more than battery can / To our fast-closèd gates, for at this match, / . . . shall we fling wide ope" (*Jn.*, II.i.447–448, 450). Noble rhetoric does not obscure the fact that the bride and groom are mere pawns in the great games of war and peace; their willingness to play those games by wedding each other is irrelevant. The complex dilemmas that ensue when marriages are made amid shifting allegiances find interesting expression in *King John*, for the union of the French heir, Louis, to John's niece, Blanche, not only buys peace at the price of English-held provinces but also bars Prince Arthur's claim to the throne. "Commodity," as the Bastard Falconbridge puts it, controls the proceedings from first to last.[38] Appropriately, his famous speech on commodity uses terms associated with a debased courtship—"break-vow," "smooth-faced gentleman," "This bawd, this broker," "fickle," "virtue," "vice." Commodity "wins of all, / Of . . . maids,— / Who having no external thing to lose / But the word 'maid,' cheats the poor maid of that," says the Bastard, though "he hath not wooed me yet" (570, 574, 583, 584, 596, 597, 570–573, 589).

"Since kings break faith upon commodity" (598), it comes as no surprise that the pledges of national amity which accompany the wedding of Blanche and Louis are broken too. King Philip at first describes his promises to England in terms of holy matrimony, not the Bastard's baser—if truer—language.

> This royal hand and mine are newly knit,
> And the conjunction of our inward souls

---

[37] On this point, see also David Scott Kastan, " 'To Set a Form upon that Indigest': Shakespeare's Fictions of History," *Comparative Drama* 17 (1983): 9.

[38] See Alan Lewis, "Shakespeare and the Morality of Money," *Social Research* 36 (1969): 373–388, on the ramifications of the Bastard's use of the term "commodity."

> Married in league, coupled and linked together
> With all religious strength of sacred vows;
> The latest breath that gave the sound of words
> Was deep-sworn faith, peace, amity, true love,
> Between our kingdoms and our royal selves.
>
> (III. i. 152–158)

However, continuing the same metaphors, he raises dreadful questions about the possibility of severing his "sacred vows" when he uses phrases like "play fast and loose with faith," "unconstant children," and "unswear faith sworn," which clearly echo the Bastard.

> And shall these hands, so lately purged of blood,
> So newly joined in love, so strong in both,
> Unyoke this seizure and this kind regreet,
> Play fast and loose with faith, so jest with heaven,
> Make such unconstant children of ourselves,
> As now again to snatch our palm from palm,
> Unswear faith sworn, and on the marriage-bed
> Of smiling peace to march a bloody host,
>
> (165–172)

Philip's last futile protest, "I may disjoin my hand, but not my faith" (188), still images the outward symbols of betrothal and marriage, as well as the permanent union they should represent.

Touchingly, Blanche voices the pain of one bound to a spouse yet also bound to her kinsmen—a sacrifice to the callous political expediency dictating now peace, now war. Her language juxtaposes nuptial celebration with military carnage and thus spells out the issue that has always been married to her marriage.

> LOUIS THE DAUPHIN. Father, to arms!
> BLANCHE.   Upon thy wedding day?
>   Against the blood that thou hast marrièd?
>   What, shall our feast be kept with slaughtered men?
>   Shall braying trumpets and loud churlish drums,
>   Clamours of hell, be measures to our pomp?
>   *She kneels*
>   O husband, hear me! Ay, alack, how new
>   Is "husband" in my mouth! Even for that name
>   Which till this time my tongue did ne'er pronounce,

247

Upon my knee I beg, go not to arms
Against mine uncle.[39]

(226–235)

In this realm, the claims of love and marriage that Blanche advances take second place to more powerful claims. The young bride affectingly utters her misery at being, in a sense, fatally handfasted to both sides in the conflict so that "each army hath a hand, / And in their rage, I having hold of both, / They whirl asunder and dismember me" (254–256).[40] It is fitting that the machinations to seize or maintain royal power, which have controlled Blanche's courtship, continue to control her marriage. When Arthur's death is plotted, Louis inquires, "But what shall I gain by young Arthur's fall?" Pandolf responds, "You, in the right of Lady Blanche your wife, / May then make all the claim that Arthur did" (III.iv.141–143). With another dismissal of peace and a cynical use of the word "honour," Louis later asks, "What is that peace to me? / I, by the honour of my marriage bed, / After young Arthur, claim this land for mine" (V.ii.92–94).

While Shakespeare explores the consequences of marital alliances either sacrificed or sealed for political ends, he also explores the consequences of unions that disregard political advantage. In the *Henry VI* trilogy, one of the many parallels characterizing these plays involves a properly conducted state courtship that is abrogated because the king prefers another woman. All sorts of conditions beneficial to the state attend the approved negotiations. Hence, when Gloucester urges a reluctant Henry VI to marry, he presses the suit of a French noblewoman to ensure the uneasy truce and enlarge the treasury:

The Earl of Armagnac, near knit to Charles—
A man of great authority in France—
Proffers his only daughter to your grace
In marriage, with a large and sumptuous dowry.

(*1H6*, V.i.17–20)

[39] Robert B. Pierce, *Shakespeare's History Plays: The Family and the State* (Columbus: Ohio State University Press, 1971), p. 129, dismisses this lament as "purely conventional" and says, p. 130, that Blanche represents all women "whose marriages are hopelessly corrupted by a world of commodity."

[40] Phyllis Rackin, "Anti-Historians: Women's Roles in Shakespeare's Histories," *Theatre Journal* 37 (1985): 339, says that the "dismemberment" speech images all the divisions in the play's actions and audiences, with Blanche the embodiment of the divisions that her exchange between men is designed to heal.

Though Henry protests, "Alas, my years are young, / And fitter is my study and my books / Than wanton dalliance with a paramour" (21–23), he nonetheless agrees to marry any bride who "Tends to God's glory and my country's weal" (27). Thus formally empowered by the king, Gloucester promises the French ambassadors, "He doth intend she shall be England's queen" (45). That promise Henry immediately ratifies: "In argument and proof of which contract / Bear her this jewel, pledge of my affection" (46–47). Thus the suit proceeds along entirely legal and conventional lines, with public consent and a token of love to seal the proxy wooing.

However, in a departure from the sources, Suffolk enters into a separate courtship of Margaret. "Fain would *I* woo her" (V.v.21; italics mine), he admits, but he also acknowledges an insuperable impediment: "Fond man, remember that thou hast a wife; / Then how can Margaret be thy paramour?" (37–38). His solution—to sue on Henry's behalf and thus bring Margaret to the English court—sets up a highly improper situation, ironically anticipated in the king's earlier reference to "wanton dalliance with a paramour." Not only are the negotiations with the woman's father, the Neapolitan king, Regnier, undertaken without Henry's authority or knowledge, but the suit is actually designed to secure a mistress in the guise of a wife, a motive Margaret endorses with her response to Suffolk's proxy spousal kiss: "That for thyself" (141). A sexual taint attaches to her entire family, for her father is one of those whom Joan la Pucelle names as sire of the unborn child she invents to save herself from the stake.[41] Even more damaging, from England's standpoint, is the meanness of a marriage to the daughter of "a worthless king, / Having neither subject, wealth, nor diadem" (*2H6*, IV.i.81–82); "our nobility will scorn the match" (*1H6*, V.v.52). The situation is compounded by the outrageous gifts to Regnier of Maine and Anjou as the bride-price. Nothing about this betrothal augurs well for either the sovereign or the kingdom—a situation that the enactment of a debased marriage negotiation underscores. The procedure follows the details of the betrothal ritual but not its intent.

Nevertheless, when Suffolk manages to beguile Henry with descriptions of Margaret's beauty, the king reverses his earlier commitment to Gloucester and the French bride, requesting of Gloucester, "Therefore, my Lord Protector, give consent / That Marg'ret may be England's royal queen"

---

[41] Marcus, *Puzzling Shakespeare*, p. 89, says that "Margaret is, symbolically at least, Joan's daughter" because of this charge.

(V.vii.23–24). The earl, having dealt with Armagnac in good faith, rightly protests,

> So should I give consent to flatter sin.
> You know, my lord, your highness is betrothed
> Unto another lady of esteem.
> How shall we then dispense with that contract
> And not deface your honour with reproach?
>
> (25–29)

Far more than a choice between two women is involved here. Not only does the prior contract affirm a prior legal commitment, but it also affirms peace, wise counsel, a strong treasury, the retention of French lands dearly bought with English blood, the precedence of the kingdom's welfare over the sovereign's personal desires. Opting for Suffolk's bargain with Margaret means repudiation of law and custom, resumption of war, reliance upon corrupt advice, loss of land and money, the triumph of private passion over public prudence. Politically, Henry decides to honor the wrong contract, thereby insulting both Gloucester and the French, plunging his country into conflict abroad and at home.[42] Personally, too, Henry errs, ironically uniting himself with a treacherous, unfaithful wife.

In the sequel to Henry's reign, the York king, Edward IV, also agrees to a French match.[43] As soon as the coronation is over, Warwick proposes to "cut the sea to France, / And ask the Lady Bona for thy queen. / So shalt thou sinew both these lands together" (3H6, II.vi.89–91). With Edward's full consent, Warwick presses the suit before the French king, Louis. He comes

> to crave a league of amity,
> And lastly, to confirm that amity
> With nuptial knot, if thou vouchsafe to grant
> That virtuous Lady Bona, thy fair sister,
> To England's King in lawful marriage.
>
> (III.iii.53–57)

---

[42] Pierce, *Shakespeare's History Plays*, pp. 60–61, points out the shame of this marriage, which is doubly suspect because it also breaks a spousal promise, p. 87n. 15. See also David Bevington, "The Domineering Female in *1 Henry VI*," *Shakespeare Studies* 2 (1966): 57–58; Irene G. Dash, *Wooing, Wedding and Power: Women in Shakespeare's Plays* (New York: Columbia University Press, 1981), p. 157; Marilyn L. Williamson, " 'When Men Are Rul'd by Women,' " *Shakespeare Studies* 19 (1987): 42.

[43] Both Holinshed and Hall trace Henry's political woes back to his unwise marriage; see Geoffrey Bullough, *The Narrative and Dramatic Sources of Shakespeare* (London: Routledge and Kegan Paul, 1960), 3:71–72.

The negotiations proceed quite conventionally. Louis assures himself that Edward is now the rightful English ruler, Lady Bona assents, both jointure and dowry are mentioned, and Queen Margaret is asked to "be a witness / That Bona shall be wife to the English king" (138–139). Like Gloucester, Warwick acts lawfully and in good faith to secure an advantageous alliance.

However, a rival wooing occurs in the scene preceding negotiations at the French court. Again, as in Part 1 of *Henry VI*, the motive is sexual attraction, but here the king himself sues an unworthy wife, the Lady Gray, "a subject fit to jest withal, / But far unfit to be a sovereign" (III.ii.91–92). Like Suffolk, Edward makes no secret of his motives: "To tell thee plain, I aim to lie with thee" (69). When his offer to return her dead husband's lands fails to corrupt the lady, he determines that "she shall be my love or else my queen" (88). Unlike the wooing of Margaret, no trappings of parental consent or tokens or contracts mask this naked display of appetite and power. In its way, Edward's courtship is quite as corrupt as Suffolk's has been. Moreover, it undercuts the properly constituted suit to Lady Bona in the following scene, for the audience knows of Edward's perfidy before that news reaches France. As with Henry VI, a ruler who sacrifices his country's welfare for a pretty face, seen or unseen, courts more trouble than his bride is worth. Louis's outrage, fully justified, raises ominous questions.

> What! Has your king married the Lady Gray?
> And now to soothe your forgery and his,
> Sends me a paper to persuade me patience?
> Is this th'alliance that he seeks with France?
> Dare he presume to scorn us in this manner?
>
> (III.iii.174–178)

The consequences of "matching more for wanton lust than honour, / Or than for strength and safety of our country" (210–211) involve a radical shift in alliances, also cemented by marriages, as well as a new round of foreign and domestic wars.

Insulted by his sovereign's rash marriage to Lady Gray, the kingmaker, Warwick, abandons Edward IV in favor of a new power base with Louis of France, Margaret, and her son. Once more the familiar signals of betrothal bind the new confederacy.

> KING LOUIS. What pledge have we of thy firm loyalty?
> WARWICK. This shall assure my constant loyalty:
> That if our Queen and this young Prince agree,

I'll join mine eldest daughter and my joy
To him forthwith in holy wedlock bands.
QUEEN MARGARET. Yes, I agree, and thank you for your motion.
(*To Prince Edward*) Son Edward, she is fair and virtuous,
Therefore delay not. Give thy hand to Warwick,
And with thy hand thy faith irrevocable
That only Warwick's daughter shall be thine.
PRINCE EDWARD. Yes, I accept her, for she well deserves it,
And here to pledge my vow I give my hand.

(239–250)

When word of this betrayal reaches England, Clarence plans a defection of his own by the very same method Warwick has employed and for much the same reasons. Affronted that the king would "bury brotherhood" by bestowing noble brides on the brother and son of Lady Gray, when they "better would have fitted" Richard or himself, Clarence vows, "I will hence to Warwick's other daughter, / That, though I want a kingdom, yet in marriage / I may not prove inferior" to Edward (IV.i.54, 53, 118–120). Warwick greets his new follower with "But come, sweet Clarence, my daughter shall be thine" (IV.ii.12). And thus the bargain is sealed. No niceties of love or courtship here, just a pact between powerful partners who hope to take over a kingdom.

Ironically, the aborted betrothal to Lady Bona is later advanced by Richard III as grounds for disinheriting Edward's children by Lady Gray.

You say that Edward is your brother's son;
So say we too—but not by Edward's wife.
For first was he contract to Lady Lucy—
Your mother lives a witness to his vow—
And afterward, by substitute, betrothed
To Bona, sister to the King of France.
These both put off, a poor petitioner,
A care-crazed mother to a many sons,

. . . .

Seduced the pitch and height of his degree
To base declension and loathed bigamy.
By her in his unlawful bed he got
This Edward, whom our manners call the Prince.

(*R3*, III.vii.167–174, 178–181)

Technically, Edward's marriage would be bigamy only if either of the two prior contracts mentioned were consummated, though the existence of such a commitment might have been grounds to prevent his marrying Lady Gray in the first place. In actuality, Part 3 of *Henry VI* makes it clear that the king's wedding occurs before the French negotiations begin, while the Lucy contract, though in the sources, appears in the play to be Richard's egregious invention. Even so, the folly of Edward's sacrifice of political interests to private inclinations brings chaos that reaches beyond his very grave, just as it does for Henry VI.

As if he has been taking lessons from his predecessors in the political advantages and disadvantages of matrimony, Richard III can pretend to the passion of a "jolly thriving wooer" (IV.iii.43) while advancing his ambitions far more ruthlessly than a Suffolk or a Warwick or a Clarence. To debase a potential rival, he will "Enquire me out some mean-born gentleman, / Whom I will marry straight to Clarence' daughter" (IV.ii.55–56). He brilliantly manipulates the language of love and the conventions of courtship in his encounter with the Lady Anne, who has earlier been bestowed in marriage so arbitrarily by her father, Warwick.[44] But in private Richard readily admits to "another secret close intent, / By marrying her, which I must reach unto" (I.i.158–159). In taking to wife the widow of the Lancastrian heir, Richard moves nearer his ultimate goal, the crown itself. Once used to attain that end, Anne is discarded in favor of a more valuable wife, the surviving York heiress, Elizabeth.[45] "I must be married to my brother's daughter, / Or else my kingdom stands on brittle glass" (IV.ii.62–63). His situation becomes even more perilous because "Richmond aims / At young Elizabeth, my brother's daughter, / And by that knot looks proudly o'er the crown" (IV.iii.40–42).[46] The long argument

[44] Andrew and Gina Macdonald, "The Necessity of the Wooing of Anne in *Richard III*," *University of Dayton Review* 15 (1981): 125–127, say the wooing represents Richard's seduction of England at a time when the kingdom, like Anne, is grieving for loss of kinsmen and countrymen. Rene Girard, " 'To Entrap the Wisest': A Reading of *The Merchant of Venice*," in *Literature and Society*, ed. Edward W. Said (Baltimore: Johns Hopkins University Press, 1980), p. 118, after mistakenly identifing the corpse of Henry VI as Anne's father, says she and later Queen Elizabeth both succumb to Richard's "temptation of power." Marilyn French, *Shakespeare's Division of Experience* (New York: Summit Books, 1981), p. 71, feels that Anne and Elizabeth yield because they value the future and their children. Note that Richard identifies Anne as Warwick's younger daughter, while *2H6* says the prince married the elder, Clarence the younger. The birth order stated in *R3* accords with the sources; see Bullough, *Narrative and Dramatic Sources*, 3:189.

[45] For another analysis of Richard's wooing scenes, see Pierce, *Shakespeare's History Plays*, pp. 109–110, 116–117.

[46] C. L. Barber and Richard P. Wheeler, *The Whole Journey: Shakespeare's Power of Development* (Berkeley: University of California Press, 1986), p. 103, say Richard's wooing for these motives "shows the falseness of romantic pretense in such matches."

Richard holds with the former queen about this alliance climaxes not with words of love but with warnings of political disaster: "Without her, follows—to myself and thee, / Herself, the land, and many a Christian soul— / Death, desolation, ruin, and decay" (IV.iv.338–340). He concludes, "Urge the necessity and state of times, / And be not peevish-fond in great designs" (347–348). However, those "great designs" overshadowing all state marriages favor Richmond, for "the Queen hath heartily consented / He should espouse Elizabeth her daughter" (IV.v.17–18).[47] And so the Tudor dynasty is founded, involving, like its dramatic predecessors, a matrimony with profound implications for the health of the entire kingdom.

Hard on the heels of his history plays, Shakespeare wrote *Hamlet*, where he also explores the relationship between a royal marriage and a state's soundness. That Claudius's adulterous, incestuous union, achieved by fratricide/regicide, rots Denmark is obvious enough. Yet Hamlet, no less than his father or uncle, brings inescapable political implications into a courtship.[48] As Laertes rightly tells Ophelia,

> His greatness weighed, his will is not his own,
> For he himself is subject to his birth.
> He may not, as unvalued persons do,
> Carve for himself, for on his choice depends
> The sanity and health of the whole state;
> And therefore must his choice be circumscribed
> Unto the voice and yielding of that body
> Whereof he is the head.
>
> (I.iii.17–24)

---

[47] Pierce, *Shakespeare's History Plays*, p. 91, feels "the union of Richmond and Queen Elizabeth's daughter, symbolizes the triumph of Providence," with "Richard's marriage to his foe's widow, a grotesque parody of the union that ends the play," p. 110.

[48] Tennenhouse, *Power*, p. 89, misunderstands the nature of Danish royal succession; it is not a matrilinear system in which "Claudius's authority comes by way of his marriage to Gertrude." As in Norway, where the throne has gone to an adult brother rather than to an infant son when Old Fortinbras is slain, the crown of Denmark goes by election. Lisa Jardine, *Still Harping on Daughters: Women and Drama in the Age of Shakespeare* (Totowa, NJ: Barnes and Noble, 1983), p. 92, says that "Claudius terminates a possible betrothal to Ophelia" for Hamlet so that his own children with Gertrude will be next in line to the throne. Even assuming the queen is fertile after so many childless years, the succession is decided by election, for in a primogenitural system Hamlet would already wear the crown and would certainly not yield his claim to younger half-siblings. Moreover, Polonius, not Claudius, ends the Ophelia-Hamlet relationship, which never bears the marks of a betrothal.

With a prince, unauthorized visits to an unmarried aristocratic girl, involving "many tenders / Of his affection" (99–100), look like seduction because he "in his particular sect and force / May give his saying deed . . . no further / Than the main voice of Denmark goes withal" (26–28). Moreover, Polonius's handling of this affair involves not just his daughter's honor but his own position as chief counselor to Claudius. At first treating Hamlet's solicitation as a private matter, he feels obliged to disclose it only after the heir to the throne seems to have gone mad when rejected by Ophelia. Yet strategically Polonius needs to put himself in the best light, both as careful father and loyal courtier, lest he appear to have ignored a dalliance or, worse, secretly angled to marry his daughter into the royal family or, worse still, deliberately plunged Hamlet into insanity. In private with Ophelia, he twice says, "I am sorry" (II.i.107, 112). Belatedly, he sees that his fears for a daughter's chastity may have led to a national crisis.[49]

His lengthy explanation to Claudius and Gertrude, often dismissed as incorrigible loquaciousness, also stems from an understandable nervousness. Polonius is revealing a situation fraught with possible disaster for his political fortunes. With a tediously oblique introduction, he produces Hamlet's love letter, reads it, and then defensively reports as follows:

> POLONIUS. This in obedience hath my daughter shown me,
>   And more above hath his solicitings,
>   As they fell out by time, by means, and place,
>   All given to mine ear.
> KING.   But how hath she
>   Received his love?
> POLONIUS.   What do you think of me?
> KING. As of a man faithful and honourable.
> POLONIUS. I would fain prove so. But what might you think,
>   When I had seen this hot love on the wing,
>   As I perceived it—I must tell you that—
>   Before my daughter told me, what might you,
>   Or my dear majesty your queen here, think,

---

[49] Richard Adams, "Polonius: Did Dover Wilson Miss a Trick?" in *Essays by Divers Hands* 44 (1986): 24–45, notes this difficult situation, but he thinks Polonius blocks the courtship because Hamlet "is a fallen star in the contest for power," p. 32. Lynda E. Boose, "The Father's House and the Daughter in It," in *Daughters and Fathers*, ed. Boose and Betty S. Flowers (Baltimore: Johns Hopkins University Press, 1989), p. 31, says that "despite the obvious kinship benefits potentially available to the Polonius family," they prefer to preserve Ophelia "as an unusable family commodity."

If I had played the desk or table book,
Or given my heart a winking mute and dumb,
Or looked upon this love with idle sight—
What might you think? No, I went round to work,
And my young mistress thus did I bespeak:
"Lord Hamlet is a prince out of thy star.
This must not be." And then I prescripts gave her,
That she should lock herself from his resort,
Admit no messengers, receive no tokens.

(II.ii.125–144)

Carefully edited with the craft of self-preservation, this account does not accuse the prince of the seduction both Polonius and Laertes have feared. Nor does it mention Ophelia's questionable entertainment of Hamlet in private. Nor does it refer to his wild intrusion into her closet, though Polonius has come directly to the king upon learning of it. Instead, an experienced courtier portrays his daughter as dutiful, himself as prudent, diligent, virtuous, above all faithful to the crown. The refrain "What might you think of me?" both affirms his own trustworthiness and tests royal approval on this slippery ground. Where the heir to the throne is an eligible bachelor, politics dictate that counselors with unmarried daughters tread warily to avoid the springes of suspicion.

The foolishness of marrying simply on the basis of personal attraction, without considering the political desirability of a union, finds perhaps its most surprising treatment not in a history play but in a comedy—*Love's Labour's Lost*. Though other comedies escape into imaginary realms such as the Forest of Arden, where unlikely noble matches are made, this play intentionally invites identification with the outside world. The names of several male characters are historical, while the figures of Holofernes, Armado, and Mote have long appeared to satirize individuals well known in courtly circles.[50] Besides presenting personages no less important than the King of Navarre and the Princess of France, from the outset *Love's Labour's Lost* gently insists upon serious concerns of state. After all, the princess has come upon a diplomatic mission, the official representative of her father, the king, to settle the rightful ownership of Aquitaine and a disputed payment of a hundred thousand crowns for the cost of a war.[51] Already the

[50] See, e.g., Mary Ellen Lamb, "The Nature of Topicality in 'Love's Labour's Lost,'" *Shakespeare Survey* 38 (1985): 49–59; Albert H. Tricomi, "The Witty Idealization of the French Court in *Love's Labor's Lost*," *Shakespeare Studies* 12 (1979): 25–33.

[51] Dash, *Wooing, Wedding*, p. 18, praises her diplomatic abilities, though the interpre-

comedy's terms echo the long tradition of Anglo-French conflict so central to the histories and so frequently involving courtship either as a solution or as a motive for continued hostility.

Besides affairs of state, references to a noble world just below the royal level abound. "At a marriage feast / Between Lord Périgord and the beauteous heir / Of Jaques Fauconbridge solemnizèd / In Normandy saw I this Longueville" (II.i.40–43), says Maria. Both Biron and Dumaine have visited the Duke of Alençon, while Katherine is "heir of Alençon" and Maria "an heir of Fauconbridge" (195, 205). In these sophisticated circles an interlude of play—compliments, love poetry, hunting, masking, dancing, pageantry—offers acceptable diversion. But it would be unthinkable for casual amusement to substitute for the serious negotiations of a royal or noble marriage, especially with men who so lightly regard their oaths of commitment. This interlude is truly "a time, methinks, too short / To make a world-without-end bargain in" (V.ii.781–782). Though the princess promises that "by this virgin palm now kissing thine, / I will be thine" (799–800), her pledge and those of her ladies are all conditional in nature, with their injunctions to be carried out for a full year before any betrothal will take effect. The males may be persuaded of their own sincerity, but neither the females nor the audience ever abandon a clearsighted detachment from the frivolity in which all indulge.[52]

How could it be otherwise at Elizabeth's court? And there is no doubt that *Love's Labour's Lost* was performed at court, regardless of whether it was specifically written for performance there.[53] The comedy's ending, with the death of a king, the priority of state responsibilities, and the feminine rejection of romantically irresponsible offers of marriage, provides a graceful affirmation of the Queen's public policies.[54] Elizabeth herself might have said,

---

tive perspective is John Stuart Mill's views on the training of princesses (p. 13), a perspective hardly available to Shakespeare or his audience. See also Louis A. Montrose, " 'Sport by sport o'erthrown': *Love's Labour's Lost* and the Politics of Play," *Texas Studies in Literature and Language* 18 (1976): 544–545.

[52] See also Ralph Berry, *Shakespeare's Comedies: Explorations in Form* (Princeton: Princeton University Press, 1972), p. 81; Richard David, ed., *Love's Labour's Lost*, Ardèn Shakespeare (London: Methuen, 1956), pp. xxvii–xxxi, xxxviii–xlviii; Montrose, " 'Sport,' " p. 537.

[53] See David, ed., *LLL*, p. 2.

[54] Curiously, Leah S. Marcus, "Shakespeare's Comic Heroines, Elizabeth I, and the Political Uses of Androgyny," in *Women in the Middle Ages and the Renaissance*, ed. Mary Beth Rose (Syracuse: Syracuse University Press, 1986), p. 146, who sets the Queen's depictions of herself against the plays, makes no mention of *Love's Labour's Lost* when she concludes

We have received your letters full of love;
Your favours, the ambassadors of love,
And in our maiden council rated them
At courtship, pleasant jest, and courtesy,
As bombast and as lining to the time.
But more devout than this in our respects
Have we not been, and therefore met your loves
In their own fashion, like a merriment.

(770–777)

This is not to suggest yet another crude historical correspondence between the comic world and the courtly world nor to rule out purely aesthetic interpretations of the action's conclusion. But here Shakespeare does seem to adapt the dramatic materials of recognizable names and figures, royal personages, and court entertainments to the restrictive requirements for proper behavior in a powerful political milieu. Such behavior did not include hasty marriage, either onstage or offstage, at least not without potentially bitter consequences. Only the sluttish Jaquenetta and the foolish Don Armado subject themselves to wedlock, with its mocking echoes of "Cuckoo" (886).

It would be a mistake to think that public considerations affect only aristocratic or royal nuptials in Shakespeare. In fact, virtually every courtship involves a circle that widens beyond the lovers themselves. Family, friends, and ruler busy themselves about the mating of Beatrice and Benedick; for their own advantage or amusement servants and kinsmen promote Sir Andrew Aguecheek and Malvolio as suitors to Olivia; all the villagers of Windsor seem to sponsor the claims of one candidate or another for the hand of Anne Page. The possibility of bringing civil peace leads Friar Laurence to unite Romeo and Juliet, while the imminence of Turkish invasion relegates Othello's elopement with Desdemona to secondary importance in Venice. A lucky alliance with the richly left Portia redeems the impoverished Bassanio's aristocratic status, but Claudio's passion for Juliet degrades him to imprisonment and a sentence of death. To a striking degree, the same currents swirling about the marriages of the mighty also affect the courtships of lesser figures. Ambition, family loyalty, and submission to authority vie with love, sexual attraction, and the pleasures of wooing—even when crowns and kingdoms are at stake.

---

that Shakespeare's heroines "settle down into wifehood and fertility: do the things which Elizabethans yearned for their Queen to do in the interest of stability and continuity."

Yet Shakespeare never provides facile answers about which claims take precedence at the highest social level. He never presents simple solutions guaranteed to achieve a nation's best interests. If unions like Henry VI's and Edward IV's, contracted solely on the basis of personal preference, bring disaster, so do purely political alliances like Antony's and Richard III's. Blanche's faith and honor no more ensure success than do Falconbridge's treachery and commodity. From Mortimer's perspective, his marriage to Glyndŵr's daughter stems from love, but in Henry IV's view, it looks like a treasonous conspiracy with Wales to seize the throne. Thus the closer one stands to the throne, the more complex are the facets of matrimony.[55] Small wonder, then, that the fictional Princess of France and her ladies distrust the "words that smooth-faced wooers say" (*LLL*, V.ii.815). In the political realm, courtship is considerably more than a pleasant game of love.

[55] Pierce, *Shakespeare's History Plays*, p. 36, calls this a situation of "correspondences." As he explains the matter, "Since what infects the kingdom infects everything in it, marriage becomes just another part of the struggle for power and loved ones are hostages to fortune in a violent world." Thus, he says, "in the *Henry VI* plays marriage is a tool of ambition and wedded life a microcosm of the disorder in the state," p. 99.

{ CHAPTER X }

Happily Ever After?

A man may woo where he will but he must wed
where his hap is.
—Morris P. Tilley, *A Dictionary of Proverbs*

In love the heavens themselves do guide the state;
Money buys lands, and wives are sold by fate.
—*Wiv.*, V.v.219–220

I F AT THIS POINT, readers know far more about how courtship functions in the Shakespearean world, they may still wonder what conclusions can be drawn from so complex a set of possibilities. Despite certain limits to the range of available options, no uniformity of behavior or opinion imposed itself on England's subjects. Women were more apt to marry than men, though by far the majority of both sexes married. Some wed only once, but others wed again when a spouse died. While rank affected the age when matrimony began and brides tended to be younger than their grooms, there were always exceptions, as in the case of William Shakespeare and Anne Hathaway. Over some unions fathers, guardians, family, friends, or masters exercised an influence that could vary from absolute authority to mere advice, yet a good many couples felt free to make their own matches, especially at the lower social levels. While few could afford to marry with no regard for financial security, the impulse of love or desire sometimes swept away a prudent regard for money or position, land or living. And if romantic attraction did not characterize all marital commitments, it was hardly foreign to the English. Although the stages of courtship conventionally proceeded from acquaintance to negotiation to acceptance, from betrothal to banns to wedding, from feasting to entertainment to bed, not everyone followed the usual route. Intercourse could and did precede marriage; clandestine engagements and elopements evaded the strictures of public scrutiny; some difficulties even rendered unions invalid or provided grounds for separation.

With such a diversity of experience surrounding him, it would be remarkable if Shakespeare did not make dramatic capital out of the rituals of mating. In exploiting the technicalities of handfasting, *de futuro* and *de praesenti* spousals, dowry and jointure, or nuptial impediments, he resembles the modern playwright who explores a homosexual relationship or a palimony suit or a custody battle. The culture produces both the materials for creativity and the audience for a critique of those materials. Nor is it surprising that courtship should occupy so central a position in most of the canon, since the movement from the unmarried to the married state usually represented the single most important alteration in one's private and public life. Examining the nuances of this transitional experience touches upon sensitive codes of belief about the self and the society. Onstage, at least, the fantasies, frustrations, follies, futilities, and fictions that sustained the matrimonial system could be held up to scrutiny. Within the limits of censorship and the market, Shakespeare had an opportunity to deal with anything related to wooing in any way he found appropriate. However, a critical impasse occurs the moment one tries to generalize about this dramatist's handling of courtship.

His only consistency in treating the subject is his inconsistency. The canon betrays no fixed perspective from which we are invited to view a variety of situations; instead, each situation generates a different perspective or even a complex of contradictory perspectives. Those who claim that in Shakespeare love always leads to marriage reckon without *Love's Labour's Lost*, where "Jack hath not Jill" (V.ii.862). A host of hopeful suitors in other plays also fail to win a bride—Paris, Gremio, Dr. Caius, Cloten, Sir Andrew Aguecheek, Roderigo, William, perhaps even Vienna's Duke of dark corners. Nor is matrimony the only approved context for sexuality, as some have charged. The carnality of characters like Lancelot Gobbo or Costard, Mopsa or Dorcas, Doll Tearsheet or Mistress Quickly merits a casual acceptance not accorded to the fornication of Angelo or Bertram's supposed deflowering of Diana. Extramarital intercourse can be a fulfillment of spousal promises as in *Measure for Measure*, a willing seduction as in *Troilus and Cressida*, or a bid for political power as in *Henry VI*. In presenting adultery, the dramas range from the brutal sensuality of Tamora and Aaron to the lethal desire of Gertrude and Claudius to the dazzling splendor of Cleopatra and Antony. While some kings like Richard III nakedly maneuver for advancement through royal alliances, rulers like Henry V or Henry VIII show their intended brides genuine affection, however qualified it might be by the demands of statecraft. Following the rules of a proper wooing may comically succeed for a Petruccio or tragically fail for a Paris. Though the secret courtship and elopement of Desdemona raises questions of impropriety, Romeo and Juliet's clandestine union seems lyrically appropriate, as fated as it is fatal. Money moves to the foreground of *The Merchant of Venice* but virtually disappears in *Twelfth Night*, and the issue of social rank similarly dominates *All's Well* but recedes in *As You Like It*. When depicting the parental role in marriage, Shakespeare offers the arbitrary Egeus, the indulgent Leonato, the suspicious Polonius, the outraged Polixenes, the heartbroken Brabanzio. On every hand, in each play, with any variable, the attitudes revealed stubbornly resist predictability.

Are there then no fixed points regarding courtship for Shakespeare? A limited set of options lies beyond the borders of acceptability—child molestation, rape, incest, bigamy. Yet virtually any other possibility can be variously treated with approval, contempt, amusement, cynicism, sympathy, satire, toleration, parody, indifference, denunciation, or some combination of approaches. With such a quicksilver elusiveness, in Shakespeare, any attempt to force a uniform design upon the plays inevitably fails. They cannot be reduced to categories like dominating fathers and defiant daughters, to advocacy of a new Puritan ethic, to codes of courtly love, to proto-feminism or misogynist chauvinism, to support for political dogma or subversion of authority, or even to motifs of genre. Instead of adhering to any one pattern, Shakespeare constantly shifts the patterns, developing new configurations for each context. Like a kaleidoscope, he arranges the minutiae of the wooing experience into ever-changing designs. And precisely this volatility represents his most radical challenge to the institutions of Elizabethan-Jacobean culture. The centrality of marriage to the self, the family, the community, the church, the state, the very cosmos meant that it was guarded by rules, rituals, customs, and beliefs designed to ensure its stability. Onstage, however, stability disappears. Any aspect of courtship may be questioned. None of the usual restrictions with regard to protocol or ethics need apply. By continually altering the options for his characters, Shakespeare relentlessly exposes the presuppositions of his audience, regardless of what those presuppositions might have been. Whether consciously aware of this exposure or not, all spectators watched alternative possibilities of behavior that implicitly denied the fixities in their own modes of making a match. Though some will see in Shakespeare's characteristic treatment a spirit stubbornly opposed to the orthodoxies of his time, others will interpret such treatment as artistic free play. Whatever the case, he never handles any aspect of courtship in a predictable fashion.

Contemporary critics will find nothing new in the idea of Shakespeare's inherent instability of perspective. In the wake of modern theory, hardly anyone claims for the dramatist a unified worldview or philosophy or politics. From the New Critics' passion for paradox to the deconstructionists' unraveling of meaning altogether, there is at least agreement on the amorphous nature of the texts. What the present study does show, however, is the way in which that amorphousness functions. Instead of beginning with a theoretical position and then adducing examples to demonstrate its validity, *Making a Match* begins with a particular kind of situation, as familiar to the audience as to the characters, a situation that cuts across the lines of genre, gender, and status, in order to investigate the dramaturgical uses of social custom. Methodologically, this represents an inside-out process. Even though it eventually reaches widely shared conclusions, they emerge from the research itself instead of from a priori assumptions. Moreover, the interpretation of the plays is partnered with the most comprehensive documentation of historical and critical materials relating to courtship that has yet been undertaken. Thus *Making a Match* provides a new resource valuable for many areas of study in the English Renaissance, as well as an exploration of the multiple manifestations of wooing wherever they appear in the canon. The information presented here not only demonstrates in detail how this crucial system functioned in Shakespeare and his society but also provides a richer, more reliable framework for other critical perspectives—the intent throughout being complementary rather than polemical.

Four centuries ago, matrimonial practices differed, sometimes radically, from the ones now followed. Examining all the earlier intricacies and implications not only creates an account of intrinsic interest but also enables one to see Shakespeare afresh. Like his countrymen, he is deeply rooted in the assumptions, laws, and conventions governing English matrimony, as his plays amply reveal. But they also reveal him capable of digging up those roots and tossing them about whenever he wishes or whenever aesthetic demands seem to require it. For him, the theater provides an arena where the conventional and the unconventional can intersect in an almost endless number of patterns. Both restless and arresting, Shakespeare brilliantly illuminates the courtship codes he knew. In turn, our deeper understanding of those codes brilliantly illuminates his unique artistry.

Appendixes

AGE AT FIRST MARRIAGE

THE FOLLOWING studies show a surprisingly consistent range of ages when men and women first married, regardless of date or place.

Source	Parish(es)	Date(s)	Average for Men	Average for Women
Joel Berlatsky, "Marriage and Family in a Tudor Elite: Familial Patterns of Elizabethan Bishops," *Journal of Family History* 3 (1978): 8–9.	various parishes	1558–1603	36.6[a]	
Alan D. Dyer, *The City of Worcester in the Sixteenth Century* (Leicester: Leicester University Press, 1973), p. 37.	3 parishes in Worcester	1580–1639	27–31[b]	23–27
Vivien Brodsky Elliott, "Single Women in the London Marriage Market: Age, Status and Mobility, 1598–1619," in *Marriage and Society: Studies in the Social History of Marriage*, ed. R. B. Outhwaite (New York: St. Martin's Press, 1981), pp. 83, 87.	London and environs	1598–1619	28.4 (London) 28.2 (environs)	20.5 (London born) 24.2 (migrants to London)
Roger A. P. Finlay, "Population and Fertility in London, 1580–1650," *Journal of Family History* 4 (1979): 31–32.	4 London parishes	1580–1650		24 (poorer parishes) 22.3 (wealthier parishes)

Age at First Marriage (cont.)

Source	Parish(es)	Date(s)	Average for Men	Average for Women
Peter Laslett, "Introduction," in *Household and Family in Past Time*, ed. Laslett and Richard Wall (Cambridge: Cambridge University Press, 1972), p. 75.	Ealing, Middlesex	1599	none married under 25, 23% by 29	none married under 20, 15% by 24, 43% by 29
David Levine, *Family Formation in an Age of Nascent Capitalism* (New York: Academic Press, 1977), p. 61.	Shepshed, Leicester-shire	1600–1699	29.4	28.1
Levine and Keith Wrightson, "The Social Context of Illegitimacy in Early Modern England," in *Bastardy and Its Comparative History*, ed. Laslett, Karla Oosterveen, and Wall (Cambridge: Harvard University Press, 1980), pp. 159–161.	9 parishes throughout England	1600–1649		26
Wrightson and Levine, *Poverty and Piety in an English Village: Terling, 1525–1700* (New York: Academic Press, 1979), p. 47.	Terling, Essex	1525–1724	25.3	24.6
E. A. Wrigley, "Family Limitation in Pre-Industrial England," in *Population in Industrialization*, ed. Michael Drake (London: Methuen, 1969), p. 164.	Colyton, Devon	1560–1599	28.1	27
		1600–1629	27.4	27.3
		1630–1646	25.8	26.5
Wrigley and R. S. Schofield, "English Population History from Family Reconstitution: Summary Results 1600–1779," *Population* 37 (1983): 162–163.	13 parishes throughout England	1600–1649	28.1	25.6

Age at First Marriage *(cont.)*

Source	Parish(es)	Date(s)	Average for Men	Average for Women
Wrigley and Schofield, *The Population History of England, 1541–1871* (Cambridge: Harvard University Press, 1981), p. 424.	12 parishes throughout England	1575– 1599	28.2	26
		1600– 1624	28	26
		1625– 1649	27.6	26.6

[a] The earliest age at which any bishop married was 26.

[b] In one parish there was an anomalous average of 23.5 for the decade 1600–1609.

[c] Out of 1,175 males, only 7 married younger than 18, 20 at 18, 38 at 19; out of 1,591 females, only 39 were under 18, 30 were 18, 60 were 19.

LIST OF PLAY TITLES AND ABBREVIATIONS

Ado	Much Ado about Nothing	*Mac.*	Macbeth
Ant.	Antony and Cleopatra	*MM*	Measure for Measure
AWW	All's Well That Ends Well	*MND*	A Midsummer Night's Dream
AYL	As You Like It	*MV*	The Merchant of Venice
Cor.	Coriolanus	*Oth.*	Othello
Cym.	Cymbeline	*Per.*	Pericles
Err.	The Comedy of Errors	*R2*	Richard II
Ham.	Hamlet	*R3*	Richard III
1H4	Henry IV, Part 1	*Rom.*	Romeo and Juliet
2H4	Henry IV, Part 2	*Shr.*	The Taming of the Shrew
H5	Henry V	*TGV*	The Two Gentlemen of Verona
1H6	Henry VI, Part 1	*Tim.*	Timon of Athens
2H6	Henry VI, Part 2	*Tit.*	Titus Andronicus
3H6	Henry VI, Part 3	*TN*	Twelfth Night
H8	Henry VIII	*Tmp.*	The Tempest
JC	Julius Caesar	*Tro.*	Troilus and Cressida
Jn.	King John	*Wiv.*	The Merry Wives of Windsor
LLL	Love's Labour's Lost	*WT*	The Winter's Tale
Lr.	King Lear		

Index

Allington, Sir Gyles, 198n

All's Well That Ends Well, 31, 33, 37, 38, 62–65, 68, 69, 92–93, 95–96, 102, 103, 110, 118, 180, 182n, 200, 227–232, 241, 261, 262

Altham, Joan, 82

Anglican doctrine, 13, 18, 21, 75, 88, 157–159, 161–162, 186, 196–200, 214n, 215n–216n, 222n, 229n

Anne of Denmark, Queen of England, 161, 235–236

Antony and Cleopatra, 91, 224–225, 225n, 226n, 231n, 243–246, 259, 261

Archdell, Sara, 107

Arden, Mary, 8

Arden, Robert, 8

As You Like It, 3, 58–61, 68, 91, 93, 94n, 97, 103, 134, 135n, 166, 181, 182n, 209n, 215, 221–223, 232, 261, 262

Aston, Sir Walter, 86

Bacon, Sir Francis, 26, 44, 108, 164

Bacon, Sir Nicholas, 27, 128

Baker, Jane, 21, 107

Baker, Lady, 237

Bandello, Matteo, 28

Banister, Jane, 107

Barham, Alice, 26

Barnardiston, Anne, 23–24, 45n, 152

Barrington family, 45, 81, 108n

Bate, Robert, 84

Bedford, Francis Russell, Earl of, 82, 108n

Bellamy, Anne, 129

Belott-Mountjoy law suit, 128

Berkeley, Sir Thomas, 26, 81–82

Bevington, David, 14

Blague, Mrs. Alice, 107

Boccaccio, Giovanni, 63

Boose, Lynda, 14

Boulmer, Mrs. Jane, 85

Boyle, Francis, 26

Boyle, Mary. *See* Rich, Mary

Braddedge, John, 83

Breton, Nicholas, 81

Bristol, John Digby, Earl of, 82

Brooke, Arthur, 28

Brooke, Sir Calistines, 191

Buckingham, George Villiers, Duke of, 239, 240

Bucknell, Mary, 25

Bullinger, Heinrich, 17, 161

Burghley, William Cecil, Lord, 23, 44, 108, 124n, 238, 240

Burles, Grace, 193

Cambridge Group, 12

Candish, Mr., 81

Carey, Elizabeth, 82

Carleton, Sir Dudley, 161

Cary, Robert, 239

Catholic doctrine, 13, 88, 214n

Cecil, Elizabeth, 194

Cecil, Thomas, 23

Cecil, William. *See* Burghley

Chancery Court, 128, 157

Charles I, 236

Cholmley, Sir Richard, 85, 130

Churchman, Joan, 131

Clifford, Lady Anne, 27, 131

Clifford, John, 130

Cocke, Elizabeth, 83

Cogan, Thomas, 22

Coke, Anne, 27

Coke, Sir Anthony, 27

Coke, Sir Edward, 194, 239

Coke, John, 107

Comedy of Errors, The, 31, 38, 47, 48, 67–68, 94, 102, 134, 241

Compton, Lord William, 131, 194

Cordwell, Henry, 107

Cordwell, Julian, 107

Coriolanus, 181, 182–183